Photoshop® CS4 for Nature Photographers

A Workshop in a Book

Ellen Anon

Josh Anon

WILEY

Wiley Publishing, Inc.

Acquisitions Editor: Mariann Barsolo
Development Editor: Candace English
Technical Editor: Al Ward
Production Editor: Dassi Zeidel
Copy Editor: Liz Welch
Production Manager: Tim Tate
Vice President and Executive Group Publisher: Richard Swadley
Vice President and Executive Publisher: Joseph B. Wikert
Vice President and Publisher: Neil Edde
Assistant Project Manager: Jenny Swisher
Associate Producer: Kit Malone
Media Quality Assurance: Angie Denny
Book Designer: Franz Baumhackl and Lori Barra
Compositor: Chris Gillespie, Happenstance Type-O-Rama
Proofreader: Kathy Pope, Word One
Indexer: Ted Laux
Project Coordinator, Cover: Lynsey Stanford
Cover Designer: Ryan Sneed
Cover Image: Ellen Anon

Library of Congress Cataloging-in-Publication Data

Anon, Ellen.

Photoshop CS4 for nature photographers : a workshop in a book / Ellen Anon, Josh Anon. —1st ed.

    p. cm.

ISBN-13: 978-0-470-38127-4 (paper/cd-rom)

ISBN-10: 0-470-38127-2 (paper/cd-rom)

1. Nature photography. 2. Adobe Photoshop. I. Anon, Josh. II. Title.

TR721.A5663 2009

778.9'302856686--dc22

                    2008042929

Dear Reader,

Thank you for choosing *Photoshop CS4 for Nature Photographers: A Workshop in a Book*. This book is part of a family of premium-quality Sybex books, all of which are written by outstanding authors who combine practical experience with a gift for teaching.

Sybex was founded in 1976. More than thirty years later, we're still committed to producing consistently exceptional books. With each of our titles, we're working hard to set a new standard for the industry. From the paper we print on, to the authors we work with, our goal is to bring you the best books available.

I hope you see all that reflected in these pages. I'd be very interested to hear your comments and get your feedback on how we're doing. Feel free to let me know what you think about this or any other Sybex book by sending me an email at nedde@wiley.com, or if you think you've found a technical error in this book, please visit http://sybex.custhelp.com. Customer feedback is critical to our efforts at Sybex.

Best regards,

NEIL EDDE
Vice President and Publisher
Sybex, an Imprint of Wiley

In loving memory of Max Lurie, our father and grandfather.
You laid the foundation for our love of photography.
8/5/1920–8/28/2008

To Dr. Gary Brotherson—whose skill restored my vision and whose confidence and patience keep me going.
—*Ellen Anon*

To my family, for continuing to set the alarm before sunrise; and to Eric Gold for the fun times we had shooting—so long, and thanks for all the Nikon vs. Canon debates.
—*Josh Anon*

Acknowledgments

In the past I've always dedicated my books to my family. And indeed I hope that they are well aware that I am very grateful for their continued support. But this book is dedicated to Dr. Brotherson. When photographers talk about their vision, we usually mean it figuratively. We take the literal for granted until something stops us in our tracks, which can be absolutely terrifying. Dr. Brotherson's skill and patient, confident, and pragmatic approach have carried me through some rough times. It's hard to know how to adequately thank someone who not only restored my vision but continues to be a rock as I weather this storm. And I want to thank Dr. Stratton as well. He too has played a vital role in helping me regain my vision. Both of them are outstanding doctors who have gone out of their way to help me. *Major thanks to you both!*

It's been a special pleasure to collaborate with my son Josh on this book. Josh is a very talented photographer and has been my computer guru for as long as I can remember! He was responsible for adding the information for Elements users.

Every successful book project reflects not only the work of the authors, but of the entire team. And as nearly every author will agree, there are good editors...and well, let's just say those that aren't. But on this project we've been blessed with an extraordinarily great team! The Sybex team of Mariann Barsolo (acquisitions editor), Candace English (development editor), and Dassi Zeidel (production editor) are unbeatable. It's been a pleasure and honor to work with each of them. They truly facilitated the process in every way possible. Thank you each so much! Thanks also to Liz Welch, who copy edited the book and did her best to ensure that we are grammatically correct and communicate clearly. Once again I want to thank Al Ward for tech-editing this book and for his excellent sidebar. His careful attention to detail helps ensure that everything is accurate. Lastly, thanks to the compositor, Happenstance Type-O-Rama, who has done a great job of laying out the book so that details in the figures are more readily visible.

I am extremely grateful to our contributors who were so generous with their time, writing, and images: Peter Burian, Charles Glatzer, Darrell Gulin, Rick Holt, George Lepp, Joe McDonald, Arthur Morris, Michael Reichmann, John Shaw, and Tony Sweet. All are busy professionals, yet they made time to help us. Thank you!

Finally, I also want to thank the readers of the first two editions of this book for making this third edition possible. It's quite an honor to do a third edition of a book, and I want you to know how much your praise, feedback, and support matter!

—*Ellen Anon*

First, I want to give special thanks to my mother Ellen for including me on this book as her new coauthor. More importantly, however, I really appreciate how easy she made the whole process for me. She assembled the material and was more involved with reviewing the different drafts, which made it possible for me to write with her even though I was working 70-plus-hour weeks for part of the process. I also want to say thanks to my dad for putting up with the times I called the house to talk to Mom instead of him about some aspect of the book. Thanks to my brother Seth for always supporting me in my endeavors and for being willing to drive his car over rocky terrain so that I could get a shot.

I want to second the thanks that Ellen passed along to Sybex's talented staff and to our photographer friends and contributors; you all are always inspiring and genuinely fun people to shoot with!

Day to day, I'm fortunate in that I get to interact with another inspiring group, the Pixar Photoclub. Its members (including Eben Ostby, Trish Carney, Heesoo Lee, Ralph Hill, Craig Good, and more) create and share impressive images nearly every day. I also want to thank my coworkers in the Camera and Staging (Layout) department for continuing to turn my photography skills into cinematography skills, especially Patrick Lin, Mahyar Abousaeedi, Andrew Cadelago, Matt Silas, and Mark Sanford.

Last but not least, I continue to be grateful to Claudia Skerlong for teaching me to write well. Although she slightly disputed my claim that she thought hell would freeze over before I wrote a book, I'm certain she felt it would freeze before I coauthored a second.

—*Josh Anon*

About the Authors

Ellen Anon got her start with photography at age five, but for years it remained a hobby as she took a very long fork in the road, eventually earning a PhD in clinical psychology. Finally in 1997 a broken foot forced her to take a break from work as a psychologist, and she used the time to study John Shaw's photography tapes. (Thank you, John, for starting me on the road to photography as a career.) She debated briefly between building a traditional darkroom in her home and creating a digital darkroom. Since she's not fond of being closed up in small dark spaces with strong smells of funky chemicals, she opted for the latter. Ever since, photography has been a two-part process for her. Making the image in the field is step one, and optimizing it in the digital darkroom is step two. Being creative with it is the icing on the cake!

Ellen is now a freelance photographer, speaker, and writer who specializes in expressive photography. Ellen's images, based on nature, are sometimes realistic and sometimes abstract but are always designed to elicit emotional reactions from the viewer. Her goal with her photographs is to go beyond the ordinary in ways that she hopes stimulate others to pause and appreciate some of the beauty and wonder of our earth. Ellen's images are included in collections in several countries. She is represented by several stock agencies, and her photos have been showcased in galleries, used in numerous publications (including Sierra Club's *Mother Earth* and *Inner Reflections* 2007 calendar). In addition she has been Highly Honored in Nature's Best Photography Windland Smith Rice International Awards, and Highly Commended in the 2008 BBC/Shell Wildlife Photographer of the Year competition. She is a member of the Aperture Advisory Board and is an Apple Certified Trainer for Aperture 2.

In addition to *Photoshop for Nature Photographers: A Workshop in a Book*, Ellen is the coauthor of *Aperture Exposed: The Mac Photographer's Guide to Taming the Workflow* (Sybex, 2006) with her son, Josh Anon, and has contributed chapters to several other books. Ellen leads both photographic- and digital darkroom–oriented workshops for Santa Fe Workshops and the McDonald Digital Wildlife Institute. She is a featured speaker at various events, and is also a frequent contributor to a variety of photography magazines and blogs. Ellen is an active member of the North American Nature Photography Association (NANPA) and is an instructor for its high school scholarship program. She is also a member of the National Association of Photoshop Professionals (NAPP) and the American Society of Media Photographers (ASMP).

Josh Anon has been a nature photographer for over half his life, with his interest in photography starting when he received his first Kodak 110 camera at the ripe old age of 4. Camera in hand, he received a BS in computer science from Northwestern University in Evanston, Illinois.

After graduating, Josh started working at Pixar Animation Studios in Emeryville, California. There he has worked on *Finding Nemo*, *The Incredibles*, *Ratatouille*, and more. Currently he is a layout artist (camera and staging), and his past positions have included crowds simulation, Linux and Mac software development, and model and render optimization.

His photographic work, which has appeared in a variety of publications, is represented by the Jaynes Gallery and is available for direct sale from his website (www.joshanon.com). Recently, Josh won best Man and the Environment Image for the Art Wolfe Environmental Photo Invitational, took second place in the Environment at Risk category in the International Conservation Photography awards, was a finalist in Nature's Best Photography Windland Smith Rice International Awards, and was a semi-finalist in the world-renowned BBC/Shell Wildlife Photographer of the Year competition. He has traveled the globe searching for the next great picture, be it 100 feet deep on the Great Barrier Reef or at 2 a.m. during the winter in the Arctic Circle. On the weekends and evenings, Josh teaches photography, both online and in-person. He also writes for the O'Reilly Inside Aperture blog, and with Ellen, he is a coauthor of *Aperture Exposed* (Anon and Anon, Sybex, 2006).

Josh continues to develop software in his free time, currently focusing on FlipBook, which is movie-making software for iPhone and iPod Touch.

When not shooting, making cartoons, or coding, Josh can be found kiteboarding.

Contents

Chapter 5   **Workflows and First Steps**   **185**

Chapter 6   **Exposure Adjustments**   **215**

Foreword

In a digital world, the blend of nature and digital is an interesting one. When looked at with a wide perspective, change in nature comes at an incredibly slow pace. Sitting on your porch watching the grass grow is nothing. How about watching a glacier advance (or retreat) across a frigid landscape? Or the motion of tectonic plates building mountains? Nature, by and large, never seems to be in a hurry.

If only that were true with photography. Compared to nature, photography develops with blinding speed. And we don't even need to limit the discussion to digital photography for this to be the case. From early beginnings—daguerreotypes, glass plates, black-and-white film, color film, and on to digital technology—no matter your perspective, things move quickly. And with digital, well, let's just say that keeping up isn't exactly easy.

So today, nature photography represents the collision of two extremes. But that's not to say they aren't a perfect fit. Quite the contrary, digital has expanded the horizons for nature photographers. The latest imaging sensors have by and large surpassed the capabilities of film. In fact, they are starting to exceed the capabilities of many lenses that have long been hailed as being almost preternatural in their ability to resolve even the finest details found in nature.

Software, too, has expanded the possibilities in nature photography. The ability to blend multiple exposures to record the oftentimes blinding dynamic range in nature. The ability to manage many thousands of images so photographers really can capture all they find in the world and still be able to find the right image when they need it. The ability to capture with confidence, knowing our cameras will faithfully record what is before the lens, and that with postprocessing that doesn't involve unpleasant chemicals, we can truly realize our vision for a photographic image.

There are countless sources of information on digital photography, Photoshop, and all the related pieces of the puzzle confronting today's photographer. But when you say "photographer," you're casting a rather wide net. In this book, image experts Ellen Anon and Josh Anon don't just shed light on the issues facing photographers today, they deftly translate that information so it makes the most sense to nature photographers. Thanks to Ellen and Josh and this book, you will improve your photography, inform your perspective on all things digital, and most importantly, truly realize your photographic vision.

So happy reading, happy travels, and happy photography.

Tim Grey
Author of *Photoshop CS4 Workflow,* and Photoshop World instructor

Introduction

Adobe Photoshop, Elements, and nature photography are a logical marriage. Although there are some people who regard Photoshop as an evil that degrades the purity of nature photography, in reality nature photography has long been a two-step process. The first step involves making the best possible picture in the field. The second is creating the best possible output from that capture. Ansel Adams is widely acclaimed as one of the greatest black-and-white nature photographers of all times. Yet if you had a chance to view some of his prints before he optimized them in his traditional darkroom, you might not have looked twice at them. Although he was an excellent photographer, he was truly a master of the darkroom. Today, Photoshop and Elements enable many more people to become masters of the darkroom—the digital darkroom.

Becoming a master of the digital darkroom can be a daunting task. Trying to learn the programs by trial and error is a most time-consuming—and frustrating—approach. Finding the time and money to spend a week at a workshop devoted to Photoshop for photographers involves a major time commitment, to say nothing of the significant expense involved.

You'll find lots of Photoshop how-to books on the bookstore shelves, but many address the needs of graphic artists more than photographers. Graphic artists need to use vector tools such as the Pen tool or Shape tool, which aren't of much use to most photographers. And although some books do target photographers, few specifically address the unique needs of nature photographers. Many of these books focus on areas unimportant to nature photographers. For example, they may spend many pages dealing with retouching portraits or repairing scans of old photos.

We've updated this edition to include specific instructions for Elements users as well. Our intent is not to provide a comprehensive Elements book; there is a plethora of Elements books available to guide you in the basics of the program. Our goal is to help nature photographers who use Elements optimize their images in the best possible ways using techniques similar to those Photoshop users employ.

When we decided to add coverage for Elements, we faced a challenge. We didn't want to annoy Photoshop users by having them read through information about Elements that wasn't relevant to them. And similarly we didn't want Elements users to wade through long sections of text that aren't useful for them. Our solution was to write the book as we had done in its earlier editions, but to include a symbol by any section that pertains only to Photoshop users **Photoshop ONLY** . That way Elements readers can skip those sections if they choose.

> Whenever possible we added sections like this one describing similar techniques or modifications for Elements users, and they have a distinct blue background. That way, Photoshop users can easily skip over the blue sections. We hope these visual cues make it easy for our readers to quickly find the information they're after.

Most nature photographers need a straightforward workflow that pertains to nature photography and that's easy and efficient to follow. That's the goal of *Photoshop CS4 for Nature Photographers: A Workshop in a Book*. In addition, it addresses some of the unique concerns nature photographers experience, such as white balance and color corrections. Of course, all photographers deal with white balance, but many are concerned with making their images truly neutral. As nature photographers, we often get up before dawn to capture the beautiful early-morning light. That light that we go to great lengths to capture is far from neutral. In fact, it's the warmth of it that makes so many of our images. If they were portrayed as neutral, many would lose their impact.

Photoshop offers a multitude of ways to accomplish almost every task. Which method is the best to use in a specific situation often depends on the type of image you are modifying. Throughout the book we bear in mind that your subjects are nature and gear the techniques to those that are likely to give you the best results the most easily.

We want this book to be easy to use and have organized it to follow the basic workflow. Each chapter lays a foundation for the following chapters. You'll also notice that we incorporate an element called Try It! in this book.

> **Try It!** These sections offer a chance to take a break from reading and to practice the techniques that have just been covered using your own images or those that we provide on the companion CD. Reading about a technique is one thing, but for most people, it doesn't sink in until you actually do it. By providing you with images to practice on, we hope to make this book more like a workshop.

In addition we have green backgrounds on sidebars that contain tips from various highly regarded nature photographers. Lastly there are some sections with tan backgrounds that offer additional information from us. These include notes, sidebars, and the Try It! boxes.

Who Should Use This Book

Every nature photographer who wants people to look at their pictures and say "Wow!" should use this book.

Photoshop CS4 for Nature Photographers: A Workshop in a Book is designed for nature photographers who want a straightforward workflow customized to make their images have the most impact. If you are new to Photoshop, you'll find we start off with the basics and gently build your abilities. We give you plenty of opportunities to practice what you're learning using images we provide as well as your own. We write in an informal, casual, but clear way, providing lots of examples and color illustrations to help you develop your skills. If you're an Elements user, we'll show you the most effective tools to use to make the most of your images.

If you already have some familiarity with Photoshop and want to update your workflow to take advantage of the new features in Photoshop CS4, we'll show you how. If you've found in the past that you don't always get the best results or that your workflow is inconsistent, we'll help you hone your skills. We'll provide techniques that will allow you to efficiently optimize your images. And if you'd like to get some ideas for how to be creative with your images, this is the book for you! We cover a variety of ways of compositing (combining) images as well as creating various digital montages, filter effects, and even digital multiple exposures.

If you take other types of photographs as well as nature photographs, our workflow and techniques will still work well for you. You'll gain the tools and abilities you need to make your pictures come alive.

Note: Although Photoshop is available in Standard and Extended configurations in CS4, every technique that we describe can be done using the Standard version. The Extended version of Photoshop contains additional features that are of particular benefit when working with 3D, motion, architecture, and construction, as well as comprehensive image analysis such as a forensics expert might need to do. It's one of the few times that we nature photographers get to buy the less expensive version of something!

What's Inside

The organization of this book follows the general workflow that we recommend. Here is a glance at what's in each chapter:

Chapter 1: Thinking Digitally discusses the photographic techniques you need to use in-camera to get the best results. It covers choosing RAW versus JPEG, understanding exposure, understanding the various types of histograms, setting white balance, and shooting for composites, as well as ethical considerations.

Chapter 2: Bridge explains how to customize and use Bridge to download, view, compare, sort, and edit your images. You'll learn how to streamline this process and organize your images so you can easily find them.

Chapter 3: Adobe Camera Raw covers using the raw converter to make most of the global changes to your images, and localized adjustments using the new Adjustment Brush. The adjustments you make here are the foundation of your workflow and will help you create the best possible image.

Chapter 4: Foundations lays the foundation to make Photoshop or Elements work in a predictable way for you, including color-management issues as well as setting the Preferences. It also covers using some of the basic selection and brush tools you'll be using later as you optimize your images.

Chapter 5: Workflows and First Steps describes how to create a flexible workflow using Smart Objects and Smart Filters as well as the traditional workflow. It also covers cropping, rotating, and image cleanup and introduces the concept of layers.

Chapter 6: Exposure Adjustments introduces you to using layer masks and guides you through making various tonal adjustments, including Levels, Curves, and Shadow/Highlight.

Chapter 7: Color Adjustments continues the use of adjustment layers to help you fine-tune the color in your image using Hue/Saturation, Selective Color, and Color Balance.

Chapter 8: Composites covers a variety of ways to combine images to create effects not possible in a single image, including creating panoramas, replacing skies, creating extended depth of field, creating extended exposure latitude, and combining parts of various pictures into a single image.

Chapter 9: Creative Effects presents ways to become more expressive with your images, including converting to black and white or partially colorized images, using various filters, creating digital montages, and even making digital multiple exposures.

Chapter 10: Output covers the workflow after you have created your master file in order to resize, reduce noise, and sharpen your images for print or the Web.

Chapter 11: Time-Savers presents ways to become more efficient, including actions and batch processing. It also covers ways to create watermarks and copyright brushes.

What's on the CD

The companion CD contains a series of training videos to augment the materials in the book. The training videos cover many of the new features introduced in Photoshop CS4 as well as instruction on some basic techniques for both Photoshop and Elements users.

The CD also provides sample images for you to use to practice the techniques in the book. Use them to follow along with the instructions and to try each new technique. Taking the time to use these images will reinforce what you're reading. It also includes some auxiliary information including how to create greeting cards from your images and more details about creating web pages for Elements users.

How to Contact the Authors

Both of us welcome feedback from you about this book or about books you'd like to see from us in the future. You can reach Ellen by writing to ellenanon@mac.com or Josh by writing to joshanon@mac.com. For more information about Ellen's workshops and photography, visit her website at www.ellenanon.com. To learn more about Josh's writing and appearances, visit www.joshanon.com.

Sybex strives to keep you supplied with the latest tools and information you need for your work. Please check www.sybex.com/go/nature for additional content and updates that supplement this book.

Thinking Digitally

The first step in digital photography is to create the best possible picture in the field. The second step is to optimize that capture and use software to present the final image in the best possible way. Digital photography requires embracing certain concepts in addition to the traditional photographic tools. The better your photographic techniques and the more efficient your digital workflow, the less time you'll spend on the computer doing mundane tasks and fixing mistakes. That will leave more time for photography itself as well as creative interpretations of the images using Photoshop.

This chapter covers some of the basic digital concepts you need to consider while in the field as well as some common digital concerns.

Chapter Contents
Photographic Techniques
Choosing RAW versus JPEG
Understanding Histograms
Exposure
White Balance in Nature Photography
Color Management
Photographing Elements to Composite Later
Aperture and Lightroom
Storage Considerations

Photographic Techniques

With the advent of digital photography, some people erroneously thought that they didn't need to be as conscientious in the field; they assumed they could "fix" the image in Photoshop. In fact, nothing could be more harmful to the quality of your images than to be sloppy in the field with plans to "fix" the images later. Whether digital or film, the basics of photography remain the same. You still have to do everything possible to take the best pictures you can in the field. That way, you can devote the time you spend at your computer to optimizing images, being creative, and perhaps other business, rather than trying to compensate for mistakes you made while taking the pictures. Using Photoshop in conjunction with good photographic techniques will enable you to create images that are closer to what you envision than was ever possible in the past.

With digital cameras, you still need to use most of your photographic tools to help create the best images possible, including tripods, mirror lockup, and cable releases when appropriate. Although we claim to sharpen images in a raw converter or Photoshop using the Unsharp Mask or Smart Sharpen filter (techniques described in Chapter 10, "Output"), this sharpening is not designed to fix an out-of-focus picture. Rather, its intent is to compensate for the slight softening that occurs in the digital process.

Focus carefully and accurately so that you capture the sharpest picture you can. Use a tripod whenever it's reasonable. In fact, using a tripod is essential when you want to combine images to expand exposure latitude, and it's highly recommended when you intend to create a panorama by stitching together several individual photographs. If you don't use a tripod when taking several pictures at various exposure settings in order to create an exposure latitude composite, then when you try to combine them into a single image (discussed in Chapter 8, "Composites"), the images may not combine properly; in fact, they may not merge at all. If you try to shoot a panorama without a tripod, you're likely to encounter a variety of complications when you try to stitch them together, a topic also covered in Chapter 8.

You need to use a polarizer or split neutral-density filter when appropriate, even though it's essentially possible to create a custom neutral-density filter digitally by combining exposures or by using adjustment layers and layer masks, all of which are covered later in this book. If the scene lends itself to using a split neutral-density filter, as in Figure 1.1, it will save you time and effort later, so use it! However, you no longer need to use a warming or cooling filter since adjusting the white balance will alter the image in very similar ways.

Choose your camera settings such as Aperture Priority, Shutter Priority, or Manual to create the type of image you have in mind. Planning to use Photoshop is not an excuse to suddenly rely on the fully automatic shooting modes. Many nature photographers shoot in Aperture Priority or Manual because controlling the depth of field is their primary concern. If you envision a picture with a shallow depth of field, photograph it that way using a wide aperture to begin with rather than relying on one of the blur filters within Photoshop. Use a filter later to accentuate the effect if desired. Occasionally nature photographers choose to use Shutter Priority for a specific need, such as to create a blur of birds in flight (like the ones shown in Figure 1.2) or to create a pleasing softness to moving water. Although you can create motion blurs in

Photoshop, planning your image ahead of time (for example, using a slow shutter speed combined with panning) enables you to capture images with motion effects that would require a lot more time to make digitally. In some cases you can capture motion effects that would be nearly impossible to re-create in Photoshop, because objects closer to you blur more than objects that are farther away.

PHOTO BY ELLEN ANON

Figure 1.1 Use good photographic techniques, including tripods, cable releases, and even split neutral-density filters, when appropriate, to capture the best images possible and then optimize them in Photoshop for impact.

PHOTO BY ELLEN ANON

Figure 1.2 It is doubtful you could re-create this blur effect in Photoshop.

Throughout this book, we've asked some of the top nature photographers in the world to share some of their insights and favorite tips for using Photoshop effectively. Here, in the first of these "pro" sidebars, Charles Glatzer, M. Photog., briefly shares some thoughts about shooting digitally. Glatzer, a professional photographer and teacher for more than 20 years, hosts "Shoot the Light" instructional photographic workshops throughout the United States and abroad. His images are recognized internationally for their lighting, composition, and attention to detail.

Getting It Right in the Camera

by Charles Glatzer

Consistency is key to my livelihood. When capturing images in the field, I eliminate as many variables as possible.

To consistently transpose the images we see in our mind to the capture medium, it is necessary to previsualize the result. Previsualization is possible when one has gained technical proficiency. Knowing the photographic fundamentals and being able to see and understand light, its quality and quantity, its physical properties, etc., and how they relate to your subject and capture medium will allow you to take control of your imagery.

And although Photoshop affords me the ability to apply levels, curves, contrast, and saturation adjustments while tweaking exposure and color balance to an image, I prefer to get it right in the camera. In doing so, my workflow is now faster and more productive, allowing me to transpose the image I captured on my CF card to the printed page more efficiently.

Translation: I can spend more time in the field.

Compose carefully. Take the time to create a pleasing composition so you can use all the pixels your camera is capable of capturing. Of course you can crop the image later, but that means you will be cropping away pixels, leaving fewer pixels. With fewer pixels your final image may not be able to be printed as large as you had hoped.

Careful metering is as important as ever, but easier since you now have a histogram to give immediate feedback as to whether the exposure is correct. Meter as you always have, but make it a habit to check the histogram, at least for the first image in a series, to see whether you need to tweak your exposure.

Note: A full discussion of photographic techniques is beyond the scope of this book, but we recommend *Mastering Digital Photography and Imaging* by Peter K. Burian (Sybex, 2004).

Choosing RAW versus JPEG

It's funny how this became such an emotionally charged topic for some, almost akin to the classic "which is better?" debates, such as Nikon versus Canon or Mac versus PC. The truth is both formats have advantages and disadvantages, which we'll discuss. However, the evolution in software to convert raw images has made it just as easy, and in most cases more efficient, to use raw files rather than JPEGs. Most professionals now agree that it's best to shoot in RAW whenever possible.

Before considering the benefits of each format, we'll define what each one is. RAW is actually a pseudoformat used to refer to a lot of camera manufacturers' proprietary formats: Canon CR2 and CRW, Nikon NEF, Olympus ORF, Fuji RAF, and more. It's a category of files rather than a specific file format like JPEG and TIFF. Raw files are similar to film negatives. They're files containing all the information about the amount of light that was captured by each sensor. Parameters such as color space, white balance, sharpening, saturation, contrast, and so on are recorded as metadata or tags, but they're not applied to the image in-camera. You can still readily modify all these parameters at the time of conversion.

JPEG is a file format that uses lossy compression each time you resave your file in order to decrease the file size. This means as the pixels are compressed, data is thrown away, even the initial time when the camera first writes the image. Each time thereafter that you *resave* your image, it is recompressed, and more data is lost. Although you may not notice any problem with the initial image, if you resave an image often, you are likely to see some degradation in image quality. Figure 1.3 presents sections of the same image at 100 percent magnification. The first version was a raw file saved as a TIFF file; the second version was resaved numerous times as a JPEG to illustrate the potential image degradation that can occur.

TIFF is a generic file format people often use to save their raw files after conversion or to save images that were initially shot as JPEGs. TIFF files can be compressed, but they use lossless compression, so you can resave your files with no loss of image quality. TIFF files are larger than JPEG files, meaning that they require more space on a hard drive.

PHOTO BY ELLEN ANON

Figure 1.3 A section of an image originally captured as a raw file and the same section after being resaved multiple times as a JPEG.

Another difference among these formats has to do with something called *bit depth*. Many nature photographers start to feel over their heads when computerese slips into the discussion, but bit depth isn't very complicated. In simple terms, a *bit* is the smallest unit of information that can be recorded digitally—either a 1 or a 0—and it refers to black or white (even in a color image). In an 8-bit image, each color channel (red, green, and blue) contains 2^8 or 256 possible tonal values. Since each channel has 256 possible tonal values, each pixel has 16.7 million ($256 \times 256 \times 256$) possible color values, as shown in Table 1.1.

Table 1.1 Colors and Bit Depths

Bit Depth	Typical Format	Possible Colors per Component	Possible Colors per Pixel
8 bits	JPEG	256	16.7 million
12 bits	RAW	4,096	68.7 billion
16 bits	PSD, TIFF	65,536	281 trillion

Now, 16 million color choices may seem like more than enough, but in reality, at times the transitions between tones in an 8-bit image are not smooth, which is called *posterization* or *banding*. Twelve-bit images, which is what many cameras can capture in RAW, have 4,096 tonal values for each color channel, which means a choice of 68.7 billion ($4,096 \times 4,096 \times 4,096$) possible colors. Some of the newest high-end digital SLR cameras capture 14-bit images, which means nearly 4.4 trillion color choices ($16,384 \times 16,384 \times 16,384$). Tonal gradations are much smoother with so many possible values for each pixel.

JPEG images are limited to 8 bits, so some JPEG images may demonstrate posterization. Although not a problem for many images, some images, particularly those requiring smooth gradual transitions of color and tone, such as sunset pictures, may show evidence of banding. Clearly, more detail can be accurately conveyed the higher the bit depth. Eight-bit color files used to be common, but 16-bit images are now the standard for most photographers. Thirty-two-bit files are starting to emerge and can be created using Photoshop's Merge to HDR, which we'll cover in Chapter 8. (HDR stands for *high dynamic range*.)

It can seem confusing initially that in Photoshop you have options to choose 8-bit or 16-bit images (even 32-bit if you've created an HDR image) when a JPEG image is clearly an 8-bit file and a raw file is either a 12- or 14-bit file. Converting a 12-bit capture into an 8-bit file results in a smaller file in which you have discarded 3,840 possible tonal values per color channel, and even more if the image was a 14-bit file. That's a lot to throw away!

When you convert a raw file that is initially 12 or 14 bits into 16-bit space, you retain all your original data. You can use the additional tonal values as you make adjustments to the image. In other words, as you tweak the color and tonal values within the image, the adjustments can take advantage of the additional tonal options. Way back in Photoshop 7, there was minimal support for 16-bit images, but all of the more recent versions of Photoshop offer considerable support, making it logical to convert into 16-bit space.

What's So Great about RAW?

A lot of things! As just described, you have many more possible tonal values, which offer the possibility of more accurate detail in your photos and smoother tonal transitions. But RAW has other advantages as well. For example, you can "expose to the right" (as we'll describe shortly, in the "Exposure" section of this chapter) to optimize the signal-to-noise ratio and then correct the exposure in the raw converter to yield the most accurate tonal information with the least problems from noise.

More important, all the information captured by the sensor is available, and during the conversion process, you determine how it appears. A tremendous amount of flexibility and control is available to you as to how to present the information you captured on the sensor, as you can see in Figure 1.4. The raw capture (top) was converted with settings that revealed significantly more color than was captured in the JPEG version (bottom) of the same image. No pixels have been damaged, and yet the image is significantly more dramatic.

PHOTO BY ELLEN ANON

Figure 1.4 Notice the increased color and impact of the raw capture as compared to the rather bland JPEG capture.

You can modify the exposure of raw files after the fact, making the image lighter or darker, sometimes significantly lighter or darker. In most cases, you can tweak the exposure in the raw converter such that there is rarely a need to bracket exposures by a third of a stop in the camera anymore, except when you are in danger of clipping your highlights. *Clipping highlights* means you have overexposed your image and captured no detail in the highlights. In the latest raw converters, including Adobe Camera Raw (ACR), you can recapture some highlight and/or shadow detail that initially may appear to be clipped as long as the information was recorded on the sensor. You may be able to recapture roughly one stop worth of information from clipped highlights, and two stops worth of information from clipped shadows. Although you can instruct the converter to distribute the information the sensor captured in ways that will maximize the contrast, decrease it, or change the white balance, and so on, what you can't do is re-create information that isn't there. So if you have highlights or shadows with no information, you may be able to lighten or darken them, but you won't be able to re-create detail within them.

That may make it seem that you would be wise to underexpose rather than overexpose, but the fact is that more noise may become visible in the image when it is lightened, as shown in Figure 1.5. For the best results, try to limit lightening in a raw converter to one stop or less. We'll talk more about this issue later in this chapter when we discuss exposing to the right.

PHOTO BY ELLEN ANON

Figure 1.5 Lightening the rocks revealed considerable color noise— the magenta, green, and blue blobs on areas of the rocks should be shades of gray.

In addition to being able to make final decisions about parameters such as exposure, contrast, white balance, color saturation, and more in the raw converter, you can even select the color space there. Usually you will want Adobe RGB (1998), which is a wide color space that correlates well to the colors most ink-jet printers can print. When capturing as JPEG files, most cameras use the sRGB color space, which has fewer colors available. sRGB is particularly suited for web use and projection. We'll talk more about color spaces in Chapter 4, "Foundations."

Note: If your camera allows you to select a color space, Adobe RGB (1998) is a good choice for nature photographers.

RAW also offers you the ability to easily fix some problems that occur in some images, such as noise reduction for images taken using higher ISOs, chromatic aberration that occurs with some lenses resulting in fringing, and vignetting. We'll explain how to identify these potential problems and how to easily minimize or eliminate these issues in Chapter 3, "Adobe Camera Raw."

It used to be that the downside of all this flexibility and capability was that in order to use raw images you had to convert them. Although you still have to convert a raw file before final output, new software such as Aperture and Lightroom make it as easy to work with raw files as with JPEGs. We'll talk more about those programs later in this chapter. Additionally, ACR is now so powerful that you can do nearly all your optimizing right in the raw converter within an easy-to-use interface. Photoshop CS4 improved a feature called *Smart Objects*, which enables you to place a raw image directly in your PS file and adjust it at will. We'll cover this more extensively in Chapter 5, "Workflows and First Steps."

The one remaining notable downside of shooting in RAW is that you will need a lot more storage space, both in your camera and on your computer, when you capture in RAW than if you use JPEG.

Advantages and Disadvantages of Shooting JPEGs

Shooting JPEGs does offer some conveniences. For example, capturing in even high-resolution JPEG means you need less storage space; a 1GB compact flash card will make you feel like you can shoot forever. Also convenient is that JPEG images are ready for you to edit or resize and show others in slide shows, emails, or whatever you desire (although programs such as Aperture offer these same conveniences for raw files).

But JPEGs have two *huge* downsides. One is that whatever your camera settings are, including color space, contrast, sharpening, white balance, exposure, and saturation, they are applied to your image at the moment of capture. Any changes must be done within Photoshop itself to this 8-bit image and will result in some destruction of pixels and therefore image degradation. In reality, this may often be so slight that it's not noticeable, but it's there. And sometimes the differences may be huge. For example, if you accidentally use the wrong white balance, a JPEG image may be nearly useless at first and at best may require extensive corrections in Photoshop. But the extent of the exposure corrections you'll be able to make will be less because you'll have only an 8-bit image to work with, and extensive Photoshop corrections may result in posterization or noise. Furthermore, as discussed earlier, a JPEG file is compressed lossy, which means that even when you first open it on your computer, it has already thrown away some information the sensor captured when you took the picture. Sometimes this is not noticeable, but at other times it can result in banding and other strange artifacts.

Which is right for you, JPEG or RAW? For most serious amateur and professional photographers, RAW is the way to go. If you make large prints and want the best images you can get, RAW is without a doubt the way to go. If limited storage space is your main priority and if you primarily post your images on the Web, email them to friends, and make only an occasional tiny print, then JPEG may be for you. If you plan on selling your images or entering contests, check with your intended clients or the contest rules, because some will require you to provide the original raw file as well as the converted image.

Try It! Shoot a series of images in RAW and in JPEG. Expose them to the best of your ability in JPEG and then use the same settings for the raw version. Then shoot one set with an incorrect white-balance setting. Capture a variety of scenes, including some with shadow areas, some with significant highlight areas, and some more average-toned scenes. See whether you can detect a difference in the optimized versions. You may have to wait until you finish a few more chapters so you can optimize both versions of the pictures to their maximum potential for your final decision.

Understanding Histograms

Without a doubt one of the most important advantages of shooting digitally is the ability to check the histogram to ensure you are exposing your images correctly. In the old days—that is, just a few years ago, before digital cameras were so common in the field—wherever there was a group of photographers shooting similar subject matter, you'd inevitably hear someone ask, "What are you shooting at?" People felt comfortable with their compositions but always worried about setting the exposure correctly, knowing that as little as $\frac{1}{3}$ stop difference could mean the difference between an awesome image and a throwaway.

With digital cameras you can review your shots on the small LCD screen on the back of the camera. Although this may be somewhat helpful for double-checking your composition and to a certain extent to check for sharpness, the real value lies in displaying the histogram. Get in the habit of checking the histogram in the LCD on the camera back (like the one shown in Figure 1.6). In addition, if your camera has a flashing highlight-overexposure alert feature, be sure to enable it. The alert will cause the area of the picture that appears to have clipped highlights to blink or have marching ants. That way you'll know immediately what areas may not have highlight detail, and you can decide whether you need to modify your exposures.

Note: The highlight alert feature on most cameras is calculated based on a JPEG version of the image using the current camera settings. Therefore it may indicate clipping when the data may exist in the raw file. Use it as a guideline for potential clipping rather than an absolute indication of clipping. Also use it to note what areas of the image are in danger of clipping so you can make an informed decision whether to alter the exposure.

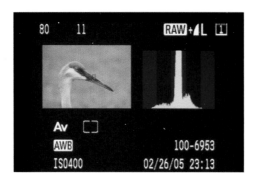

Figure 1.6 The major value of the LCD screen on your camera back is the chance to review the histogram and double-check your exposure.

What is a *histogram*? It's simply a bar graph showing the distribution of the tonalities (lightness/darkness) of the pixels you captured in the image. Each pixel not only describes a color value, but also a brightness value. The tonal range extends from pure black on the far left to pure white on the far right, with the different tonalities in between. This means that dark tones are toward the left, middle tones are in the middle, and light tones are toward the right. The higher the peak corresponding to any particular value, the more pixels there are of that particular tonality within the image.

Types of Histograms

Not all histograms are the same. Many cameras display an RGB histogram that is a combination of the pixel values in each of the three channels. This is different from a luminosity or brightness histogram that other cameras use. The data in a luminosity histogram is a weighted combination of the values in each channel. Still other cameras display histograms that show each channel individually. Each type of histogram has advantages and disadvantages.

Luminosity histograms are easier to use to determine if you have areas within your image that are pure white or pure black, lacking detail. The only time a pixel will register against the far-right or far-left side of a luminosity histogram is when all three channels have a value of 0 or all three have a value of 255. With a luminosity histogram, there is no question that if you have a spike of data on either edge, you have pure black and/or pure white areas in your image, as shown in Figure 1.7.

RGB histograms sometimes look very similar to their luminosity counterparts, while at other times, they differ substantially. An RGB histogram presents all the data from each channel, so if just one channel has a value of 0 or 255, you will see data peaking against the edges of the histogram. It will appear that you could have highlights or shadows that are pure black or white when in fact that may not be the case, as shown in Figure 1.8.

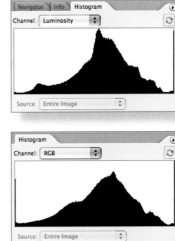

Figure 1.7 When a luminosity histogram has a spike on one or both edges, you can be certain that the image has areas that are pure white, like the windows in this image, or pure black.

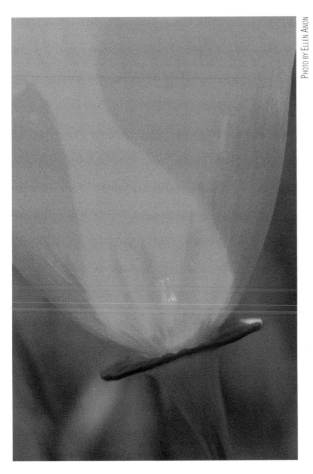

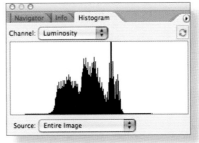

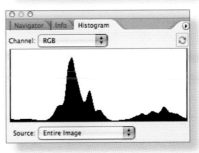

Figure 1.8 If your image contains very saturated colors, the RGB histogram may indicate potential blown-out and/or blocked-up areas, whereas a luminosity histogram will clearly indicate that these areas are not close to being pure white or pure black.

RGB histograms may have spikes on the edges when there are no white or black areas because some colors legitimately have one or more channels with values of 0 or 255. For example, pure red is represented by RGB values of 255, 0, 0; pure green would be 0, 255, 0; and pure blue would be 0, 0, 255. Similarly, cyan is 0, 255, 255; magenta is 255, 0, 255; and yellow is 255, 255, 0. But those are not the only colors that use the extreme values of 0 and 255.

Any color that has a value of 0 or 255 in a single channel will contribute to a spike on the edge of an RGB histogram. For example, the purple in Figure 1.9 has a color value of 132, 0, 189. In an RGB histogram, any pixel that shade of purple will contribute to a spike in the shadows, making it appear as if there are blocked-up shadows when there may not be. That same shade of purple will be represented by data at the point corresponding to a tonal value of 60 in a luminosity histogram...far away from either end of the histogram. Figure 1.9 shows the differences in the histograms for this shade of purple.

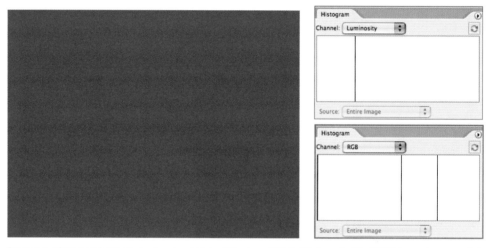

Figure 1.9 A histogram for this shade of purple, which has RGB values of 132, 0, 189, shows that the RGB histogram is composed of three lines, one at 0, one at 132, and one at 189, whereas the luminosity histogram has a single line at 60.

That may make it seem like it would always be easier to use a luminosity histogram. The issue is that if you have a subject with very saturated colors, such as a poppy or a bright-red cardinal, in reality the colors vary slightly to allow you to perceive detail in the flower petals or the bird's feathers. So, you need to have the tonal values varying. If a lot of the pixels use values that contain 0 or 255, the chances are that you don't have as much detail in those colors as you may need. A luminosity histogram would give you no indication of any potential trouble, whereas an RGB histogram would clearly indicate potential trouble. By subtracting or filtering the light from an exposure, you may be able to capture those areas of the flower or bird with more detail.

Which type of histogram should you use? That depends. It used to be that most cameras offered only one or the other type of histogram; however, some of the newer models offer a choice. What's most important is to be aware of what type of histogram you're viewing so you will understand precisely what the data is saying.

Interpreting Histograms

Some people mistakenly think that an ideal histogram would be a bell-shaped distribution of pixels. *In fact, there's not a single ideal histogram for all images.* The histogram just reflects the tones in the scene that you are capturing given that particular exposure setting. The ideal exposure for most scenes will yield a histogram that indicates all the data has been captured without any clipping. Let's look at a series of pictures and their histograms.

Figure 1.10 shows a good histogram for an average scene with a full range of tonalities. Note that the pixels extend across the entire histogram, but there are no spikes at either end. Spikes at the ends would mean you have pixels that are overexposed or underexposed and therefore areas with no detail. Since all the pixels fall within the bounds of the histogram, this picture will have detail throughout.

PHOTO BY ELLEN ANON

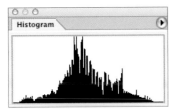

Figure 1.10 This is an ideal histogram for a scene with a full range of tonalities.

Figure 1.11 shows an underexposed picture. Most of the pixels are in the left portion of the histogram, indicating no light tones. Since you know that the pelican is in fact white, a proper exposure would have the pixel distribution moved to the right. If you are shooting a subject with a large light area and you see a histogram that looks like Figure 1.11, you need to add light to your exposure.

Figure 1.11 This picture is underexposed. Note that all the data in the histogram is skewed toward the left and there are no light tonalities.

Compare the image and histogram in Figure 1.11 with those of Figure 1.12. The latter is a well-exposed picture with an ideal histogram of an overall dark scene with a few important bright areas. If the exposure had been any brighter, the whites would have been *blown out* and lost their feather detail. *Blown-out highlights* means that no detail has been captured in the brightest areas of the picture. It's another way of referring to clipping. Since I want to retain feather detail in the white areas, it's important to safeguard against clipping the highlights. Although the darker portions of the picture may need to be lightened in the raw converter or in Photoshop, this is the ideal in-camera capture for this image because it captures all the detail information in the highlights and most of the shadows. However, if the white areas were in the background or less important areas, then I would recommend adding light to this exposure to capture all the detail in the dark areas. It would be likely that although an additional ½ stop of light in the exposure might initially appear to clip the highlights, they may be recoverable in the raw converter.

Don't get confused between an ideal in-camera histogram for the capture and the final histogram of the optimized image, which may be noticeably different. The goal in-camera is to capture as much information as possible, particularly in your main subject. Once you have the information, you can modify it as you tweak the image, but information you don't capture in the first place is not going to be there no matter what!

Figure 1.13 shows an overexposed image. Note the spike on the right side of the histogram, indicating blown-out highlights. Unfortunately, no amount of Photoshop magic can restore data that was not captured. Checking your camera's histogram regularly and using the highlight alert feature in your camera can avoid the frustration of taking an entire series of pictures like this.

Figure 1.12 Overall dark scenes with small important bright areas will have histograms that look like this. This is not underexposed for the raw capture even though the data is skewed toward the left, as in Figure 1.11.

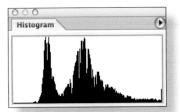

Figure 1.13 The whites in this image are blown out, as indicated by the spike on the right side of the histogram.

Now compare the histogram and picture in Figure 1.13 with those in Figure 1.14. This picture of white birds on a nearly white sky is not overexposed, although most of the pixel data is skewed toward the right. This is the type of histogram you want in this kind of situation—light background and light subject with minimal dark areas.

PHOTO BY ELLEN ANON

Figure 1.14 A light subject with a light background will have a histogram that is skewed toward the right.

Figure 1.15 shows a histogram of a high-contrast scene. It has a spike on the left side of the histogram, although the data extends through the tonalities all the way toward the right of the histogram. There is no way to capture this shot at this time of day without losing either some highlight detail or some shadow detail. Ordinarily it's better to preserve the highlights and sacrifice some shadow detail, as was done in this image. An alternative appropriate for some situations, which we will discuss later, is to shoot multiple exposures and combine them in one image.

Finally, let's look at the histogram of a silhouette in Figure 1.16. As you may expect, the far-left side of the histogram shows a spike, but in this case, it doesn't mean the image is underexposed. On the contrary, we want silhouettes to be pure black! Sometimes when you shoot a silhouette, the spike won't be all the way toward the left. The reason for this is you will need to expose the image so that you capture the most detail possible in the rest of the image. This will mean exposing to the right (which we'll discuss later in this chapter) even if the silhouette is then too bright. It's a simple matter to darken the silhouette in the raw converter or in Photoshop. By exposing to the right and then darkening part of the image, the darkest tones will have less noise.

Figure 1.15 This scene has too much contrast to capture in a single shot. The spike on the far left of the histogram shows that there is some loss of information in the shadows, but the highlights have been preserved. (Note that the small spike on the right is just before the end of the histogram.)

Figure 1.16 Silhouettes will often have histograms that have a thin spike on the left edge, indicating areas of pure black.

The bottom line is that there is no single ideal histogram for every situation. You have to think about the tonalities in your image and where they should fall on the histogram to know what is ideal for any particular situation. It's important to make sure you don't have spikes at the extreme ends of the graph, since that could mean shadow or highlight areas without detail. However, when the lighting has so much contrast that you can't avoid spikes on one or both ends of the histogram, you must consider the tonalities of your subject and preserve as much detail as possible in the subject. If necessary, you can forgo some detail in the background. Normally the order of priorities is to preserve detail in the subject; don't clip the highlights, even in the background; and maintain shadow detail, including in the background. If your subject has a very dark area and the background has bright areas—such as bright clouds— you may opt to maintain the detail in the dark areas of your subject at the expense of the detail in the clouds. Of course, if you are shooting a silhouette, a spike at the left side of the histogram indicating black for the silhouette is acceptable, while any specular highlights may be fine as pure white. (*Specular highlights* are those extremely bright areas that occur when the sun reflects off water or metal or other highly reflective surfaces. We expect those areas to be pure white without detail.) But for most images, in order to capture detail in both the shadows and the highlights, you want the tonalities to fall within the boundaries of the histogram.

Note: Some photographers new to digital and Photoshop think they don't have to worry about exposure anymore because they can "fix it" later in Photoshop. The harsh reality is if you blow out the highlights or totally block up the shadows, the only "fix" will be to clone in pixels from other areas. Photoshop gives you lots of ways to tweak the exposure, which we'll explain in Chapters 3, "Adobe Camera Raw," and 6, "Exposure Adjustments," but if the data isn't there because of overexposure or underexposure, Photoshop isn't going to create it for you.

Exposure

If you check the histogram and see that you have a spike at the far right and room on the left side, you need to modify your exposure to have less light. If you are shooting in Aperture Priority, you may choose to put in some minus exposure compensation, or if you are using manual mode, either use a smaller aperture or increase your shutter speed. Because you're shooting digitally, you have a third option—to switch to a slower ISO. Although you still need to set the correct exposure compensation, you can use the same depth of field/aperture setting as you originally wanted (perhaps in an effort to keep the background out of focus) and/or the same shutter speed (perhaps in an attempt to blur your subject).

Similarly, if the histogram is indicating a spike at the black end and has room on the right side, you'll want to add light via plus exposure compensation, slower shutter speeds, wider apertures, and/or possibly a faster ISO to allow you to use the desired apertures and shutter speeds. Faster ISOs—those with the larger numbers—

mean that less light is required to hit the sensor to achieve the proper exposure. The problem with this is that the faster the ISO, the more noise the picture may have. Some cameras have less noise while using higher ISOs than do other cameras. Test your own camera to determine the highest ISO you can use without noise becoming an issue. When using a higher ISO, be extra careful not to underexpose your image, because when you go to lighten it the increased noise will become apparent. In general, use the slowest (smallest number) ISO that you can. We usually leave our cameras set to ISO 200 and change the ISO according to the situation.

> **Note:** Usually, the lower the ISO, the less noise you will encounter. Noise is in many ways the digital equivalent of film grain, except that it tends to be more evident in darker shadow areas. It appears as variations in color and tonality in areas that should be smooth.

Technically, not only should the ideal histogram for a raw image contain all the pixels with no spikes at the ends, but also it should be exposed as far to the right as possible with no blown-out highlights. This is to obtain the best signal-to-noise ratio possible. (It is important to keep in mind that this applies to raw images but not to those captured as JPEGs because the main benefits occur in the process of the conversion. If you are shooting in JPEG, make the most accurate exposure you can, and make sure you're not clipping data on either end.)

Michael Reichmann does an excellent job of explaining this, so we asked him to share that explanation with you. The following section, "Expose Right," was written and contributed by him. For more information on Reichmann and his work, please visit his website, www.luminous-landscape.com.

"Expose Right" by Michael Reichmann

In the beginning there was the light meter. Photographers used them and saw that they were good. Then there was through-the-lens metering, and the people rejoiced. Automatic exposure followed, and photographers thought that the millennium had arrived. Eventually the millennium actually did arrive, and with it digital cameras with histogram displays; and the world changed again.

What hasn't changed over the years is the need for accurate exposure, which all of this technology is ultimately in aid of. But what constitutes proper exposure is quite different between film and digital. In this section, you'll see why and how to take best advantage of it.

Don't Blow It

Digital is very much like color slide film in that you want to avoid overexposure. Although it's often possible to recover some information from the shadows of an underexposed digital image (especially if a low ISO is being used), once overexposed beyond 255, there is no information to be retrieved. The individual photo sites or pixels have simply recorded 100 percent of the information that they can absorb, and this is a featureless white.

Note: We authors interrupt Michael here to say the exposure scale of a histogram goes from black at 0 to white at 255 in 8-bit capture; the same principle applies for 12-bit capture, where the maximum value is 4,095. For the sake of convenience, the convention is to describe histograms as extending from 0 to 255, whether for 8-bit, 12-bit, or 16-bit images.

This would lead most people to think that the best thing to do would therefore be to bias their exposure toward the left of the histogram—toward underexposure. This would avoid the risk of blown-out highlights, and since it's often possible to retrieve detail from underexposed shadow areas, what have you got to lose?

A lot, actually, as you'll see.

Signals and Noise

Film has *grain*. These are particles of silver or organic dyes that, when exposed to light, turn dark to varying degrees. Fast films have more grain because they have more of these light-sensitive particles with which to absorb light.

Digital uses very tiny photo sites—sensor elements made of silicon that are sensitive to light. Essentially, if no light hits a sensor element, no voltage is generated, and a value of 0 or black is recorded. If the sensor element is flooded with light (over-exposed), it records a maximum value of 255 (in an 8-bit image) and a corresponding voltage level is produced. Light levels in between are recorded as some value between 0 and 255.

Although silicon doesn't suffer directly from what we describe as grain, it does have a comparable issue. This is described as *noise*. Noise in this context is any form of non-image-forming energy (light is just one form of energy). Various things can cause noise to be recorded by the sensor. These include heat, cosmic rays, and several other exotic sources. All silicon chips have an inherent noise level. As a percentage of the total signal being recorded, it is usually quite small and unnoticeable. But it's always there, and depending on the exposure being recorded, it can become visible and annoying. This is somewhat akin to the noise that one sees on a TV screen when there's no channel broadcasting or antenna attached.

Note: We authors interrupt to add that usually the energy that causes noise is low enough in its intensity that it falls to the left (dark) side of the histogram.

This is where what we call the sensor's *signal-to-noise* (s/n) ratio comes in. If there's a lot of signal (data to the right side of the histogram), then the s/n ratio is high, the signal predominates, and the noise isn't visible. But if the signal is low (to the left of the histogram), then the s/n ratio is low, and you see the noise because it represents a relatively high percentage of the total signal present.

So, the solution is clear. Take a photograph, check the instant review histogram, and make sure that the exposure is as far to the right of the histogram as possible without touching the right edge.

But wait. This has a problem. If you do this and you're shooting JPEGs, you'll see some fairly nasty-looking exposures—ones that appear very bright, inappropriately so. Of course, you can try to fix the shot in an image-editing program such as Photoshop. But because JPEGs are prebaked images (reduced to 8-bit mode and with predetermined exposure and color-balance characteristics embedded in the file while in the camera), such adjustments can't always be performed while still retaining decent image quality. So, with JPEGs at least, the idea of biasing your exposures to the right of the histogram appears to be good in theory but not terribly practical.

Raw Mode

The answer is to shoot in raw mode. In raw mode, the file contains the data that the sensor recorded. In addition, *tags* describe the camera's settings, such as white balance, sharpening, contrast saturation, and the like. But these tags are just that. The raw file itself is not changed in any way. It is also in 12-bit or 14-bit mode and in a 16-bit space (more on this in a moment). Finally, a raw file isn't compressed the way a JPEG file is. If it is compressed, which a few manufacturers do, it's done so losslessly.

Dynamic Range and Bit Mode

The concept of *bit mode* is important to properly understanding digital image quality. Assume for the purposes of illustration that a digital SLR has a dynamic range of five stops. (It's usually closer to six stops, but let's not quibble.) When working in raw mode, most cameras record a 12 or 14-bit image. (Yes, we say it's in 16 bits, but the reality is that the camera is recording only 12 or 14 bits of information in a 16-bit space. This is better than 8 but not as good as a real 16 bits would be.)

A 12-bit image is capable of recording 2^{12} = 4,096 discrete tonal values in each component. You would therefore think that each f/stop of the five-stop range would be able to record some 4,096 ÷ 5 = 850 of these steps. But, alas, this is not the case. The way it really works is that the first (brightest) stop worth of data contains 2,048 of these steps—fully half of those available.

Why? Because CCD and CMOS chips are linear devices. And, of course, each f/stop records half the light of the previous one and therefore half the remaining data space available. Table 1.2 tells the tale.

Table 1.2 Where Light Levels Are Stored on Chips

F/Stop	Number of Levels Available
Within the first f/stop, which contains the brightest tones	2,048
Within the second f/stop, which contains bright tones	1,024
Within the third f/stop, which contains the midtones	512
Within the fourth f/stop, which contains dark tones	256
Within the fifth f/stop, which contains the darkest tones	128

This realization carries with it a number of important lessons, the most important of them being that if you do not use the right fifth of the histogram for recording some of your image, you are in fact wasting fully half of the available encoding levels of your camera.

But we all know (or at least should by now) that the worst sin in digital imaging is to blow out the highlights—just as it was when shooting slide film. Once they're blown (past the right edge of the histogram), it's bye-bye, data.

The Lesson

The simple lesson to be learned from this is to bias your exposures so that the histogram is snuggled up to the right (as illustrated in Figure 1.17) but not to the point that the highlights are blown. This can be seen by the flashing alert on most camera LCD screens. Just back off so that the flashing stops.

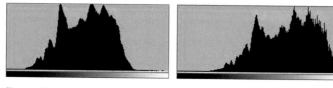

Figure 1.17 A normal exposure shows a centered histogram (left). This histogram is shifted to the right for maximum signal/noise ratio (right).

Now when you look at the raw file in your favorite raw-processing software, such as Camera Raw, the image will likely appear to be too light. That's OK. Just use the available sliders to change the brightness level and contrast so that the data is spread out appropriately and the image looks "right." This accomplishes a number of goals. First, it maximizes the s/n ratio. Second, it minimizes the posterization and noise that potentially occurs in the darker regions of the image.

Please be aware, though, that for proper results you need to make these corrections while working in 16-bit (12-bit) mode in a raw converter. Unlike what some people think, in raw mode the camera is not doing any nonlinear processing. All nonlinear processing takes place in the raw converter. This is why if you're going to try this trick, you must shoot in RAW and then manually readjust the image in the raw converter before exporting the file into Photoshop. By doing this, you'll be maximizing the data bandwidth of your entire system.

Also be aware that by doing this, you are in fact effectively lowering the ISO used to capture the image, requiring slower shutter speeds and/or larger apertures. If you are holding the camera by hand or shooting moving objects, the trade-off may not be worth the reduced noise level.

But, if ultimate image quality is your goal and you have the ability to control all the variables, *exposing to the right* is a technique that will serve you well.

© 2004 Michael H. Reichmann, `www.luminous-landscape.com`

White Balance in Nature Photography

With film cameras, you use specific types of film according to the lighting conditions, and you use filters to further control the color casts. With digital, you have a somewhat equivalent but far more flexible choice, which is white balance. As you know, the color (or temperature) of light varies throughout each day. It's a "warmer" color in the morning, and the world takes on a reddish/yellow glow. Your eyes adapt to that and compensate because you know that white is still white. (Think about when you put sunglasses on and a few minutes later the colors look "normal" again.) Later, when the bright sun is overhead, the color appears "cooler," or bluer. Your eyes continuously adapt so that you see neutral colors as neutral, and most people are rarely aware of color casts.

Your cameras are more literal—they record the colors exactly as they see them. With digital cameras you can use the white balance setting to render the neutral tones (any shade from white to black where the red, green, and blue values are all the same) as neutral, rather than rendering them with a color cast. For example, you need a different white balance in the cool bluish light of an overcast day than in the warm reddish light of a sunset. All digital cameras offer an automatic white balance setting in which the camera makes a best guess as to the correct lighting temperature. Surprisingly, most do quite a good job, as shown in Figure 1.18.

Some photographers think the best way to be certain of getting the correct white balance is to set it themselves. However, most of these photographers are content to use one of the presets supplied with the camera, such as Flash, Sunny, Cloudy, Shade, Fluorescent, and so on.

PHOTO BY ELLEN ANON

Figure 1.18 Auto white balance was used to capture this photo in the warm light of early morning.

If you don't use Auto White Balance and you shoot JPEGs, you must be vigilant about changing lighting conditions and altering your white balance accordingly. As you can see in Figure 1.19, if you use the wrong white balance setting, your picture may have a strong color cast. If you shot the image in RAW, you can easily correct this during the conversion process; but if you shot it in JPEG, a mistake like this could ruin the image.

Figure 1.19 The white balance here was accidentally set to Tungsten. A mistake like this can be deadly if the image is shot in JPEG.

But if you've ever gotten up before dawn to go out and photograph in the beautiful, warm, early morning light, you know that nature photographers aren't always seeking to make neutrally colored images! Often, nature photographers want a color cast in their images, particularly a warm cast, as shown in Figure 1.20. This is one of the reasons we prefer to shoot in raw mode; we don't have to make a final decision about the precise white balance until we're converting the image, whereas with JPEG mode, the white balance is "baked" into the image. We retain the option to set the final white balance to be as accurate as possible or to set it to reflect the mood we want to portray rather than the exact lighting conditions at the time.

PHOTO BY ELLEN ANON

Figure 1.20 This picture, taken at dawn, actually has a warmer, pinker color cast than what existed at the time, but the result is pleasing. Altering the white balance lets you convey a mood effectively.

If you are shooting in JPEG, you may want to experiment with using the auto white balance feature, along with setting the white balance specifically. You may not only want to set the white balance for an accurate rendition of the scene, but you may also want to experiment a little. For example, if you use the Cloudy or Shade setting in fairly sunny conditions, it's similar to adding an 81A or 81B filter to your camera lens; these settings will add a warm cast to your picture. Product photographers must be concerned with absolute color accuracy in their photography. Nature photographers have the luxury of being able to be creative with the white balance and create, augment, or remove color casts as it suits their vision. You can use the white balance settings rather than filters to do this both with JPEG and with RAW.

When you capture your images as raw files, because the white balance you selected in the camera is not actually applied until you convert the image, you have the luxury of time to adjust the white balance as you want. Most raw converters provide continuous temperature and tint sliders to set the white balance that best fits the mood of the image. You can tweak it in small increments to precisely obtain the effect you want. Because of this, many photographers elect to leave their cameras on auto white balance and then use the sliders in the converters to impart or remove color casts. Others still select what they believe is the best white balance setting while in the field so they can recall what the lighting was and how the image actually appeared. They prefer to have their images be as close to accurate, realistic color as possible. Who's right? Both are! It's a matter of your personal goals and preferences with your photography.

Note: If you are using auto white balance, using a warming or cooling filter may have no effect, because most cameras will compensate for the filter and try to make everything neutral!

Color Management

For any photographer, achieving accurate color is a key concern. You need to know that the way the image looks on your monitor is how it will look when it's output. While you may take artistic license in how you optimize an image, you want to ensure that a print or image you show in a slideshow or on the Web is an accurate reflection of your interpretation of the image. That means producing output that matches the monitor display to the extent possible. This is the job of color management, and it can help you achieve greater consistency in your workflow. The workflow and settings we recommend throughout the book will help you establish a color-managed workflow.

Monitor Calibration

The first step in a color-managed workflow is to calibrate and profile your monitor. We can't stress how important this is. If you don't have a calibrated display, the images you are evaluating and optimizing are likely to be at least slightly—and possibly significantly—inaccurate. They might look good to you on your monitor, but your prints are unlikely to match what you see. If you don't calibrate your monitor, you also have no valid reason to complain about prints that don't match your monitor. Calibrating your monitor is a critical first step to producing the results you are looking for with your images.

As far as we're concerned, calibrating your monitor is done properly only by using a package that uses a colorimeter (a type of sensor) to measure the color values of your monitor so that appropriate compensation can be applied (see Figure 1.21). There are several packages available that include a colorimeter, and we're perfectly comfortable with any of them. We asked Jon Canfield, an expert on color management, to describe some of the current devices.

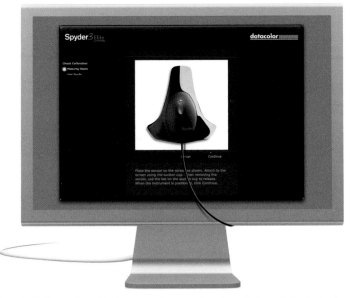

Figure 1.21 For monitor calibration, use a software package that includes a colorimeter to measure the color behavior of your monitor and apply compensation to ensure an accurate display.

Color Management Essentials

by Jon Canfield

PHOTO BY JON CANFIELD

Having a calibrated monitor is a critical part of the digital workflow. There are plenty of options, from the free Adobe Gamma on Windows (included with Photoshop in the Extras folder), to the Color Calibration Assistant that ships with Apple's OS X. Both of these programs let you make adjustments to your display by visually comparing different color patches. While this is better than nothing, it's far from ideal.

Continues

Color Management Essentials *(Continued)*

The best option is hardware calibration. These small devices measure different colors directly from the screen with a colorimeter, evaluating them for accuracy. Once this is done, a profile is created that sets your monitor to the optimum settings. At the low end in cost is the PANTONE huey. At less than $100, it does a good job of calibrating your monitor and has a feature to adjust the display as the ambient light changes. The next step up in accuracy and options are the X-Rite i1Display 2 and the Datacolor Spyder3Elite. Both of these devices give you the option to set color temperature and gamma. By using more color patches, both of these tools can create very accurate profiles. Expect to pay approximately $250 for either of these products. The final option is a spectrophotometer, which can also create printer profiles. The options here are the X-Rite ColorMunki, the Spyder3Studio, and the i1Photo. The ColorMunki is a new addition to the field and can profile monitors, printers, and digital projectors as well as do spot color measurements. If you use specialty papers, at less than $500, the ColorMunki can easily pay for itself with custom profiles. It's priced substantially less than the i1 Photo.

Note: Although Adobe Gamma is no longer installed by default in PCs, it may still be in your Startup folder if you are using an older version of the OS. If it's present, it overrides any custom profiles you try to use. To remove it, do the following:

1. Click Start.

2. Select All Programs.

3. Select Startup.

4. Right-click on Adobe Gamma and select Delete.

Working Conditions

A calibrated monitor display ensures accurate color (to the greatest extent possible) but doesn't ensure consistent color. That may sound a bit contradictory, but it emphasizes the importance of working under consistent conditions. As a nature photographer, you are well aware of the considerations of good lighting. You look for optimal conditions, with the sun at an optimal angle to produce a golden glow, for example. Just as varying lighting conditions can affect both the appearance of your subject and the ultimate quality of your photos, the conditions under which you work can affect the appearance of your monitor display. Different ambient lighting conditions will cause you to perceive the colors and tonalities differently on your monitor.

It is very important that you work under lighting conditions that are as consistent as possible, and ideally somewhat dim. The monitor you are using as the basis of all your evaluations about an image emits light, and your perception of that light can be influenced by the light in the room. If the room is too bright, you won't be able to see subtle details on the monitor. If the light isn't relatively neutral, it can have an effect on the color appearance of the monitor display.

The ideal situation is to work in an environment that is consistently somewhat dark. That doesn't mean you need to work in absolute darkness. It just means that you want to minimize the lighting to the extent you are comfortable with, and do everything you can to ensure the lighting is neutral and remains consistent from one session to the next. If you work on an image with early morning light filling the room and making the image on your monitor look warmer than it really is, you may overcompensate by adjusting the image to look too cool.

If you can minimize the amount of artificial light in the room, perhaps by using a dimmer to keep the light at an appropriate level, that is an excellent start. If you have windows in the room where you're working on your images, it is a good idea to close the blinds (or install blinds) so you can minimize the influence of outside light.

The bottom line is that you want to be working in an environment where the monitor is accurate by virtue of the fact that it has been calibrated, and is consistent because your working conditions are likewise consistent. This helps ensure that you are seeing accurate color on your monitor, which is the reference both for adjustments you're making to your images and for evaluating the accuracy of your prints.

Photographing Elements to Composite Later

How many times have you looked up and commented on the great clouds or beautiful sunset but not taken the picture because foreground elements were missing? Or the opposite—you found a great subject, perhaps a bird posing wonderfully or a gorgeous scene, but the sky or background was completely blah? Or you could tell there was just too much contrast to be able to capture the picture? When you are in the field with your camera, it's important to remember that Photoshop enables you to combine images in a seemingly infinite variety of ways. You have to adjust your thinking to include seeing the potential for an image.

Expanding Camera Capabilities

Sometimes you see a situation and know that you can't capture it in a single shot because of the technical limitations of your equipment. Photoshop provides ways to combine shots to create images close to what you can see but that are not possible to capture with a single exposure.

Your eyes can see a much greater range of tonalities than can your camera, where the dynamic range is limited to five to six stops of lights for digital captures and slide film. This means although your eyes may be able to see detail in both the highlights and the shadows in a scene, today's cameras may not be able to do so within a single exposure. The solution is to take a series of exposures, making sure you capture detail in all parts of the pictures. This could mean two or more exposures varying at least one stop each.

Dynamic Range and HDR Images

It's helpful to understand exactly what "dynamic range" means and what constitutes an HDR image.

Dynamic Range The range between the brightest and darkest points of an image.

High Dynamic Range (HDR) Images An HDR image contains a far wider dynamic range than can be displayed on a screen or printed on a printer. HDR images are often created from multiple exposures of one image and are stored in special file formats. They are of interest to photographers because you can convert them back to 8-bit or 16-bit images and compress the dynamic range, allowing you to get images with detail in both shadow and highlight areas of an image, more like what your eye saw when looking at the scene rather than what your camera captured.

If you're dealing with a static subject and shooting from a stable platform, you can take a series of exposures to later combine using Merge to HDR to create a 32-bit file. This file is called a *high dynamic range (HDR)* file, and we'll discuss it more in Chapter 8. In addition, there are several other ways to combine 16-bit exposures within Photoshop to extend the latitude. So even if your subject matter is not completely static, take at least two or three exposures: one that captures all the detail in the shadows, one for the midtones, and one that captures all the highlight detail. Be certain to keep your camera in precisely the same spot, and don't change the focus or aperture between the exposures; vary only the shutter speed. Chapter 8 will explain several techniques to put these pictures together to create a picture with at least as much detail as your eyes are accustomed to seeing.

Photographing Parts of the Scene Individually

Another limitation of your camera sometimes arises when you need more depth of field and shutter speed than what the amount of light will allow. This happened to Ellen in Bosque del Apache, New Mexico, when she saw the beautiful mountains and sunset in the distance with the cranes flying fairly close to her. Although she could see it, there was no way to capture the entire scene with adequate depth of field to have the cranes in focus as well as the mountains and have enough shutter speed to freeze the motion of the birds. Her solution was to photograph the birds in one frame and the background separately. Then she combined the two in Photoshop, as shown in Figure 1.22. In reality, the moon was behind her while taking those shots, but in the end she decided to add it to the picture because she wasn't trying to create a documentary image but, rather, one that captured how it felt to be there. Photoshop made that possible.

Figure 1.22 There was no way to capture the birds and the mountains in a single shot because of the low light levels. Instead, individual shots were combined in Photoshop.

Image Components

Some nature photographers prefer to create only images that literally convey what they saw, which is fine. However, others are looking to create artistic renditions of what they saw and may want to add elements to their images. A number of situations lend themselves to photographing parts of a picture that you will later combine in Photoshop. You can create libraries of these image elements to use at some later time. Perhaps the most obvious elements to store are skies and moons. Whenever you see a dramatic sky, photograph it! Place the images in a special folder labeled "skies," or keyword them with the word "sky." You'll need more than one replacement sky, because one of the keys to creating believable composites is to match the direction and quality of the lighting. Sunsets are great to photograph, as are clouds—the blue-sky-with-puffy-white-cloud types as well as the impending-storm types. When you start paying attention to clouds, you'll soon see that different types of clouds tend to occur more in certain seasons. By having a collection of skies, when you find a great subject (perhaps that leopard in the tree while in Africa) or a beautiful scenic landscape, you'll be able to remove the distracting white sky and make it appear that luck was with you in the field.

Figure 1.23 shows a picture that could have occurred but didn't. Capturing all these landing cranes in one shot was wonderful, but unfortunately the sky behind them was boring. A few minutes earlier, the sky in the very same spot had been dramatic, but there were no birds. This image is a combination of the birds with the sky that had been there a few minutes earlier.

PHOTO BY ELLEN ANON

Figure 1.23 Sometimes nature doesn't cooperate and gives you a great subject but a boring sky, or vice versa. In Photoshop you can combine them to have the best of both worlds.

Don't limit yourself to just skies and clouds, though. You can add all sorts of elements to pictures to add impact or create a sense of your own style. It can be helpful, for example, to keep a folder of moons to use as accent elements in pictures. You can shoot full moons, crescent moons, moons against black skies, and moons in daylight skies. You'd be amazed at the variety of color casts in the moons. Then when you think a picture needs a little extra pop, you can put one in. (We'll explain how to do that in Chapter 8.) Sometimes you might make them a realistic size, and sometimes you might enlarge them. A photographer we know adds boat docks, and so he has a collection of docks to add to scenic water pictures. You're the artist, and the choice is yours. Use your imagination, and keep your eyes open for other elements to collect to add to your images.

When photographing something that you're likely to want to later extract from the picture and use elsewhere, try to design your photograph to make it easier to remove the desired object. For example, it will often be easier to remove an item from a blurred background than from a cluttered one, so consider using a wide aperture. You may need to take a step or two left or right or perhaps get down a little closer to the ground to help separate intricate background objects from your subject. A little care in the field can make your work in Photoshop much easier!

Be sure to store these photo elements in a consistent place that's easy for you to find. You don't want to have to look through all your pictures to find them. Of course, adding keywords to them will also make it easy to locate them when you need them.

Ethical Considerations

Is the image manipulated? It sounds like such a straightforward question. But answering honestly may be more difficult than it appears, especially when responding to people not well versed in digital photography.

If you shoot in RAW, you essentially have a negative that needs to be processed during conversion. The settings you apply determine the appearance of the image, but these really aren't manipulating the image any more than chemicals do in a darkroom. Similar adjustments done in Photoshop, as opposed to in the raw converter, are considered by some to be manipulations. Many accept that it is necessary to clone out dust and to perform some sharpening since there is some slight softening of digital images by their very nature. A few people are bothered by basic exposure and color modifications, but most accept this as part of the processing, as long as the overall intent of the capture remains the same. Modifying the colors or tonalities within only a section of the image is more troublesome for some, and such changes are not allowed by several prestigious contests such as the Shell Wildlife Photographer of the Year or *Nature's Best Photography* magazine. If you enter your image in a contest, be sure to follow their rules for what changes are and are not permitted.

Although cloning out dust is usually acceptable, there is debate about how much of an object one can clone out before the image is considered manipulated. Sometimes it's more environmentally responsible to clone out an object rather than remove it in reality (see the sidebar "Removing Objects in the Field or Later in Photoshop" for more on this). Sometimes it's impossible to remove it in reality. Unfortunately, for some this crosses the line into a manipulated image. Maybe it's an area that needs to be thought through more carefully.

Many gray areas exist. For example, it's common practice when photographing hummingbirds at feeders to put up a man-made background so that the birds are photographed against a pleasing, nondistracting background rather than clutter. This is acceptable. But if you took the image photographed with the cluttered background and, in Photoshop, replaced the background with a simpler one, many would insist the image is manipulated.

Ellen's feeling is that when she composites elements within an image, the image is manipulated, and she is careful to indicate this whenever reasonable. When asked, she responds honestly, and labels images accurately. The bottom line for her is that photography is an art form, and her goal is to create images that express what she feels. For those who are more inclined toward scientific documentary types of nature photographs, the lines may be different. You have to decide what's right for you!

Removing Objects in the Field or Later in Photoshop

There's an old adage that reminds us to "Take only pictures and leave only footprints, and barely those if possible." But as nature photographers, we know that sometimes there are distracting elements that interfere with our pictures. There may be an ill-placed stick, a wayward branch, or maybe a rock that's too light and bright. It seems harmless enough to move it and create a cleaner photo. Many times doing so may be fine. But have you considered that perhaps that rock or branch was serving a purpose to one of the many critters in our world? Perhaps the branch provided some protection against the wind or shielded visibility from a predator; maybe the rock provided a safe resting spot while looking for food. We know and see the world through our human perspective, and what seems inconsequential to us may have a significant impact on a variety of wildlife.

Does that mean you should never move anything in the environment? That would be an extreme and unrealistic position, but the reality is you may want to consider whether it would be smarter to remove the offending item later in Photoshop. Although it may create more work for you, you will be creating less stress on the nature around you. You have to use common sense in making this choice. (We'll cover how to remove objects in Photoshop in Chapter 5.)

Aperture and Lightroom

A few years ago the software choices for digital photography were fairly limited. Photoshop has dominated the market for quite a while, and its sister products, such as Photoshop Elements, provide a reduced selection of tools offering some of the basic adjustments. Many photographers, amateur as well as professionals, have based their workflows entirely on using Photoshop or Elements for years. In fact, Photoshop and Elements offer good workflows (which are what we're teaching you throughout this book), but they're not perfect. Photoshop was developed not only for photographers, but also for graphic artists. The result is that it has numerous features that photographers don't need. And there are some features that photographers need but that Photoshop doesn't do quite as well as we wish. For example, Photoshop is not an image-management device; it doesn't help you keep track of where you've stored the images. (Eventually, if you shoot enough, you can't keep all your images on your computer's internal hard drive—you must export them to external hard drives or gold DVDs, and so on.) Further, because Bridge is a separate program from Photoshop, you actually encounter three different user interfaces—Bridge, Camera Raw, and Photoshop. This can be confusing for some and is a little time-consuming as you go back and forth among them.

Apple introduced Aperture in late 2005, followed shortly by Adobe's announcement of a beta version of software called Lightroom. These newer programs are designed from the ground up to meet the needs of photographers. In addition, they make working with raw files virtually indistinguishable from working with JPEGs or TIFFs. No separate converter software or interface is needed. Currently, they are intended to be used in conjunction with a program such as Photoshop, rather than as a complete replacement for Photoshop although you can optimize many images using only Aperture or Lightroom.

Aperture and Lightroom are designed to make your workflow easy and efficient from the moment you download images from your camera through locating your best images and showcasing them to others. When you connect your camera or card reader, an import window appears and nearly instantaneously so do low-res previews of your images. You choose where to store these images and how to name them. In addition, you can quickly add any metadata you choose, such as basic contact information and keywords. After importing the images you can easily edit them, using a magnifying loupe to check for sharpness and details—and comparing similar images side by side.

In Aperture, a single keystroke causes a dialog to appear that contains most of the adjustments you're likely to need to make, whereas in Lightroom you proceed through different modules. You can save commonly made adjustments as presets, or you can adjust the sliders to tweak all aspects of the exposure and colors. These adjustments are stored as instructions while the master file remains untouched. The adjustments go beyond those typically available currently in most raw converters and include all the expected features as well as an outstanding Highlight/Shadow tool, individual color controls, Retouch tools (Aperture), red-eye reduction, cropping and straightening, toning, and more.

One of the major innovations of Aperture, also incorporated into Lightroom, is the ability to generate versions of the image that are stored with the master file simply as instructions. That way, you can create several variations of an image (see Figure 1.24)—perhaps a different crop, a black-and-white version and a sepia version, and so on—yet the demands for storage space on your hard drive are greatly reduced because the master file is not recopied each time. This makes your computer more efficient, and it makes it easy to find the different variations of your image. In both Aperture and Lightroom, you can add keywords at any time, search for images (including those you store offline), send emails, or create slide shows with a single click.

If you opt to use Aperture or Lightroom, you're likely to find that you will not need to use Photoshop for all your images. You'll still need Photoshop when you have more complicated cloning to do, when you want to create composites, or when you want to use any of the filters available in Photoshop. When using Aperture or Lightroom, if you want to open an image in Photoshop, it's just a keystroke away. The image will open in Photoshop, and you can make the desired changes. When you're done, you click Save, and Aperture (or Lightroom) will automatically update the image preview to reflect the changes you made in Photoshop. You can save all your layers when you work in Photoshop, and although the individual layers are not accessible from within Aperture, if you reopen that same file in Photoshop all the layers will still be there.

Photo by Ellen Anon

Figure 1.24 Experimenting with different variations of an image in Aperture is easy and requires only minimal additional storage space on your hard drive.

Aperture provides equally efficient methods for creating slide shows, sending emails, creating books, creating websites, and making prints. We've adopted Aperture as our primary workflow tool. For more about Aperture, see *Aperture Exposed: The Mac Photographer's Guide to Taming the Workflow* by Ellen Anon and Josh Anon (Sybex, 2006).

Lightroom provides similar functionality. It too provides a workflow enabling you to use raw images as easily as JPEGs or TIFFs. It has an intuitive interface that enables you to make many of the global color and tonal modifications that you may want to make and has a good keywording system to make it easy to find your images. Lightroom 2 has some exciting new features including the ability to make some types of localized adjustments, similar to what's available in ACR. Lightroom has the advantage that it is available for both PC and Mac, whereas Aperture is a Mac-only application. One of the main disadvantages of Lightroom, in our opinion, is the need to change modules depending on what task you're doing. That makes the initial edit through your images slower.

If you opt to adopt Aperture or Lightroom as the basis of your workflow, you'll find that you make many or all the global exposure and color changes we discuss in this book in those programs. You'll still find it advantageous to work in Photoshop for some tasks. For example, if you use Lightroom, it's likely that you'll still use Photoshop for most of your cloning. We also use Photoshop at times when

CHAPTER 1: THINKING DIGITALLY ■

we want to make a change to part of the image and not have it affect the rest of the image—which means when we'd like to use a layer mask. In earlier versions of Photoshop, we used layer masks a lot. With the latest raw converters offering localized controls, we don't use layer masks quite as often as we did in the past, but we most assuredly still use them. The ability to make a change and have it affect only the targeted area gives you precise control over the final appearance of your images. We also use Photoshop when we want to use any of its filters as well as for all types of creative ventures, including creating composites of all types. Even if you use Aperture or Lightroom, it's worthwhile having a solid understanding of Photoshop. That way, if you encounter a difficult image, you'll have more tools available to you to work with it.

Storage Considerations

A comprehensive discussion of storage media is beyond the scope of this book. We'll cover only a few aspects here, which are especially pertinent for nature photographers.

Many nature photographers often do at least some of their photography away from home. We know one photographer who buys enough compact flash cards so that he can use a new one when needed rather than having to download and/or edit images while on the road. Although the cost of compact flash cards has come down considerably in the past few years, for most photographers, this is not a practical solution. Even if you can justify it monetarily, it's impractical because it means you will have all your editing to do when you get home, and that can be overwhelming. In addition, it eliminates one of the major advantages of digital shooting—the ability to review the shots you took during the day and to learn from what went right and what went wrong so you can adjust your shooting the next day accordingly. Being able to view your images, preferably reasonably large, allows you to fine-tune your shooting skills and experiment with new techniques while still on location. That way, you can return to a location if necessary or build upon a creative approach you tried.

Various independent handheld image storage and viewing devices have come on the market during the past few years. All of them have been promising, but most have had their issues. In addition, the screen size on most is too small to be as helpful as needed, although large enough to be tantalizing and tempting. At best these devices should be used as a secondary backup in our opinion.

When we're on a photographic trip, we prefer to take a laptop along and make certain that it has plenty of space on its hard drive. That way, we can download our images and view them at a reasonable size. (In addition, having the computer enables us to have email access while on the road.) Also, we take small external portable hard drives along. These drives are the size of a deck of cards. We back up all the images we store on our computer on this hard drive. That way if something happens to the computer, we still have a copy of all the files. If we're on a long trip that will involve a lot of shooting and not much time for editing, we may bring along a second external portable hard drive for overflow images when the computer's hard drive becomes full. Ordinarily we recommend doing at least a first pass of editing each day to delete the images you are certain you don't want, but sometimes that's not possible. When we return home, we transfer the images to our main computer for further editing and archival storage.

After editing our images, we establish a Best Of folder for each shoot containing the images we want to keep. That folder gets backed up onto a *RAID* (Redundant Array of Independent Disks) system. A RAID system consists of two or more hard drives that function together. There are several different types of RAID devices, but we use RAID-5 (one of the most popular implementations). When you back up to a RAID-5 hard drive, the data is automatically copied to all the drives. If one hard drive develops an error, it uses the information on one of the other drives to correct it. We think this provides one of the best storage systems currently available.

A newer option is to use a Data Robotics Drobo device (www.datarobotics.com). This is similar to a RAID device but a lot more flexible. You fill it with hard drives as needed to give you as much storage as you need. It calculates how much space is available and acts accordingly. If you insert a single hard drive, it acts as a single hard drive. If you put in three drives, even if they have different capacities, it configures them automatically as a RAID-5 type of device. It makes the entire process of backup far easier and may be the wave of the future.

Some photographers still prefer to use DVDs or CDs. If you have a lot of images, the volume of DVDs and/or CDs will become unwieldy unless you have a clear-cut system for storing and identifying the discs. In addition, it's imperative to use gold discs, which are archival and are reported to last 100 years or so. On the relatively rare occasions that we use DVDs for storage, we use the gold discs that are available from Delkin Devices. DVDs and CDs that are not gold may become unreadable in as little as one year! If you have been using regular DVDs or CDs to archive your images, we urge you to copy them to a gold disc.

Another relatively new option is online storage. Services such as Amazon S3 (www.amazon.com/gp/browse.html?node=16427261) and Mozy (http://mozy.com/) act essentially as an online hard drive. You pay a certain amount each month, in some cases for data transfer as well, and upload your data to their site, where it will be stored in an encrypted format. You can upload any types of files to these services. Other companies, such as PhotoShelter (http://psc.photoshelter.com) and Digital Railroad (http://digitalrailroad.net), offer photo-specific online storage. In addition, some allow you to showcase your work and may even serve as stock agencies. The advantage of online storage is that you maintain copies of your images in a location that's physically separate from your main storage. The potential disadvantages are cost, image-transfer time, and issues if the company providing the storage goes out of business. Nonetheless, it is a good option to consider in conjunction with your other storage.

Note: Whatever storage system you adopt, be consistent so that you protect your images and can locate them easily when you need them. You never know when "disaster" will strike. Having backup copies of your images readily available may save the day!

Bridge

After you're done photographing, you need an easy way to get your images from the memory cards onto your computer and to see how the pictures look. Although you may be eager to start optimizing them right away, first you need to sort through them and decide which files to keep and which to delete. Adobe Bridge, a stand-alone application that comes with Photoshop and Elements, and Organizer in the PC version of Elements, have a lot of features to help with this task. We'll show you how to take advantage of these features to make this part of your workflow as efficient as possible.

2

Chapter Contents
Customizing Bridge
Downloading Images
Bridge Views and Workspaces
Sorting and Editing
Additional Features
Organizer

Customizing Bridge

Bridge is a program designed to be customized for each user's individual needs. It's used not only by photographers, but also by graphic artists and others using any of the programs packaged in the Adobe Creative Suite series. Bridge's interface has been radically changed in CS4 to make its features more discoverable. However, the default views and behaviors may not match your workflow needs, so it's worth spending a little time learning to set it up in the most convenient way for you. We'll take you through the program step by step and make recommendations about what works best for us. That way, you can customize your version according to your needs.

> **Note:** Bridge is aptly named because it is the "connector," or "bridge," between the various applications that make up Creative Suite 4, such as Adobe InDesign, Illustrator, GoLive, Version Cue, Stock Photos, and so on, as well as Photoshop. It enables files created in one application to be viewed and opened in one or more of the other applications.

Bridge and Organizer

Mac Elements users can follow along with the Bridge descriptions for Photoshop even though Bridge in Elements is slightly different and sometimes has fewer options. We'll highlight the key differences as we go along. For PC Elements users, there's a separate section devoted to Organizer at the end of the chapter.

Setting Bridge Preferences

Bridge includes a Preferences dialog box where you can set a wide variety of options to adjust the behavior of Bridge to your liking. You access the dialog box by selecting Edit > Preferences (Bridge > Preferences on Macs) from the menu in Bridge. Because there are so many settings and many of them are a matter of personal preference, we'll simply highlight the major settings:

General This section (see Figure 2.1) contains general settings related to the appearance and behavior of Bridge. Use the sliders in the Appearance section to control the background of the user interface as well as the backdrop for your images. The Accent Color drop-down menu enables you to choose a color and style for the highlight in the user interface. We find that the default settings work well, but this is largely a matter of personal preference.

> **Note:** If you opt to experiment with the Appearance sliders, be aware that there is no way to automatically return to the default settings.

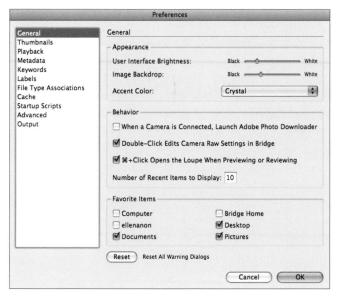

Figure 2.1 The General section of the Bridge Preferences contains settings related to the display of images within Bridge.

The Behavior section includes three options. The first automatically launches Adobe Photo Downloader. Unless you are specifically using another program such as Aperture or Lightroom for your image importing (which we'll discuss later in this chapter), check the option to launch Adobe Photo Downloader when a camera is connected. This will launch the downloader when a memory card is connected and will save you time.

We recommend checking the option Double-Click Edits Camera Raw Settings in Bridge. When this check box is cleared, raw files open into ACR hosted by Photoshop. When you check the box, the ACR dialog box opens without launching Photoshop. This may seem like a subtle distinction, but it may enable you to adjust settings more rapidly than you otherwise could; for example, you could be working in Photoshop while Bridge processes a large number of raw files in the background. In addition, it may allow you to process a larger volume of images at once.

The option to use Control+click/⌘ + click Opens the Loupe When Previewing or Reviewing is a personal preference. (This is a Photoshop-only preference.) If you're annoyed that you're accidentally eliciting the loupe by clicking while navigating around the interface, then check this option. By doing so, a single click will no longer call forth the loupe; instead you'll have to add the modifier key (Ctrl or ⌘) as well. We find we prefer to keep this checked.

The Favorite Items section allows you to choose the image sources to be included on the Favorites tab. The Reset button at the bottom of this section allows you to reset the warning dialog boxes so that all are shown, even if you have previously checked the box to not show a particular message.

JPEG and TIF Options

Bridge for Adobe Elements 6 for Mac does not allow you to open JPEG or TIFF files in Camera RAW and does not have the File > Open in Camera Raw command. However, within Elements, if you select File > Open, choose a JPEG or TIFF file, and set the Format pop-up to Camera Raw, Elements will open the image in Camera Raw.

Thumbnails   The Thumbnails section includes options for the appearance of the associated metadata as well as for file handling.

First is the Do Not Process Files Larger Than option, which determines the size, in megabytes, above which Bridge will not generate a thumbnail for the image. It can be useful to create such a limit (the default is now 1000MB), because building thumbnails for such large images can be time-consuming, resulting in reduced system performance. However, for photographers who frequently produce extremely large files, such as panoramas, setting such a limit can be a source of frustration, because they aren't able to see thumbnails for many of their images. Consider this setting based on the relative advantages of placing a limit on the building of thumbnails for large files.

Four check boxes with drop-down menus allow you to specify additional information about the image to be displayed below the thumbnail. Again, it's a matter of personal preference and what information you want to have at your fingertips about each file. As shown in Figure 2.2, we opt to show the date created, dimensions, depth, and file type. With that information we can easily identify which version of an image we want at a glance.

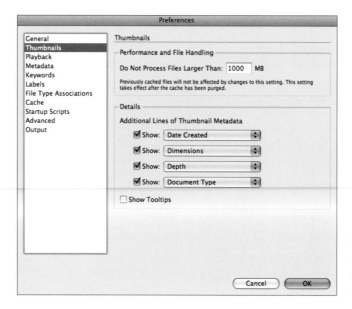

Figure 2.2 The Thumbnails section of Preferences contains settings to control what metadata is displayed with the thumbnails.

The Show Tooltips check box determines whether information about the image is displayed as a pop-up tooltip when you hold the mouse over a thumbnail. We generally leave this off because we find it distracting, but you could opt to use this feature rather than display the additional lines of thumbnail metadata information.

Playback Playback is not relevant for most nature photographers unless you are doing time-lapse photography. Therefore, we leave these options set to their default values.

Metadata This section (shown in Figure 2.3) allows you to specify which fields are displayed in the Metadata panel for each image. This extensive list includes a variety of metadata formats and fields that are not necessarily supported by all image formats. This section can be used both to include fields you're most interested in to maximize the amount of information displayed, as well as to remove those items you're not interested in to keep the display more manageable. For example, most users don't need the GPS data (and only a few cameras, such as some Nikons, even support it), but it's a good idea to include the IPTC Core information that contains your contact and copyright information (if you added it during import or later) as well as some of the Camera Data (EXIF) and ACR information.

Figure 2.3 The Metadata section of Bridge Preferences allows you to specify which metadata fields should be displayed on the Metadata panel.

Keywords   These options control what happens when you click on a keyword to apply it, as well as Bridge's ability to read hierarchical keywords. When you check the first option, applying a subkeyword (such as Egret) automatically applies the parent keyword category (such as Birds). This can be a time-saver, so we select it. We also want Bridge to be able to read keywords that input in a hierarchy. (See Figure 2.4.)

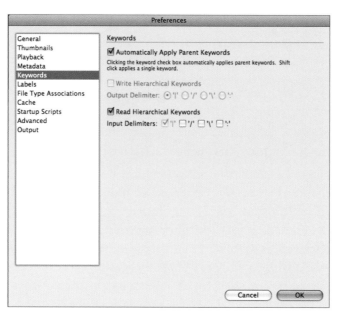

Figure 2.4   Use the keyword preferences to control whether parent keywords are applied automatically when a subordinate keyword is chosen.

Labels   This section (see Figure 2.5) allows you to set preferences related to the labels you can use to rate and flag images. The check box at the top determines whether the Ctrl/⌘ key must be held to apply a rating or label to an image. We recommend you clear this check box so that you can simply press the appropriate number key rather than holding the Ctrl/⌘ key while pressing that key. The section below the check box allows you to change the description of the colored labels by clicking on the text and typing. We opt to leave these descriptors blank because if you change them after you've applied labels to a group of images, when you view the images that were labeled with the old descriptors, their labels turn white rather than remain colored. We consider this to be a major flaw.

File Type Associations   This section is a long list (see Figure 2.6) of the file types supported by Bridge. By default, most image formats are opened by Photoshop automatically. However, you can change the association so that files open in a different application. For example, you might choose to have Nikon NEF files open in Capture NX. Similarly, you can set different associations for specific file types within Bridge, if you prefer, using the drop-down menu to the right of a given file format to choose an application or to browse for the executable for the preferred application.

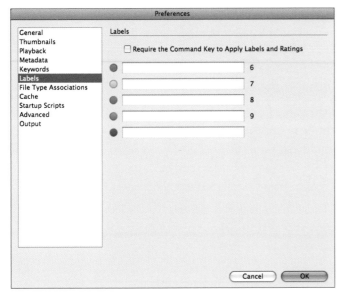

Figure 2.5 The Labels section of Bridge Preferences allows you to adjust the names of the colored labels and determine how keyboard shortcuts for rating and labels behave.

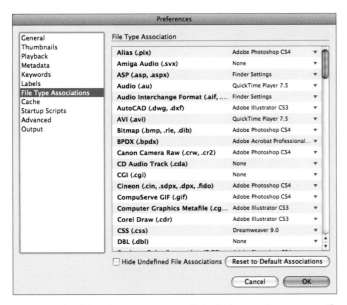

Figure 2.6 The File Type Associations section in Bridge Preferences allows you to specify which application should be used to open each supported file type.

Note: If you find you are unable to open a file in Photoshop, check the File Type Associations. Sometimes loading a new application or an upgrade will change the settings and cause files to open in another program.

Cache   The Cache options (Figure 2.7) control how quickly you'll see a preview of your image. The cache stores information about the file so that it can display it with any changes you've made, including ratings, rotations, and so forth. We recommend checking the option Keep 100% Previews in Cache because it makes it faster to load files. Of course, enabling this option does take up more room.

In the past we recommended checking the option Automatically Export Cache to Folders When Possible; however, the way CS4 is utilizing the cache makes this less useful and takes up more memory. But if you frequently export folders of images to DVDs or elsewhere, you may want to check this option rather than having to remember to do it manually at the time of export (via Tools > Cache > Build and Export Cache).

The larger the cache size, the more disk space it consumes but the less often you'll be faced with a full cache. We leave this near its default setting but if you are processing large quantities of images, you may want to increase it.

If Bridge's performance has become erratic or slowed way down, you may want to use the Compact Cache option, and if that fails to improve the problem, use the Purge Cache option.

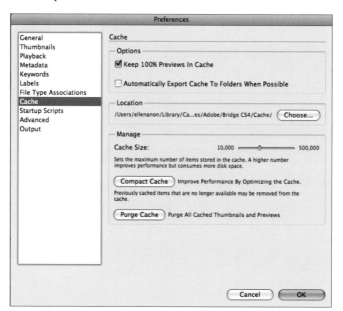

Figure 2.7 Remembering to use the Cache options will help your computer to operate more efficiently.

Using the Cache Options

Elements users should select Automatically Export Cache to Folders When Possible since Elements utilizes the earlier form of Bridge.

Startup Scripts   This section enables you to select which scripts run automatically when you launch Bridge. We recommend turning off those you don't need since doing so may help Bridge run faster. As shown in Figure 2.8, check Adobe Bridge, Adobe Output Module, Adobe Photoshop CS4, and Auto Collection CS4.

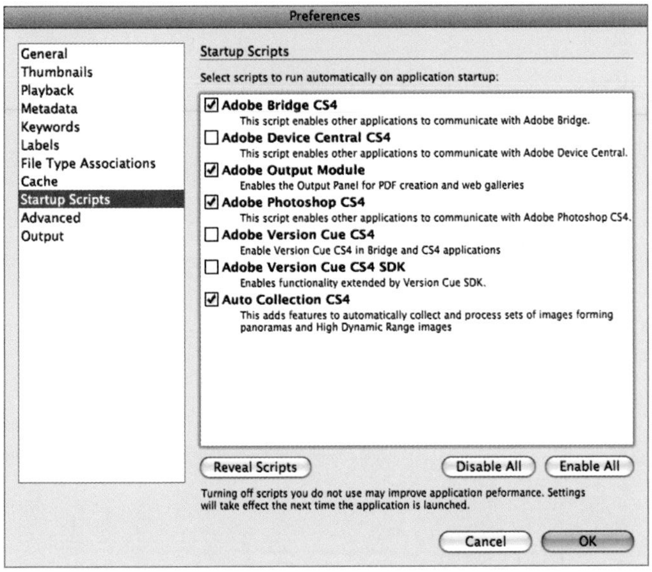

Figure 2.8 Select only those scripts that you need in order to improve Bridge's performance.

Advanced   This section (shown in Figure 2.9) contains several settings. These are matters of personal preference and we leave them unchecked.

Software rendering can be helpful for those with older computers and/or lesser graphics cards whose hardware can't take advantage of some of the features in Bridge. For those with better graphics cards and newer computers, it's better to use the hardware acceleration. If you're not sure, you can easily try checking this option to see which way Bridge works better for you.

If you want to use previews that match the resolution of your monitor to more easily assess critical sharpness in your images, check the option Generate Monitor-Size Previews. If you always want Bridge to launch when you log in, check that option.

Output   We leave the Output Preferences options set at their default values.

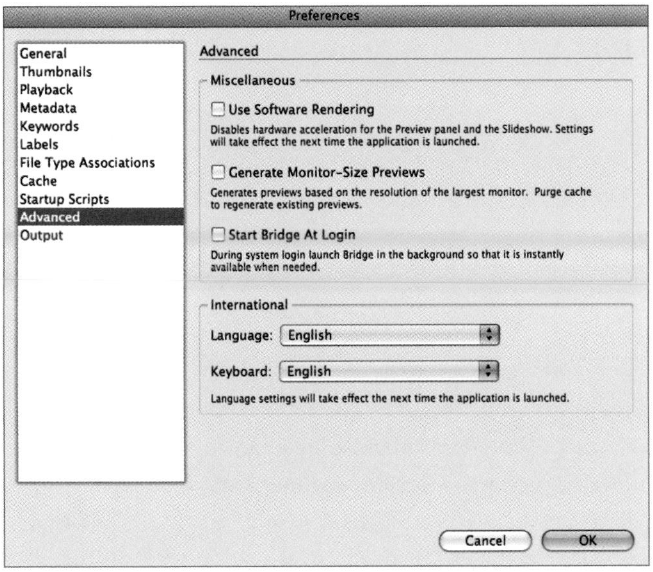

Figure 2.9 The Advanced section of the Bridge Preferences contains a number of additional settings.

Downloading Images

We're sure that you are anxious to look at your images immediately after returning from a photo shoot. Of course, you need to download the images from your memory cards before you can get started. CS4 includes an excellent downloader that makes this task easier than ever.

Start by inserting your digital media into the card reader. In Bridge, click the camera icon near the top left of the interface ![camera icon]. Choose File > Get Photos from Camera. A dialog box appears for the Photo Downloader. Click the Advanced Dialog button in the lower-left corner to access the interface shown in Figure 2.10.

CHAPTER 2: BRIDGE ■

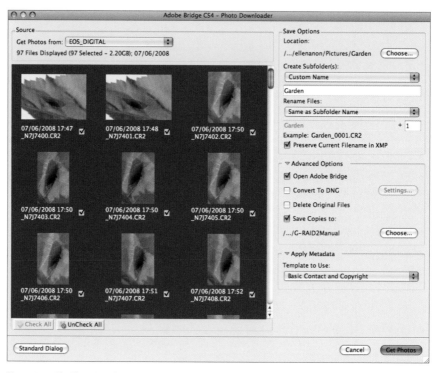

Figure 2.10 The Photo Downloader is an extremely efficient way to download and rename your images.

Note: We recommend using an accessory card reader rather than connecting your camera directly to the computer. This is partly because we just find it more convenient to use a card reader, especially when we have a relatively large number of images to download. However, we also prefer keeping the camera safely in the camera bag rather than sitting on the desk with a cord attached, with the risk that the cord might accidentally get pulled and the camera might crash to the floor.

Begin by choosing a location for your pictures. Click the Choose button to navigate to the desired location on your computer, and use it to create a new folder if necessary. Which folder you copy them to depends on your own organizational structure. Hopefully you've set up folders to organize your images systematically, such as by the location, date, or other attributes of the images. If not, now is a good time to start.

Ellen stores her images in a location folder she created within Pictures. Then in the Create Subfolders drop-down menu, she chooses Shot Date. That creates a subfolder within the location folder for each day so she can use the same location folder for multiple days of shooting while still keeping her images organized by date. At a minimum, create a new folder to reflect the event you've just photographed or the location.

One of the handy features of the Downloader is the ability to rename the files while importing them. We usually select the Custom Name option and choose a name that reflects the location, although some people prefer to use the species or subject name. It's a good idea to check the option Preserve Current Filename in XMP so that if the file gets saved and renamed again later, you can more easily find the original raw file.

Although it may seem silly since Bridge is already open, we recommend checking the option Open Adobe Bridge. Doing so opens a second Bridge window that automatically displays the images you are downloading. That saves you from having to navigate to them later.

We do not recommend converting the images to DNG unless you have a specific reason to want DNG files. We also recommend against using the Delete Original Files option. It's safer to wait and reformat the card in your camera.

We recommend that you always store your files in at least two places since hard drives can fail. Photo Downloader enables you to simultaneously save copies of the images to a second location by checking the Save Copies To box and then choosing the desired location. Obviously, if you want to use an external hard drive as your backup, it must be connected to the computer.

It's a good practice to create a metadata template containing your basic contact information such as your name, email, website, phone, or whatever information you want to include. Then you can select that template within Downloader, and it will apply the information to each file during the import. We'll explain how to do that shortly.

Lastly, if you want to import only some of the files from the card, click the Uncheck All button, and then manually check those you want to import.

When you're ready, click Get Photos. A new Bridge window will appear, preset to the folder containing the newly imported pictures, which will already be renamed and have your contact metadata attached. That's pretty slick!

Once you've copied the images, the originals are still on your digital media card. Until you need to use that card, it serves as a backup copy just in case something goes wrong in the meantime (though you should still be backing up the images on your hard drive as well). When you're ready to use that digital media card again, reformat it in the camera to remove the existing images and reinitialize the card.

Creating a Metadata Template

In the days of slides, nature photographers used to label each slide with their name and contact information, helping to ensure that their slides were not lost. In today's digital world it's equally important to label your digital images with your contact information. The easiest way to do so is to create a template that can be applied to all your images as you import them.

To create a metadata template, go to the Metadata panel, click the small fly-out menu in the upper-right corner, and choose Create Template, as shown in Figure 2.11, or go to Tools > Create Metadata Template. In the resulting dialog box, fill in the desired fields. Be sure to check each field that you want to include in the template. Even if text appears, if the field is not checked it won't be included in the template. Name the template—for example, Contact Info—and click Save. The template you just made will be available in the Downloader to apply to all images as you import then, as well as in the Metadata panel. You can apply the template from the Metadata panel by selecting the images and then going to the same fly-out menu and choosing Append Metadata. Select your template from the list that appears.

Figure 2.11 Create a metadata template to quickly add contact and copyright information to your files.

> **Note:** To view the metadata information you add, either go to the Metadata section of Bridge or choose File > File Info. Although you can add information to an individual image from File Info, you cannot save the information as a template there.

Renaming Your Images After Import

Sometimes you may import images without renaming them and want to rename them later, or perhaps you want to change the name you initially used. Fortunately, it's quite easy to rename all or some of the images in a folder. To rename your images, take the following steps:

1. Either select the particular files you want to rename or select a folder in the Folders panel. In the latter case, the renaming will be applied to all the files in the folder.

2. Choose Tools > Batch Rename in the Bridge menu to open the Batch Rename dialog box (see Figure 2.12).

3. Select whether you want your renamed files to be in the same folder, copied to another folder, or moved to another folder. If you copy or move them, specify where by clicking Browse.

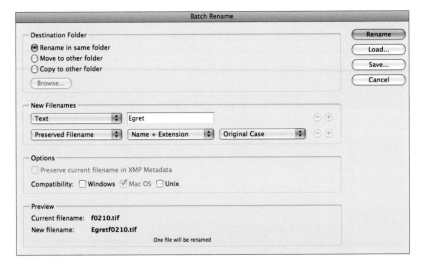

Figure 2.12 To rename images after you've imported them, use the Batch Rename dialog box.

4. For New Filename, we like to create a name that tells us essential identifying features about the images. This could be text that describes the place (such as Holland) or the subject (tulips), along with a date and/or the original preserved filename and an extension. The number of components you use is your choice:

- In the first drop-down box under New Filenames that says Current Filename by default, choose Text. The next box to the right will prompt you to type text. This is where you type the location, subject, name, and so on.

- To the far right of this row are + and – radio buttons. Click the + button to get another drop-down box to add more parameters to your name. We recommend using the Preserved Filename because it creates a distinct filename for each image.

- If you do not use the Preserved Filename, then we suggest that you choose a sequence number (or letter) from the drop-down menu. Usually we specify a three-digit number, but if you don't use the date in your naming schema, you may prefer to use at least a four-digit number.

> **Note:** Bridge will automatically preserve the file extension, so you don't have to use Extension as your final choice.

You'll see a preview of your new name at the lower right.

5. Under Options, if you did not previously save the original filename to the XMP metadata, you can choose to keep the original filename in the metadata for the file. If you are renaming copies, this can be helpful in the event you ever want to refer back to the original files.

6. Under Compatibility, it's a good idea to select both Windows and Mac (your current operating system is selected by default).

Bridge Views and Workspaces

We know you're eager to check out your images, but most nature photographers find that the default configuration (see Figure 2.13) of Bridge isn't a very efficient way to work. Fortunately, Bridge is easy to customize, and making a few changes can mean the difference between thinking that Bridge is awkward to use and thinking that it's wonderful. The Bridge interface is composed of *pods* that can be moved and adjusted in size either manually or by using one of the presets, or a combination or both, to enable easier access to whatever features you're using. We'll show you several of the variations that we find most helpful.

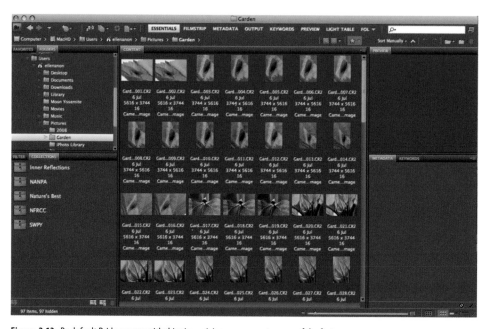

Figure 2.13 By default Bridge opens with this view, giving you access to many of the features.

There are numerous preset workspaces available from the Workspace Chooser in the toolbar. If some of them are not visible, drag the thin double line at the beginning of the spaces to the left. It will act like a drawer and reveal more choices. Alternatively, click on the drop-down disclosure arrow on the right side of the Workspace Chooser, above the Sort Manually button, to reveal a drop-down menu of choices. (See Figure 2.14.)

Figure 2.14 The new Workspace Chooser makes it easy to access different workspaces so that you can work more efficiently.

Filmstrip Views

Most nature photographers use a version of a "filmstrip" view (Figure 2.15) to sort through their images. The preset called Filmstrip has a large Preview area with a much larger version of the selected thumbnail, along with a horizontal filmstrip view of all the thumbnails beneath the image preview. The large preview makes it much easier to decide which images to keep and which to delete. In addition, the Favorites, Folders, Filter, and Collections tabs are on the left, making it easy to find the images you want to see.

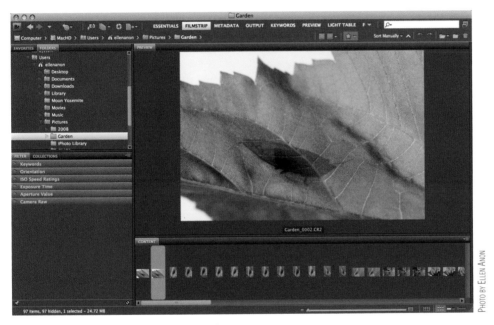

PHOTO BY ELLEN ANON

Figure 2.15 The filmstrip view is a good starting place for viewing images.

The slider at the bottom right of the interface will scale the thumbnails up or down. The thumbnail size and image layout adjust dynamically as you move the slider, making it easy to decide exactly what setting works best for you. You'll want the thumbnails to be large enough that the metadata you've chosen in Preferences to appear with the thumbnails is visible. If the thumbnails are too small, the metadata won't appear. The idea is to make the thumbnails just large enough to reveal enough information to know which image is which but small enough that they don't unnecessarily take space away from the Preview pod. Click the small icon to the left of the slider to have Bridge automatically make the thumbnails as small as possible while maintaining your configuration, and click the button to the right to make them as large as possible within the confines of the allotted space.

Although the default horizontal filmstrip view is usable, there is also a vertical filmstrip preset called Preview. This workspace has the content appear as a vertical filmstrip and leaves the preview unencumbered so that vertical images are displayed considerably larger in this view (Figure 2.16).

Figure 2.16 We find that a version of the vertical filmstrip is the best choice for reviewing our images as we edit.

Ellen prefers a modified version of this view. She prefers to have the filmstrip appear vertically on the right side, as shown in Figure 2.17. To create that view, it's easier to begin with the filmstrip. Next, hover your cursor on the right edge until it changes shape into a double-edged arrow. Then click and drag to the left to expose the third pod. Click the Content tab and drag it into the third pod.

You can resize any of the pods by hovering the cursor over the heavy line that separates them, then clicking and dragging.

To adjust the size of the filmstrip, place the cursor over the vertical line separating the Preview pod from the Content pod. The cursor will change to a double-facing arrow, as shown in Figure 2.18. Click and drag to the right or left to increase or decrease the width of the Content pod. Just above the scroll bar is a tiny, somewhat difficult-to-see icon at the top right of the Content pod. Click it to reveal choices to display the thumbnails vertically, horizontally, or in the auto layout. For the vertical filmstrip view, Ellen prefers the vertical thumbnail display.

Figure 2.17 Using a vertical filmstrip affords more room for the image previews.

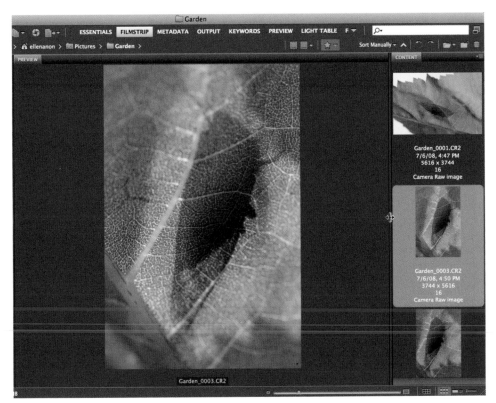

Figure 2.18 Adjust the size of the Content pod so that it's large enough to view the thumbnails comfortably but small enough so that you maximize the size of the image previews in the Preview pane.

Customizing the Left Pod

On the left side of the interface is a pod containing the Favorites and Folders panels, and beneath it is one containing the Filter and Collections panels. You can adjust the width of these pods similarly to the way you adjusted the width of the Content pod. In addition, you can allocate more or less vertical space to each of these pods by clicking the horizontal line just above the Filter tab. Drag it up or down as you want. You can opt to have just a single pod on the left by clicking the Filter tab and dragging it on top of the Folders tab. In addition, you can view keyword or metadata information in these pods by choosing Window > Metadata Panel or Window > Keyword Panel. Then drag each panel to whichever pod is most convenient.

To reposition a panel, point your mouse at the title tab for that panel, and click and drag it to whatever pod is convenient for you. If several panels share a pod, simply click the tab of the panel you want to view to bring it to the forefront.

> **Note:** If you drag both the Filter and Collections panels from their default locations and place them by Folders and Favorites, the pod that originally contained the Filter and Collections panels will collapse unless you have placed another panel there. That's true of the Content and Preview panels as well.

> **Note:** Any panel in Bridge can be positioned in any pod by clicking the tab at the top of the panel and dragging it to the desired location. By doing this you could place the filmstrip on the left and the folders on the right, or create any other configuration that suits your needs.

When initially viewing images, we usually select the Folders tab and navigate to the desired folder so we can have the Folders panel fill the left pod. (If you have used Adobe Photo Downloader, it will automatically open a new Bridge window and navigate to the folder containing the newly imported images.) However, while we sort through our images, we like to have the Filter and Keyword panels visible on the left. Occasionally we like to use the Light Table view to scan the contents of a folder. Ellen has created a custom view called Ellen 1. The new workspace is automatically added to the list of presets, as shown in Figure 2.19. That way, she can use any of the other presets but still quickly return to her preferred layout.

To create and save a customized workspace, take these steps:

1. Choose the default workspace that initially is closest to what you want to use.

2. Adjust the size of the pods as described earlier.

3. Select which panels to have visible by choosing Window > Workspace and toggling the check marks on and off.

4. Drag the panels to the desired pods.

Once you have configured the space the way you want it, save the workspace by choosing Window > Workspace > Save Workspace or by clicking the Workspace-changer drop-down menu in the top of the interface and choosing Save Workspace.

A new dialog will appear in which you name your workspace. There are also options to save the current sort order and the physical location of the window. After you save your workspace, it's available from Window > Workspace or from the workspace-changer icons at the top of the interface, as shown in Figure 2.19.

Figure 2.19 Choose a name for each workspace you save that clearly describes it, so you can quickly select the best workspace for any task.

Customizing Bridge

Bridge in Elements is similar to the version of Bridge that was in CS3. The interface contains fewer icons and controls than CS3's Bridge, but you can still customize it, and we recommend creating a view as shown here.

PHOTO BY ELLEN ANON

Other Views

Sometimes it's helpful to be able to see more of the images at once without seeing a larger preview of a single image. The Light Table view (Light Table) shows only the Content panel (see Figure 2.20). This can be helpful when you want to get an overall look at the images. We often use this view when looking for a specific image or checking to get a sense of the images that are in a folder.

This view is also excellent if Bridge didn't automatically rotate your verticals so they appear with the proper orientation (which requires that your digital camera support this feature). To rotate images, simply select them, and click the appropriate rotation button at the top of the Bridge window—these buttons have circular arrows indicating the direction of rotation. To select a group of images to be rotated, click the first one, then Shift-click the last one in the group, and finally click a rotation button.

To rotate noncontiguous images, Ctrl+click/⌘+click the desired images, and then click a rotation button. When you rotate an image in Bridge, only the thumbnail preview is rotated. The actual image isn't rotated until you open it.

Resize the thumbnails using the same procedure as described earlier. Usually you'll want the thumbnails to be fairly small in this view since you're not checking the individual files for details but rather getting a sense of what images are in the folder.

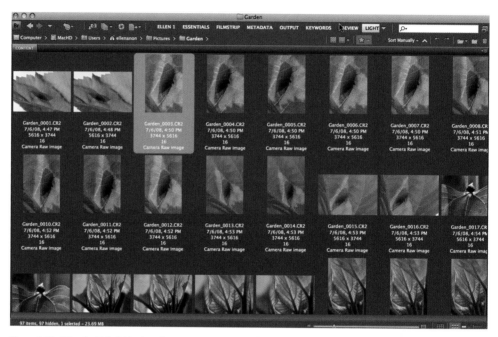

Figure 2.20 Using the Light Table view allows you to see as many of your image thumbnails as possible for an initial sort.

If you want to see a full-screen preview of your image at any time, press the spacebar. The interface will change to reveal only the selected image. Press the spacebar again to return to your regular workspace. To view multiple images in a full-screen view, click the Refine icon ![icon] and choose Review Mode.

> **Try It!** To get more comfortable with the many options available in Bridge, point it to a folder containing some of your images, and adjust the various options we've discussed here for changing the interface, including the view, pod size, and panel locations.

Recognizing the Icons

Photoshop ONLY

CS4 changed the information that's accessible on the interface and added a lot of functionality to the toolbar at the top of the interface, as shown in Figure 2.21. We've labeled the icons for you in the figure, but when you hover the cursor over them on your monitor, a tooltip will appear with their names. Still, it helps to know what functions are available from the icons rather than having to go to the menus.

Figure 2.21 The new icons in the Bridge interface make it easy to access a multitude of features with a single click.

The top bar is always visible but if the bottom bar, called the Path bar, is missing, choose Window > Path Bar and click to toggle its visibility.

Notice that there are icons to control the quality of the thumbnail previews. When you want to browse quickly, click the ▣ icon. To specify the overall quality used for the thumbnails and size of the previews, use the ▣▾ icon. We tend to set the Quality to Always High and then use the Quick Browse icon when we're anxious to see the images and don't want to wait for high-quality preview generation. You can choose whichever setting best meets your needs.

Stacking Images

As you go through your images, if you're like most nature photographers you'll see that you have a series of very similar images. This is particularly true if you are a wildlife photographer seeking just the right head angle and subject position. Or perhaps you're taking shots to composite into a panorama. Sometimes it helps to organize your images into stacks. That way, you can rapidly glance through the stacked view to have a general idea of what you've captured, and you can edit each stack individually.

To stack a group of images, first select them by Ctrl+clicking/⌘+clicking the images you want to group. If the images were shot in sequence and are all next to each other, click the first one and Shift-click the last one to select the entire series; press Ctrl+G/⌘+G to group them as a stack. Alternatively, you can stack them by choosing Stacks > Group as Stack. The stacked images will appear with an outline around them and a number on top indicating how many images are in the stack (see Figure 2.22).

We find the following techniques helpful when working with stacks:

- To open an individual stack, click the number at the top of the stack. Click the number again to close that stack.

- To open all stacks, choose Stacks > Expand All Stacks, and to close all stacks, choose Stacks > Collapse All Stacks.

- To move an image in or out of an existing stack, click and drag it in or out of the stack.

- To unstack images, select the stack and choose Stacks > Ungroup from Stack (Ctrl+Shift+G/⌘+Shift+G).

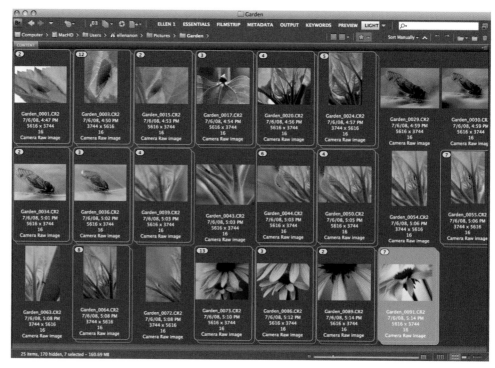

Figure 2.22 Stacking groups of similar images makes it easy to find specific sequences of images.

The image on top of the stack will be the image that's the farthest to the left in the group when you open the stack. You can click any image in the stack and drag it to the right or left, thereby selecting which image will be on top of the stack. Usually you'll want to choose the best image from the group, as shown in Figure 2.23.

Figure 2.23 The image farthest to the left will appear on top of the stack.

To open just the top image in ACR, make sure that only the top image is selected. You can tell because the top image will have a gray background, and there will be a rim of black on the right and bottom before the outline of the stack, as shown in Figure 2.24.

Figure 2.24 When there is a black space to the right and bottom of the stack, only the top image is selected.

To open an entire stack in ACR, first click in the black space, which will then fill with gray. When the entire stack outline is filled with gray, the entire stack is selected, as shown in Figure 2.25. Double-click in the main part of the thumbnail to open the images in ACR. To select just the top image, click in the space on the right and bottom so that it returns to black.

Figure 2.25 When there is no black space to the right and bottom of the stack, all images in the stack are selected.

In CS4 if a stack contains 10 or more images, when you hover your cursor over the stack a "play" arrow appears along with a small window with a marker in it. Click the play button to have Bridge rapidly scroll through all the images in the stack while leaving the stack closed (Figure 2.26). Move the marker slightly to the right to manually scroll through the images in the closed stack.

Figure 2.26 By using the play option or the manual advance, you can view stacked images without opening the stack.

CS4 added the option to have Bridge automatically create stacks for images that you shot to composite into panoramas or HDR composites. After selecting the folder containing the images, go to Stacks > Auto-Stack Panorama/HDR. You can help Bridge do this by making certain to shoot a blank frame (such as sky or your hand) between the last segment in one series and the first image in the next.

Try It! Practice working with stacks on a folder of your own images. Create stacks, rearrange the files in them to change the one that appears on top, drag images in and out of the stack, and so on. We think you'll like this new feature once you get comfortable with it.

Sorting and Editing

Getting your digital images onto your computer and creating a good way to view them is certainly a start. But as you've probably noticed, images seem to accumulate quickly, and keeping them organized can be a bit of a chore, especially if you have a backlog of images stored in many folders. When you download your latest images, chances are you want to get started working with them right away. But the first step, of course, is to figure out what you have, which images are worth keeping, and which should be deleted. Then you can select the images you'd like to start optimizing.

A good approach is to plan to do at least two passes through your images. Ellen finds it helpful to reject the images that are obviously poor on the first pass and to mark those she's excited about with a star rating. She then takes a second look at the rejects before deleting them. That way, no files are accidentally deleted. After that, she may stack the images and go through them a second or third time, assigning more careful ratings as well as labels. We'll go into more detail about this process later in this section.

If you haven't already navigated to the folder containing your images, do so using the Folders panel. It's a directory of everything on your computer. If you will be returning to this folder frequently, you may want to drag the folder to the Favorites panel. That way, you can find it quickly without needing to look through the entire directory. To place it on the Favorites panel, right-click/Control-click the folder, and choose Add to Favorites, as shown in Figure 2.27. If both the Favorites panel and Folders panel are visible, you can simply drag the folder to the area under the words *Drag Favorites Here* on the Favorites panel. Then click the folder in Favorites to view the contents.

Figure 2.27 Placing frequently accessed folders in the Favorites panel makes them easier to find.

Instead of using your mouse to haphazardly click images that you want to view in more detail, we recommend taking a close look at all of the images in the folder. Click the first image on the list (scroll to the top of the list if necessary), and then use the up and down arrow keys on your keyboard to navigate through the images. As you move up and down, the preview is updated based on the currently active image. This gives you a much better idea of the overall composition, exposure accuracy, and image quality so you can decide whether you should delete or keep the image. You can also start to get a better idea of which images deserve more attention as you sort through them.

Zooming and Comparing Images

As you go through your images, you need to know whether they are critically sharp. It's easy to tell when things are grossly out of focus, but judging critical sharpness can be challenging, especially on smaller laptop monitors. The Loupe tool enables you to quickly check sharpness, as shown in Figure 2.28. To access it, simply click the image preview or Ctrl+click/⌘+click if you have checked the option in Preferences to require a modifier key, and then drag the loupe wherever you'd like. The pointed corner of the tool points at the area it will magnify. Alternatively, click anywhere on the image that you'd like to view at 100% magnification.

By default, the Loupe tool is set to 100%. To adjust the magnification, up to 800%, press the + and – keys. The magnification percentage is visible by the filename beneath the image preview. To remove the loupe, click the X on the outer-rim corner of the magnifier.

Sometimes it's helpful to be able to look at two or more similar images simultaneously to decide which one is the best (Figure 2.28). To see more than one image in the Preview panel, Ctrl+click/⌘+click the thumbnails in the Content panel. The previews will automatically resize and move to accommodate as many images as you want to compare. To remove an image from the Preview panel, Ctrl-click/⌘-click it in the Content panel. You can create a loupe for each image that's currently in the Preview panel, as shown in Figure 2.28.

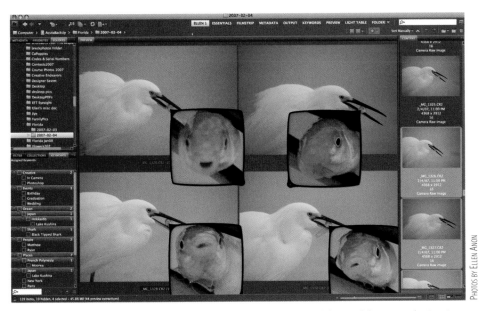

Figure 2.28 Being able to view multiple images simultaneously with a loupe to check for critical sharpness makes it easier to decide which image is the best.

Rating Images

Bridge includes a rating capability that allows you to assign a value of one to five stars or "reject" to your images, much like you might rate a movie. In so doing, you can quickly go through your images and rate them so that when you've finished with the sorting and editing process, you'll know exactly which images are your favorites and which ones need to be deleted.

As you sort through your images, begin by rejecting those you definitely don't want to keep. To apply a Reject rating, press Alt+Delete/Option+Delete. The image will remain in the folder but will be marked with Reject in red. You could opt to delete each throwaway image instead, but then there is no safeguard if you accidentally reject/delete one that you later decide you should have kept. We strongly believe it's better to first mark the throwaways with a Reject rating.

You'll also want to start thinking about which images are your favorites, since those are the ones you'll want to spend the most time optimizing. To assign a rank, simply press a number from 1 through 5 to assign a star rating.

Note: You must change the Label preference in Bridge preferences to enable you to assign labels and ratings without pressing the Ctrl/⌘ key. Otherwise, the keyboard shortcut for applying ratings is Ctrl/⌘ plus a number key from 1 through 5. We have found no advantage to using the additional keystroke; it's much faster to do the rating by simply pressing a number key.

If you prefer to not use the keyboard shortcuts to apply ratings, select an image (or images), and move your mouse over the row of five dots below the thumbnail. The dots represent the possible star ratings, so click the first dot to rate it as one star, the second dot to rate it as two stars, and so on (these dots are visible only if the image is selected, but the star rating you've applied to an image will display regardless of whether it is selected). If you have multiple images selected when you click, the rating will be updated to the same value for all the selected images. You can also remove a rating by clicking to the left of the row of dots. The star-rating display replaces the dots below the image, so you can see at a glance what you rated a given image (see Figure 2.29).

Figure 2.29 When you apply a rating to an image, that rating is reflected with stars displayed below the image thumbnail.

Labeling Images

The labeling feature in Bridge allows you to take the rating system a step further by assigning a color code to your images. You do this by applying a colored label to images in a way very similar to ratings. You can then filter the display to show only the images that are labeled or only those labeled with a specific color. The available colors for labels are red, yellow, green, blue, and purple.

To use these effectively, you'll first want to come up with a system that identifies what the colors mean. You might, for instance, use the labels to identify categorizations of images. For example, you might use a yellow label to mark images to use for a contest or competition, a green label to mark images to illustrate an article, and a blue label to designate images for a slide show. It's a good idea to document your system so you won't get confused later as you are reviewing images that have been previously labeled or as you are trying to remember what color specific images should be labeled in a new group of images. Consistency is important to taking full advantage of this capability. To label an image, you simply select it (or several images) and press the numbers 6 through 9; 6 for red, 7 for yellow, 8 for green, and 9 for blue (purple doesn't have a shortcut key). Alternatively, you can choose Label and then the desired color from the menu. You can turn off the label by pressing the number key a second time or by selecting Label > No Label.

When you label an image, a colored bar appears below the thumbnail (see Figure 2.30). This allows you to see at a glance which images were marked for a particular purpose, based on the system you're using for color-coding with labels.

Figure 2.30 When you apply a label to an image, a colored bar appears below the thumbnail in Bridge.

Of course, just seeing a colored bar or a star rating below the thumbnail image doesn't quite provide you with a powerful way to review your decisions about the images. By using the Filter panel, you can make even better use of the rating and labeling options.

Using the Filter Panel

When you have assigned a rank and/or label to all the images in your current project, you can sort the images by a particular parameter such as ratings or labels by clicking the Sort Manually icon Sort Manually ▾ ⌃ . You can also opt to display only a subset of the images—in other words, to filter them from the Filter icon ★▾ or from the Filter panel.

The Filter icon enables you to view only images that have a certain rating or label by clicking on the desired option. To specify images that have a certain rating or higher and a label, Ctrl+click/⌘+click on the additional option. Toggle off a criterion by clicking on it again.

The Filter panel enables you to choose which images to display at any one time according to a larger variety of parameters. In addition, Bridge shows how many images in the folder match each parameter. You can select just one parameter such as stars, labels, or Reject, or multiple parameters. If the parameters are within the same category, such as Ratings, then selecting more than one parameter is the equivalent of saying, "Show all images with this rating *or* that rating." When you choose an additional parameter from a different category such as Labels, then you are instructing Bridge to show only those images that meet the conditions checked in both categories; for example, in Figure 2.31 they must have a rating of five stars and a yellow label. If you clear a label or rating for an image at this point, it will disappear from the current view if it no longer meets the display criteria. When you want to see all the images again, toggle off all the check marks in the Filter panel.

Figure 2.31 Use the Filter panel to selectively display images meeting specific criteria.

You may want to combine using the sort and filter options. For example, you may choose to view images with three or more stars or those containing a label. You can then use the Sort Manually options to reorder the images according to a variety of parameters, including file type, bit depth, rating, labels, and so on.

In our workflow, after we have made the first pass through our images and rejected some of them, we filter the images to show only the rejects. We then quickly look through the images to make certain there are none we want to keep. To delete the images, we select them all (Ctrl+A/⌘+A) and then press Delete. A warning dialog will appear asking whether to delete or reject the images. Choose Delete.

Note: You may opt to check the box to prevent the warning dialog from appearing in the future since by rejecting the images first, you have introduced a safety step. It's a matter of personal preference to keep or eliminate this particular warning.

Creating Collections

Collections are a new feature in CS4. The idea is that you may want to view certain groupings of your images even though the files are housed in different folders. To begin, click on the Collections panel. If it's not visible choose Window > Collections Panel. Then click the ▨ icon. Name the collection, then click and drag one or more images into it. To remove an image from a Collection, right-click/Control-click on the thumbnail in the Content panel and choose Remove from Collection.

By clicking the Refine icon ▨▾ and choosing Review, you can view all the images currently visible in the Content panel in a full-screen Preview-only mode. If there are more than a few images, the images will appear in a carousel. By clicking the arrow, you can delete images from view. Click the ▨ icon to place the remaining images into a collection. A dialog will appear in which you name the new collection.

You can opt to have Bridge create collections for you based on certain parameters that you specify as shown in Figure 2.32. To begin, click the new Smart Collection icon ▨. In the new dialog box that appears, specify where Bridge should check for potential images. You could choose a folder or a broader part of your computer. Then specify the criteria. The first drop-down window says Filename by default, but by clicking within it you can choose from among a huge number of options. If you want to specify more than one parameter, click the + sign at the end of this line and then repeat the process until you have specified all the criteria. Next choose between If any criteria are met and If all criteria are met in the drop-down window. To create the collection, click Save. The Smart Collection will have a blue icon in the Collections panel. To edit the criteria, click the Edit Smart Collections icon 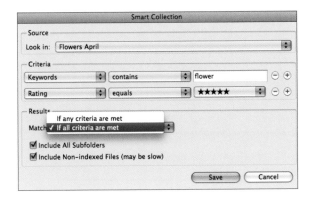 in the lower left of the panel.

Figure 2.32 Smart Collections help you organize your images in groupings that are meaningful to you.

Using Keywords

Applying keywords to your images is essential if you want to be able to easily find particular images, or types of images, in the future. Although it may feel like a nuisance, it's important to apply keywords to your images early in your workflow. It's all too easy to procrastinate and figure you'll do it later so that you can get on with the fun part of optimizing your images. But if you skip adding the keywords, you're likely to wind up with thousands of images stashed in various folders without an easy way to locate any particular image. By applying keywords, you can later search for an image using the Find command in Photoshop or using the search function on your computer.

Using Keywords to Locate Images

To find images using Bridge, choose Edit > Find. A new dialog box appears in which you specify the criteria for which to search. In the Criteria drop-down menu, choose Keywords. By using a series of keywords, you can do a more comprehensive search than just searching by filename. At the end of the line, click the + radio button to add additional keywords to use in the search. Under Results, choose If any criteria are met or If all criteria are met. Then proceed with your search.

Assign keywords every time you import images. In Bridge, you do so by highlighting one or more images, clicking the Keywords tab, and checking the keyword(s) to apply. It's really quite simple!

Keywords are organized into sets containing specific nested subkeywords in each set. By default Bridge has a few keywords, but for most nature photographers these will not be of much use. You'll need to create your own. Fortunately, it's easy. First you need to think of what organizational scheme you want to use. Since Bridge

CS4 is able to create nested keywords, you can create multiple levels within a set. For example, we might begin with a set called Places, then add a subkeyword Japan. We'll click on Japan and then click the subkeyword icon to add yet another more explicit location called Hokkaido. We'll click on Hokkaido and add a new subkeyword called Lake Kushira. Or, as in Figure 2.33, we might create a keyword called Birds, with a subordinate keyword of Shore Birds with a subordinate keyword Egret and subordinates of Cattle, Great Egret, Reddish, and Snowy.

Figure 2.33 Organize your keywords in a logical way with main keywords and nested subordinate keywords.

Note: At the very least, you should have a keyword for the location of each shot and the subject matter. If you submit your images to stock agencies, you'll want to add keywords according to their recommendations.

To create new keywords, click on an existing keyword at the desired level. Then click the New Keyword icon ⊞ and type the name. To create new subkeywords, first select the parent keyword by clicking on it, and then click the New SubKeyword icon ⊞. To create an additional keyword at the same level, click the Add Keyword icon rather than the Add Subordinate Keyword icon. To delete a keyword or keyword set, select it, right-click/Control-click, and choose Delete.

Before creating a new keyword, you can search to see if it already exists in your keyword list by entering the text in the search field (see Figure 2.34). Then any place that word exists in the keyword structure will be highlighted, as shown in the figure.

Figure 2.34 Searching for a keyword avoids creating duplicate, nearly identical keywords as well as misspellings.

You can also import or export keyword categories by right-clicking/Control+ clicking and choosing the Import/Export options. Keywording is now even easier than ever and should be a routine part of your workflow.

Try It! Create a new keyword set and several new keywords, and apply them to various images. Although it may seem intimidating at first, once you do it, we're confident you'll see how easy it is to do.

Additional Features

Bridge contains a variety of additional features that we find useful. For example, we use Tools > Photoshop > Image Processor (see Chapter 11, "Time-Savers") to quickly batch-convert images to other sizes and file formats, and we use Tools > Photoshop > Photomerge to stitch together a series of images into a panorama (see Chapter 8, "Composites"). We also use Tools > Photoshop > Merge to HDR to combine a series of shots in Bridge into a 32-bit file (see Chapter 8), and we use Tools > Photoshop > Contact Sheet to create contact sheets (see Chapter 10, "Output").

In addition, Bridge has a cool feature that quickly generates a slide show of your images. That can be useful to show off some of your best images or to help you with your sorting and editing.

To create a slide show in Bridge, choose View > Slideshow from the Bridge menu, or press Ctrl+L/⌘+L. This will start a slide show of the selected images (or all images in the current folder if none are selected). By default, the images will change every five seconds, but you can press the spacebar to play or pause the slide show. To move through the images manually, click the mouse or use the arrow keys on the keyboard.

Choose View > Slideshow Options (Shift+Ctrl+L/Shift+⌘+L) to access a dialog box (see Figure 2.35) to specify options for the slide show. You can opt to have the slide show repeat, set the timing for the advances, whether the captions show, whether the images are scaled, as well as the transitions and transition speed. We think that the Dissolve feature is quite good and makes for a nice transition between images.

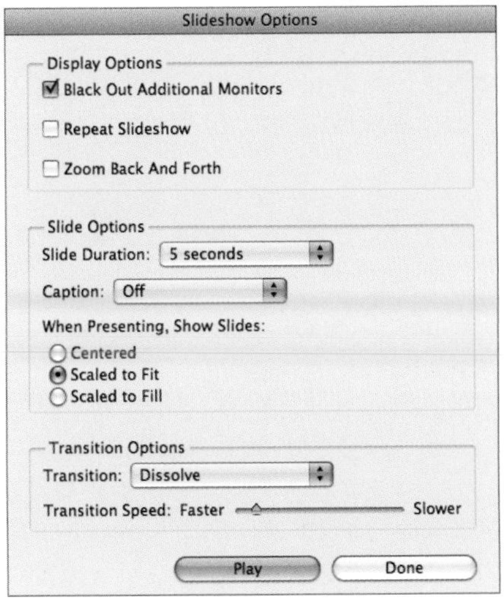

Figure 2.35 Add transitions and other controls to your slide show using the Slideshow Options dialog box.

While viewing a slide show, press the H key to access additional slide show commands, as shown in Figure 2.36. Notice that you can apply or change labels and ratings while viewing images in a slide show. Sometimes it's easier to decide which image you like the best by viewing the series of images in a slide show. Bridge makes it simple to remember which file you want by applying a label or rating. Press the 1–5 keys to add the appropriate number of stars and 6–9 to add a colored label.

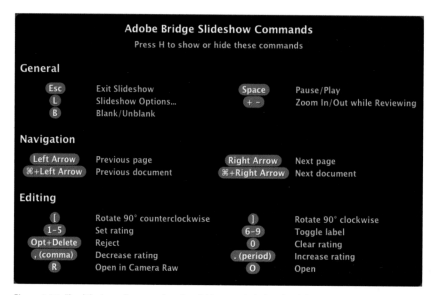

Figure 2.36 The slide show offers a number of useful features, including the ability to easily add labels and ratings to images while viewing the slide show.

Try It! Open a folder in Bridge and create a slide show. Try using the various commands and controls to customize the show. We think that once you try this feature, you'll like it a lot!

We'll talk about Adobe Output Module, which is based in Bridge, in Chapter 10. You can use it to generate web pages and PDFs directly from Bridge.

Additional Tools

Bridge > Tools provides other useful tools for Elements Mac users, including quick access to the Process Multiple Files tool. This is similar to the Image Processor that we cover in Chapter 11.

Organizer, the PC version of Bridge

Instead of using Bridge, Elements 6 for Windows has its own photo-organization tool, Organizer (shown in the image here). To open Organizer, click the Organizer button in the toolbar ⬚⬚ Organizer. In many ways, Organizer is more like iPhoto or Lightroom instead of Bridge. Unlike Bridge, it doesn't let you browse files or folders. Instead, it requires you to import your images into Catalogs (many users typically have just one Catalog) and then organize them into Albums (we'll discuss both Catalogs and Albums in more depth later in this sidebar). However, Organizer makes it easy to store your images on a CD, search your images, and more. Because Organizer is available only with Elements for Windows, we will cover only the features in Organizer that are most useful for nature photographers and won't explore every feature of the program.

Tip: We recommend avoiding the simplified Fix tools within Organizer and instead use the more powerful tools within Elements.

Setting Organizer Preferences

Open Organizer's Preferences dialog by selecting Edit > Preferences. Here are the useful areas for photographers:

General

This section controls the display options for Organizer. The default options work well, although we recommend setting Print Sizes to your preferred unit of measurement: inches or centimeters.

Continues

Files

This section controls how Organizer handles files, as shown in the following image. We recommend checking each option within this dialog. Checking Use "Last Modified" Date if EXIF Date Is Not Found ensures that your images have a date set in their metadata, and Import EXIF Caption causes Organizer to automatically pick up any caption you've written elsewhere for the image.

Automatically Search for and Reconnect Missing Files causes Organizer to search for any files it doesn't find (for example, if you go into Windows Explorer and move a file outside of Organizer).

Automatically Prompt to Backup Files and Catalog is a helpful reminder to create a backup of your library database, although if you find it annoying, uncheck this option.

We recommend selecting Rotate JPEGs Using Orientation Metadata and Rotate TIFFs Using Orientation Metadata so that you don't have to rotate your images manually.

Organizer is slightly confusing because there are two different places where you need to specify where to store your images. Folders for Saved Files is the first place, and this affects where images you import from any disk (for example, your hard drive or a CD) are stored. You also must specify where Organizer stores any files it creates. Change this folder by clicking the Browse button and picking a new folder.

Another useful option here is the Preview File Size setting. We won't cover Offline Volumes in this chapter, but the short of it is that Organizer lets you store your images in locations other than your hard drive (such as on a DVD) but still see previews within Organizer, even when the disc isn't in the drive. Preview File Size controls that preview image's resolution. The larger the preview file, the higher the quality and the more disk space it requires.

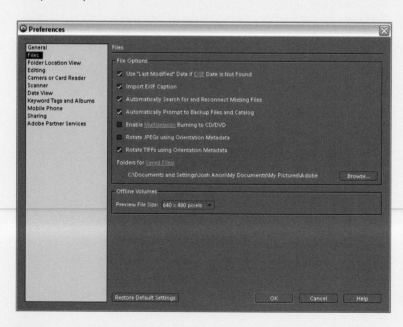

Editing

If there's another application you like to use to edit your images in addition to Photoshop Elements, the Editing pane lets you add that application to the Edit menu.

Continues

Camera or Card Reader

Organizer has a Photo Downloader that's nearly identical to the one in Bridge. The Camera or Card Reader settings section, shown below, allows you to customize its initial behavior. We change the default Save Files In location that specifies where Organizer stores the images that it downloads from your camera or card reader. To change this setting, click the Browse button and choose a location that's convenient for you. We recommend using the same folder that you set in the Files Preferences pane.

We recommend unchecking Automatically Fix Red Eyes to avoid having Organizer do any unintended image corrections.

The Download Options box allows you to determine whether the Photo Downloader opens automatically, and if so, what mode it opens into. We recommend always using Advanced mode. To set this option, select the profile for your card reader or camera, click the Edit button, and select Show APD Dialog (Advanced) from the pop-up menu.

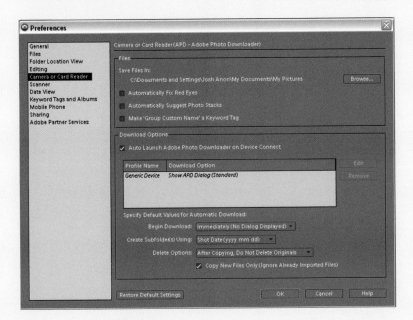

Keyword Tags and Albums

It's a good idea to specify whether keywords and albums sort manually or alphabetically. We recommend Alphabetical sorting over manual sorting, but some people prefer their own organization and like the option to use Manual sorting.

Color Settings

The Color Settings preferences, shown here, are located under Edit > Color Settings rather than being grouped with the other preferences. Here you can select No Color Management (not recommended), Always Optimize Colors for Computer Screens (Organizer will convert images to sRGB), Always Optimize for Printing

Continues

(convert images to Adobe RGB), or Allow Me to Choose. We recommend selecting Allow Me to Choose so that Organizer does not adjust the color in your image without asking you what to do.

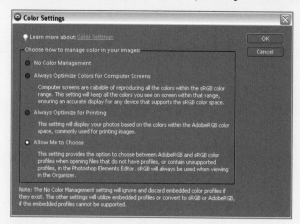

Bringing Images into Organizer

Organizer enables you to import images from the hard drive or other disks as well as by using the Photo Downloader to access images that are currently on a memory card or in your camera.

Adding Images From the Hard Drive or Other Disk

Choose File > Get Photos from Files and Folders. Use the Open dialog that appears to select either a set of images or folders containing images to import to Organizer. Uncheck Copy Files on Import to have Organizer leave the images in their original location. If you do select Copy Files, Organizer provides an option to automatically remove red-eye in the Open dialog. We recommend deselecting this option so that Organizer does not modify your images without your knowledge.

Alternatively, to add existing images to Organizer you can drag the images from Explorer directly into Organizer.

Photo Downloader

To open Photo Downloader from Organizer, choose File > Get Photos and Videos > From Camera or Card Reader. Alternatively, click the Photo Downloader button  in the Windows System Tray.

The primary differences between Organizer's Photo Downloader, shown here, and Bridge's are that Organizer will also let you download movie and audio files from your camera and the Advanced Options are different. In Organizer, there is no option to make a second copy of the images and no option to convert to DNG. Instead, you'll find an option for fixing red-eye (which we recommend unchecking), an option for automatically stacking photos, and an option for specifying what to do with the originals after copying. We recommend leaving this pop-up set to After Copying, Do Not Delete Originals so that if something goes wrong with the download, you will still have your original files. Furthermore, by not deleting the originals it's easier to make a backup copy of your storage card.

Continues

We suggest you follow the instructions in the next section to create a custom metadata template to apply on import. That way, important information such as your contact and copyright information will be contained in your image.

Once Photo Downloader finishes, Organizer will prompt to show only the new files. We recommend deselecting this option so that you don't wonder why your old images disappeared.

Creating a Metadata Template

To create a metadata template in Elements for Windows, take the following steps:

1. Within Elements (not Organizer), open any file.

2. Choose File > File Info.

3. Type in your preset information.

4. Click the triangle at the top.

5. Select Save Metadata Template.

Note that the fields Elements allows you to set are limited compared to Photoshop CS.

Renaming After Import

Although Organizer does not have a robust renaming tool, it is possible to rename multiple images.

1. Select the images to rename.

2. Choose File > Rename.

3. Type the base name and click OK. Organizer will rename each image as base name-#, starting at 1.

Catalogs

Catalogs are unique to Organizer. They are databases that hold a collection of links to your original image files with extra metadata (like keywords and captions) associated with your images. For example, a catalog might include every image you've ever taken, all of your shots from 2008, or all of your shots from a given assignment. Within each catalog, you can further organize images into albums. For example, if you have a catalog for a specific trip, you might have albums for each subject that you photographed. To manage your catalogs, select File > Catalogs (Ctrl+Shift+C) to open the Catalog Manager.

Under the Catalogs box, you have a choice between seeing Catalogs Accessible by All Users (meaning every person who has a login on your computer), Catalogs Accessible by the Current User, or Custom Location (which lets you specify a custom folder to store your catalog files in). We recommend choosing Custom Location and selecting a folder within My Documents to store your catalogs so that you can easily access your catalog files if necessary.

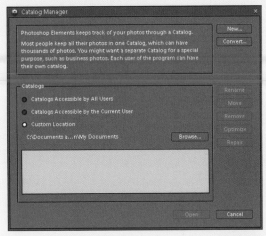

Continues

Click the New button to create a new catalog, use Rename to change the catalog name, use Move to move the catalog to a new location, and click Remove to delete the selected catalog. Clicking Optimize can help improve Organizer's performance if you have a lot of files in your catalog, and Repair can recover a damaged catalog. To switch catalogs, select the catalog from the list and click Open.

Ultimately, how you organize your catalogs is up to you. If you're new to digital photography, we recommend starting with just one catalog and using albums to organize your images so that you have one less thing to worry about. If you're an experienced digital shooter, then you should have some idea of how you like to group your images, such as by shoot, which is our preferred working style.

Tip: If you go to the File menu at the top of the monitor, the option Backup Catalog to CD, DVD, or Hard Drive will let you quickly make a backup copy of all the images in your catalog. Backup Catalog even has an Incremental Backups option, which will cause Organizer to back up only files that have changed since the last backup. This can be a huge time-saver when working with large image collections, because you won't have to make a copy of every image each time you back up.

Restore Catalog from CD, DVD, or Hard Drive provides a way to load a backup catalog into Organizer, optionally copying the images to a new location.

You might wonder why Backup and Restore are useful. Well, if you are using a laptop with a small hard drive, after editing your images from a shoot, you could back up the catalog to a DVD and delete the images from your hard drive to recover the disk space. Later on, you could quickly restore those images to your hard drive by using the Restore Catalog command. Another practical example is that even if you don't use the Restore function, the Backup tool provides a quick way to collect all of your images in the catalog, wherever on your hard drive they may be, and copy them to a backup location.

Albums

Albums are a way of organizing subcollections of images within a catalog. For example, a catalog for a weeklong shoot might have an album for each day. Organizer has normal albums, where you manually add and remove images to the album, as well as Smart Albums. Like a Smart Playlist in iTunes, a Smart Album automatically adjusts its contents based on a certain criterion—for example, all images created within the past week.

To make a new album, click the Create New Album button ➕ in the Albums pane and select New Album. Type in a name and click OK. Drag images from the Photo Browser onto the album to add them to the album. Select Find > Items Not in Any Album or click the Show All button at the top of the Photo Browser to see the images not grouped into albums.

To create a new smart album, click the Create New Album button in the Albums pane and select New Smart Album. In the dialog that appears, pick the criteria you want for your smart album.

An album group represents a collection of albums. For example, if you were photographing Zion National Park and Bryce Canyon, you could have one album group for Zion and another for Bryce. Then, within the album group, you could make an album for each day. To create an album group, click the Create New Album button in the Albums pane, select New Album Group, and give the group a name. Drag and drop albums into or out of the group as needed.

Continues

Viewing Images

By default, Organizer shows the Thumbnail View for the Photo Browser, shown earlier. We recommend adding the Properties pane to the display, so that you can quickly see image metadata, by selecting Window > Properties and clicking the Dock to Organizer Pane button ⬇. Change the size of the thumbnails by using the slider in the top middle of the window. Check the Details check box to see image ratings, filenames, and more. This view is very similar to Bridge's Light Table view.

Click the Display button in the toolbar 🖥 Display ▾ to reveal the various display options. Import Batch will show you your images grouped by when they were imported, and Folder Location will reveal the folder that each image is in (and allow you to move the image by dragging it elsewhere in the folder hierarchy). We recommend using the Folder Location view when moving images around.

These first three modes are considered Photo Browser views. Date View, shown here, is a completely different mode that lets you view your images based on the day they were taken. You can toggle between viewing the Year, Month, or Day by using the buttons on the bottom, and there is a note field on the right side of the window to add daily notes, such as location information.

PHOTOS BY JOSH ANON

For most purposes, we recommend using the Photo Browser over Date View in the default Thumbnail View mode. The View menu lets you customize which fields are visible below each thumbnail. We recommend selecting Details and Show File Names.

Opening Images in Adobe Camera Raw

In all views, double-clicking an image will take you to a larger view of the image. Unfortunately, you cannot set up Organizer so that double-clicking a raw file opens Camera Raw. To open a raw file with Camera Raw, instead choose Editor > Full Edit. When finished in Camera Raw, click the Done button, and Organizer will update to show the changes you made to the raw conversion.

Continues

Full-Screen Modes

Organizer has two different full-screen modes, Full Screen and Side by Side, which let you take advantage of your entire screen for photo organizing. Select Display > View Photos in Full Screen or Display > Compare Photos Side by Side to begin. The difference between the two modes is that Full Screen shows one image at a time, and Side by Side shows two images at once to make it easier to pick between similar images.

The first time you select View Photos in Full Screen, Organizer will open another dialog with various slide show options. To disable this dialog, uncheck the option that says Show this dialog before viewing photos in full screen and click the OK button. We also recommend deselecting Include Captions so that Organizer does not show your image caption on top of your image. These options are shown here:

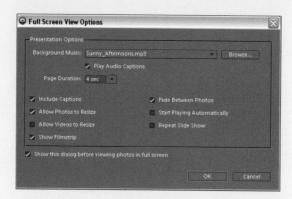

At the top of the screen, Organizer presents a toolbar (shown here) with common tools, such as Rotate, Zoom, and Rate. We recommend clicking the Action Menu button ▣ and selecting Show Filmstrip to reveal a non-movable Filmstrip on the right side of the screen. The Filmstrip makes it easy to jump between images in the current collection. Use the Full Screen and Side by Side View buttons in the toolbar to toggle between the two modes

Full Screen   Side by Side

To exit Full Screen, press the Esc key.

Stacking Images

Take the following steps to stack images in Organizer:

1. Select the images to stack.

2. Choose Edit > Stack > Stack Selected Photos.

3. If you are in an album and the Stack menu is not enabled, try exiting the album by clicking the Show All button and then reselect your images.

Continues

4. Organizer will show a rounded rectangle around the image stack, as shown here. Open and close the stack by clicking the disclosure triangle halfway up the right side. (The yellow icon indicates that keywords have been added.)

To set an image as the top image in the stack, select the stack, expand the stack, select the desired image, and choose Edit > Stack > Set as Top Photo.

To edit all images within a stack, be sure to expand the stack and select all of its images before selecting Editor > Full Edit. Otherwise, Organizer will edit the selected image only.

To remove a photo from the stack, expand the stack, select the image, and choose Edit > Stack > Remove Photo from Stack.

Sorting and Editing

In Organizer, we like to start by placing all of our images from a shoot into an album (or albums) and using the Thumbnail View to look through our images. We find this more useful than Import Batch because we often have more than one card's worth of images from a single shoot, and creating an album lets us conceptually group our images together so we can quickly return to the right album later on to find specific images.

As we mentioned earlier, to move images into an album, simply drag and drop them onto the album name in the Albums pane. To view an album, click the album name in the Albums pane.

To actually begin our editing, we find Full Screen view the most useful because it provides a way to see our image at 100%, a filmstrip to see what's next, a rating control to mark our images, and the Side by Side view to compare two images.

Although there is no Loupe tool in Organizer, the Zoom slider in the toolbar will let you zoom from 6% to 1600%. Click and drag directly on your image to view different parts of the image.

To quickly rate an image, press the number 1–5 that corresponds to the image's rating. Press 0 to clear the rating. Since Organizer does not have a Reject flag, we recommend using a one-star rating to indicate "This image should be deleted." Once you've made an initial pass through your images, exit Full Screen and set the ratings filter field in the top right of the Thumbnail view to be one star. This will show you all of your "rejected" images. Select all of those images and choose Edit > Delete from Catalog to remove the images. Be sure to check Also Delete Selected Item(s) from the Hard Disk in the dialog that appears so that your image file is removed, too.

Organizer does not provide labels.

Filtering Images

In the Photo Browser view, Organizer provides the ability to sort your images by date, or you can define your own order. To change this sorting, change the Photo Browser Arrangement on the top toolbar. The Ratings Filter on the top right of the Thumbnail view allows you to specify what images are visible based on their rating. For example, to see your best images, you would set this to show four-star and higher images. To

Continues

clear the filter, click on the highest selected star (for example, in the previous example, you would click on the fourth star).

Organizer also provides a useful Find menu, with many default searches, but the most useful is the Find by Details (Metadata) command shown in the following image. This window allows you to build up search expressions, such as finding all three-star or higher-rated images taken on a Canon camera. If you are rating and keywording your images in Organizer, this is a powerful way to find images. Furthermore, you can make a smart album easily from your search results by clicking Create New Album and selecting Save Search Criteria as Smart Album.

To close the search results, click on an album or click the Show All button to see all the images in the catalog.

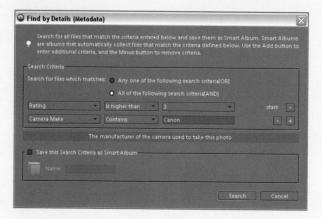

Keywords

To create a new keyword tag in Organizer, click the Create New Keyword Tag button in the Keyword Tags pane of the Organize tab and select New Keyword Tag. The dialog shown here will appear; there you enter the keyword, group the keyword under a category, set an icon, and add notes about the keyword.

To apply a keyword tag or a group of keywords to an image, select the image and drag the keyword or keyword group from the Keyword Tags pane onto the image. To remove a keyword, right-click on the image, choose Remove Keyword Tag, and select the keyword to remove.

When you've finished applying keywords, it's smart to use File > Write Keyword Tag and Properties Info to Photo so that Organizer will save the keywords with the photo (instead of just storing them in the Catalog database). That makes the keywords accessible to other programs, such as Bridge.

Continues

Other Features

Watch Folders and Slide Shows are both very useful additional features in Organizer. Watch Folders are folders on your hard drive that Organizer "watches" for new files. When you add new files to the folder, Organizer will either notify you that there are new files or import them automatically. To set up Watch Folders, select File > Watch Folders, and in the dialog that appears, shown here, add and remove folders to watch.

There are two ways to create a slide show in Organizer. To start a quick slide show, select Display > View Photos in Full Screen and click the Play button in the toolbar. To modify the slide show settings, click the Action Menu button in the toolbar and select Full Screen View Options.

The second method is to create a more sophisticated slide show project. We won't go into detail here, but to start a project, switch from the Organize to the Create tab and click the Slide Show button. Configure the basic preferences however you'd like, and then use the Slide Show Editor to adjust transitions, add text, and customize your show.

Adobe Camera Raw

Adobe Camera Raw (ACR) has been significantly improved in Photoshop CS4 and is the foundation of our workflow. Camera sensors capture information that needs to be converted to a form that we can see. Shooting in RAW gives us the chance to modify the algorithms used to convert the images. We now do most image adjustments within ACR, in its powerful and easy-to-use interface. What's more, we can even use ACR to adjust TIFF or JPEG files. We'll show you how to use ACR to adjust your images so that you're starting with the best possible files!

3

Chapter Contents

Using the ACR Interface

The new ACR interface packs a lot of features and controls into its intuitive and easy-to-use interface. You can choose to make only basic corrections to your image or perform some quite sophisticated adjustments, including targeted adjustments. We'll go through the interface step by step so you'll know precisely where to find each control.

Note: It's worth mentioning that ACR is different from the converter supplied by your camera manufacturer. The one that came with your camera may be able to take advantage of some proprietary information captured by your camera, and this can, in a small percentage of cases, result in better image quality in the conversion. However, there is a huge convenience factor in using the very user-friendly and generally faster converter included within Photoshop. You'll rarely, if ever, encounter a problem by using ACR.

The Elements Version of Camera Raw

The Elements version of ACR is quite similar, although more limited, as seen here. It has only two tabs and lacks some of the more sophisticated tools of the Photoshop version.

PHOTO BY JOSH ANON

Seeing Your Image Within ACR

By default when ACR opens, the image is set to Fit in View, so you see your entire image within the workspace. As shown in Figure 3.1, the small box in the lower left of the dialog box gives the current magnification of your image. To zoom in or out, click the – or + box there, or click the arrows next to the number to get a drop-down menu revealing a variety of common magnifications. To check for critical sharpness within your image, zoom to 100%. To return to the original view, select Fit in View from the drop-down menu, or use the keyboard shortcut Ctrl+0/⌘+0.

Figure 3.1 You have the option of seeing your entire image or zooming in to closely examine parts of the image.

When you are zoomed in beyond the Fit in View size, you can click the hand icon in the strip of icons at the top left of the ACR window and then click within the preview and drag to inspect various parts of the image. Alternatively, you can simply hold down the spacebar while clicking and dragging within the preview. Note that you can also click the magnifying-glass icon in that same strip of icons to zoom into your image and hold down the Alt/Option key while clicking to zoom out. Many other important tools are available from this strip of icons, as indicated in Figure 3.2. We'll discuss them in more depth throughout the chapter.

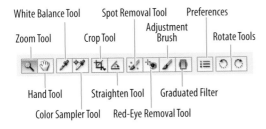

Figure 3.2 This strip of icons allows you easy, one-click access to a number of important features in ACR.

If your image needs to be rotated, click one of the circle arrows ⟲ ⟳ , or press the R key to rotate the image 90° to the right (clockwise) or the L key to rotate it 90° to the left (counterclockwise).

Use the Preview check box to toggle between a preview of the file with and without your changes. The preview is continuously updated. The ⬦ icon toggles the ACR interface between a full-screen version and a smaller adjustable size. Usually we prefer the full-screen version so we can see the image in more detail.

In the upper-right corner of the interface is the histogram. It shows a graph for each color channel with the white luminosity histogram superimposed on top. In the upper corners of the histogram, as shown in Figure 3.3, you'll see two triangles. Clicking these triangles toggles the clipping previews on and off. When they are on, any highlights that are being clipped will appear solid bright red, and any shadows being clipped will appear solid vivid blue. This way, you can readily see when you may have made an adjustment that would lead to accidentally throwing away detail in your highlights or shadows. With this obvious warning enabled, it's easy to modify your settings to retain as much detail as possible within your image. In addition, the triangles change colors to indicate which channels are being clipped. When there is no clipping, the triangles are black.

Note: *Clipping* means forcing pixels above or below a certain value to become pure black or pure white, thus losing detail in either your highlights or shadows.

Figure 3.3 Checking the Preview box and the clipping triangles in the histogram allows you to see whether there is any clipping in your image, either from the way it was captured or because of the changes you make within ACR.

As your cursor hovers over any point in your image preview, a readout of that point's RGB values appears beneath the histogram. In addition, some basic information about your lens, ISO, aperture, and shutter speed appears there.

Cropping and Rotating Within ACR

Photoshop CS4 offers the ability to crop and rotate within ACR. Since you can embed your raw file in your image file as a Smart Object (see Chapter 5, "Workflows and First Steps," for more details), you can crop nondestructively using the cropping tool in ACR. By *nondestructively*, we mean that you can change your mind at some future time and change the crop without any loss of image quality. (Obviously when you crop, you're eliminating certain pixels from your final file.)

To use the Crop tool, simply click its icon 🔳 or press C on your keyboard, then click a beginning point in the image preview and drag diagonally across the image. You can refine your selection by clicking any one of the small boxes appearing on the boundaries of the image and dragging them inward or outward as desired. You can move the crop around on the image by placing the cursor within the center of the area to be cropped and then clicking and dragging. To apply the crop, press Enter.

If you click and hold on the Crop tool, you'll see a drop-down menu listing various preset cropping options, so you can crop the image to an aspect ratio of your choosing (see Figure 3.4). You can even create custom settings for other aspect ratios that you use frequently, such as 8×10. To do this, simply click the Custom option to reveal a Custom Crop dialog box. Fill in the boxes with the appropriate numbers, and click OK. To remove a crop, press Esc while the Crop tool is still selected, or choose Clear Crop from the Crop drop-down menu.

Figure 3.4 You can crop to a preset size or to a custom size within ACR. The Size menu will reflect the cropped file size.

As you set the crop to the desired size, notice that the size listed in the center bottom in the Workflow Options has changed and reflects the size of the image after the crop. We'll talk more about the Workflow Options later in this chapter.

ACR also enables you to easily straighten horizons. To do so, click the Straighten icon ▲, or press the letter A. Then click at the beginning of the *horizon*, or area that should be straight, and drag across to the opposite side. You are telling ACR what part of your image should be a straight horizontal or vertical line. When you release the cursor, you will see the preview rotated, and automatic crop lines will have been set, as illustrated in Figure 3.5. The Crop tool icon will automatically be highlighted or selected. To apply the rotation and crop, press Enter. To quickly reset your image to its original position, in the event that the straightening didn't work as planned, press Ctrl+Z/⌘+Z, or select Clear Crop from the Crop tool drop-down menu.

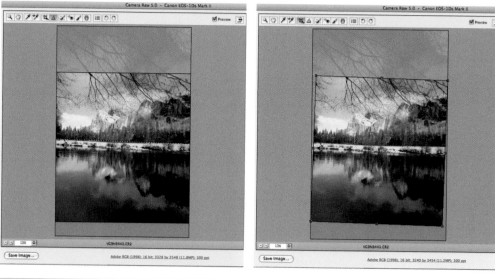

Figure 3.5 The Straighten tool automatically crops and straightens your image.

One potential drawback to cropping and rotating within the converter is that ACR limits your crop to the boundaries of the image, meaning you cannot rotate and crop in such a way that the boundaries extend beyond the pixel information at any point. If the placement of your subject matter dictates that you need to clone in additional background area after straightening the image, wait to crop and straighten the image within Photoshop.

Try It! Open the raw image named ConvertRaw.dng on the accompanying CD or one of your own, and practice cropping and rotating it.

Using the Spot Removal Tool

The Spot Removal tool 🖌 is similar to the Clone and Healing Brush tools in Photoshop, although not quite as powerful. The Spot Removal tool is particularly well suited to removing the dust that plagues most digital photographers. Unfortunately, since retouching in ACR is limited to circular spots, it is not well suited for object removal. That type of retouching is best done later in Photoshop.

If you are using a Smart Object–based flexible workflow (see Chapter 5), it's helpful to do as much as possible of your dust removal in ACR. That way, anytime you change the Smart Object, your retouching will automatically change as well. If you use the flexible workflow but do your cleanup in Photoshop, some changes you may make later to the Smart Object (your background layer with the raw file) may force you to have to redo the cleanup layer. For instance, if you make tonal or color corrections to the raw file, any cloning and healing that was based on the previous settings will no longer match.

To use the Retouch tool, follow these steps:

1. Zoom into your image to 100% magnification.

2. Begin at one corner and systematically work your way through the image.

3. When you find a speck of dust, click the Spot Removal tool. As shown in Figure 3.6, several new options appear to the right of the image.

4. Select either Heal or Clone in the Type drop-down menu. Clone will copy the pixels from another area that you choose to replace the dust, whereas Heal will copy the texture and blend the color just as the similar tools do in Photoshop. (For more in-depth coverage of cloning and healing, see Chapter 5.)

5. Check Show Overlay so a circle will remain showing areas that have been retouched, as well as the source for the retouching. That way, if you need to modify an area, you can redo it easily.

6. Click and drag over the dust to create a circle just slightly larger than the dust. A red circle appears to indicate this is the spot you are currently working on. As you drag, the size of the circle changes. You can also modify the size of the circle, before or after you've created it, by adjusting the Radius slider.

Figure 3.6 After clicking the Spot Removal tool, specify the Heal or Clone tool, as well as the radius, opacity, and whether to show an overlay of the corrections.

7. Whether you are cloning or healing, a second circle will appear with broken green lines. That indicates the source for the cloning or healing. To change the source, click within that circle and drag it to the desired location.

8. Once you click the next spot, the previous red circle changes to a broken circle indicating the area that was retouched.

9. To modify a previously retouched area, click within the circle. If you place the cursor directly on the outline of the circle, you can drag to change its size. To change the source, click within the source circle and drag.

10. To remove a single retouched spot, click within the circle and press the Delete key on the keyboard. To remove all the retouching, click the Clear All button in ACR.

Note: The Red Eye Removal tool works similarly to the Red Eye Removal tool in Photoshop. Click and drag over the red pupils, and drag the Darken slider until the eye looks natural. Because red-eye removal is not a task faced by most nature photographers and the tool is straightforward to use, we won't go into more detail about using it.

Controlling the Default Appearance of Your Image

Bridge generates thumbnails and initial previews of your images to help you edit your images based on the ACR settings. These previews also serve as a starting place for your ACR adjustments. By default, they are set to use Auto Tone Adjustments and to apply some sharpening to generate these previews. You may decide that you would rather edit your images in Bridge, viewing the file previews with the settings you used to shoot them or some other combination of settings. ACR allows you to specify what settings it should use to generate the default thumbnails and previews. Click the Preferences icon in the toolbar ▤ to open the dialog box shown in Figure 3.7.

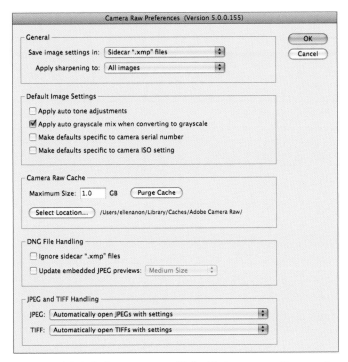

Figure 3.7 Click the Preferences icon to modify the default appearance of image previews in Bridge and ACR.

Specifying the General Settings

We recommend you use the default setting and save your image settings in sidecar XMP files. These are the settings that contain the adjustments you make to the image, and it's useful to have them go with your image if you opt to open it in another application. More applications are able to read XMP files and thus maintain consistency with the appearance of your image.

By default, ACR applies some sharpening to each image. This is to balance the slight bit of softening that is inherent within digital capture. In the past, we recommended that you change the Apply Sharpening To option to preview images only. However, the sharpening algorithms have been improved substantially in the most recent versions of ACR, and we have yet to see an image that was adversely affected by applying the default low levels of sharpening as a first pass of sharpening. Therefore, we now leave the sharpening option set to All Images.

Specifying the Default Image Settings

ACR includes several options for determining how you want to preview your images. There is an option to preview your images using auto-tone corrections for exposure, shadows, contrast, and brightness. For images from some cameras, these auto-corrections work fairly well and give you a good start on optimizing your images. With images from other cameras, the settings can be too extreme and result in clipped data or other less-than-ideal presentations. By default, CS4 ships with the Auto setting functionality turned on. This means that when you view your images in Bridge, you're seeing the raw files with the Auto settings applied. In reality, your raw file is still a raw data file; the settings are applied only to the previews, not to the raw files themselves. *When you open the image in ACR, you not only can but should modify any and all settings to customize the conversion as you desire.* The Auto settings are useful primarily as starting points.

We prefer to set ACR so that Auto is not applied to raw files. That way, when you edit in Bridge, you'll see your files as you shot them. Therefore, we recommend that you deselect the Apply Auto Tone Adjustments check box.

In the Default Image Settings section, we do enable Apply Auto Grayscale Mix When Converting to Grayscale. In addition, if you use more than one camera body, we recommend checking the option Make Defaults Specific to Camera Serial Number. That way, you can establish different settings for each camera if necessary. In particular, you may find that one camera requires a different amount of default color noise reduction or camera-calibration settings.

We leave the other settings at their defaults. However, you may want to consider the TIFF and JPEG options.

- The Automatically Open All Supported JPEG/TIFF Files setting causes all JPEGS and TIFFs to open in ACR when you double-click on them in Bridge.

- The default setting, Automatically Open JPEG/TIFF Files with Settings, means that ACR will open any JPEG or TIFF file with editable settings from ACR (ACR tags) in them. For example, with the preference set this way, if you select a JPEG file in Bridge; open it in ACR by using right-click/Control-click, and choosing Open in Camera Raw; edit it; and click Done, this file will always open in ACR. However, any JPEG that you haven't opened and modified like this will not open by default in ACR. JPEGs you edit within ACR and *save* in ACR will not reopen in ACR by default as they already have the AlreadyApplied CRS tag because the settings are "burned in" and can no longer be modified.

- To force a JPEG or TIFF file to open in ACR, right-click/Control-click, and choose Open in Camera Raw.

Using Camera Raw with JPEGs and TIFFs

To open TIFF and JPEG files in Camera Raw with Elements, take these steps:

1. Choose File > Open.

2. Change the Format pop-up menu setting to Camera Raw.

3. Select the TIFF or JPEG file.

4. Click Open.

Saving Settings

You may find with images shot under certain conditions that you frequently make similar adjustments. To save time, you can save these settings as a preset. At other times you may want to return to the ACR default settings, or you may want to establish new ACR default settings. To do any of these, click the fly-out menu icon ▤◢ that's on the right side of the ACR interface about one third of the way down. It's actually on the far right edge of each adjustment tab. A new menu appears, as shown in Figure 3.8.

Figure 3.8 ACR enables you to save a group of settings as a preset or as the new default settings.

To save the settings for a particular image so that you can use them later for other images taken under similar conditions, choose Save Settings. A second dialog box appears, as shown in Figure 3.9, in which you select which parameters to save. Clicking Save will cause another dialog box to open in which you give the setting a name. We suggest you give it a name that's specific enough that you will easily recognize its purpose. Unless you have a clear reason for changing it, store the settings in the default location.

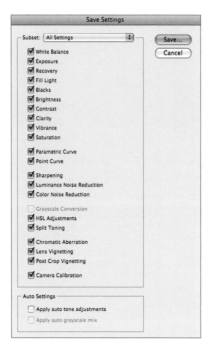

Figure 3.9 When saving a group of settings, you can select as many or as few of the parameters as useful for any particular situation.

To use these settings, choose Apply Presets or click the ⊞ icon to go to the last adjustment tab, which contains a list of your presets.

Custom Defaults

Elements does not support saving or loading settings, but it does allow you to save new Camera Raw defaults.

To save your settings as the new default for ACR to use for all images (before they are individually adjusted), adjust the sliders and settings as desired, and then choose Save New Camera Raw Defaults. You will not see a dialog box asking which settings to save—it saves all of them. If you later change your mind, you can click Reset Camera Raw Defaults.

Using the Basic Tab

Whether or not you choose to use the Auto settings as your default, chances are that you will often want to make some tonal and color adjustments to your images. The ability to easily make subtle tweaks, as well as major corrections, to your exposure is one of the many advantages of working with the ACR interface.

The Basic tab ⊚ icon is visible by default when the ACR interface first opens; it contains the white balance adjustments as well as some exposure and color adjustments.

Setting White Balance

One of the major advantages of using the ACR interface is the ability to fine-tune the white balance, or color cast. If you decide that you want to make your picture as neutral as possible, then including a gray card such as the WhiBal card (available at www.rawworkflow.com) within one frame of your pictures makes it easy to determine the correct white balance. Just use the White Balance tool ⚲ and click the gray tone in the card in your image. In fact, you can use this eyedropper to click any pixel within any image that you want to define as neutral—that is to say, any shade of pure gray from the lightest to the darkest gray—and the tonalities within the entire image are remapped accordingly.

However, for most nature photographers pure neutral is not the goal for most images. We nature photographers tend to like the warm color casts of early morning and late daylight. Sometimes we even like the cool colors of shadows and/or the harsh blue light on winter snow. And sometimes we like to pretend those color casts were present even when they weren't! In such cases, the white balance you ultimately select may be *correct*, but perhaps *not accurate*. Fortunately, there are no "white balance police" running around demanding that your choice of white balance must be true to life! However, if you're trying to depict your images more documentarily, then you'll want to make your white-balance choices as accurate as possible.

> **Note:** There is a difference between accurate white balance and correct white balance. *Accurate* white balance portrays the lighting as it existed when you photographed the scene. *Correct* white balance is the ideal setting that gives the image the feeling you seek to express.

The Basic tab has two sliders that control the white balance or color cast of your image:

- The Temperature slider refers to the temperature of the light (in degrees Kelvin). What you really need to know is that moving the slider to the left adds a blue cast to your image, similar to using an 80 A, B, or C filter. Moving the Temperature slider to the right adds a warm yellow cast, similar to using an 81 A, B, or C filter. There's a blue/yellow gradient associated with the Temperature slider, making it obvious which direction to move the slider.
- The Tint slider controls the green/magenta color cast. Moving this slider to the left increases the greenish cast; moving it to the right increases the magenta cast. We find that we tend to adjust the Tint slider less than the Temperature slider in general.

The major advantage the white-balance sliders have over using a filter is that the adjustments are continual and gradual, so you can choose the precise amount of warming or cooling to apply to convey the mood you have in mind.

Unless you are color-blind (and we're being serious here, not sarcastic, having had several color-blind students), it's well worth getting into the habit of spending a little time adjusting the white balance because the changes you can make to the colors of your image here are subtly different from what you can do within Photoshop (see Figure 3.10). And if you are color-blind, you may want to get into the habit of setting the cursor on a specific point in the image and noting the RGB values that appear above the histogram. You can learn to interpret the values so you know when your image is slightly warm or cool.

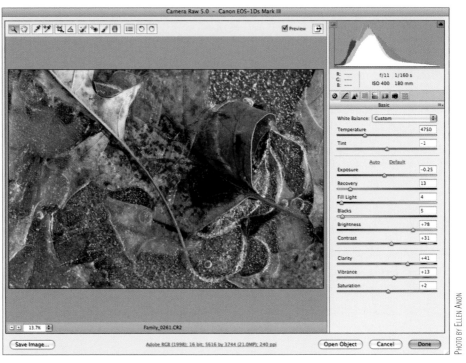

Figure 3.10 Adjusting the temperature and tint sliders allows you to make finer adjustments to the color cast in your image than would be possible using traditional filters.

Adjusting Tonalities

The next group of sliders on the ACR Basic tab enables you to fine-tune the tonalities in your image, such as increasing or decreasing the exposure, contrast, and so on. We'll describe the sliders in the order that we usually set them.

> **Note:** Although we usually follow a certain order adjusting these sliders, if one aspect of an image is significantly off, we'll adjust that first. Since you can readjust these sliders as much as necessary, you can set them in whatever order seems most logical to you.

Setting the Exposure and Blacks Sliders

The Exposure slider is similar to using Levels in Photoshop to set your white point. In plain English, this means you are selecting which tonal value (pure white, almost but not quite pure white, and so on) to make the lightest pixels within your image, and all pixels in the image are remapped accordingly. In many ways it's similar to modifying your in-camera exposure, but instead of being limited to a half or a third of a stop, or multiples thereof, you can choose from continuous values using tiny increments, up to four stops over or under the in-camera exposure. However, remember that if you over-exposed your image in-camera to the point that no details were captured in the brightest highlights, using the Exposure slider does not restore the details. ACR cannot produce detail that was never captured in either highlight *or* shadow areas. However, it may make those blown-out areas a little less obvious by making them a light shade of gray instead of bright white.

Note: To quickly reset any of the sliders in ACR to their default values, double-click the small triangle that specifies the value on the slider. It will automatically return to its default setting.

Use the Blacks slider to set the black point. You are telling ACR how close to pure black you want the darkest pixels within your image to be. Simply drag the slider to the desired value. Usually you won't have to drag the slider far, because you're working on the linear-gamma data—that is, preconverted information.

To set your Exposure and Blacks sliders without accidentally clipping any pixels, do the following:

- Hold down the Alt/Option key, and drag the Exposure slider; the preview box turns completely black. Drag the slider to the right (or left) until you see a few colored pixels appear. These are the first pixels that start to become pure white with no detail. Reduce the exposure slightly so there is no clipping, and release the mouse button.

- Hold down the Alt/Option key while sliding the Blacks slider to set the black point with no clipping. With the Blacks slider, the preview becomes totally white. When you see colored pixels begin to appear, back off slightly. By doing this, you have distributed the pixels in your image over the maximum tonal range using clipping previews.

Although you could just rely on the clipping warnings in the preview, holding down the Alt/Option key makes it easier to see clipping in small areas.

It's tempting for some photographers to assume that all pictures should have as wide a range of tonal values as possible. Indeed, many images look their best utilizing the full range of tonal values—which is what you're doing if you set the white and black points using the Exposure and Blacks sliders while utilizing the clipping previews. However, especially within nature photography, not all images are suited to using the full range of tonal values. For example, if you take a moody picture of a lovely foggy scene, as shown in Figure 3.11, you most assuredly don't want maximum contrast. You want a limited tonal range reflecting the limited tonalities visible through the fog. You need to look at each image and decide whether it should utilize the full range of tonalities.

Figure 3.11 Some pictures, like this foggy scene, must not use the full range of tonal values. Note that the histogram does not extend all the way to each end but rather is limited to more of the middle and light tonalities.

Using the Recovery and Fill Light Sliders

The Recovery and Fill Light sliders, which are similar to the Highlight/Shadow tool in Photoshop, are extremely useful when, despite your best efforts, there is some clipping of the highlight and/or shadow values because of contrasty lighting. You can use the Recovery slider to recapture as much highlight detail as possible, while the Fill Light slider recovers shadow detail, as shown in Figure 3.12.

The best approach is to first set the Exposure slider so that the exposure is correct for most of the image. Then adjust the Recovery slider as necessary to regain as much highlight detail as possible.

> **Note:** If you overexposed or underexposed the image to the point that you didn't capture some of the highlight or shadow data, the Recovery and Fill Light sliders will not be able to recover it. It can't create information that you didn't capture. But if you were able to capture it on the sensor, then the Recovery slider will reveal it. Remember that the sensor contains more information than can be displayed initially—usually up to about ½ stop more information in the highlights and up to 1½ stops more information in the shadows.

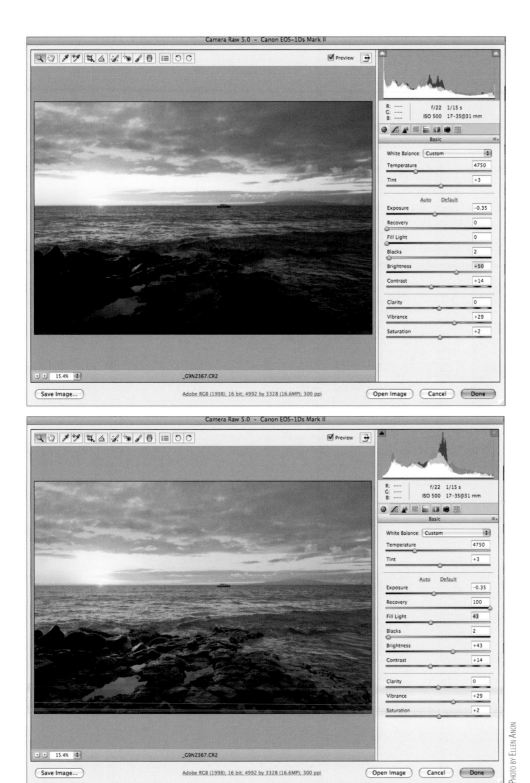

Figure 3.12 The Recovery and Fill Light sliders can help expand the exposure latitude of an image so you can see detail in the highlights and shadows in contrasty scenes.

Set the Fill Light slider as necessary to recover detail in the darkest shadow areas. You may need to modify the Blacks slider setting as well. The trick is that you still want some true blacks in your image, but you want to see detail in the not-quite-black shadow areas.

Using the Brightness and Contrast Sliders

The Brightness slider shifts the majority of the pixels lighter or darker to make the overall image appear lighter or darker. Watch how the bulk of the histogram shifts as you move this slider each way. It's similar to moving the center slider within Levels in Photoshop. The more extreme the adjustments you make with the Exposure slider, the more likely it is you'll need to make adjustments using the Brightness slider. Don't forget to keep an eye out for any clipping you may introduce by increasing or decreasing the brightness.

The Contrast slider is similar to applying an S curve within Curves in Photoshop to increase or decrease the contrast within the bulk of the pixel values. If you watch the histogram as you adjust this slider, you'll see the bulk of the pixels being shifted away from the middle toward the extremes.

Contrast is primarily modified to those pixels in the middle tonalities, with the lightest and darkest tonalities being less affected. Increasing the amount to greater than the default of +25 lightens values above the midtones and darkens values below the midtones. Similarly, reducing the value darkens values above the midtones and lightens values below the midtones to reduce the overall contrast. If you decide to adjust the contrast in ACR, be sure to check that you have not introduced any clipping to your highlights or shadows. You may have to readjust the other sliders.

Note: Given the ability to make some fairly dramatic changes in exposure, it may seem as if you don't have to worry about capturing the correct exposure in camera. In fact, as discussed in Chapter 1, "Thinking Digitally," the better your initial exposure, the better the final product will be. If the image is initially underexposed, you'll find that although you can correct the exposure, there is likely to be a lot of distracting noise in the final image. If you "expose to the right" (again, see Chapter 1), you will have the least amount of noise within your image, although you may have to adjust the Blacks slider, and possibly the Brightness slider as well. Exposing to the right with raw captures ultimately gives you the best possible result as long as you make certain you don't clip the highlights.

Modifying Saturation

Both the Saturation and Vibrance sliders affect the saturation or purity of colors in an image. Saturation increases the purity of all colors equally whereas Vibrance is a "smart" saturation tool. It affects colors differentially as it increases (or decreases) the saturation to reduce the chances of introducing clipping in any color. Instead of applying increased saturation uniformly to all colors, Vibrance applies it heaviest to the less saturated colors and less to the more saturated colors. It also tends to saturate yellows and oranges less in order to try to preserve skin tones. Although nature photographers are not often concerned with skin tones, we may want to saturate some colors more than others. In fact, we find that the Vibrance slider often creates a more pleasing result. We find that we can use higher settings with the Vibrance slider and create images that pop but still look natural.

At times you may want to use the Saturation slider in addition to or instead of the Vibrance slider. Be sure to check for unexpected clipping within the different color channels.

The Saturation and Vibrance sliders affect all the colors in your image. If you want to adjust specific color ranges, use the HSL/Grayscale tab, which we'll cover shortly.

There is also a check box to convert the image to grayscale, which immediately sets the Vibrance and Saturation sliders all the way to the left. You can further modify the appearance of a black-and-white image in ACR by using the HSL/Grayscale tab that we'll describe shortly.

Note: Some images may benefit from reduced saturation or vibrance. Be sure to watch the histogram as you make any changes.

Setting the Other Tabs

ACR includes a total of eight tabs, as shown in Figure 3.13, that have features to help you optimize your image. Many photographers are more than happy with the results they get simply by adjusting the sliders on the Basic tab. However, if you want to have even more control, you should venture into these other tabs after you've made your initial corrections on the Basic tab. We'll describe how to use the other tabs in the order they appear.

Figure 3.13 Click each of the tabs to reveal additional tools to fine-tune and adjust your image.

Setting the Tone Curves: The Tone Curve Tab

The next tab is the Tone Curve tab . By default this tab opens to the Parametric Curve. Ellen calls Parametric Curves "Easy Curves" because they're much easier and more intuitive for novices to use. But in addition to being easy, they're quite powerful and useful. Although we used to use point curves primarily, we routinely start with the Parametric Curves in ACR. As shown in Figure 3.14, there are four sliders beneath the Parametric Curves graph, and the histogram is superimposed within it. Adjusting the Highlights slider primarily adjusts the brightest quarter of the tonalities. Adjusting the Lights slider primarily affects the midtones to light tones but may affect the lightest tonalities or the darks as well. The effect is most pronounced within the midtones to light tones. The Darks slider primarily affects the middle to darkest quarter of tonality, while the Shadows slider affects the darkest quarter of tonal values. As you adjust any

**Photoshop
ONLY**

of these sliders, the more dramatic the adjustment you make, the wider the range of tonal values that will be affected. To change the tonal range controlled by each slider, click on the triangles at the bottom of the graph and move them left or right.

We suggest you spend a little time experimenting with these sliders and getting comfortable with them. They can be quite useful.

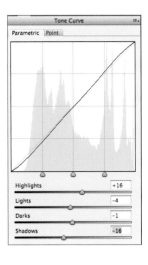

Figure 3.14 Creating customized curves to adjust midtone contrast is easy using the Parametric Curve slider controls.

Note: Parametric Curves are also available in Elements and Lightroom, but not within Photoshop.

The Tone Curve tab offers another tab to access the Point curve. This is the type of curve that is found in Photoshop.

When you click the Point tab (illustrated in Figure 3.15), you'll see a drop-down menu for the Tone Curve, which by default is set to Medium Contrast. You'll also see a graph showing the actual tone curve superimposed over a graph showing the distribution of pixels. By clicking within the drop-down menu, you can choose the Linear curve option, which causes no additional contrast to be added to your image, or the Strong Contrast option, which uses a preset tone curve that adds more contrast to your image.

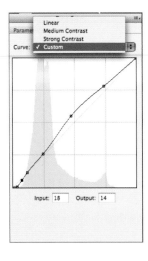

Figure 3.15 By using the Point tab, you can access various preset tone curves or make a custom curve to further refine your image.

However, the really useful part of the Point tab is that you can begin with any of the Tone Curve presets and modify the curve, using the preset points as well as any points you want to add, to create a custom curve for each image. The advantage of doing this here in ACR rather than later in Photoshop is that the curve is still operating on the linear data. As long as you have the clipping preview boxes checked in the histogram in ACR, you can see whether the changes you make are causing any clipping. If you're comfortable using curves, you may want to experiment with the Point Tone Curves within ACR. If curves are new to you, you may want to stick with Parametric Curves until you are more familiar with using them.

> **Note:** By holding the Ctrl/⌘ key and hovering the cursor over a pixel in the image preview, a circle will appear on the tone curve indicating where that point falls. To create a point on the curve at that location, click while holding the Ctrl/⌘ key.

Sharpening and Reducing Noise: The Detail Tab

The Detail tab ▲ contains four sliders to adjust the sharpening in ACR. It's important to remember that the sharpening you're applying in ACR is a first pass only. The final sharpening should be based on the output size of the image. Therefore, your setting should be conservative. We often use the default settings. However, you may want to adjust them.

- The Amount slider controls the amount of sharpening or contrast to add to the edges.

- The Radius slider determines how far out the effect extends. If the image has very fine details, it may need a lower setting, and if it has larger details, it may benefit from a larger radius. However, large radius settings can cause unnatural results, so be careful.

- The Detail slider controls the extent to which the sharpening process creates halos to emphasize the edges. Lower settings remove blurring from edges, whereas higher settings make textures more pronounced.

- The Mask slider controls where the sharpening is applied. At 0 everything in the image receives the same amount of sharpening, while at 100 sharpening is restricted to areas near the strongest edges.

Zoom into 100% magnification and experiment with the sliders. Err on the side of caution and avoid oversharpening, which can cause obvious halos and/or a crunchy appearance.

The remaining two sliders help control noise. Noise is a by-product of digital captures, and is more problematic when using higher ISOs, extremely long exposures, and/or correcting underexposed images. It's a bigger problem with some cameras than with others. Noise may be seen primarily in areas of darker tonalities, although it can extend into the midtones as well. As you can see in Figure 3.16, noise appears as variations in tones and colors in areas that should be smooth, such as skies or skin tones.

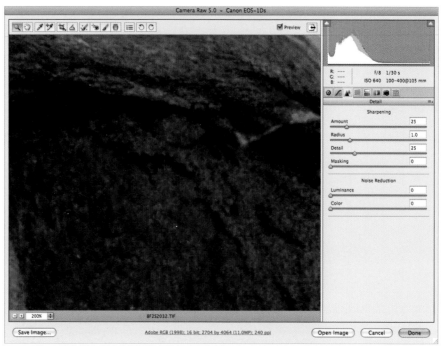

Before

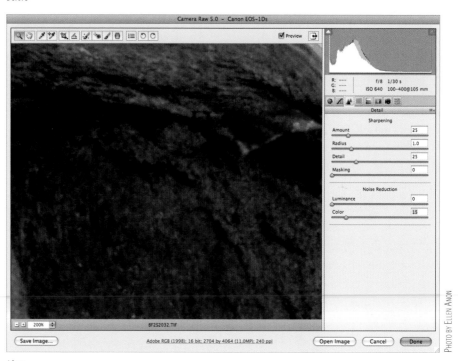

After

Figure 3.16 Noise appears as random variations in tones and colors in areas that should be smooth. Using the noise-reduction sliders is an easy way to eliminate it.

- The Luminance Smoothing slider deals with *grayscale noise*, the unexpected and unwanted variations in tonal values that appear. This type of noise is similar in appearance in many ways to film grain. By reducing these tonal variations, this type of smoothing may reduce the overall sharpness of your image, so keep these corrections to a minimum. It's a good idea to zoom into various critical areas of your image to 100% or even 200% to see how they're being affected as you make adjustments.

Since luminance smoothing can reduce overall sharpness and blur fine detail, we prefer to do most luminance noise reduction in Photoshop. That way, we can use a mask to apply it only to problematic areas and retain full detail in our subject matter.

- The Color Noise Reduction slider reduces *color noise*, the unexpected color variations that often appear. Although this noise is most common in the darker tonalities, it can also sometimes be seen as green and magenta blobs in areas that should be neutral gray and as rainbow artifacts in the highlights. Again, zoom to a 100% or 200% view of the areas demonstrating problems with noise, and move the slider to reduce the color variations. Make the minimum amount of adjustment necessary to decrease the noise. We tend to use the Color Noise Reduction slider in ACR to remove as much color noise as possible when noise is an issue.

Note: Although the default value is set to 25, Ellen finds that with her camera a setting of 15 works well for most images. She saved this setting and created a new default as described earlier in this chapter. Occasionally she uses higher numbers with extremely noisy images.

Correcting Color: The HSL/Grayscale Tab

The HSL/Grayscale tab ▦ (HSL is short for *hue, saturation,* and *luminance)* is a very visual tool offering the ability to fine-tune each color range on a variety of parameters. For example, you can modify the yellows so that they are closer to orange or closer to green. You can also adjust the saturation of the yellows and then the *luminance*—or lightness/darkness—of them. This means you can make subtle—or not-so-subtle—adjustments to individual color ranges in your image without affecting other colors.

Photoshop ONLY

When you click the Hue, Saturation, or Luminance subtabs, the eight color range sliders change to gradients, as shown in Figure 3.17, indicating how moving the slider will change the appearance of the colors. You set each color individually.

Clicking the Saturation or Luminance tabs changes the eight color sliders so that they reflect increased and decreased saturation or modifications in luminance.

Spending the time to fine-tune the colors in your image may not be something you do to every image, but for some images, these tweaks can take an image from ordinary to extraordinary!

If you checked the Convert to Grayscale option on the Basics tab, then a Grayscale Mix tab will appear in place of the HSL tabs. Adjusting the sliders for each color lightens or darkens that color range. By using these sliders, you can alter the contrast within your image and create dramatic black-and-white versions of your images, as shown in Figure 3.18.

Figure 3.17 By using the HSL controls, Ellen fine-tuned the colors in this sunflower image.

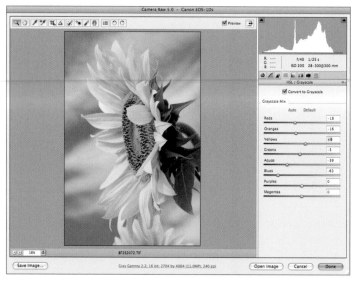

Figure 3.18 A Straight-forward grayscale conversion is often lackluster, but by using the grayscale controls you can create a more vibrant image.

Alternate Interpretations: The Split Toning Tab

The Split Toning tab ▤ is not one that we have found a lot of use for with nature photography. However, you may well find that a specific image lends itself to this creative interpretation based on a grayscale version of the file. The concept (seen in Figure 3.19) is that you assign one color for the highlights and a different color for the shadows so that you "split" the tones of the image.

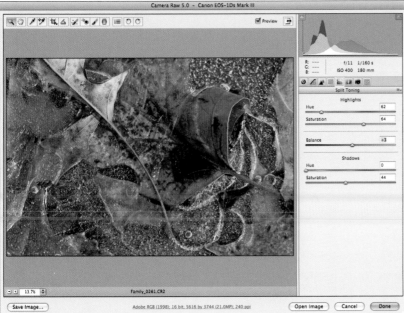

Figure 3.19 A Split Tone version of this image increases the feeling of fall colors but may or may not be to your taste.

Fixing Aberration and Vignetting: The Lens Corrections Tab

The Lens Corrections tab ▦ offers solutions to some issues—specifically vignetting and fringing (chromatic aberrations)—that may result when using particular lenses with digital cameras. Some photographers either never have or never notice these problems, and that's fine. Others perceive them readily and are quite bothered by them.

Chromatic aberration, also known as *fringing*, occurs when the lens fails to focus the red, green, and blue wavelengths of light on exactly the same plane (the camera's image sensor); this causes color fringes along high-contrast edges. Chromatic aberration seems to be more of a problem with wider-angle shots, especially those made with lenses not optimized for digital cameras. It may be more noticeable toward the corners of the image, as shown in Figure 3.20.

- The Fix Red/Cyan Fringe slider helps you to reduce or remove red/cyan fringing.

- The Fix Blue/Yellow Fringe slider addresses any blue/yellow fringing.

- The Defringe drop-down determines whether defringing is applied to just highlight edges or to all edges.

Before using these sliders, it's a good idea to zoom in to 200% or more to easily see the fringing and the results of moving the sliders. Holding down Alt/Option while dragging these sliders limits which color channels are visible and makes it significantly easier to locate the best setting for each slider.

Vignetting is darkening in the corners of your images. It typically occurs when a lens originally designed for 35mm film photography, and not optimized for digital cameras' sensors, is used with a digital camera that has a sensor that is smaller than the film area would have been. However, vignetting also sometimes results when using a lens hood with wide-angle lenses or even from using filters with wide-angle lenses. The Vignetting controls enable you to reduce or eliminate the darkening in the corners:

- The Amount slider controls the amount of lightening or darkening that is applied to the corners.

- The Midpoint slider controls where the adjustment gets applied. Larger values on the Midpoint slider increase the area that is affected, while smaller numbers reduce it.

Make adjustments in small increments while closely watching the effect on your image.

CS4 added Post Crop Vignetting controls to enable you to add a vignette after cropping an image. In addition to the Amount and Midpoint sliders, you can control the shape of the vignette with the Roundness slider and how gradually the vignette blends into the image with the Feather slider. The best way to get comfortable using these sliders is to experiment by setting the Amount very high so the effect is easy to see. Then adjust the other sliders. Finally back off the Amount until you achieve the desired effect.

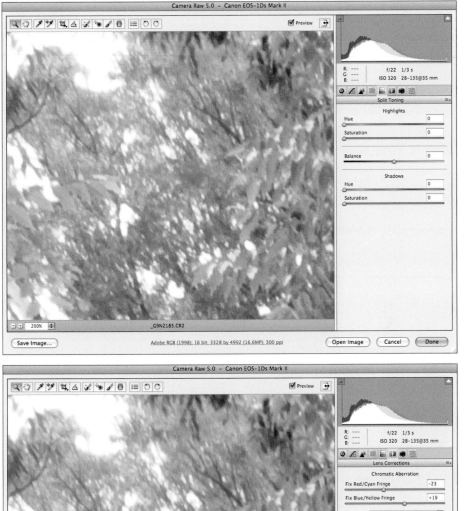

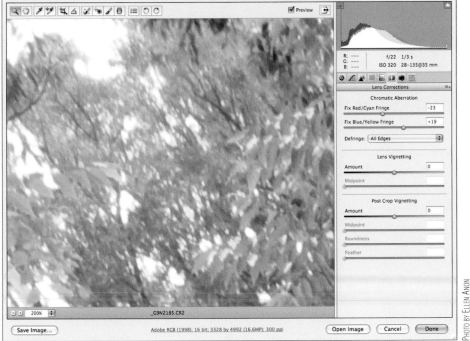

Figure 3.20 Chromatic aberration (fringing) is noticeable along the branches in this image, when viewed at 100–200% magnification, but you can easily remove it by adjusting the Chromatic Aberration sliders.

Accounting for Camera Variation: The Camera Calibration Tab

Photoshop
ONLY

The Calibrate tab ▓ is one that most nature photographers never touch; those of you who do will need to use it only rarely. The purpose of the Calibrate tab is to tweak the performance of the built-in camera profiles to account for any variations between your camera and the one they actually used to build the profiles in ACR for that specific camera model. If you notice that your images routinely have a slight color cast, rather than removing it in the Adjust tab, you can use the sliders here to set a correction. To do this accurately, you need to shoot a color checker chart, such as those available from GretagMacbeth (www.gretagmacbeth.com), and then compare it to a downloaded version with known values. You then move the sliders to match up the colors. To modify the reds, use the controls in the Red Primary section; to adjust the greens, use the ones found in the Green Primary section; and to adjust the blues, use the sliders found in the Blue Primary section. You can also adjust the tint of the shadows.

After creating settings for a particular camera, save them as the Camera Raw defaults by using the fly-out menu as described earlier in this chapter. Then go to the toolbar in ACR, and click the Preferences icon to access the Preferences dialog box. Check the option Make Defaults Specific to Camera Serial Number. That way, if you have several cameras, ACR will use the correct camera calibrations for each one.

Preset Tab

Photoshop
ONLY

The Preset tab ▓ contains a list of all the presets you've created. To create a preset, adjust the sliders and options. Then access the fly-out menu by clicking the ▓ icon to the right of the name of the tab and choose Save Settings. That way, you can use the same settings on other images by choosing the particular preset.

Making Localized Adjustments

Photoshop
ONLY

ACR in CS4 added the ability to make localized adjustments right in the raw converter. This is a huge addition to the power of ACR. It means that you can make adjustments to specific geographic parts of your image while still accessing all the information your sensor captured rather than having to wait and use the converted file in Photoshop with selections and layer masks. It's worth spending the time to get comfortable with these new tools. At first they may seem a bit quirky, but if you follow our instructions, you'll have them under control in no time!

There are two tools you can use: the Adjustment Brush ▓ and the Graduated Filter ▓.

Using the Adjustment Brush

When you click the Adjustment Brush icon, the interface changes, as shown in Figure 3.21. The first controls consist of three radio buttons that let you specify whether you're making a new adjustment, adding to or modifying an existing adjustment, or erasing part of an adjustment. Every time you use a new Adjustment Brush on the image, a pin ▓ appears on the image. You can toggle the visibility of the pins by checking Show Pins in the lower-left part of the interface. To remove a pin, click on it and press Delete.

Figure 3.21 When you brush in an adjustment, toggle the mask overlay visibility to help fine-tune the changes.

Lower in the interface are sliders to control the features of each brush. *Size* refers to the size of the brush, and *Feather* controls whether the edges of the adjustment blend in gradually to the image or have a discrete edge. *Flow* controls the rate the correction is applied or, in other words, how rapidly the effect flows out of the brush. Density refers to the opacity of the effect.

Near the bottom of the panel are options for Auto Mask, Show Mask, and a color swatch. The Auto Mask option helps you constrain your brushed effects to a certain area based on the color range. By checking the Show Mask option, you'll see a mask showing what areas are affected by your adjustment. The color swatch indicates the color that will be used for the mask overlay. Click on it to access the Color Picker, shown in Figure 3.22, for further control of the overlay. When you hover the cursor over a pin with Show Mask selected, you'll see the mask associated with that pin.

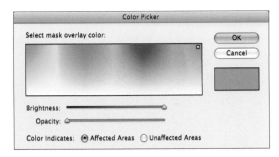

Figure 3.22 The Color Picker enables you to control the appearance of the mask overlay.

The bulk of the interface contains seven parameters that you can apply either singly or in combination. By default the sliders are not set to 0. We double-click them to set them to 0, and then adjust them according to whatever effects we're after. The settings are *sticky*, meaning that the next time you access the Adjustment Brush controls, they will be set the way you left them.

Note: It's hard to know exactly what values to set in the sliders before you use the brush. Remember that you don't have to guess the initial settings exactly right. When you change to the Add mode, you can refine the settings visually. That makes it a lot easier!

The +/– buttons to the sides of each slider access presets and adjust the sliders in increments.

The Color option, which by default is set to a blank rectangle with an X in it, contains presets to use to warm or cool parts of the image. Click on it to access more options, as shown in Figure 3.23.

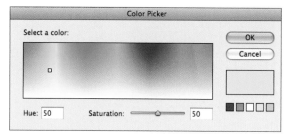

Figure 3.23 Clicking the color box accesses additional options for modifying the color cast.

Begin by clicking New and then setting the sliders for the desired effect. Most of the time you'll want Auto Mask selected. Then begin brushing in the effect. When you stop, the top radio button will automatically change to Add. At that point you can brush an additional area with the same settings, or you can modify the sliders to tweak the change you just brushed. Click the Erase button to change the brush into an eraser to remove the effect from an area. Remember to zoom in as far as necessary to work accurately!

We have no doubt that the more you use Adjustment Brushes, the more impressed you will be with them!

Using the Graduated Filter

The Graduated Filter is similar to the Adjustment Brush in terms of the adjustments it can apply. The difference is that rather than brushing the adjustments directly where you want them, you apply them using a gradient.

To begin, select the New radio button and then adjust the sliders. Initially you're making a best guess with the slider settings. You can refine your choices when you click the Edit radio button.

Each time you click and drag on the image, a new gradient appears, beginning and ending where you clicked and dragged. To remove a gradient, click on one of the pins and press Delete.

Using the Graduated Filter, you can simulate not only a graduated neutral-density filter, but also a filter that controls saturation, contrast, clarity, and so forth.

These two new tools in ACR are extremely powerful. Be sure to take advantage of them!

Setting ACR Workflow Options and Saving Files

At this point you're almost done with the ACR interface, but first you have to instruct ACR how you want the converted file saved.

Directly below the image preview in the ACR interface is a series of information that looks like a web link. Click on this information to reveal the ACR Workflow Options dialog box, shown in Figure 3.24.

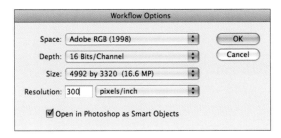

Figure 3.24 Several important settings are found in the Workflow Options dialog box.

Workspace Options

Camera Raw in Elements does not allow you to change the color space, size, or resolution of your raw files, but it does allow you to change the depth by using the Depth drop-down menu. Furthermore, Elements does not support Smart Objects.

Choosing the Space

The Space drop-down menu gives four options for the color working space:

Photoshop ONLY

- Adobe RGB (1998)
- ProPhoto RGB
- sRGB IEC61966-1
- ColorMatch RGB

Only the first three options are useful for nature photographers (we'll tell you why shortly).

Adobe RGB 1998 is the most frequently used color space for nature photographers seeking to make prints and archive their files because it is a reasonably wide color space and corresponds fairly well to the color spaces available in most inkjet printers. Many people prefer to use this space as their default color working space.

If you're planning to work with images in 16-bit color (and we recommend you do), you may consider using the ProPhoto RGB workspace, particularly if you have a printer that uses 16-bit files. It's a wider space than the commonly used Adobe RGB 1998 and will allow you to use some colors that your camera may have captured but that are outside the gamut of Adobe RGB 1998. Some inkjet printers can print some of these colors. Further, if you have some clipping—that is, pixels that are at the extremes of the tonal values—in one or more channels, you may want to see whether changing to the ProPhoto RGB space allows you to capture more detail in those channels. The disadvantage is that if you are converting back to an 8-bit image, you may have more colors that need to be converted than if you had limited yourself to Adobe RGB 1998. This may lead to some posterization or banding.

Occasionally, some people may want to use sRGB IEC61966-1. This is a narrower color space, but it's useful if your intended output is limited to projection, email, and/or web usage. If you think that there's any chance you may want to print the file, we recommend you use either Adobe RGB or ProPhoto RGB and convert to sRGB for the specific use. (See Chapter 4, "Foundations," for a more complete discussion of color spaces.)

ColorMatch RGB is a space that is wider than sRGB and narrower than Adobe RGB. This means it may have more colors than you can utilize for web use or projection but fewer than your inkjet printer is capable of printing. Therefore, one of the other spaces is usually a better choice.

Choosing the Depth

You have the choice of converting your image into a file with 256 possible tonal values (8 bits/channel) or a file with 32,768 possible values (16 bits/channel). The clear advantage to 16-bit is accurate and smooth reproduction of tonal variations. The workflow is as easy for a 16-bit file as for an 8-bit file. The only slight disadvantages are that since the 16-bit file is larger, your computer may process adjustments a little more slowly, you may need more RAM to process the files, and the files will take up more space in memory.

> **Note:** Although it would seem logical that "16-bit" implies 2^{16}, or 65,536, tonal values, in fact Photoshop uses 2^{15}, or 32,768, when dealing with 16-bit files. Since most high-bit scans and digital captures currently range from 10-bit to 14-bit, this isn't an issue.

Choosing the File Size and Resolution

Photoshop ONLY

ACR provides a drop-down menu, found under the Size option, listing various file sizes specific to the camera used to take the image. Some of the sizes are marked with a plus sign (+) and some by a minus sign (–). One size has neither; it refers to the native resolution of the image with no interpolation. Most of the time this is the choice you'll want. If you are optimizing images for a slide show, you may prefer to use a smaller size.

Some people prefer to use a larger size if they know they will be creating huge files, believing that the interpolation done by ACR is better than the interpolation done later in Photoshop. We have not found any significant benefit to enlarging the file in ACR, and the drawback is that you are dealing with a larger file size that requires more memory space and longer processing times.

If you have cropped the image, the sizes available will reflect the crop. In that case you may prefer to use one of the sizes with a + depending on the magnitude of the crop and the size of your intended output.

As we discuss in Chapter 4, the resolution, expressed in ppi (pixels per inch), merely refers to how tightly or loosely packed the pixels are; it doesn't change anything about the total number of pixels. The actual number of pixels is controlled by the file size that you choose. The resolution you set determines whether pixels are distributed 72 to an inch, 300 to an inch, and so on. Since one of the most common outputs is for print, we recommend setting your resolution to your print resolution (usually 300 ppi). That way, when your image opens in Photoshop it is sized according to an output resolution of 300 ppi. We'll cover resizing images for print further in Chapter 10, "Output."

Opening an Image as a Smart Object

If you opt to follow our flexible workflow (see Chapter 5) we recommend checking the option to open the file as a Smart Object. If you prefer to use the traditional workflow, then leave this option unchecked. The Open Image button in the lower corner of the ACR interface will say Open Object if this option is checked or Open Image if it is not.

Photoshop ONLY

When you're done with the Workflow Options dialog box, click OK. Most of the time you'll leave the workflow options set without changing them. The settings are sticky.

Finishing Up in ACR

After optimizing your image in ACR using as many of the features as necessary to make the file the best it can be, you have five choices:

Done The Done button applies the changes but does not open the image. The image is still a raw file, and the changes are still tags. The thumbnail preview in Bridge will reflect the settings you chose in ACR, and those settings will reappear when you reopen the image in ACR.

Note: If you are working with a JPEG or TIFF file in ACR, Done applies the changes, but you can see them only when you view the file in ACR. This is because the file itself remains untouched and the changes you made are stored as instructions to that file. To see the changes in Bridge, you will need to use Save.

Open Image/Object The Open button applies the changes to the selected image and opens that image in Photoshop. The image is now converted, and the changes are a permanent part of the file. To toggle between Open Image and Open Object, hold down the Shift key.

> **Note:** In JPEG and TIFF files, the changes you made in ACR are applied to the image when you open it in Photoshop, but you will need to save the file to have the changes remain If you previously checked only Done.

Open Copy The Open Copy button is available if you hold down the Alt/Option key. This allows you to apply the current changes and open another copy of the same raw file within Photoshop using different settings. This is useful when you are trying some creative techniques such as a black-and-white version of your image or experimenting with different crops.

Save Image The Save button converts the image and saves it; another dialog box appears, prompting you to choose a location, name, and format (such as DNG, JPEG, TIFF, or PSD) for your converted image. (If you don't want this dialog box to appear, hold down the Alt/Option key when you click Save.)

Cancel The Cancel button closes ACR, and the settings you chose are not retained.

> **Note:** Digital negative (DNG) is a universal raw file format developed by Adobe to allow users to archive their raw images in a format that hopefully will continue to be accessible for years to come as converters become more sophisticated. DNG was developed as a response to the ever-increasing number of different raw formats and concerns that files archived in the camera manufacturer's proprietary raw format may one day be unable to be opened as camera manufacturers abandon older raw formats. The downside to the DNG format is that it's unable to store some information that exists within the original raw file but is proprietary to the camera manufacturer.

> **Try It!** Now that we've covered the basics of using ACR, it's time for you to try it. Open the raw file ConvertRaw.dng on the CD that accompanies this book, or open one of your own.
>
> Take the following steps:
>
> 1. Begin by dragging the Exposure slider and then the other sliders. Don't forget to hold down the Alt/Option key while setting the Exposure and Blacks sliders to avoid clipping any pixels. Move the other sliders as needed. Experiment with each of them to become familiar with them.
>
> 2. Next, adjust the white balance. Try clicking the eyedropper in various areas to see how it affects the image. Fine-tune your results with the Temperature and Tint sliders.
>
> 3. Click the Detail tab, perform any noise reduction that you need, and then experiment with the Lens Correction sliders.

4. Use the HSL/Grayscale tab, and create a black-and-white as well as a color version of the image.

5. Select the Brush tool and make several localized adjustments.

Be certain to keep an eye on the histogram as you make your adjustments to ensure you don't accidentally clip any pixels!

Batch-Converting Multiple Images

If you have a series of images that you want to convert, you can select them all in Bridge and then open them in ACR by double-clicking on one of the selected thumbnails. Pressing Ctrl+R/⌘+R will open the ACR dialog box while remaining in Bridge, and pressing Ctrl+O/⌘+O will open the ACR dialog box hosted by Photoshop. (You can set an option within Preferences in Bridge to indicate whether double-clicking opens the Camera Raw dialog box in Bridge or in Photoshop.)

Note: Hosting ACR by Bridge can be a time-saver so that ACR can convert images in the background while you continue to optimize other images in Photoshop.

When ACR opens, it opens in Filmstrip mode, as shown in Figure 3.25. The images to be converted appear in a vertical column on the left. Mark images to delete by pressing the Delete key. Those thumbnails will have a large red X on them.

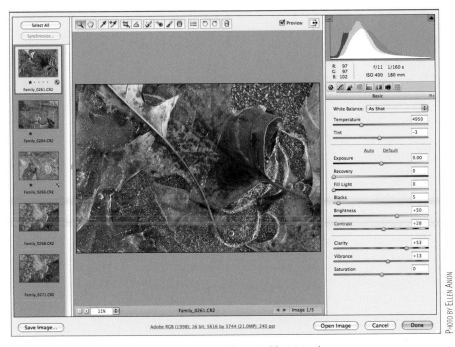

Figure 3.25 When selecting multiple images to convert, ACR opens in Filmstrip mode.

PHOTO BY ELLEN ANON

Selecting a number of images that you want to convert and having them open within a single ACR dialog box can save time. You can choose settings for them individually, or in Photoshop you can select a group to share some of the same settings. Although you are most likely to want to customize the ACR settings for each image, if you have a series of images that were shot under similar conditions and that need some of the same settings, batch-converting can be a huge time-saver. To batch-convert a group of images in ACR, take these steps:

1. Click one of the images to select it, and then make all the adjustments you want to perform in ACR.

2. In the left pane, click the image(s) to which you want to apply these same settings. To assign the settings to more than one image at a time, Ctrl+click/ ⌘+click all the desired files or click Select All.

3. Next, click the Synchronize button. A dialog box appears where you choose the parameters you want to copy from the file you just optimized to the other selected files (see Figure 3.26). Sometimes you may want to copy all the changes you made; other times you may want to select only a few, such as white balance or the dust removal. (Yes, you can even copy the retouching!)

4. When you have finished, click one of the buttons at the bottom: Done, Open, or Save.

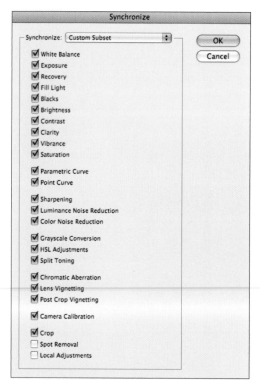

Figure 3.26 You can choose which parameters to apply to all the highlighted images in ACR in Photoshop by checking them in the Synchronize dialog box.

Batch Processing

Elements enables you to open multiple images into Camera Raw, but you must adjust the settings individually for each image. When done, click the Select All button and then click Done, Open, or Save.

Foundations

We know that you want to continue working on your images as soon as possible, but there's some groundwork to be laid. Much of the work you'll do in Photoshop, and in fact most of the advanced work, involves using the various tools in the Tools panel. In this chapter we'll introduce you to some of these tools to help you build a strong foundation for the adjustments we'll cover in later chapters. But before we do that, we'll help you set up Photoshop so that you can be as efficient as possible. In later chapters, you'll put these choices and tools to good use, in some cases extensively.

4

Chapter Contents

Customizing Settings

It might seem tempting to assume that Photoshop's default settings will be fine, and to skip ahead and get to work on your images. However, the fact is that spending a few minutes carefully adjusting the settings will prevent frustration and save you considerable time in the long run. That way, you'll work more efficiently and more effectively. Once you customize the settings, you'll rarely need to revisit them. The settings that you need to customize fall into two categories: Color Settings and Preferences.

Color Settings

Photoshop allows you to establish color-management settings that determine its behavior related to the color in your images. Establishing appropriate settings is important to ensuring that your workflow results in accurate color and maximum image quality. You can adjust these settings by choosing Edit > Color Settings, which opens the Color Settings dialog box, shown in Figure 4.1.

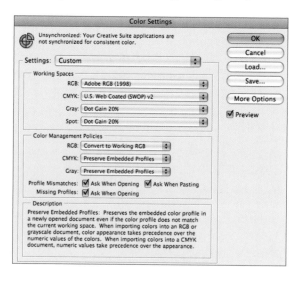

Figure 4.1 The Color Settings dialog box allows you to establish settings related to color management within Photoshop.

The Color Settings dialog box includes a More Options button that, when clicked, enlarges the dialog box to include additional controls. (It also enlarges the list of profiles on the Working Spaces drop-down menus to include all profiles available rather than only those designated as working space profiles.) Once you've clicked this button, it changes to Fewer Options, which returns you to the "basic" dialog box. Since we recommend leaving the advanced settings at their default values anyway, you'll rarely need to use the More Options button.

Note: In versions of Photoshop prior to CS2, access the More Options settings by selecting the Advanced Mode check box.

A *working space* profile defines the range of colors (the color *gamut*) that will be available for your images. The Working Spaces section includes options for specifying which profile should be used as the working space for each of the color modes available (RGB, CMYK, Gray, and Spot). For most photographers, the only working space you need to be concerned with is RGB, which is the mode we recommend working with for all images until you have a reason to convert them to a different color space (for example, if a printing service insists that you perform the RGB-to-CMYK conversion). In most situations (including printing to most desktop printers), you will work on your images in RGB and keep them in RGB for the entire workflow.

> **Note:** Most of the time you want to work in RGB because either you're printing to what is effectively an RGB device (photo ink-jet printers are RGB devices, even though they use CMYK inks) or your print service prefers to receive RGB images and perform CMYK conversions for you.

For the RGB working space, we generally recommend using the one named Adobe RGB (1998). This is a good general working space with a relatively wide gamut, providing an appropriate space for a wide range of output options. This doesn't mean it's the best answer for everyone, but when in doubt Adobe RGB (1998) is a good choice, and it is what we recommend unless you have a good reason to use something else. For example, some photographers may want to utilize the sRGB space as their working space if their printer uses a workflow based on sRGB or if their images will be displayed primarily on the Web or via digital slide shows. Others may want to use the ProPhoto RGB space because it contains a few colors that most printers can print that are not contained in the Adobe RGB space. The downside of working in ProPhoto RGB is that it contains many colors that will be out of gamut when you go to print, so more colors will have to be converted.

> **Note:** If you are using Adobe RGB (1998) as your working space in Photoshop, it makes sense to capture in the same color space if your digital SLR camera offers it. This really matters only if you're not shooting in RAW, because you can specify the color space to use in your raw converter.

Within the Color Settings dialog box, the Color Management Policies section provides settings that allow you to determine what Photoshop should do when you open an image that has a different embedded profile than the one you are using for your working space. As with the Working Spaces section, here you need to be concerned only with RGB. We recommend using the Convert to Working RGB setting most of the time with the assumption that if you've decided on a working space profile that's appropriate for your workflow, it makes sense to use that as the working space for all your images. Should you decide to use an image on a website, you can always convert to sRGB as part of the process of preparing the image. However, if you're doing further editing of some images that have already been converted to sRGB for output purposes, you might want to open them in sRGB. For that reason we set the Profile Mismatch option to Ask When Opening.

In order to maintain maximum control over what is being done to our images, we also prefer to have options for what action should be taken for each image. Therefore, we usually select all three check boxes next to Profile Mismatches and Missing Profiles at the bottom of the Color Management Policies section. The effect is that the options selected from the drop-down menus will be the default (for instance, RGB images will be converted to the current working RGB space), but each time an image is opened that has a different profile embedded than your working space or no profile embedded at all, you'll be prompted so you can apply a different action on a case-by-case basis.

Once you've established the preferred options in Color Management Settings, click OK to apply the settings. You don't need to restart Photoshop for the changes to take effect.

Color Settings

Elements 6 has a far simpler, but less robust, approach to color management than Photoshop CS4. It limits you to no color management, sRGB, or Adobe RGB. Select Edit > Color Settings to bring up the color settings window you see here.

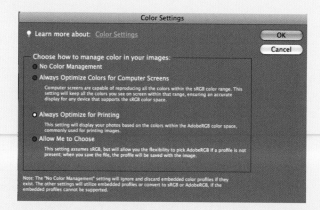

The first option, No Color Management, is obvious, and you should never use it.

The second, Always Optimize Colors for Computer Screens, means that if an image already has a profile embedded it will be converted to sRGB, and any images without a profile will be assumed to be sRGB. For most point-and-shoot cameras, this gives something roughly correct.

Continues

Preferences

In addition to the color settings, there are a large number of preference settings you can establish within Photoshop. As the name implies, many of these are a matter of personal preference. However, we do have recommendations for some of the settings. Access the Preferences dialog box by choosing Edit > Preferences > General from the menu. (On a Mac, choose Photoshop > Preferences > General.)

> **Note:** Because the Preferences dialog box contains so many settings, we won't cover all of them. Instead, we'll focus on the settings we think are most important. Elements users will find a sidebar with specifics for them at the end of this section, but there is considerable overlap, and for full details they should read through this entire section.

General Settings

The General page includes a variety of settings that affect your overall experience in Photoshop, as you can see in Figure 4.2.

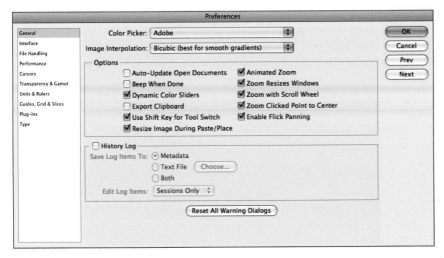

Figure 4.2 The General section of the Preferences dialog box includes settings that affect your overall experience in Photoshop.

Here are the settings you should be concerned with:

Color Picker: Adobe   Leave Color Picker set to the default of Adobe rather than using the color picker from the operating system.

Image Interpolation: Bicubic   This is the best general option for interpolation, while other settings are useful in specific situations. We'll address the details of interpolation in Chapter 10, "Output."

Options Check Boxes

The General page in the Preferences dialog box is dominated by a large number of check boxes that allow you to set a range of preferences. Here are some of the settings we find helpful in this section:

Auto-Update Open Documents: Off   This option causes Photoshop to automatically update files that are opened and modified in another application. Since this rarely pertains to nature photographers, we leave it unchecked.

Beep When Done: Personal Preference   Turning on this setting causes Photoshop to beep when a task is completed. That way, you can turn your attention to other matters while waiting for a major task to complete, knowing you'll be alerted when you're ready to continue. Ellen finds it annoying to have machines beep at her and prefers to check to see when a task is done. She finds that she rarely has to wait long enough for it to be an issue.

Dynamic Color Sliders: On   When selecting a color in the Color panel, it can be helpful for the sliders to change color as you adjust the color value so you can get a better sense of what color you'll achieve by moving a slider in a particular direction. We don't use the Color panel very often, but we keep this setting enabled for situations where we put the panel to use.

Export Clipboard: Off   This setting determines whether anything copied to the clipboard in Photoshop will be exported so other applications can use it. We recommend turning off this feature to reduce the amount of memory being used.

Use Shift Key for Tool Switch: On   Each tool in Photoshop has a shortcut key associated with it, allowing you to activate the tool quickly. Some tools have more than one tool associated with the same shortcut. By default, to switch among tools with the same shortcut key, you need to add the Shift key. We recommend leaving this option set because otherwise you can get some unexpected changes in tools when you press the shortcut key.

Resize Image During Paste/Place: On   When you are compositing images, this setting causes components to be automatically resized to fit, which is often helpful. If you don't composite images, you can leave this option unchecked.

Animated Zoom: Personal Preference   This is new to CS4 and determines whether zooming is animated. It's nice to have but not essential, and requires OpenGL drawing, which may not be available on some older computer systems.

Zoom Resizes Windows: On   This determines whether a document window will automatically be resized as you zoom in or out in Standard Screen mode. When this setting is turned on, as you zoom out on an image, the document window becomes smaller when the image no longer fills the screen; when you zoom in, the document window enlarges until the image exceeds the space available on the screen. This setting is a matter of personal preference, but we find it helpful.

Zoom with Scroll Wheel: On   If you have a mouse with a scroll wheel, this setting can be helpful. It allows you to zoom in and out on your image by scrolling the wheel. We recommend turning this setting on.

Zoom Clicked Point to Center: On   When using the Zoom tool, this option, new in CS4, will center the magnified version of your image around the point where you clicked. That's a real time-saver.

Enable Flick Panning: Personal Preference   This option, new in CS4, enables you to move within the document by "flicking" the hand tool (click, drag, and abruptly let go). After you give a flick, the visible part of the image will continue to move and will drift to a halt. If you're checking for dust in an image with very few dust spots, this can be a less tiring way of navigating through the image. Besides, the animation is fun! However, if you don't have OpenGL, turn it off.

> **Note:** Use the Reset All Warning Dialogs button in this interface if you have opted to have Photoshop not show some of the warnings while working, and then later discover you'd prefer to have the safety cushion that some of these warnings provide.

History Log

The History Log section provides settings that can help you figure out how you performed a particular action on an image. When you enable this setting, you can have every step you perform on an image recorded in metadata so you can review the information later. We generally prefer to leave this setting unchecked because there isn't an easy way to remove the information later. However, it can save the day if you apply a series of steps on your images and then want to know how to apply the same changes on another image. This option is particularly helpful, for example, when you're applying a series of filters to an image or experimenting with any creative technique.

When you select the History Log check box, additional settings become available. If you're going to use this option, we recommend setting the Save Log Items To option to Metadata so the information will always be saved with the image file. We also recommend you set the Edit Log Items option to Detailed so the information you collect is actually useful. The other options—Sessions Only and Concise—don't record the actual settings you used. Although they are helpful for other fields, such as forensic work, they are not useful for most nature photographers.

> **Note:** If you save the log information to a text file, the information for *all* images is saved in a single file, which isn't very efficient.

If you use the History Log option, you can review the saved information (which accumulates only after you enable the setting) by selecting File > File Info and clicking the History option in the left column (see Figure 4.3). Alternatively, you can view the information by selecting Bridge > Metadata > Edit History. Edit History will appear only if the History Log has been enabled.

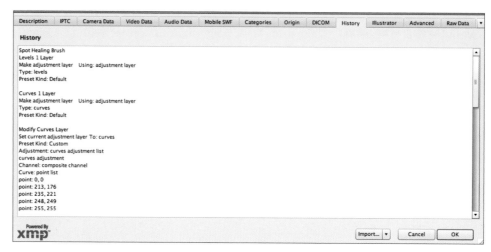

Figure 4.3 If you use the History Log feature, you can review everything that has been done to your image in the History dialog box (File Info > History).

Interface

The options in the Interface section of Preferences (Figure 4.4) relate to the appearance of your workspace. We'll talk more about setting up your workspace later in this chapter; however, you establish some of the basics here.

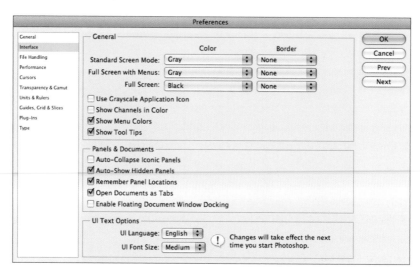

Figure 4.4 We recommend configuring these options as shown here.

The first options are drop-down menus offering choices as to the background color for the interface. We suggest using Gray since it's easiest to make the most accurate color and tonal adjustments against a gray background than any other color.

CHAPTER 4: FOUNDATIONS

Black often looks dramatic, but it can mislead you about some of the contrast and tonalities within the image. For that reason we choose Black only for Full Screen mode, which we might use to showcase an image, but not for those modes we use when we're actively working on an image.

For similar reasons, we turn off the options for a border. Although a line or drop shadow can enhance the final presentation of an image, it can be disconcerting if you're trying to create a drop shadow on your picture or when you're making other decisions about the edges of your image. If you opt for a color other than Black for Full Screen, you may want to use the drop shadow or line options for presentation purposes.

Use Grayscale Application Icon: Personal Preference   This determines whether the application icon is shown in color or grayscale on the Application bar. (We're surprised this is important enough to warrant a preference!)

Show Channels in Color: Off   We prefer to view the individual channels in grayscale so we can easily assess what detail information is contributed by each channel, so we leave this option off. Turning this on causes the channels viewed through the Channels panel to be displayed in their actual colors (red for the Red channel, for example), rather than as grayscale images. Although this sounds like a good idea in terms of being able to interpret the color values for each channel, it actually becomes a challenge, because each of the component colors has a different perceived tonality, making comparison (and even viewing at times) difficult.

Show Menu Colors: Personal Preference   This option is useful if you are new to Photoshop and use some of the preset workspaces that make certain menu items more obvious. We rarely take advantage of these features.

Show Tool Tips: On   We recommend turning on this option so that as you hover the cursor over an icon in the workspace, a brief explanation of the function associated with that icon appears.

Auto-Collapse Iconic Panels: Off   Although it can be handy to save space on your monitor by collapsing the panels, when we expand a panel, such as the Layers panel, we prefer it to stay open.

> **Note:** Only one panel at a time can be expanded when the panels are set to the collapsed mode.

Auto-Show Hidden Panels: Personal Preference   When this option is checked, panels that are hidden are temporarily visible as the cursor rolls over them. We don't often use hidden panels, so we don't often use this feature.

Remember Panel Locations: Personal Preference   This setting determines whether the panel arrangement you see when you start Photoshop will be the same arrangement you set when you last closed Photoshop. In general, if you moved panels within Photoshop, you probably did so for a reason; therefore, this setting can be a good thing. On the other hand, if you have saved a particular panel arrangement (as discussed later in this chapter), you may want to have Photoshop always open that way. In that case, you'd want to disable this setting. We prefer to leave it unchecked.

Open Documents as Tabs: Personal Preference   Checking this option causes new documents to open as tabs in the window rather than as individual floating windows. We have become accustomed to using the tab view for most of our work, but if you prefer floating windows, leave it unchecked.

UI Font Size: Medium or Large   This setting provides relief for the tiny text size that results from running our monitors at extremely high resolutions. You'll find it very helpful from a readability standpoint to set this to Medium or Large. Note that this setting does not take effect until you restart Photoshop.

Enable Floating Document Window Docking: Personal Preference   Checking this option makes it possible to dock a window into the tab by dragging it. This can be convenient, but we've found it's quite easy to accidentally dock images when you're trying to move them on the monitor. We prefer to leave this option unchecked. Then if we want to dock the floating window we right-click/hold down the Ctrl key while dragging.

File Handling Settings

When you're finished with the General settings in the Preferences dialog box, click Next to continue to the File Handling section, shown in Figure 4.5. This section contains options related primarily to how files are saved.

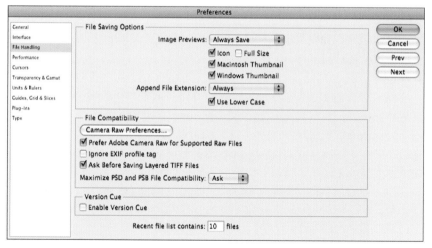

Figure 4.5 The File Handling section of the Preferences dialog box contains settings that affect how files are opened and saved.

Two topics appear under File Saving Options:

Image Previews: Always Save   The Image Previews setting determines whether a small preview thumbnail will be stored as part of the image file. We leave this setting on Always Save and check the option to save an icon for use in the Finder. We don't feel that it's worth the extra memory space to store a Full Size preview, but an icon is useful.

Append File Extension: Always   The File Extension drop-down enables Photoshop to automatically append the filename with the correct extension. In addition, you can choose between uppercase and lowercase file extensions. This is not a significant concern because either will work fine with current software.

Several options appear under File Compatibility in addition to a link to the Camera Raw Preferences (which we cover in Chapter 3, "Adobe Camera Raw").

Prefer Adobe Camera Raw for Supported Raw Files: On   This option causes all supported raw files to be opened in the ACR interface. We recommend using this option because we think ACR does an excellent job with most raw files. However, if you are using other raw conversion software (including Lightroom, your camera manufacturer's proprietary software, or other third-party software), you should leave this box unchecked.

Ignore EXIF Profile Tag: Off Unless Necessary   We recommend you leave this option off *unless* you're encountering problems with the color space embedded in your captures. This option shouldn't be an issue for most photographers. If activated, it causes Photoshop to ignore the embedded color space in your digital captures. It's an issue only for images that have problems caused by their embedded profile, which is rare.

Ask Before Saving Layered TIFF Files: Personal Preference   This setting controls the display of the TIFF Options dialog box. This option is based on your particular workflow. If you usually save TIFF files flattened (saving the master file with layers as a PSD instead), leave this option turned on to be reminded if you're starting to save a TIFF file with layers. We tend to save TIFF files with layers (or flatten them manually), so we turn off this option to avoid the extra click on the OK button in the dialog box.

Maximize PSD and PSB File Compatibility: Personal Preference   This option essentially controls whether a full-resolution composite image will be saved as part of the image file in Photoshop's native formats. The primary reason to enable this feature is to ensure that you're able to open the image as you intended it to appear with other versions of Photoshop—even if the algorithms determining how adjustments are applied get changed—or to enable applications that aren't able to build a thumbnail or preview from the layered file to utilize the full-resolution composite instead. It also provides a solution for situations where you have created a PSD file in a recent version of Photoshop and are sending that file to someone using an older version that doesn't support all the latest features. The disadvantage to using this setting is that file sizes are increased considerably (potentially doubled) when this option is used.

N o t e :   The PSB file format can be opened only with Photoshop CS or later.

You'll see one check box under Version Cue:

Enable Version Cue: Off Unless Necessary   Version Cue is a separate Creative Suite application (not included with the stand-alone version of Photoshop) that allows multiple people to work from one set of files without conflict or allows one person to work on a file with multiple versions.

The final option in the File Handling settings deals with the Recent File list:

Recent File List Contains: 10 Files This option allows you to specify how many files should be listed on the Open Recent list found on the File menu. We find the default of 10 is usually adequate.

Performance

The Performance section of Preferences controls some of the behind-the-scenes issues that help Photoshop run smoothly and quickly. There are four sections in this part of Preferences: Memory Usage, Scratch Disks, History & Cache, and GPU Settings, as shown in Figure 4.6.

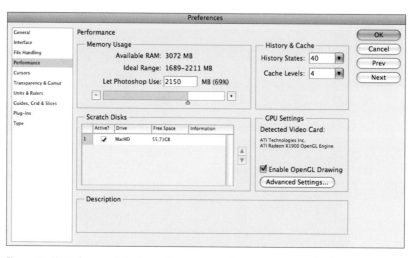

Figure 4.6 The Performance dialog box enables you to control computer memory–related options.

Memory Usage The Memory Usage setting is quite important for overall system performance. As you have no doubt figured out, Photoshop wants to have access to as much memory as possible. The Memory Usage setting determines how much memory Photoshop reserves for its use. Although you would generally expect to benefit from setting this to the maximum value, that can lead to problems. Very high settings can lead to stability issues, and on many computers, setting the value to 100% can even prevent Photoshop from loading.

Photoshop assesses the amount of RAM that's available on your computer after the operating system and other programs stake out their portion, and then it suggests an ideal range for how much to allocate to it. We recommend setting the value at the high end of the recommended range to provide as much memory to Photoshop as possible without running the risk of system-stability problems.

> **Note:** For best performance, your computer should have a *minimum* of 2GB of RAM and ideally more. Although Photoshop can operate with less, you'll find yourself spending time waiting for things to process.

Scratch Disks   In the Scratch Disks section of the Preferences dialog box, it's important to establish appropriate settings to ensure optimal performance for Photoshop. Whenever Photoshop doesn't have adequate memory to perform a task, it depends on hard drive space to simulate additional memory; the hard drive space used is referred to as a *scratch disk*. (Think of it as providing a scratch sheet of paper for Photoshop to use for figuring out complicated problems.)

When Photoshop must resort to scratch disk space, you want to make sure it's working optimally. If you have more than one internal hard drive, you can specify which drive Photoshop should use for startup and which for memory-intensive processing tasks. To maximize performance in this situation, use the arrow keys in the dialog box to point Photoshop toward a secondary internal hard drive that isn't being used by the operating system. If you have more than two drives installed, you can also establish settings for the third and fourth, keeping in mind that you want to set these in order of optimal performance, with the fastest drive first and the drive used by the operating system listed last. Most external drives offer much slower performance than internal drives, so they either should not be used for this purpose or should be last in the order.

If you have a drive separated into multiple partitions, you won't achieve a benefit by making these changes. You achieve the benefit by using a separate physical drive for the scratch disk usage.

History States: 40 to 60   This determines how many steps you'll be able to undo in the History panel. In other words, if you've made a mistake, how many individual steps can you undo in order to get back to the point where you actually made the mistake? The default setting of 20 is relatively low, especially for certain tasks, such as image cleanup with the Clone Stamp tool. However, setting the value too high consumes a relatively large amount of memory when you are doing a lot of work on your images. Therefore, we recommend that you strike a compromise, using a value of 40 to 60. This is usually adequate for being able to go back and correct a mistake, even if it takes some time to realize what you've done, while not consuming a huge amount of memory.

Cache Levels: 4   The Cache Levels setting determines how many zoom settings are stored in memory for your image so the image and histogram can be drawn more quickly when zooming in and out on your image or performing adjustments. The performance difference here is minimal, so we generally leave the setting at the default value, which is 4.

GPU Settings   We leave the GPU Settings options in their default checked positions. To take advantage of some of the smooth zooming features in CS4, you must have Enable OpenGL Drawing checked.

Cursors

Setting Preferences for accurate cursor displays (see Figure 4.7) is essential. Otherwise, although you may be using an icon that shows you what tool you're using, you won't know precisely where you are creating the effect on the image. In the Painting Cursors area of the Cursors section, you can adjust the cursors used for your mouse pointer when working with brush tools within Photoshop. We recommend Normal Brush Tip and Precise.

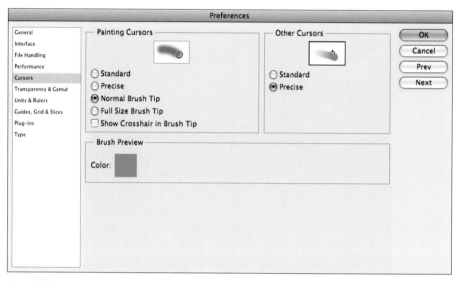

Figure 4.7 The Cursors section of Preferences is used to control the appearance of the pointer so that it is as useful as possible.

Standard   The Standard option causes the mouse pointer to display a small icon of the tool you're using. Although this helps remind you of which tool is in use, it doesn't help much in evaluating the size of the brush being used or the specific area to be affected.

Precise   The Precise option uses a "target" display that makes it easy to see exactly where you'll paint on the image with a given tool, but it doesn't give you any size information.

Normal Brush Tip   The Normal Brush Tip option uses a mouse pointer that matches the shape and size of the brush you're using, with softness accounted for by showing the perimeter of the brush at the point where the opacity of the brush edge is 50%. (See the left image in Figure 4.8.) That means the soft edge of the brush actually extends beyond the shape shown for the brush, but the shape represents the primary area being affected.

Full Size Brush Tip   The Full Size Brush Tip setting uses a full display of the actual brush size, with a fuzzy edge to the mouse pointer representing a soft brush. (See the right image in Figure 4.8.) However, this brush size represents the full extent of the brush, which can be a bit misleading for soft-edged brushes since they generally have no effect all the way out to the edge of the full brush size.

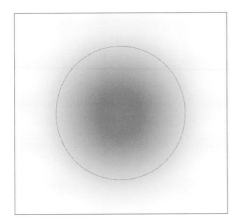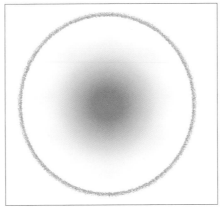

Figure 4.8 The Normal Brush Tip setting (left) causes the brush edge to be defined at the point where the opacity of the brush is at 50% for soft-edged brushes. The Full Size Brush Tip setting (right) causes the full extent of the brush to be shown (including a representation of a soft edge), even though there may not be any effect out to that distance when painting.

There is one additional option under Painting Cursors:

Show Crosshair in Brush Tip   The Show Crosshair in Brush Tip check box allows you to specify whether you want to see a crosshair in the center of the brush, so it's easier to see exactly where the center of the brush is. This can be helpful in a variety of situations, and we don't find it to be a distraction, so we recommend leaving it turned on.

> **Note:** The Caps Lock key toggles the display of brush cursors between Precise and the brush options, so if you're not getting the display you expect based on Preferences, check the status of your Caps Lock key. This is one of the most common problems we see in our workshops!

For Other Cursors, use the Precise option so you can see exactly where in the image you're clicking when using one of the nonbrush tools. In most cases, this option displays a crosshair, or "target," for the nonbrush tools.

We leave the Brush Preview set to the default color of red. Although we don't often use the Brush Edit feature, it's easy to see the Brush Edit previews on most images. However, if red doesn't stand out, click on it to call up the Color Picker and choose whatever color you wish.

The next three sections of preferences can be left at their default settings, but be sure to have Print Resolution for New Documents set to 300 (or whatever resolution you use for printing). That way, whenever you create a new document it will be set to the correct resolution.

Plug-Ins

If you use a number of plug-ins, you can opt to store them in a separate folder and have Photoshop automatically access the folder. Since we don't use many plug-ins, we leave this option unchecked. To use it, click the check box, navigate to the appropriate folder in the dialog box that appears, and click Choose. If you have an older Photoshop serial number associated with these plug-ins, you can add that to the Legacy Photoshop Serial Number box.

Note: For the Transparency & Gamut, Guides, Grids & Slices, and Type settings, we recommend the default settings. The settings themselves aren't of significant consequence for optimizing photographic images, so we won't cover those sections here.

Setting Preferences

The Elements Preferences dialog, seen here, is similar to the Photoshop Preferences, but Elements generally has fewer choices. We'll highlight any options that are noticeably different. Otherwise follow the choices selected in the figures and detailed earlier in the Photoshop section.

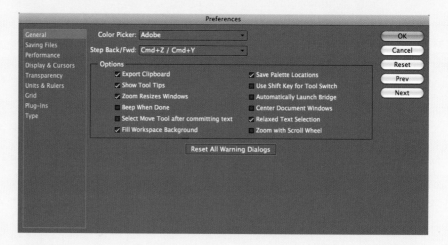

General

The Mac version of the Elements 6 General tab has a preference to Fill Workspace Background. This option fills the workspace, the space behind your images, with a neutral gray color, making it easier to judge colors accurately. We recommend turning this option on.

Elements also has an option to Center Document Windows. This option causes Elements to automatically center the window within the workspace when opening an image. We consider this a personal preference.

Note that Elements does not have a History Log.

Saving Files

The Elements File Handling preferences pane is called Saving Files. Its options are similar to those in Photoshop CS4, but it does not have support for Camera RAW for JPEG files, saving layered TIFF files, or Version Cue.

Continues

Setting Preferences *(Continued)*

Performance

The Memory Usage, History & Cache, and Scratch Disk options are similar between CS4 and Elements 6, but Elements does not have options for OpenGL drawing or 3D acceleration.

Display & Cursors

In addition to CS4-like cursor preferences, the Elements Display & Cursors preference pane has options for the crop shield. The crop shield is what hides the part of the image being cropped. If Use Shield is checked, Elements will darken that area with whatever color you set in Shield Color and by however much you set with Opacity. We recommend using a black color and a 50% opacity so that the region to be cropped becomes darker with no color cast.

Units & Rulers

Elements has an option called Photo Project Units. A photo project includes things like photo calendars and greeting cards. Set this option to the unit of measurement you are comfortable working with.

The remaining preference panes are quite similar to those in CS4.

Views and Zoom

With Photoshop set up just the way you like it, you're ready to start looking at your images. Photoshop provides a variety of ways to do just that, including ways to display images with Photoshop and ways to navigate within your images using various tools. Some of these are new to CS4.

Application Bar

The Application bar has been changed in CS4 and has increased functionality and features. The Windows CS4 Application bar, shown in Figure 4.9, combines the main menu bar as well as features previously found in the Application bar. The Mac Application bar does not contain the main menu items but shares the other new features.

The PC Application bar

The Mac Application bar

Figure 4.9 The new Application bars have increased functionality.

The Application icon is on the far left; it identifies the application (helpful if you're using more of the Creative Suite than just Photoshop). Clicking the Application icon in Windows will display the standard system menu and follows other expected Windows behaviors, including having a double-click close the application. On a Mac it doesn't do anything. Windows items previously found in the menu bar are next, but on a Mac they remain at the top of the monitor.

The next series of icons are new in CS4:

- First there is an icon for Bridge [Br]. Click it to access Bridge.

- Next is the View Extras icon [⊞▾]. Click the arrow next to it to access options to apply Show Grids, Show Guides, and Show Rulers.

- The next icon [36%▾] changes to reflect the current level of magnification on the selected image. Click the arrow by it to access options to change to 25%, 50%, 100%, and 200% magnification views.

- The Hand icon [✋] is a shortcut to the Hand tool to enable you to pan through the image when part of the image is hidden due to the magnification. In some screen modes, you can also use it to change the position of the image in the interface.

- The Magnifying Glass icon [🔍] is a shortcut to the Zoom tool. Use it to change the magnification of the image in steps.

- The Rotate tool [✋] is new in CS4 and enables you to rotate the image. This is more useful to graphic designers than nature photographers, but it's still worth knowing about.

- The Arrange Documents icon [⊞▾] is new in CS4 and provides access to a multitude of ways to arrange your images on screen, as shown here:

- Next is the Screen Mode icon [□▾]. Use the arrow next to it to toggle from Standard Screen to Full Screen Mode with Menu Bar to Full Screen Mode. We'll talk more about these modes in the next section.

- On the far right is the Workspace icon. The currently selected workspace is displayed, and other choices are available from the dropdown menu.

Windows and Workspaces

Although Windows users have always had a gray background for their workspace, Mac users have not. CS4 offers the option to use an application frame, which provides a solid background and hides the desktop. We find this very helpful so that we aren't distracted by the clutter on the desktop. If for some reason you want to be able to see your desktop behind your images, go to Window > Application Frame and toggle it off.

The first thing we recommend doing when you open an image is to size the document window appropriately. In general, this means maximizing the document window so you can see as much of the image as possible (as illustrated in Figure 4.10). To do this, press Ctrl+0/⌘+0. We're always a bit surprised at the number of people in our workshops who are working with their images sized so small that the majority of their monitor is filled with blank gray space. You can work far more accurately when you can see the image in more detail.

Figure 4.10 It's generally best to maximize your document window so you can see as much of the image as possible while working in Photoshop.

Screen Modes

Photoshop CS4 offers three screen modes: Standard Screen, Full Screen with Menu Bar, and Full Screen. These screen modes change the background surrounding your image as well as how you view your image. To toggle through the screen modes, press the F key; each time you press it, the mode will change to the next one in the series. You can also access the screen modes from the Change Screen Mode icon in the Application bar or from View > Screen Mode.

If you have selected Open Documents as Tabs in Preferences, your images will open in Standard Screen mode as tabbed images, as shown in Figure 4.10. Initially only one image at a time is visible. If the magnification renders the image larger than the screen space, scroll bars appear to help navigate through the image. You control which image is selected and visible by clicking its tab. Click the small X on the right side of the tab to close an image.

To view more than one image at a time, you have several options. N-Up is new in CS4. It refers to the option to divide the workspace among as many images (*N*) as desired in Standard Screen mode, as shown in Figure 4.11. To view multiple images simultaneously, first open the images, then click the Arrange Document icon and choose the layout you want.

Figure 4.11 By using N-Up, you can view multiple images simultaneously and scroll through them independently.

You can also opt to view one or more images in their own floating windows. To float an image, click the tab and drag it down and away from the Application bar, or click the Arrange Documents icon and choose Float All in Windows. To return them to tabbed documents, click on the section with the document name and drag them back next to the Application bar.

In Full Screen mode with or without the menu bar you can only view a single image at a time. Click the Hand tool and drag the image to control its placement in the window. No scroll bars appear, which makes it difficult to accurately pan through an image. For that reason we prefer to use the Standard Screen mode with the Application Frame on for most of our work. Full Screen mode can be useful when showing your work to others.

Note: Press the Tab key to hide both the toolbar and the panels on the right. Press Shift+Tab to hide the panels but leave the toolbar visible.

Screen Modes

Photoshop Elements does not have different screen modes; it has only one general workspace. As in Photoshop, the tools and options are on the left and top of the screen, respectively, and the palettes are on the right side. You can click on the split bar on the right side of the screen, indicated in the image shown here, to hide or show the Palette Bin.

Within the Elements workspace are five key areas. At the top (1) are the Workspace buttons. On the left (2) is the Toolbox, and on the bottom (3) is the Project Bin. The bulk of the screen is taken up by the Workspace area (4), which in this graphic is showing two different images. On the far right is the Palette Bin (5), containing palettes with information relating to the image, such as the Navigator and Histogram palettes.

To have more space for your images, we recommend closing the Project Bin at the bottom of the screen by choosing Window > Project Bin or by clicking the split bar between the bottom of the workspace and top of the Project Bin.

Configuring Panels

In versions of Photoshop prior to CS3, the panels on the right side of the monitor used a significant amount of monitor real estate. If you were working with a dual-monitor setup, it wasn't as much of an issue, but with a single monitor it was frustrating and distracting to have so much space devoted to the panels rather than your image. Now the panels are not only completely flexible as to their arrangement, but they are also collapsible.

Note: Prior to CS3, panels were called palettes.

You can customize the arrangement of the various panels within Photoshop to suit your own needs. The default arrangement in CS4 (Essentials) shown here displays certain panels that Adobe considers to be of general use. We find it beneficial to modify this arrangement. Keep in mind that your ideal configuration may vary depending on whether you are using a one- or two-monitor setup. *(below left)*

Initially the Color, Swatches, and Styles panels are visible, but we don't often use them. We remove them by clicking the ▣ icon at the right of that panel group and choosing Close Tab Group. We like to have the Histogram, Information, and History panels visible as they were in earlier versions of Photoshop. To make them visible, select Window in the Application or main menu bar and toggle them on. You'll see new collapsed iconic panel groups appear as shown here. *(below center)*

Hovering the cursor over the icon will reveal the name of the panel. If you click one of the icons, the individual panel expands as shown. *(below right)*

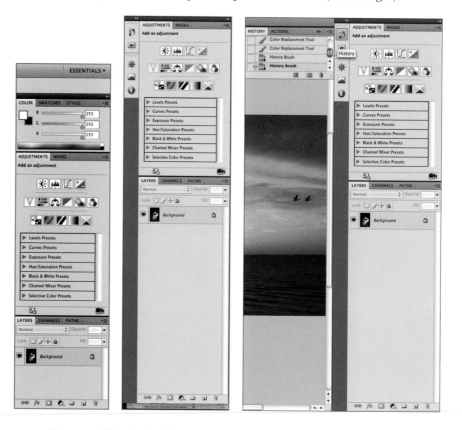

You can click the double arrow at the top of the iconic panel groups to expand them as shown on the next page. However, most of the time we prefer to either move them or keep them collapsed.

To move an icon tab group into the panel group on the right, click the thin double line at the top of the group and drag it to the desired location. A blue line appears where the group will be inserted, and the panel is automatically expanded in keeping with the others in that column. You can opt to drag the entire tab group or just an individual icon. In addition, you can group the panels any way that you want by clicking an individual tab and dragging it to the new location, regardless of whether the panel is expanded or collapsed.

We also like to have the History and Actions tab groups accessible as iconic tabs but remove Paths because we rarely use them. Our current preferred workspace is shown here.

When you have rearranged the panels the way you want them, go to Window > Workspace > Save Workspace. Give your workspace a descriptive name in case you want to create more than one. Ellen uses "Ellen's Basic." Notice that's what appears in the workspace name in the Application bar. Anytime you want to return to this arrangement, click in the Workspace Chooser and select your saved workspace.

Throughout this book you'll become familiar with many of the panels you can use, and you'll start to develop a preference for which panels you want to have visible and how you want them arranged. You may even find that you prefer to establish different configurations for different tasks or for different types of images. Fortunately, it's easy to switch between various panel arrangements by using the Workspace Switcher.

Note: Photoshop provides some preset customized workspaces under Window > Workspace. Although tempting to use, none of them are configured the way we like to work, so we prefer to create our own customized workspaces.

The Adjustments and Masks panels, new to CS4, provide quick access to adjustment tools that automatically create adjustment layers. It's the same as clicking the Adjustment Layer icon at the bottom of the Layers panel, but a bit easier to access and has options for creating masks, clipping layers, and previews that we'll talk about in Chapter 6, "Exposure Adjustments." Since the adjustments work in a nonmodal fashion in CS4, you can modify various parameters, such as blending modes and zoom, or even alter the mask, while the adjustment dialog is open. The Masks panel contains numerous options for both creating and refining a mask. We cover this in more detail in Chapter 6.

Note: If you have hidden the panels on the right by using the Tab or Shift+Tab options, you can access them by hovering the cursor over the dark translucent stripe at the right edge of your monitor. The panels will magically appear, and when you move your cursor away from that area they'll disappear again.

The Tools panel changed in CS3 to a single column as the default configuration. We prefer this view, but if you're more comfortable with the double-column setup that earlier versions of Photoshop used, click the gray area by the two triangles at the top of the Tools panel, just above the PS icon.

Configuring Palettes

In Elements, panels are called palettes. Although the default configuration has only the Effects and Layers palettes visible, with a little bit of tweaking it is possible to create a layout very similar to Photoshop CS4, as shown earlier in the sidebar "For Photoshop Elements Users: Screen Modes." Begin by choosing Full in the upper-right part of the interface. We recommend you follow these steps:

1. Choose Window > Histogram.

2. In the floating palette that appears, click the More button and select Place in Palette Bin When Closed.

3. Close the palette.

4. In the Palette Bin, click on the word *Histogram* and drag that palette where you want it.

Repeat the previous steps for each palette you wish to add to the Palette Bin. We recommend adding the Histogram, Navigator, Undo History, and Layers palettes.

To remove a palette, such as Effects, follow these steps:

1. Click on the double-arrow on the right side of the palette ▸▸.

2. Uncheck Place in Palette Bin When Closed.

3. Click on the palette name and drag the palette off into the workspace. It will appear as a floating palette.

4. Close the palette.

Note that it's also possible to group multiple floating palettes, such as Navigator and Info, together into a single floating window. To do so, have at least one palette open as a floating palette and drag the second palette onto the first palette.

To collapse or expand a palette, click the disclosure triangle next to the palette's name.

Although there is no way to explicitly save your Elements setup as a named workspace, Elements will remember your settings each time you quit, and will reopen the program configured the same way.

Zoom Tool

The Zoom tool is the most basic of navigation tools, but it does include some hidden features that can be helpful. To select the Zoom tool, click its icon on the Tools panel 🔍 or in the Application bar, or press Z on your keyboard.

> **Note:** If you're using any other tool, you can switch to the Zoom tool by pressing Ctrl+spacebar/ ⌘+spacebar. When you release the spacebar, your tool switches back.

In the most basic use, after selecting the Zoom tool, click anywhere in your image to zoom in by one preset percentage level. When you do so, not only is the image enlarged on the screen, but also the point you clicked becomes the center of the new display (if you have checked that option in Preferences). To zoom out, select the minus (–) option on the Options bar, or simply hold down the Alt/Option key while you click. When zooming out, the same basic behavior occurs in reverse. The image zooms out by one level, and the point you clicked becomes the center of the new display.

> **Note:** You can also zoom in or out (without changing the center of the view) by pressing Ctrl/⌘ and the plus (+) or minus (–) key. Also, if your mouse has a scroll wheel, you can use that for zooming in and out.

The Zoom tool also offers one special capability that makes it incredibly powerful. If you click and drag with the Zoom tool, you create a *marquee* (dashed box) on your image. When you release the mouse, the area you dragged the box around is zoomed as much as necessary to fill the document window. This is an excellent way to zoom in on a particular area of your image to give it a closer look.

Another handy hidden feature of the Zoom tool is the ability to quickly go to a 100% view of your image, which is an excellent way to evaluate sharpness and look for small problems such as dust spots within the image. To quickly return the zoom percentage to 100%, simply double-click the Zoom tool's icon on the Tools panel *or* press Ctrl+Alt+0/⌘+Option+0. You can also access some of these commands when the Zoom tool is active by right-clicking the image and choosing the desired option from the context menu. In CS4 you can use the Magnification icon in the Application bar as well.

> **Note:** In earlier versions of Photoshop, artifacts often appeared at irregular magnifications, causing distortions or making the selection "marching ants" disappear. One place this commonly occurred was with photos showing the texture in cloth. At some magnifications it may have looked as though the cloth was a fancy silk moiré rather than ordinary fabric. CS4 uses OpenGL technology to avoid many of these issues. Nonetheless, the most accurate magnification is still 100%. If something looks odd in your image, check the magnification to see whether it's a problem with the image itself or an artifact.

Evaluating Sharpness: The Proper Magnification and Practice

Determining whether an image is critically sharp is a major aspect of the image-review process that leads up to the actual optimization workflow. Many photographers, especially those who have spent many years evaluating the sharpness of images on film by utilizing a high-powered loupe, have a difficult time evaluating the sharpness of a digital image displayed on their monitor.

The first step to evaluating sharpness for a given image is to view it at 100% magnification (or Actual Pixels). To do this, you can use the Zoom tool or the keyboard shortcut Ctrl+Alt+0/ ⌘+Option+0. At this magnification, one image pixel is represented by one monitor pixel. As a result, you're seeing all the actual pixels within the image for the area that can be seen on the monitor. If you don't have the display set to 100% magnification, the monitor is either using more than one pixel to represent each pixel in the image (if the zoom percentage is greater than 100%) or is not showing all pixels for a given area within the image (if the zoom percentage is less than 100%).

After you're viewing the image at 100% magnification, look to see whether the edges within the subject matter of the image have good contrast. This is the key attribute of an image with crisp focus. Learning to see what a sharp image looks like on a monitor display takes some practice, and the only way to accumulate that practice is to evaluate a large number of images.

Besides simply reviewing the images on your monitor, it can be helpful to first make prints of some of your images and then compare the printed image (where you'll have an easier time evaluating sharpness) to the image on the monitor at 100% magnification. Comparing these images gives you a better idea of how the monitor display translates into actual image sharpness.

Hand Tool

The Hand tool provides a way to navigate around your image when the magnification is higher than 100% and it therefore spills over the document window. You can think of this tool as behaving the way your own hand would if you were evaluating a large print on a table. Instead of moving your head around to look at different areas of the image, you can simply move the "print" with your hand. You can activate the Hand tool by clicking its icon in the Tools panel or by pressing H on your keyboard.

With the Hand tool active, drag around on the image. The image moves in the direction you drag, and the display updates in real time so you can watch the image slide around as you move the mouse. In CS4, if you "flick" the Hand tool (click, drag, and abruptly let go), the image will continue moving and slide to a halt. To stop it more suddenly, left-click. This animated moving can make it easier to navigate through the image rather than having to drag all the way through it. It helps with the problem of running out of space when dragging the mouse and with hand fatigue when using a trackball. Make sure you've checked this option in Preferences. If it's not working, your graphics card may not support OpenGL, which is required for flicking.

Another handy trick is to use the Hand tool to quickly display your image at a magnification that allows it to fit within the space available without being obstructed by the panels (if they are docked to the side of the screen) or to fill the screen display area (if they are not), resizing the image window if necessary. To do so, double-click the Hand tool in the Tools panel. This is a great way to quickly get an overview of the image for evaluating overall composition, tonality, and color.

Navigator Panel

The Navigator panel consolidates many of the features of the Zoom and Hand tools into a single package and provides another method for moving around your image to evaluate various portions of it (see Figure 4.12). If the Navigator panel isn't visible, choose Window > Navigator from the menu to make it active.

Figure 4.12 The Navigator panel provides a convenient way to navigate around your image.

The Navigator panel provides a thumbnail preview of the currently active image. A red box indicates which portion of the image is being viewed in the document window, so you always have a sense of what portion of the image you are seeing. The bottom-left corner of the panel includes a zoom-percentage indicator for reference.

The zooming features of the Navigator panel are utilized primarily with the slider in the bottom-right corner of the panel window. The "little mountains" button to the left of the slider allows you to zoom out by one preset percentage level each time you click it, similar to Alt+clicking/Option+clicking your image with the Zoom tool.

The "big mountains" button to the right of the slider allows you to zoom in by one preset percentage level. You can exercise greater control over the zooming process by adjusting the slider left (to zoom out) or right (to zoom in).

The Navigator Panel

Rather than mountains, Elements has buttons labeled + and − for zooming in or out.

Within the thumbnail display for your image, the red box serves not only as an indicator of which area of the image is currently being viewed, but also as a way to change the view of the image to look at a different area. If you drag the boxed area around within the thumbnail display, the document display changes in real time to reflect the area defined by the box. This is similar to the use of the Hand tool for navigating around your image.

Note: You can't move the outline in the Navigator panel if the entire image is currently visible.

You can click a particular point in the thumbnail to center the outline on that spot. This is a great method to use when you want to spot-check various portions of the image. For example, if you're trying to evaluate critical sharpness, check various areas of the subject and even areas at various distances from the camera to see the effect of depth of field. By simply clicking those points in the thumbnail of the Navigator panel, you can check multiple areas of the image quickly and easily.

One last trick in the Navigator panel allows you to reproduce the effect of drawing a marquee on your image with the Zoom tool so you can quickly fill the screen with a particular portion of your image. To do so, hold the Ctrl/⌘ key, and click and drag within the thumbnail display of the Navigator panel to draw a box over the area you want to view. When you release the mouse button, the image is automatically zoomed and repositioned so that the area you drew the box around fills the available space.

Navigating by Keyboard Shortcuts

If you love using keyboard shortcuts to speed up your workflow, there are a variety of options for navigating around your images during the evaluation process (as well as during your optimization workflow). If you tend to keep one hand on the keyboard as you work, this may be your preferred way to navigate. Even if you prefer to use the mouse as much as possible, remembering a few of these keyboard shortcuts can help improve your workflow by adding to your arsenal of tricks for working with your images. Table 4.1 includes the most common navigational shortcuts.

Table 4.1 Keyboard Shortcuts for Image Navigation

Windows Shortcut	Mac Shortcut	Action
H	H	Activates the Hand tool
Z	Z	Activates the Zoom tool
Ctrl++	⌘++	Zooms in
Ctrl+-	⌘+-	Zooms out
Ctrl+Alt+0	⌘+Option+0	Zooms to 100% magnification (actual pixels)
Ctrl+0	⌘+0	Zooms document window to fit on the screen
Spacebar	Spacebar	Temporarily activates the Hand tool regardless of currently active tool
Ctrl+spacebar	⌘+spacebar	Temporarily activates the Zoom tool regardless of currently active tool
Ctrl+Alt+spacebar	⌘+Option+spacebar	Temporarily activates the Zoom tool in zoom-out mode regardless of the currently active tool

Note: In Windows, if you have a check box or other control active in a dialog box while trying to hold the spacebar to access the Hand tool, you may not get the behavior you are expecting. This is because you can use the spacebar to toggle such controls. To avoid this, click an empty area of the dialog box so that no control has the focus before using the spacebar as a shortcut key.

On a Mac, ⌘+Spacebar is usually set to launch Spotlight searches, even though it also activates the Zoom tool temporarily. To change the Spotlight shortcut, look in System Preferences > Spotlight.

As you've seen in this section, Photoshop offers many options for navigating around your images during the evaluation and optimization processes. Instead of trying to decide which particular methods work best for your needs, make an effort to become familiar with all of them. Doing so will ensure that you have the maximum number of techniques available for any given situation. You'll likely find that although you have your favorite methods for navigating around your images, in certain situations other methods are more convenient. By being comfortable with all the available methods, you'll have maximum flexibility and control when working on your images.

Try It! To gain familiarity with the Navigator panel, open the image NavPanel from the accompanying CD and zoom in to various areas of the image, deciding on a specific area to view and then navigating to that area so it fills the monitor display. Then, save a workspace with the panel arrangement you prefer to use when working on your images.

Selection Tools

We're including the selection tools in this chapter on foundations because making a selection is required for many of the more advanced topics we'll cover in later chapters. You can make a selection in a variety of ways, and which approach is best depends on the characteristics of the specific image as well as your own preferences. Focusing on the selection tools now introduces and reinforces the general techniques you employ when working with most of the tools in Photoshop. We recommend you experiment with and learn the different tools that perform similar basic tasks to help you get more comfortable using Photoshop and the various tools it offers. That way, you'll be able to use the best one in any given situation.

You can use selections for making targeted adjustments and for other tasks, as we'll discuss in later chapters. For example, you can select the sky to apply adjustments that affect only the sky, or you can select a foreground subject to enhance it so it better stands out from the landscape. In the following sections, we'll look at some of the selection tools most commonly employed by nature photographers, as well as some behaviors common to all the selection tools.

The Lasso Tool

The Lasso tool provides maximum flexibility and is very intuitive because it allows you to literally draw a custom shape around the pixels you want to select. This is helpful for situations where the more automated selection tools don't provide the accuracy you need, requiring you to trace by hand. For example, if you are trying to select a dark bird against a dark background, other tools may not be able to tell the difference between the two. The Lasso tool allows you to define the specific shape and location of the selection edge. Activate the Lasso by choosing it from the Tools panel or by pressing L on your keyboard.

The Options bar for the Lasso tool (shown in Figure 4.13) contains some settings that allow you to adjust the tool's behavior. These include four modifier options, which we'll discuss in the next section. Also on the Options bar for the Lasso tool are the Feather, Anti-Aliased, and Refine Edges controls. We recommend leaving Feather set to 0 px and Anti-Aliased selected (to help smooth portions of the selection lines that are not perfectly horizontal or vertical). We'll explain what feathering is and how to use Refine Edges later in the section on Refine Edges.

Figure 4.13 The Options bar for the Lasso tool lets you decide how to use the tool.

Zoom in on the area you want to select. Creating an accurate selection is easiest to do when you magnify the image to clearly see the edge you're trying to select. Carefully position your cursor along that edge; then click and hold the mouse button. Drag the cursor along the edge so you're effectively tracing that edge to define your selection, as shown in Figure 4.14. Take the time to be as precise as you can so the selection you create is as accurate as possible.

Note: For tools like the Lasso that require you to draw on your image, using a tablet such as the Wacom Intuos3 (www.wacom.com) can be a tremendous help, providing you with greater control and precision. In addition, using a pen and tablet feels more natural to many people.

PHOTO BY ELLEN ANON

Figure 4.14 When working with the Lasso tool, you can trace along any shape within your image to define your selection.

Note: For all the Lasso selection tools, use the keyboard shortcuts Ctrl++ (plus sign) /⌘++ to zoom in and Ctrl+− (minus sign) /⌘+− to zoom out while you are in the process of creating the selection.

When working on a zoomed portion of your image, the area you're trying to select might extend outside the document window. In that case, as you near the edge of the document window, press and hold the spacebar. This temporarily accesses the Hand tool, so you can click and drag the image to change the area you're currently viewing. When you finish moving the image, release the spacebar and continue dragging the cursor to extend the selection you're in the process of creating.

When selecting an area of the image, be sure to define all of it, dragging the cursor all the way back to your original starting point and releasing the mouse button to finish the selection, as shown in Figure 4.15. If you don't finish at the same point you started, Photoshop automatically completes your selection by extending a straight line from the point where you release the mouse button to your original starting point, which is obviously less than ideal in most situations.

Figure 4.15 When you finish tracing the object you want to select, returning to your starting point, the selection will be complete.

Working with the Lasso tool requires a steady hand and a bit of practice. It isn't always the fastest or easiest way to create a selection, but it does offer exceptional flexibility.

Selection Modes

Sometimes when you are making a difficult selection, you may want to make part of your selection first and then add or remove sections. With the Lasso selection tool under control, you can make more complicated selections by adding pixels to or subtracting pixels from a selection. Start by using the Lasso tool to create a basic selection. To the right of the Tool Preset drop-down list on the Options bar is a set of four buttons (these are labeled back in Figure 4.13) that allow you to modify the behavior of these (and other) selection tools.

Note: You can apply the options discussed in this section to most of the selection tools in Photoshop.

The first button, New Selection, causes the current selection tool to behave in the "normal" manner, creating a new selection whenever you use the tool. With this option active, when you click and drag to create a selection, it replaces any existing selections. Each time you click and drag with the first button selected, you are starting to make the selection from scratch.

The second button is the Add to Selection option. With this option chosen, whenever you use a selection tool to surround pixels, the new selection is added to the existing selection. For example, if you use the Lasso tool to create a selection around your subject but then realize you left a part of the subject out of the selection, choose the Add to Selection option and then select the area you missed. It is then added to the overall selection (see Figure 4.16). You can also hold the Shift key to access the Add to Selection option regardless of the current state of the tool.

> **Note:** When using the Lasso tool to add or subtract from a selection, you only need to trace carefully around the pertinent area of your selection; you can then make a quick loop through areas that are already selected (or not selected, as the case may be).

PHOTO BY ELLEN ANON

Figure 4.16 The Add to Selection option for the Lasso tool allows you to add a new area to your selection, creating a larger final selection.

The third button in the set is the Subtract from Selection option, which allows you to subtract pixels from an existing selection. When this button is selected, drawing a selection causes the surrounded pixels to be omitted from the existing selection, as shown in Figure 4.17. You access this option by holding the Alt/Option key when using any selection tool. You must still draw a closed shape to define the area of the selection you want to subtract.

Figure 4.17 The Subtract from Selection option for the Lasso tool allows you to remove an area from your selection, creating a smaller final selection.

The Add and Subtract options are extremely helpful, and you'll use them extensively as you build complicated selections that require a fair amount of fine-tuning.

The last button of the four, Intersect with Selection, is not particularly useful for most nature photography. When you choose this option, creating a new selection when you have an existing selection results in a selection of only the pixels in the areas where the two selections overlap.

Try It! To get more comfortable revising selections, open the image called Lasso Tool from the accompanying CD. Start by creating a quick but not very accurate selection, and then use the Add to Selection and Subtract from Selection options with the Lasso tool to revise the selection.

The Magnetic Lasso

The Magnetic Lasso is helpful for selecting objects within your images where reasonably good contrast exists along the edges defining that object. Instead of selecting precisely where you drag, the Magnetic Lasso defines a selection by periodically placing anchor points as you drag the cursor around an object, automatically identifying the locations of highest contrast as you move the cursor around the edge. In other words, this tool often simplifies the process of identifying exactly the area that you want, reducing the need to work extremely slowly and carefully, as you must with the Lasso tool. It makes the selection jump to the edges of the area that you're trying to select.

You'll find the Magnetic Lasso  under the regular Lasso on the Tools panel. Click and hold the cursor (or right-click) on the Lasso tool to open the fly-out menu, and choose Magnetic Lasso Tool (see Figure 4.18). You can also press L on your keyboard to activate the current Lasso tool, and then press Shift+L to toggle through the selection tools until you access the Magnetic Lasso.

Figure 4.18 You can find the Magnetic Lasso tool under the Lasso tool on the Tools panel.

Besides the standard controls found on the Options bar for the other selection tools (and discussed in the earlier section on the Lasso tool), the Options bar contains some special controls for the Magnetic Lasso tool. (Figure 4.19 shows the Options bar.) The first is the Width control; as you "paint" with the Magnetic Lasso, the Width control determines the size of the area in which you'd like Photoshop to search for contrast. You could enter a value in pixels to determine the size of the edge width for the Magnetic Lasso, but obviously this is a rather arbitrary decision. Instead, simply place your cursor along the edge where you'll start making the selection, and use the left or right square bracket key ([or]) to reduce or enlarge the size of the edge width, respectively. You want the width to be small enough that the strongest area of contrast within the sample area is the edge you're trying to select but large enough that you don't have to be overly precise in dragging the mouse pointer along that edge.

Figure 4.19 The Options bar for the Magnetic Lasso tool includes some specialized settings in addition to those found with the regular Lasso tool.

The Edge Contrast setting determines how much contrast the Magnetic Lasso should seek. For high-contrast edges, if you use a higher setting, you won't need to be as precise as you move the mouse along that contrast edge. For low-contrast edges, use a lower setting, but be more precise in dragging the mouse along the edge you're trying to select. We've found the change in behavior achieved with different settings is very slight, so we recommend setting Edge Contrast to the default value of 10%.

The Frequency setting determines how often anchor points are placed as you drag the mouse pointer over the edge. A higher Frequency value causes anchor points to be placed quickly in close proximity to each other; a lower value causes them to be placed farther apart. (Figure 4.20 illustrates both of these situations.) Lower settings are best for well-defined edges, whereas higher settings tend to work well for more nebulous edges. A Frequency value of 60 is a good general starting point, and you can then revise that number based on whether the anchor points are being placed at an appropriate rate (the allowed range is 0 to 100). It's generally better to have a higher frequency with more anchor points rather than a lower frequency so the shape of the selection better matches the edge of the object you're trying to select.

Note: The faster you move the cursor with the Magnetic Lasso tool, the farther apart the anchor points are spread as compared to when you drag it slowly.

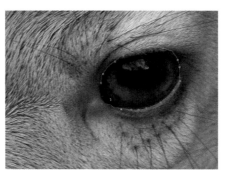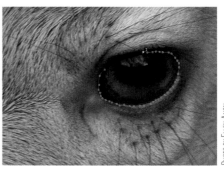

PHOTO BY ELLEN ANON

Figure 4.20 A low Frequency setting for the Magnetic Lasso causes anchor points to be spaced out relatively far apart, while a high setting causes them to be placed closer together.

The next setting on the Options bar is a Pen Pressure check box. This setting applies only if you are using a tablet. With this check box selected, varying the pressure you apply to the stylus (pen) affects the edge width. Pressing harder causes the width to decrease as though the pressure is focusing the edge width onto a smaller area. Less pressure causes the edge width to enlarge, so the Magnetic Lasso looks for contrast across a broader area.

With the Options bar settings established, you're ready to start creating a selection with the Magnetic Lasso tool. Position the cursor over the contrast edge you want to select, and click the mouse button once to place the initial anchor point. Then drag the cursor along the edge of the object you are trying to select. Photoshop automatically places anchor points at the area of highest contrast within the target area (Width), with spacing based on the Frequency setting. If you get to an area of the image where contrast isn't adequate for the Magnetic Lasso to accurately place an anchor point, click the mouse to manually place an anchor point. For example, if you have a well-defined subject such as a flower against the sky, the Magnetic Lasso will likely do a good job. But where the flower overlaps foliage or other flowers below it, the Magnetic Lasso may not be able to identify the edge, requiring you to place anchor points manually by clicking. We often find it helpful to manually place an anchor point where the selection needs to abruptly change directions.

At times you'll find the Magnetic Lasso doesn't do a very good job of placing anchor points where you want them, instead placing them in inappropriate places. When that happens, you need to delete anchor points before trying again in the problem area of the image. First move the cursor back to the last place where you want an anchor point. Then press the Backspace/Delete key once for each anchor you want to remove. They are removed starting with the most recently created point. You can then adjust the width with the square bracket keys, or change other settings on the Options bar, and drag again along the edge. If you can't find settings that work well for a particular area, place the anchor points manually by clicking the mouse.

Note: Sometimes the Magnetic Lasso tool seems to have a mind of its own and runs amok. When that happens, place the cursor over the last good anchor point before it ran off, and repeatedly hit the Backspace/Delete key. Doing so will remove all the extra anchor points and put you back in control of the tool. Knowing this trick will make using the Magnetic Lasso a lot less frustrating.

To access the regular Lasso tool while working with the Magnetic Lasso, press and hold the Alt/Option key as you click, and drag the cursor along the edge you want to define by drawing freehand. Click again without the Alt/Option key to return to the Magnetic Lasso. (Note that if you inadvertently release the Alt/Option key while dragging, you will be using the Polygonal Lasso tool rather than the Freehand Lasso tool.)

If you decide you want to cancel the selection in progress, simply press the Esc key; all anchor points are removed, and there is no active selection (unless there was a selection active before you started using the Magnetic Lasso).

Try It! To get more comfortable working with this tool, open the image Magnetic Lasso on the accompanying CD, zoom in on the eye of the owl, and use the Magnetic Lasso to create a selection of the eye.

The Magnetic Lasso tool is powerful, but it isn't perfect. Although it does a good job of selecting based on contrast in the area you drag the cursor over, in many cases it won't create a perfect selection, as you can see in Figure 4.21. However, it usually creates a good basic selection, making it an effective tool that can sometimes save you time in creating selections. By learning the nuances of each tool, you too will develop your own favorites that work best for you.

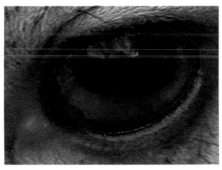

PHOTO BY ELLEN ANON

Figure 4.21 The Magnetic Lasso tool doesn't generally create perfect selections, as you can see here, but it does provide a good basic selection with minimal effort.

The third Lasso selection tool is the Polygonal Lasso tool. However, for nature photography this tool tends to be less useful than the tools described in this section because it is designed for creating selections comprised of straight lines.

The Magic Wand

When the Magic Wand tool creates a selection with a single click of the mouse, it seems truly magical. When too many clicks are required, it can be frustrating. The trick is knowing what type of image is best suited for this tool and how to configure the settings for the best result.

The Magic Wand lives underneath the Quick Selection tool. To access it, click the Quick Selection tool in the toolbar, and select the Magic Wand ✴ from the fly-out menu. (You can also press W and then Shift+W as needed to toggle between the Quick Select and Magic Wand tools.) The Magic Wand functions by sampling the pixel that you click and then comparing other pixels to see whether they are a close-enough match. If they are, they are included in the selection.

Before setting the options for the Magic Wand tool, it's important to check a setting on the Options bar for the Eyedropper tool ⟋. Although these tools don't seem related, the Magic Wand tool uses the Sample Size setting from the Eyedropper tool to determine the actual value to use in evaluating pixels for inclusion in the selection. Choose the Eyedropper tool from the Tools panel, and choose an option from the Sample Size drop-down menu on the Options bar, as shown in Figure 4.22.

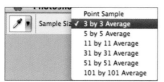

Figure 4.22 The first step in using the Magic Wand tool is to set an appropriate option from the Sample Size drop-down menu on the Options bar for the Eyedropper tool.

The most useful options available for your purposes when you select the Eyedropper tool are 3 by 3 Average and 5 by 5 Average. As their names indicate, they sample a grid of pixels (a total of 9 or 25 pixels, respectively) surrounding the one you click and average their values. This average value is then used as the basis of the Magic Wand tool selection. Averaging helps to compensate for any local variation among pixels and is more reliable than sampling a single point. We recommend using the 3 by 3 Average setting, because it provides a good balance for most images. The 5 by 5 Average setting has a higher risk of averaging the pixel values to the point that the result isn't as accurate based on the pixel area you clicked.

Note: The Point Sample option causes the Magic Wand tool to use only a single pixel as the basis for pixel comparison. This can certainly increase precision, but it also introduces potential errors. For example, you could click a dust spot or a pixel with variation caused by grain or noise, and the resulting selection wouldn't match what you were intending to create. For this reason, we don't recommend using the Point Sample option.

After you've established an appropriate Sample Size setting on the Options bar for the Eyedropper tool, choose the Magic Wand tool so you can adjust the settings and create your selection.

The key to using the Magic Wand tool effectively is the Tolerance setting on the Options bar (see Figure 4.23). This setting determines how different the pixel values can be and still be considered a match. With a low setting, pixels must be very similar to the value of the pixel you clicked to be included in the selection. With a high setting, even pixels with very different values can be included in the selection. The tolerance ranges from 0, which would mean a pixel must be identical to the sampled pixel in order to be selected, to 255, which would result in the entire image being selected.

Figure 4.23 The Tolerance setting on the Options bar for the Magic Wand tool is key to getting the best results.

The Magic Wand tool is obviously best suited to images with broad areas of similar tone and color that you want to select. An example would be the out-of-focus brown background in the image in Figure 4.24. Because the pixels already have similar values, a relatively low Tolerance setting should be appropriate. We often start with a value of 30 and work from there.

PHOTO BY ELLEN ANON

Figure 4.24 The Magic Wand tool is best suited to images with broad areas of similar tone and color.

Click the area of the image you want to select, and adjust the Tolerance setting based on the result. If too many pixels from areas you don't want to select are selected, the Tolerance is too high; cancel the selection (choose Select > Deselect from the menu) and reduce the Tolerance value.

Of course, you could spend a lot of time chasing the right Tolerance value. We recommend taking a tempered approach, trying to find a *good* value without spending too much time finding the *perfect* value. Opt for a Tolerance setting that is a bit lower than needed. Then use the Add to Selection option and the Refine Edge feature (which we'll describe later in this chapter) to build up the final selection.

It's important to keep in mind that when you add pixels to or subtract pixels from a selection by using the appropriate options with the Magic Wand tool, the selection is modified based on the pixel you click after making your initial selection. Also, keep in mind that you can adjust the Tolerance setting between mouse clicks when using the Add and Subtract options, giving you even greater control. Each time you click with the Magic Wand tool, pixels throughout the image are evaluated based on the Tolerance setting, regardless of whether the pixels are already selected.

Although the Tolerance setting is the pivotal setting for the Magic Wand tool, the Contiguous option is also important. The Contiguous option affects which pixels are evaluated. When you click a pixel with the Magic Wand, Photoshop looks outward from that pixel to find matching pixels. If it encounters a pixel that doesn't match closely enough based on the Tolerance setting, that pixel creates a border so that pixels outside the areas defined by that border aren't considered. In other words, all pixels in the final selection are contiguous, or touching each other.

Using the Contiguous option is helpful when a tonality appears not only in the area you want to select, but also in areas you don't want to select. By clicking Contiguous, the Magic Wand will not include pixels that are in other areas of the image. For example, if you wanted to select the two swans shown in Figure 4.25, by selecting Contiguous you help the Magic Wand limit the selection to the swans rather than including the snow in the mountains.

Figure 4.25 Using the Contiguous option enables you to select a subject when similar tones are present elsewhere in the image.

At other times, you need to select similar areas that are noncontiguous. For example, you may need to select a sky in an image where the sky shows between the leaves and branches of a tree. Turning off the Contiguous option causes Photoshop to evaluate every pixel based on the pixel you click with the Magic Wand tool, as shown in Figure 4.26.

PHOTO BY ELLEN ANON

Figure 4.26 Turning off the Contiguous option for the Magic Wand tool allows you to select multiple noncontiguous areas in a single step.

The Sample All Layers check box allows you to determine whether Photoshop evaluates pixel values based on all layers in the image or on only the currently active layer. Because you're viewing the image based on all visible layers, it usually makes sense to keep this option turned on. In fact, you can use this setting to make the Magic Wand tool more effective by creating a temporary adjustment layer that accentuates the difference between areas you do want to select and those you don't.

The Anti-Aliased check box serves the same purpose as it does with the other selection tools discussed earlier in this chapter, and we recommend leaving it selected.

The Magic Wand tool is best for selecting areas of an image that have similar tone and color. If the area you're trying to select contains too much variation, evaluate the image to see whether you can easily select the opposite of what you really want. For example, if you want to select everything in an image except the sky, it might be easier to select the sky and then invert the selection (Select > Inverse).

When using the Magic Wand tool, it's important to check your selection at 100% magnification. At other magnifications there may be small "blinkies" that you can't see. These "blinkies" are actually pixels that may be erroneously selected or not selected. Rather than have to click over and over with the Magic Wand and use Add to Selection/Subtract from Selection, it's often much easier to refine the selection with the Freehand Lasso set to Add to Selection/Subtract from Selection. We'll talk more about this in the next section of this chapter.

The Magic Wand is a favorite selection tool for many nature photographers, and it's one that we used frequently in earlier versions of Photoshop. However, we find that now we turn more often to the Quick Selection and Color Range Select tools.

Try It! Open the image Magic Wand on the accompanying CD, and practice by creating a selection of the sky that doesn't encroach on the clouds.

The Quick Selection Tool

The Quick Selection tool was new to CS3 and has quickly become one of our favorite selection tools. It's easy to use, and it actually gets "smarter" as you work with the Add to Selection and Subtract from Selection options. Rather than having to trace along the edges to make a selection, you click and drag the cursor over the areas you want to select. The selection grows as you drag the cursor.

The Quick Selection tool is actually a brush tool. To determine the size of the tool, set the brush size in the Options bar, or use the bracket keys to increase and decrease the size. We find that using a fairly small brush gives the best results; the larger the brush, the less precise the area that is selected. By using a small brush in detailed areas, we can make reasonably accurate selections in many cases, as shown in Figure 4.27.

PHOTO BY ELLEN ANON

Figure 4.27 It was easy to make a good selection of the horse and cowboy by using the Quick Selection tool.

If the selection is not updating fast enough, you may need to drag a little more slowly and continue to hold down the mouse.

If you stop dragging and then click elsewhere, the tool will automatically change to Add to Selection. The selection will grow to incorporate the new area but not necessarily areas in between the original selection and the new area.

To remove an area from the selection, choose the Subtract from Selection option in the Options bar and then drag over the area to be removed. You may need to reduce the size of the tool.

In areas of lower contrast, you may need to alternate between adding to and subtracting from the selection. Holding down the Alt/Option key will enable you to rapidly toggle between the two modes. As you do so, Photoshop is actually refining the algorithm to make the selection more accurately and quickly.

To further adjust the edges of the selection, click the Refine Edges button, discussed in the next section.

The Magic Wand and Quick Selection Tools

These two tools are available in Elements and work similarly to their Photoshop counterparts, but are separate on the toolbar.

Elements provides an additional selection tool to help you refine selections, called the Selection Brush. With this brush, you begin with another tool to create the initial, rough selection and then use the Selection Brush to refine the selection. You use it to paint on areas that you want to add or remove from the selection.

To access the Selection Brush, click and hold the Quick Selection icon until a drop-down menu appears; then choose Selection Brush. The menu shown here will appear at the top of the screen.

The Selection Brush is set to initially Add to Selection ▮. Click the Subtract from Selection button ▮ to remove pixels from the selection.

Tip: When using the Selection Brush, especially while removing from a selection, setting Mode to Mask makes it easier to see the selected area and to see what effect a softer or harder brush has. Mask mode places a transparent red overlay (customize the color by clicking on the color well and picking a new color) over every part of the image that's not selected.

Using the Refine Edge Controls

When using the selection tools, a Refine Edge button appears on the Tool Options bar (Refine Edge...) that is particularly helpful. It's also available from within the Masks panel from the Mask Edge button. It has become our method of choice for controlling the appearance of the edges of a selection no matter how we made the initial selection.

It's taken the place of the simple Feather command in our workflow and often eliminates the need for the elaborate method we used to use, in which we created a layer mask for a selection and blurred the edges of the layer mask.

Click the button and the Refine Edge dialog box appears, as shown in Figure 4.28. Its purpose is to enable you to modify the edges of a selection so that it blends or separates from the background as needed.

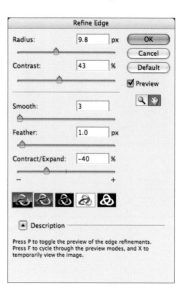

Figure 4.28 The Refine Edge dialog box provides tools to perfect the edges of the selection.

Within the Refine Edge dialog box, you'll see a series of sliders and boxes. The five boxes near the bottom enable you to preview the selection in different ways, as shown in Figure 4.29.

Standard shows the selection as the traditional series of marching ants around the edge of the selection. The presence of the marching ants can make it difficult to determine the precise location of the edges.

Quick Mask hides the background under a transparent veil of red while the selected area remains in clear view.

On Black shows the selection floating on a pure black background. In many cases, this makes it easy to see the edges. This is our default setting.

On White is similar to On Black, but the selection sits on a white background. This too can be helpful when trying to determine edge detail. Whether black or white is preferable depends on the colors in the selection.

Mask changes the preview to a traditional black-and-white mask view.

To toggle among the views, click the different boxes. Whichever view you last used is "sticky" and will be used initially the next time you open the dialog box.

In addition to the boxes, you'll see five sliders. Increase the Radius slider to improve the edge selection in areas with low contrast and/or fine detail. The larger the radius, the more gradual the edge; the smaller the radius, the more discrete the edge. Larger radius settings preserve more details along the edges but may include some artifacts. You can remove such artifacts by increasing the Contrast slider.

Standard   Quick Mask   On Black

On White   Mask

Figure 4.29 Depending on the image, different previews make it easier to see the edge detail of the selection.

Moving the Contrast slider to the right can remove artifacts along the edges. In addition, increasing the contrast retains gradual transitions in larger areas but makes slightly soft edges crisper.

Adjust the Smooth slider to reduce any jagged edges along the edge of the selection. At times this may cause some fine detail to be lost. In such cases, adjust the Radius slider to recover the detail.

The Feather slider is similar to the familiar Feather command from earlier versions of Photoshop. It produces a uniform, gradual blur along the selection edge. The Radius slider is a more sophisticated version of feathering. We recommend using the Radius slider rather than Feather.

Moving the Contract/expand slider to the left contracts the selection and moving it to the right expands the selection.

By using the Refine Selection tools, you can control the appearance of the edges of your selections to make transitions that blend naturally into the rest of the image.

Refine Edges

The Elements Refine Edge window is simpler than the CS4 tool, providing only Smooth, Feather, and Contract/Expand options, as seen here. Furthermore, the Elements version of Refine Edge has only the Standard and Quick Mask preview modes.

Color Range Tool

Photoshop ONLY

The Color Range tool has been improved in CS4. Color Range is similar to the Magic Wand tool but far more powerful. It enables you to select multiple areas of the same or different colors at one time. It's particularly useful in selecting skies when there are objects such as trees in the foreground. To access it, choose Select > Color Range. In addition, you can preview the effects of your settings as an overlay on top of your image.

The new Localized Color Cluster option is helpful when you want to make a selection of a color in one part of an image but not in another—for example, in the foreground but not the background, or blue sky but not blue water in an image. It helps you to make a more accurate selection quickly.

To use Color Range to select the sky (or anything else) in an image, take the following steps:

1. Make certain the Select box is set to Sampled Colors, and use the left eyedropper to click an area in your image to specify as the target color. (You can also use the pull-down menu from the Select box, and choose a specific color, such as blue, or highlights, midtones, or shadows; but usually it's more effective to sample the specific color in the image.) You can click directly on the image or on the small preview in the dialog box.

2. Your selection is white in the preview box. (Selected areas are white, unselected areas are black, and gray areas are blurred selection edges.)

3. Drag the Fuzziness slider to adjust the tolerance. Higher tolerances select more colors; lower values select fewer colors. The preview box shows how the Fuzziness value is affecting the selection (see Figure 4.30).

Photo by Ellen Anon

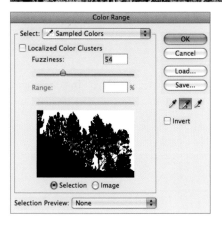

Figure 4.30 With just a couple clicks of the eyedroppers and adjusting the Fuzziness slider, you can easily select a sky from this image.

4. You'll probably need to use the Add To eyedropper (the one with the + by it) and click additional areas of the background until you have successfully identified the entire sky area. Similarly, you may need to use the Subtract From eyedropper to remove areas from the selection. As you do so, you'll have to readjust the Fuzziness slider.

5. By using one of the overlays, as shown in Figure 4.31, you can more accurately see the boundaries of your selection, making it easier to set the Fuzziness slider. Choose the selection preview that makes it easiest for you to see the edges of your selection. We often find the grayscale view helpful.

6. If you wanted to select the yellow leaves on the tall tree near the right but not the other yellow leaves, you would check the Localized Color Clusters option (Figure 4.32) and then move the Range slider toward the left to limit the geographic area that Photoshop uses for the selection. By doing this, we were able to make a very specific selection that would have required more work using any of the color selection tools. (The Range slider is only active when Localized Color Clusters is checked.)

Figure 4.31 Using the Selection Preview overlay helps you make accurate selections.

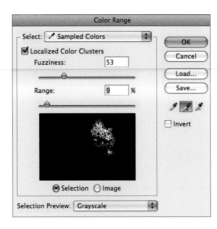

Figure 4.32 The Localized Color Clusters option makes it possible to limit the area that's selected when the color appears in multiple parts of the image.

7. When you are happy with your selection, click OK, and Photoshop turns the white area into a selection, as shown in Figure 4.33.

Figure 4.33 Selecting the sky was easy using the Color Range tool.

8. If Color Range has identified other areas that you do not want to be selected and you cannot eliminate them using the Subtract From eyedropper, the Fuzziness slider, or the Range slider, use any of the other selection tools (such as the Lasso or Magic Wand tool) to remove them from the selection.

> **Note:** You can use more than one color as the basis for your selection by selecting the middle eyedropper tool and clicking an additional color in your image. Similarly, you can use the farthest-right Eyedropper to click a color range to remove from your selection.

The Color Range tool tends to create selections with slightly blurry edges, whereas the Magic Wand creates more definite selections with anti-aliased edges. Of course, any selection can be modified using the Refine Edges tool.

The new-to-CS4 Masks panel uses the Color Range tool to help create and adjust layer masks. We'll talk more about that in Chapter 6.

Combining Tools

We've covered some of the key selection tools here to help you build a foundation for the use of tools within Photoshop as well as get you started on creating selections you'll use to apply targeted adjustments to your images. In Chapter 8, "Composites," we'll explore additional, more advanced ways of making selections. However, we want to stress here that you can *mix and match* any of the selection tools or methods in Photoshop to create the perfect selection. It's fine, and often helpful, to begin a selection with one tool and use another tool to refine it.

In the workshops we teach, we often see participants getting stuck on a single selection tool for a given task. For example, if they're trying to create a selection of the sky, they naturally start with the Magic Wand tool. If that tool isn't providing a good solution in a particular portion of the sky, we often see the person struggling to find just the right Tolerance setting and just the right pixel to click in order to get the selection perfect. The result is a lot of frustration as the photographer has to repeatedly undo a step in the selection process and then redo that step with different settings.

You can avoid (or at least minimize) this sort of frustration by combining various selection tools to create a selection. For example, when selecting a sky, you might start with the Magic Wand tool to create a basic selection and then employ the Lasso tool to clean up that selection and the areas the Magic Wand tool wasn't able to select effectively. Always keep in mind that every tool or method for creating a selection in Photoshop can be utilized in building a selection, adding to or subtracting from the selection as appropriate, using the means most appropriate for each given area of a selection as you work to create the final result.

Saving and Loading Selections

After you've created a selection, particularly if it was time-consuming and/or challenging, you probably want to save it for future use, just in case. Once you save a selection and then save the image file in an appropriate format (such as Photoshop PSD or TIFF), the selection is then saved as part of the image file, so you can always reload the selection in the future if needed.

> **Note:** Selections are saved as *alpha channels*. As you may know, RGB images are composed of individual channels that describe the amount of red, green, and blue light that should be combined to produce the color value for each pixel. An alpha channel is a special channel in addition to these RGB channels, and it is generally used to store selections for an image.

To save a selection, choose Select > Save Selection from the menu, which opens the dialog shown in Figure 4.34.

Figure 4.34 The Save Selection dialog box allows you to specify a name (as well as other settings) for the selection you are saving.

Although you can save selections in different documents with the same dimensions, it's generally best to save your selections within the image for which you've created the selection. Therefore, leave the Document setting to the default value, which is the name of the current document.

The Channel drop-down list should be set to New so the selection is saved as it is. If an existing selection has been saved, you can also choose that selection from the Channel drop-down list and merge the current selection with the previously saved selection. We don't recommend this option, because it merges two separate selections together so they can't be used separately in the future.

Name is the key setting (and generally the only one you need to change) in the Save Selection dialog box. Be sure to save the selection with a descriptive name that will make sense to you in the future when you need to load a selection, since you may be choosing a selection from a list of names when you load it.

If you're using the New option from the Channel drop-down list, the Operation section of the dialog box has only a single option to create a new channel. Otherwise, you'll have the same options as you have for each selection tool to create a new saved selection: Add to Channel, Subtract from Channel, or Intersect with Channel. When you click OK, the selection is saved as an alpha channel, which you can view on the Channels panel.

Note: Saved selections aren't truly saved until you save the image in which you stored them. If you save a selection but then close the image without saving it, the selection isn't saved.

In the future, you can "load" the selection—that is, select the same pixels once again—by choosing Select > Load Selection from the menu and choosing the name from the Channel drop-down list, as shown in Figure 4.35.

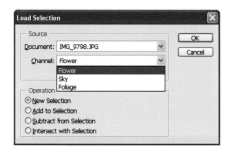

Figure 4.35 The Load Selection dialog box allows you to recall previously saved selections.

Note: Not all image file formats allow you to save selections, because they don't all allow you to save alpha channels, which is how a selection actually is stored. If you're going to save a selection, it should be part of your master image file saved as a Photoshop PSD or TIFF image file.

Saving and Loading Selections

The Save Selection dialog box in Elements, seen here, is simpler than the one in CS4 because Elements only lets you save (or load) the selection within the current document. Keep in mind that when you save a selection within a JPEG image, you will have to resave the image as a PSD or TIFF file.

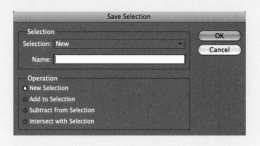

The Brush Tools

As a nature photographer using a camera to produce artistic images, you may not think you'd need to utilize the Brush tool in Photoshop. After all, if you capture an image with a camera, you certainly don't need to draw an image from scratch. However, there are actually many situations where you'll use the Brush tool while optimizing your photos. For example, we use the Brush tool extensively with Safe Dodging and Burning layers and for painting on masks to identify areas where we want targeted adjustments to apply. (We'll cover both of these topics in later chapters.)

Note: The Quick Selection tool we just covered is actually a form of a brush tool, and the Clone Stamp and Healing Brush tools are advanced types of brush tools that allow you to clean up your images. We'll cover those in Chapter 5, "Workflows and First Steps."

The Brush tool allows you to paint pixels with great flexibility. This comes in handy for a number of different adjustments you can make by painting on a layer with special properties or for painting on a mask (which you'll learn about in later chapters)—to change where adjustments will apply to your image, for example. By learning how to work with the Brush tool, you open up many opportunities for making more advanced adjustments and taking full control of your images.

To get started, create an empty document by choosing File > New from the menu. The New dialog box appears. Choose 5 × 7 from the Preset drop-down list, make sure Color Mode is set to RGB, and click OK. Then select the Brush tool either by clicking the Brush tool icon on the Tools panel or by pressing the B key.

Next, look at the color swatches on the Tools panel (see Figure 4.36). The large squares indicate the current foreground and background colors (represented by their relative positions). For painting, think of the foreground color as the color you'll actually be painting with and the background color as an alternative color you have quick access to when you need it. If you want to change either of the colors, simply click the corresponding box to open the Color Picker dialog box (shown in Figure 4.37). Click (or click and drag) the vertical color bar to define the basic color you want, click the large area to select a specific color to paint with, and then click OK.

Figure 4.36 The Color Picker area on the Tools panel shows you the current status of your foreground and background colors.

Figure 4.37 The Color Picker dialog box allows you to select a specific color value to use.

To set the colors back to the default values of black and white, click the smaller thumbnail at the bottom-left corner of the color swatches on the Tools panel. You can also set these defaults by pressing D on your keyboard.

Since the foreground and background color options are mostly a way to have two colors readily available when working with the Brush tool, you often want to be able to switch back and forth between them. At the top-right corner of the color swatches is a double-headed curved arrow. Click this icon to switch the foreground and background colors, or perform the same action by pressing X.

The Options bar contains several settings that allow you to modify the behavior of the Brush tool (see Figure 4.38). Near the far left is a Brush drop-down list where you can select the type of brush you'd like to use. Figure 4.39 shows the available options. The Master Diameter setting controls the size of the brush you're using in pixels. It's much more effective to adjust the size of the brush based on its relative size in your image, so we'll set the size in a moment. The Hardness setting determines whether your brush will have a hard edge, a soft and "fuzzy" edge, or somewhere in between. We'll discuss specific settings for various situations in later chapters, but for now experiment with different settings to get a sense of how this setting affects the brush.

Figure 4.38 The Options bar for the Brush tool contains several settings that allow you to adjust the behavior of this tool.

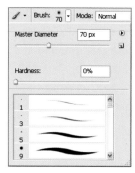

Figure 4.39 The Brush drop-down list contains several settings for adjusting the type of brush you'll use to paint.

At the bottom of the Brush drop-down list is a scrollable list containing a variety of brush shapes. The first group contains hard-edged brushes of various sizes, and the second group contains soft-edged brushes of various sizes. Below that is a variety of brushes with more artistic shapes, which you can use in a variety of applications.

Note: You can also access the options from the Brush drop-down list by right-clicking/Ctrl-clicking the image when the Brush tool is active, or at any time by clicking the Brushes panel icon in the Dock or the panel on the right .

Once you've set the basic properties of the brush, adjust the remaining settings on the Options bar. The Mode drop-down list allows you to adjust the blending mode for the brush, which affects how the "paint" you are drawing with interacts with the underlying image. We recommend leaving this set to Normal. We'll tell you under what circumstances you might need to change blending modes in later chapters.

The Opacity setting controls how opaque or transparent the paint you're drawing with appears. At full opacity, the paint completely covers the underlying pixels, effectively replacing them. At a reduced opacity, the underlying pixels show through. (Figure 4.40 illustrates these situations using both hard and soft brushes set to the same diameter.) We'll use the Opacity setting to vary the strength of the painting in several adjustments we'll discuss in later chapters, but for now play with various settings to get a sense of how they affect the behavior of the Brush tool.

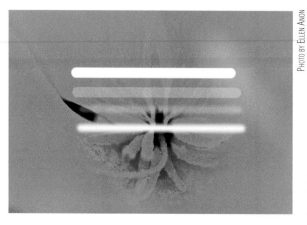

PHOTO BY ELLEN ANON

Figure 4.40 The Opacity setting allows you to determine whether your paint strokes completely cover up the pixels below them or allow them to partially show through.

The Flow setting and the Airbrush option control the variability of the Brush tool, causing it to behave like an airbrush or a can of spray paint, where the longer you hover over an area, the more the paint spreads out. Because this creates a somewhat unpredictable response from the Brush tool, we recommend leaving the Airbrush option off, which means the Flow setting is ignored.

You're just about ready to take the Brush tool for a test-drive, but you still need to adjust the size of the brush. Place the cursor on the new document you created, and evaluate the size of the brush. Then, press the left and right square bracket keys ([and]) to reduce or enlarge the size of the brush, respectively. You can hold down the Shift key while pressing the right and left bracket keys to adjust the hardness/softness, respectively, of the brush, but this isn't quite as visual as the size adjustment. For that reason we usually set the hardness/softness directly in the Brushes panel or using the dragging shortcuts below.

CS4 added the ability to drag and modify the brush tip. Once you get used to these shortcuts, they're quite useful.

- To resize the brush tip in Windows, press Alt and right-click while dragging the cursor. On a Mac, press Option+Ctrl and drag.
- To modify the softness/hardness of the brush in Windows, press Alt+Ctrl and right-click while dragging. On a Mac press Option+⌘+Ctrl while dragging.

> **Note:** To draw a horizontal or perpendicular straight line, hold down the Shift key and then click and drag the cursor.

> **Note:** The Caps Lock key toggles the mouse pointer display between Precise and the brush size settings. If you're not able to see the circle that defines the shape of your brush, check the status of Caps Lock. This is one of the most common problems we encounter in workshops!

Brushes Panel

The Brushes panel is located on the Tool Options bar when you select a brush tool, and is accessible as a panel as well. Clicking the icon opens the Brushes panel in a floating dialog box. You can select preset brushes and set the same parameters you set in the Brush Preset Picker on the Options bar, but in addition you can modify brush tip options. Most of these options are more useful to graphic artists than to nature photographers, but if you use a graphics tablet such as a Wacom, you'll need to use this dialog box to set the brush so that the opacity of your stroke varies with pen pressure. This will be useful when you're painting on layer masks. (We'll be doing that extensively in later chapters.)

To vary the opacity of your brush stroke according to the pressure applied with your stylus, follow these steps:

1. Attach the graphics tablet and install any necessary software.
2. Select the Brush tool.

3. Click the Brushes panel or go to choose Window > Brushes.

4. Select Other Dynamics. Then choose Pen Pressure from the Controls menu under the Opacity Jitter slider control, as shown in Figure 4.41.

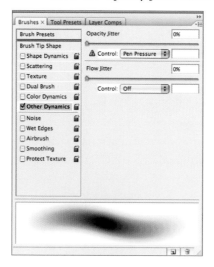

Figure 4.41 Setting Pen Pressure to control opacity is extremely useful when painting on a layer mask using a graphics tablet.

Try It! Now comes the fun part. You have an empty canvas before you, and you know how to adjust the behavior of the Brush tool. So, start painting away! Get comfortable working with the Brush tool, using the mouse (or a stylus) to paint strokes on the canvas. Be sure to adjust all the various settings for the Brush tool, including the Color, Hardness, Opacity, and the size of the brush so you get comfortable adjusting the various parameters. You can then use the Brush tool with confidence in the wide variety of situations we'll describe in later chapters.

Setting Brush Options

Elements' Brush drop-down list is simpler, having no options for Master Diameter or Hardness. To see a stroke preview, like in the Photoshop Brush drop-down, click on the More Options button ▶▶ and select Stroke Thumbnail.

Although Elements does not have a Brushes panel, if you click the Brush icon grouped with the tool options, to the right of the Airbrush Button, Elements will open the Options panel seen in the following image. Here, in addition to Hardness and Spacing, there are controls for the following:

Hardness: How discrete the edges are as you paint.

Fade: How quickly the paint fades away as you paint (similar to lifting a brush up off of a physical canvas while drawing a stroke). Lower values mean the color fades away faster, although a value of 0 means to turn fade off.

Continues

Setting Brush Options *(Continued)*

Hue Jitter: How often the brush color changes from the foreground to background color (not very useful for photographers).

Scatter: How much the brush "skips" off the page when you draw.

If you are using a tablet, clicking the small triangle ▼ grouped with the other tool options, between the Airbrush and Brush Options buttons, will bring up a panel that allows you to choose which brush options are affected by pen pressure. We recommend leaving this at the default, Size.

The Color Replacement Tool

The Color Replacement tool is a specialized Brush tool, with properties that allow you to alter the color of specific areas within your image. It produces similar behavior in most cases to what you could achieve with the Brush tool in conjunction with specific settings, but it provides extended capability above and beyond the Brush. The Color Replacement tool is useful for fixing small areas of color problems within an image, where you need to change the color without changing the tonality or texture of the area.

For this type of use, we typically work with the Color Replacement tool with the following options set:

Mode set to Color, so we're changing the color in the image.

Sampling set to Continuous (the first of the three option buttons), which causes the tool to change color anywhere we paint, not just based on an initial sampling point, for example. Occasionally we use the second button, Sampling, once to replace just a certain color.

Limits set to Contiguous, to adjust only those colors that are contiguous to those we paint over.

Tolerance at 100%, so all areas we paint on are adjusted.

When you paint with the Color Replacement tool with the settings recommended here, it changes the color of the pixels under the brush, preserving tonality and texture. For example, if you have some color contamination on a flower because a flower of a different color was very close to the lens and resulted in a wash of color that is completely out of focus, you could use this tool to paint an appropriate color to fix the flower.

Painting with a neutral color (such as black) changes the color to a shade of gray.

If you want to paint a color correction, you naturally need to find an appropriate color to paint with using the Color Replacement tool. To do so, simply hold the Alt/Option key, and click an appropriate color within the image to make that color the foreground color. You can then paint with that color in appropriate areas of the image using the Color Replacement tool to change the color as needed.

The History Brush

The History Brush tool is unique—it allows you to selectively paint certain areas of your image to take them "back in time," reflecting what they looked like before certain tasks were performed. This allows you to perform actions on the entire image and then undo those actions in specific areas as desired. Let's look at an example to help you understand this concept.

Start by opening an image and applying an artistic filter to that image. For example, you might select Filter > Artistic > Colored Pencil, adjust the settings for this filter, and click OK. Then select the History Brush 🖌 from the Tools panel. (You can also access it by pressing Y on your keyboard.)

By default, when you paint with the History Brush, it changes the areas you paint on to what they looked like when you first opened the image. However, you can change the *source* for the History Brush to any history state on the History panel. To do so, click the box to the left of the name of the history state (which defines the action performed at that step) on the History panel. This places a small History Brush icon in that box, as shown in Figure 4.42, so you know it is the source for this tool.

Figure 4.42 On the History panel, click the box to the left of the state you want to paint back to, defining the source for the History Brush tool.

For example, in your new, blank practice document, you've only opened an image and applied the Colored Pencil filter to it, so you don't have many options. However, in Figure 4.43 we changed the image from a 16-bit image to an 8-bit image in order to use the Artistic filters, so we set the History Brush to use the 8-bit history state. You can set the source to any step in the history using the same bit depth and crop to specifically select that history state as the definition of how you want to change the pixels.

With the source set, you're ready to paint. Note that you have the same options on the Options bar for the History Brush as you do for the regular Brush tool. In most cases, you want to use a soft-edged brush of an appropriate size, the Normal blending mode, and a 100% opacity. Wherever you paint, the effect of the Colored Pencil filter in this example is removed, returning those areas of the image to their original appearance, as shown in Figure 4.43. However, at times you might want to paint at a reduced Opacity setting—for example, when you want to "tone down" an adjustment in certain areas of the image rather than eliminate the effect altogether.

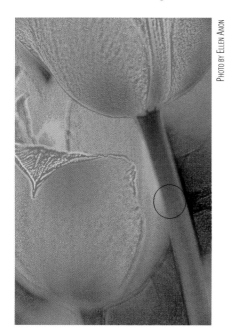

PHOTO BY ELLEN ANON

Figure 4.43 With the History Brush, you can selectively paint areas back to the way they looked before you made a particular adjustment.

Think of the History Brush as a "selective undo" tool. Anytime you've changed pixel values in an image and want to tone down or eliminate the effect in certain areas, this tool allows you to do exactly that with very good control. However, if you have made certain types of changes to your image, such as cropping it or changing the bit depth, you'll need to change the source to a state that reflects the same conditions, rather than setting it to the initial image. Otherwise, the tool refuses to work.

Building Tool Knowledge

In this chapter we explained how to use a handful of the tools you're most likely to use in Photoshop, providing you with an introduction to the use of these tools. Because so many of the tools in Photoshop behave similarly in a general sense, you can apply your knowledge of one tool to using another. Of course, in later chapters we'll describe additional tools and techniques for optimizing your images.

Workflows and First Steps

Once you have Photoshop or Elements set up the way you want it and you've used Adobe Camera Raw (ACR) to make the most of your global tonal and color changes, usually you have at least a little more work to do. If you get in the habit of following a routine approach when optimizing your images, you'll find that you work more efficiently. We'll suggest two versions of an overall workflow that you can modify to suit your particular needs. One version is more flexible and takes advantage of Smart Objects and Smart Filters, while the other is more traditional.

5

Chapter Contents

Understanding Layers

Before proceeding further with the workflow, you need to understand layers—what they are, why they're so important, and how to make them. Most Photoshop novices are initially intimidated by the concept of layers. But in reality, they're quite simple to understand.

Let's begin by thinking of a couple of prints that are the same size. If you took one print and placed it on top of the other print, you would no longer be able to see the print that's on the bottom. You know it's there, and you know if you remove the top print or make a hole in the top print that you would see the print that's underneath. But when one print is simply on top of the other, you see only the top print. Those prints are actually two layers. Agreed? In Photoshop each of these prints is called a *pixel layer*. Pixel layers contain pixels, which are the building blocks of your image. Pixel layers work much the same way as stacking prints on top of one another. Whatever pixel layer is on top is what you see.

Note: Right now we are discussing how pixel layers behave in the Normal blending mode. Later in this book we'll discuss some more advanced behaviors of layers using different blending modes. For now, we'll keep it simple.

But wait—there are actually two types of layers of concern to photographers: layers that have pixels, and adjustment layers, which don't have any pixels at all! *Adjustment layers are simply instructions for changing the appearance of the pixel layers.* For example, they may contain instructions to make the pixels lighter or darker; more or less contrasty; more or less saturated; or bluer, redder, and so on. In other words, adjustment layers modify the appearance of your image but not the content. It would be similar to putting a filter over your top print in our analogy and viewing the print through the filter. Your print would look warmer if it were a slightly yellow filter, bluer if it were a blue filter, and so on. The filter would change the appearance of your print but not the content.

Note: Adjustment layers modify the appearance of every pixel layer below them.

You could perform all the modifications you make in adjustment layers directly on your pixels by choosing Image > Adjustments and selecting the type of adjustment you want to make. *But that's exactly what we want you to avoid doing!* Every time you work directly on a pixel, you damage it and you risk losing some quality in your final output. By using *adjustment layers*, you can see the changes you have made, but they are not applied to the pixels until you either print the file or flatten it. This way, you can make multiple changes and affect the pixels only once.

Even better is the flexibility that working in layers gives you. You can return to your image at any time in the future, even after closing it, as long as you have saved the image file with the layers intact, and you'll be able to modify the adjustments you made. You can increase them, decrease them, eliminate them, and so on—all without damaging your pixels.

CS4 has made it even easier to select adjustment layers. Clicking the Adjustment panel icon ![icon] or going to Window > Adjustments opens the new Adjustment panel (shown in Figure 5.1). Choosing any of the specific adjustments automatically opens the specific Adjustment dialog and also creates a new layer in the Layers panel, Icons are shown for each of the adjustments, but when you hover your cursor over any of the icons, the name of the adjustment appears in the upper left of the dialog. Almost all the adjustments that are available from Images > Adjustments in the menu bar are available from this list. In addition, if you click the disclosure icon at the top right of the dialog , a text list of all the adjustments will appear. Alternatively, you can still click the New Adjustment Layer icon ![icon] at the bottom of the Layers panel and choose from that menu. The result will be the same and the adjustment will be performed as an adjustment layer.

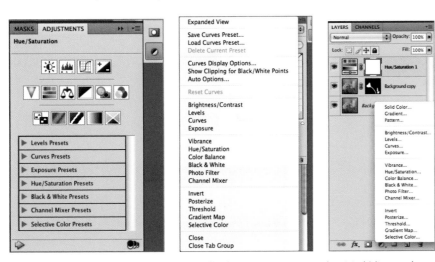

Figure 5.1 CS4 added a new Adjustment panel to use for adjustments, or you can use the original Adjustment layer icon at the bottom of the Layers palette.

Adjustment Layers

Elements users can find the available adjustment layers in the Layers panel, under the Create Adjustment Layer icon ![icon] .

We have a couple more thoughts about layers. If you place a pixel layer on top of one or more adjustment layers, the adjustment layers don't have any affect on that pixel layer because the adjustment layers are below it rather than above it. It's like taking another print and putting it on top of the stack—you're going to see what's on top, and what's underneath is not going to affect what you see.

Now imagine you have a print with a great sunset, and you have another print with a silhouette of a group of birds flying by. If you took the print with the silhouette of the birds flying and placed it on top of the sunset picture, you'd see only the silhouette picture. But you could cut the birds out of that print and lay them on top of the print below. Now you'd see the sunset with the silhouetted birds flying through it. In Photoshop this is akin to having a pixel layer that is partially transparent (the part that you removed from the print is the transparent part) and partially filled with pixels (the silhouetted birds) resting on top of the original pixel layer—the sunset. The sunset is the background layer, and the layer with the birds is only partially filled with pixels. In other words, pixel layers can be partially transparent and partially filled with pixels.

This is enough theory for now about layers, but we'll be talking more about them later in this book. Take the time to reread this section again slowly if you're feeling a little shaky about layers.

Flexible and Traditional Workflows

The goal of all the adjustments in ACR is to create the best possible file from the data collected on the camera sensor when you took the picture. Although by now the image may look pretty good, there are some things you can't do within ACR, such as applying filters, creating composites, resizing specific items, and sharpening output. And it's possible you'll want to tweak some of the exposure or color settings in parts of the image. We perform these tasks in a routine order to make the best final image possible. We'll describe how to do the various modifications in Photoshop in detail beginning here and continuing through the next few chapters, but first we need to consider our workflow.

Digital workflows are works in progress that evolve as technology and software change. With each new version of Photoshop, new features affect our workflow. For example, our workflow habits changed when adjustment layers became part of Photoshop (yes, there was a time when Photoshop had no adjustment layers), they changed when it became easy to use adjustment layers on 16-bit files, and they changed yet again when converting raw files became easy, just to mention a few of the features that caused us to modify our workflow.

With the arrival of CS3, our workflow evolved again; we established a *flexible workflow* as our recommended workflow when optimizing an image in Photoshop for future use, particularly printing. The flexible workflow takes advantage of Smart Objects and Smart Filters to maintain the most editability along with the most nondestructive workflow possible. Ultimately this leads to the highest-quality files possible.

However, there are times you may have a specific output in mind and/or need to make fewer changes and prefer to follow a more traditional workflow. We'll describe both our flexible and traditional workflows in detail so you can choose what's right for you. You'll see that both these workflows are actually quite similar. But first we'll explain Smart Objects and Smart Filters so you can better understand their roles in changing our workflows.

Note: If you are using a version of Photoshop prior to CS3 or Elements, then you'll need to follow our traditional workflow since early versions do not support Smart Objects or Smart Filters.

Smart Objects

Smart Objects were introduced in CS2, but they were of limited use for nature photographers, so we didn't readily incorporate them into our workflow. With the addition of Smart Filters and a vastly more robust ACR in CS3, we began to make use of Smart Objects.

Smart Objects are actually containers that you create within a file that can store (among other things) your original image file, including a raw file. By using a Smart Object, you embed your original raw file inside the master file you create while doing your image optimization.

The Smart Object raw file will then retain all its original characteristics and be fully editable. In other words, you can modify the settings used in ACR for your image at any time, even while in the midst of working on the file in Photoshop, and those changes will appear in the current file.

If you don't use a Smart Object, then once you choose your settings in ACR, those settings are fixed into place when you open the file in Photoshop. If you later decide that you wish you had used different settings in the conversion, you will have to start all over in ACR and then in Photoshop. But if you begin with the raw file opened as a Smart Object, double-clicking the Background layer of your file will open the ACR dialog so that you can modify the settings.

You can edit a Smart Object over and over again with no loss of image quality because the Smart Object always refers back to the original image data. This means you can repeatedly change any of the raw settings with no loss of image quality. Smart Objects also make it possible to repeatedly resize the image within Photoshop, making it larger or smaller *with no loss of quality*. For example, look at the 100 % magnification sections of water drops on a flower in Figure 5.2. The Smart Object was opened, reduced to a less than $1^2"\times 1^2$ file, then resized to a nearly 8" × 8" file. Then this process was repeated. The water droplets are still tack-sharp. The version of the file that was opened as a regular file was resized to the same nearly 1" × 1" size and then resized to nearly 8" × 8" just once, and you can easily see the tremendous loss of image quality. Being able to resize your master file offers a lot of convenience, as you'll see later. Opening your raw file as a Smart Object lends valuable flexibility to your image optimization workflow.

To open a raw file (or any other file format) as a Smart Object from ACR, check the Open in Photoshop as Smart Objects option in Workflow Options, and then choose Open Object (or in Photoshop choose File > Open as Smart Object). See Chapter 3, "Adobe Camera Raw," for more details. When the file opens, you'll see that the background layer is marked as a Smart Object, as shown in Figure 5.3.

> **Note:** A Smart Object can contain either raster or vector data from other Photoshop files or even files from other programs, such as Adobe Illustrator. You can also create a Smart Object from one or more layers of an image by selecting those layers and choosing Layer > Convert to Smart Object. You won't be able to access ACR by double-clicking those layers because in this case the Smart Object is referencing whatever was on those layers of your file rather than the raw file itself.

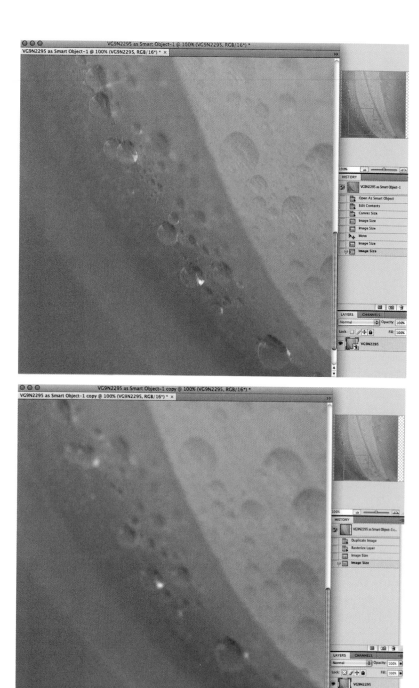

Figure 5.2 Compare the image quality in the resized Smart Object versus the resized regular image.

Figure 5.3 Smart Object layers are marked as such in the Layers panel.

Smart Filters

Smart Filters are *editable* filters. Prior to CS3 you applied a filter to a pixel layer, and once you clicked OK in the filter dialog, you had no way to modify the settings. The only exception was the Edit > Fade command, available only immediately after applying the filter, which could reduce the strength of the effect or apply it using a different blending mode. There was no way to access the filter dialog and modify your settings. Smart Filters changed that—with them your filter settings are forever editable, similar to adjustment layers.

Photoshop ONLY

The only "catch" to using Smart Filters is that they can be used only on a Smart Object layer. However, it's easy to change any pixel layer into a Smart Object by choosing Filter > Convert for Smart Filters. Photoshop will automatically change the layer so that it can receive a Smart Filter.

Any filter that can be applied as a regular filter can be applied as a Smart Filter, and a bonus is that the Shadow/Highlight adjustment can also be applied as a Smart Filter. Once you change the active layer to a Smart Object, when you select a filter, it will automatically be applied as a Smart Filter. (Pretty smart, yes?)

> **Note:** Photographers have wanted to be able to apply a Shadow/Highlight adjustment as an adjustment layer rather than directly on a pixel layer since the arrival of the Shadow/Highlight adjustment feature. Because of behind-the-scenes technical issues, it could not readily be made available as an adjustment layer. Instead, the Adobe engineers made it possible to apply the Shadow/Highlight adjustment as a Smart Filter.

An Example of Smart Filters in Action

Let's take a look at Smart Filters in action. You can follow along with the image SmartFilter on the accompanying CD.

1. Begin by opening the image SmartFilter. We'll pretend that for whatever reason we did not initially open the file as a Smart Object. (If you did open the image as a Smart Object, skip Step 2.)

2. Choose Filter > Convert to Smart Filters. A warning dialog will appear (Figure 5.4). We recommend checking the option to not have this warning reappear.

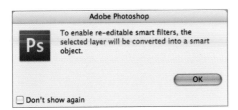

Figure 5.4 The Smart Filter warning

3. Choose Image > Adjustments > Shadow/Highlight, and adjust the settings as desired. Click OK.

> **Note:** For more details about using the Shadow/Highlight feature, see Chapter 6, "Exposure Adjustments."

4. Notice that the adjustment appears as a Smart Filter on the Background layer (Figure 5.5).

Figure 5.5 A Smart Filter in the Layers panel

There's a layer mask you can use to control which parts of the image are affected by the filters. We'll cover using layer masks in detail in Chapter 6 and in Chapter 7, "Color Adjustments."

The Smart Filter icon ⚞ leads to a new dialog, as shown in Figure 5.6, in which you can specify the opacity of the effect as well as a different blending mode. We'll talk more about these features in Chapter 9, "Creative Effects."

Figure 5.6 The Smart Filter Options dialog box lets you choose different blending modes and opacities for each filter.

To modify the settings you used in the Shadow/Highlight dialog, double-click directly on the words Shadow/Highlight in the Smart Filter layer, and make the desired changes.

5. If you want to add an additional filter, open the Filters menu and choose the desired filter. It will appear beneath the other Smart Filters in the Layers panel as shown in Figure 5.7.

Figure 5.7 You can add additional filters, and they appear as sublayers under the Smart Object layer.

6. Unfortunately, all Smart Filters are governed by the same filter mask, so if you need to apply two or more filters to different areas—for example, if you wanted to apply noise reduction to part of the image—you are forced to use a workaround.

   a. Begin the workaround by copying the initial Smart Object layer after you've applied the first filter or Shadow/Highlight adjustment. To do so, drag the original Smart Object layer to the Create New Layer icon in the Layers panel 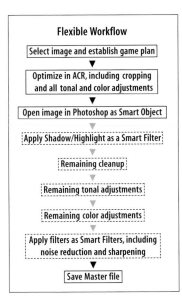. A copy of the layer is created, complete with any Smart Filters you used.

   b. Choose Layer > Smart Objects > Rasterize to change the copy layer into a regular layer containing the effects of the previous Smart Object layer.

   c. Choose Layer > New Smart Object to turn this composite layer into a Smart Object so that you can apply an additional Smart Filter, and use the associated layer mask to apply the effect to a different part of the image. Note that this Smart Object layer contains the rasterized version of the first layer, which means that if you make further changes to the first layer, they will *not* update in the second layer. Instead you'll have to re-create the second layer. This is a pitfall of the current design of Smart Objects.

As you can see, using Smart Objects and Smart Filters creates the potential for unparalleled flexibility in your workflow, with editability combined with no loss of image quality. Therefore, despite some awkwardness caused by the Smart Object mask limitations, we recommend the following to you as the backbone of your flexible workflow. Ultimately, you should modify our workflow to suit your specific needs.

The Flexible Workflow

Your image-optimization workflow begins when you initially choose an image in Bridge for further work. We find that by following a consistent series of steps, we work more efficiently. The order of the steps remains the same, although depending on the needs of each image, we may omit one or more steps. The flexible workflow is of particular benefit when working with raw files, although it can be used with JPEGs or TIFFs as well. Figure 5.8 lays out this particular plan of work.

Figure 5.8 Following the flexible workflow, and customizing it according to the needs of individual pictures, will enable you to use a single file as both the master file and the output file.

Note: To take advantage of the flexible workflow, we open raw files as well as JPEGs and TIFFs in the ACR converter, as explained in Chapter 3, "Adobe Camera Raw." If you're using a version of Photoshop prior to CS3, then you can only open raw files in ACR; JPEGs and TIFFs will open directly in Photoshop. In that case, you'll need to follow our traditional workflow and make all your modifications in Photoshop.

1. To begin, *take a good hard look at the image in ACR. Don't skip this step!* Think about what you like about the image and what aspects you want to emphasize, and decide what elements you need to modify. It's important to have an overall game plan in your head when optimizing images to keep you on track. Otherwise, it's easy not to know what to do next and even not to know when you're done! It sounds silly until it happens to you—suddenly you realize you've been working on an image for a long time and can't decide whether you're done. Having a game plan in mind makes it easier to know where you're going and when you've arrived! So, the first step is to look at the image and the histogram and decide what you want to do.

2. The next step is to use ACR to make most of the global tonal and color adjustments, in addition to cropping, straightening, and cleaning up dust. (See Chapter 3, "Adobe Camera Raw," for details.) It's important to do as much work as possible in the raw converter so that you're starting with the best image possible. Remember that with raw files almost all the settings we specify in ACR are actually changes to the algorithms used to convert the information captured by the photo sites on the sensors into a visible image, rather than changes to the pixels. Although we work as nondestructively as possible in Photoshop, ultimately all the changes we make in Photoshop modify the pixels. The greater the changes we make there, the greater the potential for some image degradation. Changes made in the raw converter do not generally result in image degradation—except when clipping is introduced or areas are cloned or cropped out. However, the changes made in ACR to JPEGs and TIFFs are changes to the actual pixels—which is one of the reasons why we recommend shooting in RAW for most nature photographers.

3. When you finish in ACR, open the image as a Smart Object. At this point your image may be done except for sizing, sharpening, and/or noise reduction, or you may need to work on it further. We consider making the following adjustments in this order. Keep in mind that on most of your images you won't need to perform all these steps.

   a. If you think your image could benefit from a Shadow/Highlight adjustment because it allows finer control than the similar Fill and Recovery tools in ACR, or because you want to apply it to only a certain part of your image, begin by making a Shadow/Highlight Smart Filter. (We'll go into detail about this in Chapter 6.) Most images will not need this step.

b. If you need to straighten and crop your image in a way that will result in needing to clone in some additional background, do that next. (Otherwise, you can crop in ACR.) We'll talk more about this later in this chapter.

c. If you need to do any further cloning/healing, it should be the next step. That way, changes to additional adjustment layers will change the work you do on this layer as well.

d. If you want to make further tonal adjustments to a particular part of your image, follow the procedures described in Chapter 6 for making targeted tonal adjustments using layer masks.

e. If you want to make further color adjustments such as a Selective color adjustment or a Color Balance adjustment taking advantage of the controls in Photoshop, or to adjust the color in a particular part of your image, follow the procedures described in Chapter 7.

f. If you want to apply any creative filters and/or noise reduction, do that next. Although some people recommend applying noise reduction earlier in the workflow, we save it for later in the process because noise is sometimes not apparent until after you make all your tonal adjustments.

g. Finally, follow the recommendations for output workflow that we cover in Chapter 10, "Output," for resizing and sharpening your images.

4. Note that by using a Smart Object as your Background layer you can do your resizing and sharpening on your master image. However, some people may feel more comfortable saving their master images without resizing and sharpening and instead create a duplicate copy, the way we recommend in our traditional workflow. The choice is yours.

No matter what workflow you follow, make it a habit to save and save often! When you first open your image after using ACR, you will need to save your image. You can opt to use PSD or TIFF formats. PSDs tend to be slightly larger, but both formats can retain the integrity of your layers. As a matter of habit, we tend to use the PSD format for layered files and TIFFs for flattened files, but you could just as easily do the opposite. By using one format for layered files and one for flattened files, it's easy to recognize which file is which. The important point is to save the image after every step that has been at all time-consuming. You never know when a computer is going to decide to crash...and in our experience, it's usually when you have been struggling and working for a long period of time and haven't saved what you're working on!

The Traditional Workflow

There are times when even those who use the flexible workflow will choose to use the traditional workflow. If you have images that you converted using another program, you may want to use the traditional workflow—illustrated in Figure 5.9—particularly if you have only a few adjustments to make.

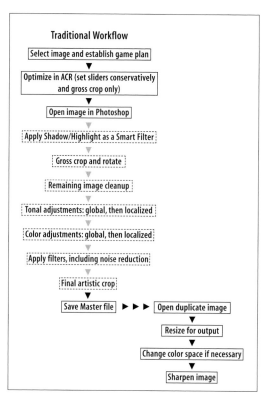

Traditional Workflow

Select image and establish game plan
▼
Optimize in ACR (set sliders conservatively and gross crop only)
▼
Open image in Photoshop
▼
Apply Shadow/Highlight as a Smart Filter
▼
Gross crop and rotate
▼
Remaining image cleanup
▼
Tonal adjustments: global, then localized
▼
Color adjustments: global, then localized
▼
Apply filters, including noise reduction
▼
Final artistic crop
▼
Save Master file ▶ ▶ ▶ Open duplicate image
▼
Resize for output
▼
Change color space if necessary
▼
Sharpen image

Figure 5.9 Following the traditional workflow, and customizing it according to the needs of individual pictures, will enable you to optimize your images efficiently.

In addition, anytime you begin by creating a composite—whether it's a panorama, creative, to extend exposure latitude, and so on—you will not have a raw file as the basis of your master file. Technically you could opt to create the composite, save it, and then open it in ACR and use the flexible workflow. The advantage would be using the ACR interface; however, many people will find it just as easy to use the traditional workflow.

Numerous combinations of these two workflows are possible, and ultimately you should establish a predictable pattern, either by following our steps exactly or by borrowing from each of the workflows to create a workflow that serves you well.

Just as with the flexible workflow, *the traditional workflow begins by looking at the image carefully and developing a strategy.* Focus on how you'll maximize the strengths of the image and remove or minimize any of its shortcomings—that's what optimizing is all about! We'll assume that this file is not a raw file and that you have opted not to use ACR to make the global adjustments, but instead have just opened it in Photoshop.

Once we have in mind the changes we want to make, we approach the adjustments in the following order:

1. If you are using a file that does not have a raw file original associated with it—for instance, if you captured in JPEG or if you created a composite file such as a panorama—begin by creating a duplicate of the image file. To do so, choose Image > Duplicate (File > Duplicate in Elements). That way you will optimize the copy and preserve the integrity of the original file in case you need to refer to it in the future. Then close the original file.

2. Begin with any initial cropping and straightening that may be needed. We'll describe how to do this using the Crop tool or the Measure tool later in this chapter. There's no sense in taking the time to correct pixels that you aren't going to use.

3. If you feel the image could benefit from a Shadow/Highlight adjustment because there are blocked-up shadows or extremely light (but not completely blown-out) areas, apply it now.

4. The next step is to remove any dust spots by using the cloning and healing tools. We'll talk more about how to do this later in this chapter. This is also a good time to remove any objects you don't want from the picture.

5. At this point you have the basic image but you need to make whatever adjustments are necessary to the exposure, including using Levels or Curves adjustment layers to bring out the details in the image. We'll explain in detail how to do this in Chapter 6.

6. After you're satisfied with the exposure, it's time to work on the color within the picture. Most images benefit from a slight boost in the saturation of the color, and sometimes you need to modify the hue or color casts within the image. You'll use adjustment layers for this, of course, and we'll talk about how to do it in detail in Chapter 7.

7. If you want to apply noise reduction or any creative filters, do so at this point.

8. With most images in the traditional workflow, you've now created the master file—the optimized version that you save without resizing it and without sharpening it.

> **Note:** Save the master file as a TIFF or a PSD file, since both allow you to save the file with the layers intact. It's not uncommon to return to an image that was previously optimized and realize that perhaps you prefer the color to be slightly different or you want more or less contrast in a particular part of the image, and so on. If the adjustment layers are there, these minor modifications are quick and easy. If you have to make them on a flattened file, then you're risking some slight image degradation by changing and therefore damaging the pixels again. In reality, such damage is likely to be slight, but since you're after the best finished product you can make, you want to save with your layers intact.

The reason to save your file without sharpening it in the traditional workflow is because sharpening must be done according to the final output size. When you resize the image—interpolating to either increase or decrease its size—you need different sharpening values. You want your master file to be at the native resolution without any interpolation since interpolation also inherently slightly degrades the image quality. We'll talk more about resizing and sharpening in Chapter 10.

Following this same basic series of steps with each image allows you to work efficiently and without needless repetitive steps that might conflict with one another.

Of course, there are times some of the steps in the traditional workflow aren't necessary, and those steps are omitted. You'll have to decide what your image needs are and how much you want to fine-tune the exposure and color within your image.

Cropping and Straightening in Photoshop

We'll begin by assuming you're using the traditional workflow and that you have opted not to use ACR with a JPEG, a slide from a scan, or a composite. We're going to go through our routine traditional workflow in detail. Of course, if you've used the flexible workflow, you could opt to use any of these steps as well.

Cropping

Many people are unaware that cropping can be done nondestructively within Photoshop. This means that in Photoshop you have the added security of knowing that you can opt to modify the crop later in the workflow if you change your mind.

To nondestructively crop an image, take the following steps:

1. *Unlock the background layer* by double-clicking it in the Layers panel and clicking OK in the dialog that appears. This is essential if you want to be able to preserve the nondestructive nature of the cropping even after you save the image.

2. Select the Crop tool ⛏ by clicking it.

3. To mark out a crop manually—without constraints on height, width, or resolution—place your cursor in any corner of the image approximately where you want to begin the crop, click, and drag diagonally, releasing the cursor after you are close to where you want the crop to end. The area to be cropped out darkens so you can preview how the image will look.

4. To crop your image to a particular aspect ratio—for example, 8 × 10—you can set these values in the Options bar at the top of your screen, as shown in Figure 5.10, and then click and drag within the image. To clear these settings, click the Clear button. Alternatively, you can use one of the Crop Tool Preset values, accessible by clicking the Crop tool icon at the left of the toolbar. (If desired, you can also specify the image resolution to use so that you can crop and resize in one step; however, we don't recommend this if you're working on your master file. We prefer to resize a copy of the master file later for specific output use.)

Note: To create a custom preset value for the Crop tool, fill in the desired values in the toolbar for height, width, and resolution. You can opt to leave the resolution blank. Click the disclosure arrow in the Crop tool's drop-down menu at the top left of the interface. Click on the small right-facing triangle and choose New Tool Preset. An interface will appear that lets you set the name for the preset. Click OK and your preset will appear in the Crop tool's drop-down menu. That can be extremely helpful if you routinely crop to a size that's not included in the presets.

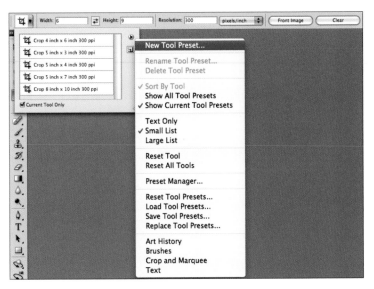

Figure 5.10 You can enter specific dimensions to crop your image to any desired size or use a preset value.

5. The Options bar changes, adding a Shield check box, which controls how, and whether, the area to be cropped away is darkened. Select the color and opacity of the shield by clicking the color swatch. We recommend leaving the Shield box checked and the color set to black at 75% opacity. This way, you get an effective preview of your crop for most images. If the outer edges of your image are quite dark, you may want to use a different color for the Shield.

6. Fine-tune the crop boundary. You can change the size and proportion of the crop (if you're using a freehand crop rather than a specific aspect ratio) by dragging the handles at the sides and corners of the boundary. To reposition the crop within your image, place your cursor within the remaining image area, click, and drag. If you entered both Height and Width values before you started, you can change the size of the crop area but not its proportion.

7. *Check the option to Hide rather than Delete,* as shown in Figure 5.11—this is what makes the cropping editable at a later point in the workflow.

Figure 5.11 Choose Hide rather than Delete in order to crop nondestructively.

Note: Although it's not often needed in nature photography, if you check the Perspective box, you can transform the crop by pulling out the corners as desired. You can use this feature to straighten buildings that appear to be tipping away.

8. Once the crop boundary is where you want it to be, to make Photoshop perform the crop do one of the following: Press Enter/Return, double-click within the image area, or click the check mark on the Options bar.

9. When you save the image, you must save the file as a TIFF or PSD with layers in order to maintain the nondestructive aspect of the cropping. If you save without the layers or as a JPEG, the cropping will become final.

Note: In Photoshop, to crop an image to match the dimensions of another image, open both images. Click the one that has the correct dimensions, click Front Image, and then click the other image. Notice that the dimensions of the first image are specified in the Height, Width, and Resolution boxes. You can now readily crop your second image to match the size of the first.

Cropping

The cropping controls in Elements are more limited and cropping remains a destructive process. Therefore, if there is some portion of your image that you're absolutely positive you would never want to be included in your final image, it's a good idea to crop it out at the beginning of your workflow. This includes cropping those black edges that often appear with slide scans. Those black edges can throw off the histograms as well as the tonal adjustments you'll be making. We recommend that you not do a final tight artistic crop initially, because by the time you're done optimizing the image, you may change your mind and want a tad less cropped out. If you did a tight crop at the beginning, you would have to start all over again. To be conservative, wait to do your final crop at the end of your workflow just prior to outputting your image.

Elements users can skip Step 1 of the PS cropping steps. Also, with Elements no additional options appear in the toolbar after drawing the initial crop. The shield is set automatically.

Elements does provide two useful options that CS4 does not. First, in the toolbar there is a pop-up Aspect Ratio menu that lets you specify preset aspect ratios to crop to, including an option called Use Photo Ratio that makes the aspect ratio the same as your image's aspect ratio.

Second, after you drag out a crop box, Elements displays two controls with the crop box, which allow you to accept or dismiss the crop.

Straightening Horizons

This is an easy way to straighten a horizon while using the Crop tool:

1. Begin by using the tool to draw a crop on the image. Don't worry about placing it precisely yet.

2. Click the small square box in the middle of the horizontal line closest to the horizon, and drag it so that it is just on top of the horizon.

3. Place your cursor outside the crop area. Notice it changes from an arrowhead to a double-arrowed icon. Click and drag it up or down to rotate the crop, and make the horizontal line follow your horizon, as shown in Figure 5.12. When you are satisfied that the crop line parallels the horizon line, release the cursor.

Figure 5.12 Drag one edge of the crop close to the horizon, and then rotate it until it parallels the horizon line.

4. Click the center box on that crop line to drag it back to an appropriate place in your image. The rotation of the crop should remain as you reset all the outside edges, as you can see in Figure 5.13.

Figure 5.13 Carefully drag the edges of the crop where you want them while leaving the rotation alone.

5. Be careful not to drag the corners of the crop beyond your image, or you'll have empty areas in the cropped version that you'll need to create a background for or recrop. However, in some instances it might actually be better to go too far than not far enough.

Now when you press Enter/Return or double-click the image to perform the crop, it rotates the image as well as straightens it in one step, as illustrated in Figure 5.14. That's pretty cool and very convenient!

PHOTO BY ELLEN ANON

Figure 5.14 Cropping and rotating the image in one step is easy and saves time.

An alternative method in Photoshop for straightening an image, and one that is particularly effective with reflections, is to use the Measure tool, located with the eyedropper tools. Click the subject's eyes or other identifiable point and then drag to the same point in the reflection. Choose Image > Rotate Canvas > Arbitrary. A dialog will appear that has the precise angle and direction needed to rotate the canvas. Click OK, and the image will be straightened. You'll need to crop the image after straightening it.

Try It! Open the image called Straighten on the accompanying CD, or an image of your own, and use the Crop tool to straighten the horizon.

Alternative Straightening

Photoshop Elements 6 provides two other ways to straighten an image, one automatic and one manual. To let Elements try to straighten your image automatically, select Image > Rotate > Straighten Image. When you straighten your image, because Elements is rotating the image there will be blank canvas around the corners. Although there is a Straighten and Crop Image option, we recommend doing the crop manually so that you can opt to fill in any blank canvas areas or simply crop them out.

Continues

Doing Cleanup in Photoshop

Although some recent cameras have automatic sensor cleaning, dirt can still accumulate on the sensor and be visible in your image. Therefore, you have to carefully go through your images and remove these blobs. Scanned images also often have dust and/or scratches on them that you need to remove. First we'll describe four tools in Photoshop that you can use, and then we'll go through the actual steps to use on an image.

Note: Even if you used ACR, you may prefer to do your cleanup in Photoshop if there are complicated areas that need work.

The Photoshop Cleanup Tools

The Clone Stamp tool, the Healing Brush tool, the Spot Healing Brush tool, and the Patch tool are all useful in removing dust spots, removing unwanted objects from your image, and even filling in areas when you need to enlarge your canvas. They're very similar tools, but they're also different in some important ways.

When using any of these tools, we always begin by creating a new layer for the cleanup. To do so, click the Create New Layer icon 🔲 at the bottom of the Layers panel next to the trash can. This creates an empty pixel layer on which you will place new pixels to hide the imperfections in your image. By doing the cleanup on a separate layer, you don't have to worry about permanently changing any pixels in the file. (You can't use these tools directly on a Smart Object layer.)

The Clone Stamp tool ![icon] may be the easiest to understand. It simply copies the pixels that you specify from one place to another place. To use it, do the following:

1. Place the cursor over the area from which you want to sample.

2. Hold down the Alt/Option key, and click.

3. Release the Alt/Option key.

4. Position the cursor over the area that you want to replace, and click. It's that simple!

If you just keep clicking to sample an area and then clicking to put it somewhere else, you're likely to end up with a series of circular replacements that are easy to spot. On the other hand, if you click and drag for long distances, you're likely to get repeated patterns that are also a telltale sign of a poorly optimized image. The trick is to just drag a smidge around the replacement area and make certain not to have an identifiable repeated pattern.

Most of the time you should make sure to use a soft brush and adjust the size of the brush, using the bracket shortcut keys as explained in Chapter 4 ("Foundations") so that the brush is just slightly larger than the smaller dimension of the dust you're trying to remove. If you are cloning out a large area, you'll have to use a small enough brush to be able to convincingly re-create the background. You need to think like an artist and select pixels to use to re-create that area of the picture.

It's important to remember to have Sample All Layers checked in the Options bar at the top of your screen. If it seems like nothing is happening, it's probably because this isn't checked. Also make sure the No Adjustment Layers icon ![icon] in the Options bar is turned on so that adjustment layers are ignored when cloning. That way, if you return to the cleanup layer after you've made some further adjustments, you won't have to manually turn off the adjustment layers as you did with versions of Photoshop prior to CS3. (Otherwise, if you clone on a lower layer after you've added adjustment layers, the adjustments are applied twice to the cloned pixels and that causes the cloned areas not to match the image.)

Most of the time, you also want Aligned checked. This means that the source you are sampling from moves in conjunction with the movement of the cursor at the destination. Otherwise, every time you unclick and then click to continue cloning, the source resets to where you initially began sampling. That tends to cause repeated patterns.

There is a Clone Source Panel (Figure 5.15) in Photoshop (but not Elements) in which you can specify several different sources for your cloning. The sources can be located in the same image or in different images. To create a source preset, click one of the Clone Source icons, then hold the Alt/Option key and click the desired point in the image; a target with a number will mark that spot. This is helpful so you can easily identify which clone source to use. Although we don't often find this too useful with nature images, you may encounter certain situations where using multiple source presets would be very helpful. For example, if you removed an object or added canvas and need to create a new area of background, it might be helpful to have several different source points preselected on other images with similar backgrounds.

Figure 5.15 The Clone Source Panel adds features to the Clone Stamp tool, including presets and the Show Overlay option.

However, we do find that the Show Overlay option can be helpful. By checking this option, an overlay of the source you're using appears superimposed on your image. That makes it easier to know how far to drag when cloning. This is particularly helpful when you're repositioning an object within an image, as shown in Figure 5.16. However, sometimes seeing the overlay follow your cursor is annoying. There is an option to use the overlay when it's helpful and turn it off at other times; it's not something that we always or never use.

PHOTO BY ELLEN ANON

Figure 5.16 Using the overlay made it easy to move the swans.

Elements does have options for showing an overlay. To reveal them, click the Overlay button ▣ in the Workspace Buttons bar.

The Healing Brush tool ⬭ operates very similarly to the Clone Stamp tool. Press Alt/Option and click to define the source area, then release the Alt/Option key and click the area you want to change (the destination). However, the Healing Brush copies the *texture* of the source area and blends the colors so that a natural-looking correction results, in which texture has been added and color has been blended from the source and destination. This can be quite useful to create natural-looking corrections, especially in areas of sky and clouds. Its behavior initially seems less predictable when used near edges with strongly contrasting tonalities. In the Options bar, make sure that Source: Sampled is checked and that Pattern is unchecked. As with the Clone Stamp tool, you usually want Aligned and Sample All Layers checked as well. Adjust the brush size and hardness as with the Clone tool.

The Spot Healing Brush ⬭ operates like a "smart" Healing Brush. You don't have to define a source; instead you simply click the tool and then click and drag your cursor over the area that needs fixing. This can work extremely quickly and efficiently in areas of low detail such as sky and clouds, but at other times you may prefer the additional control of being able to specify the precise source that the Healing Brush uses.

Make certain Proximity Match is selected in the Options bar. Usually the Spot Healing Brush works best if the brush is a little larger than the narrowest dimension of the area to replace, but just one click of the bracket keys larger than what you would use with the regular Healing Brush. We've found that the Spot Healing Brush can be a huge time-saver.

Note: If initially the Spot Healing Brush gives you an unacceptable result, adjust the size with the bracket key to slightly larger or smaller, and try again. Often a slight adjustment to the brush size or the direction that you drag enables Spot Healing to work effectively.

Using these tools well takes some practice. Be careful not to create repeated patterns that make it obvious you "fixed" something. Taking the time to do a careful job in removing unwanted areas and re-creating background areas is well worth it if you want the image to look natural.

Try It! To get familiar with the behavior of these tools, open the image called Cloning on the accompanying CD, and play with each tool, noting what happens when you sample in one colored or textured area and then try to heal or clone to the same or a different area. See how each tool behaves in each situation and near edges.

The Patch tool is the fourth cleanup tool. It can save time in repairing larger areas. To use the Patch tool, click the ⟳ icon from under the Healing Brush tool. Then choose Source in the Toolbar Options. Make a selection around the area that needs fixing, and then drag the selection to other areas of the image to find one that is suitable. Similar to the other healing tools, the Patch tool will copy texture and blend color.

Darrell Gulin offers the following cleanup suggestion based on his workflow for creating dramatic images of butterflies and moths.

Repairing Wings Using the Patch Tool

by Darrell Gulin

When I am working with raising and photographing moths and butterflies, they can damage their wings and scales so easily. The Patch tool has been a lifesaver for me to fix minor—and sometimes not so minor—damage to their wings.

Continues

Zooming, Navigating, and Layering for Cleanup

To remove dust or scratches, you first need to zoom to a 100% view by double-clicking the Zoom tool. You need to check your image in a systematic way to ensure you don't miss any areas. We recommend beginning in the upper-right corner. Make sure the blue scroll bars are as far to the right and the top as they go, as shown in Figure 5.17. To navigate through the image, you can drag one of the scroll bars. When you reach the other side, place the cursor in the white area next to the other scroll bar, and click. This advances that scroll bar to the next unit so you don't miss anything. Continue this process throughout the image.

Figure 5.17 Begin navigating through your image in a systematic way by placing the blue scroll bars at the top of the vertical axis and to the right on the horizontal axis.

CS4 added the ability to flick to scroll. If you've set this option in your Preferences (see Chapter 4, "Foundations"), you can drag the Hand tool, let go, and have the image continue to scroll. The direction and speed of your drag determine the direction and distance that Photoshop will continue to scroll after you release the cursor. Once you try it, you're likely to find that not only is it fun, it's actually an efficient way to scroll!

Next, rather than doing any cleanup directly on the Background layer, make a new pixel layer for your cloning and healing. To make a new pixel layer that initially has no pixels in it, click the Create New Layer icon ▣ next to the trash can icon at the bottom of the Layers panel. (In Elements, the New Layer button is on the top of the Layers palette, to the left of the Create Adjustment Layer button.) Notice in the panel that a new layer has appeared. To name this layer—so you know what you were doing in it if you return to the file later—double-click the words *Layer One*, and then type the new name. You want a short but clearly identifiable name, such as Cleanup or Dust and Scratches, as shown in Figure 5.18.

Figure 5.18 Make a new layer to do your cleaning up on, and be sure to label the layer.

Birds-Eye View

CS4 added a new method of zooming in and out of an image called Birds-Eye View. You begin with an image that's magnified so that only part of it is visible on the monitor. Press and hold the H key, then when you left-click and hold, the image will zoom out so that you can see it in its entirety, thus giving you the opportunity to select a new area for magnification. Drag the red navigation box to a new area to view a different part of the image at the specified magnification. When you release the cursor, the image will snap to the prior level of magnification centered on the new area.

Photoshop ONLY

This ability to easily zoom out and return to the magnified view can be quite helpful—particularly when you're not certain whether something is dirt or dust to be removed, or a part of the image.

Once you're familiar with the tools, you've examined your photo, and you have a layer available, you're ready to clean up your image.

Removing Dust

In most cases, removing the spots created by dust and dirt on your camera's imaging sensor is a relatively easy job. Create a new layer as described in the previous section, zoom in, and begin carefully navigating throughout your image, checking for dust (see Figure 5.19). Our first-choice tools for removing these spots, particularly in sky areas, are the Spot Healing Brush and the Healing Brush. Often they blend the corrections seamlessly into the image with little effort. However, sometimes you'll find that the Clone Stamp tool is a better choice, particular when working in areas of high detail. You'll know quickly whether one of the Healing brushes is going to work.

PHOTO BY ELLEN ANON

Figure 5.19 Carefully navigate through your picture at 100% magnification to find the dark blobs resulting from dust on your camera's sensor.

Whether you're using the Clone tool or one of the Healing brushes to remove dust spots, select a brush size just barely larger than the smallest dimension of the offending spot. For example, if it's a hair, the brush should be just wider than the width of the hair. Click and drag the tool along the length of the hair to remove it. The brush doesn't need to be large enough to cover the whole thing in one click. In fact, more often than not you'll run into trouble if you try to do that. Sometimes you need to zoom in even further and use a very tiny brush.

The single most important trick to remember to successfully use these tools is to click and then drag the cursor just a smidge. This avoids the appearance of "correction circles."

Try It! Open the image named Dust from the accompanying CD or open an image of your own, and practice removing the dust spots.

Removing an Undesirable Object

Eliminating an object—whether it be a branch, a bird, an animal part, or whatever has crept uninvited into your image—is very similar to removing dust. But doing a good job requires finesse, patience, and practice. In fact, careful cloning is actually an advanced technique!

> **Note:** Sloppy cloning is one of the telltale signs of a poorly optimized image. If you've done your job well, no one should have a clue that anything was removed from the image.

When you decide to remove an object from your image, you need to think even more like an artist. Imagine what the background would look like if you could see through the offending object, and then work to create that background by using the existing pixels in the rest of the picture or by borrowing pixels from another picture.

Often you'll need to begin by using the Clone Stamp tool. Zoom in to focus on that portion of your image so you can work precisely. Click and drag the cursor a small distance to "paint" over the offending object, and then sample another spot and continue working. Balance dragging the cursor with resampling.

After you have hidden an object, look at the area even more carefully. If you are creating something with distinct patterns or textures, such as grasses or ocean waves, you should probably work with the Healing Brush on top of the cloned area. Sample from a variety of different areas where the lighting, size, and direction of the textures match what you need to fill the spot. You can also vary the opacity of the Clone Stamp tool or the Healing Brush, along with their sizes, by changing the Opacity setting in the Options bar. By combining these different approaches and tools, you can create a very natural-looking replacement area.

Cloning from a Separate Image

You can use an entirely different image as the source for your cloning. Open both images, making certain they are the same size, resolution, and color space. Place your cursor on the image you want to copy from, and click while holding the Alt/Option key; then release the Alt/Option key, place the cursor on the other image where you'd like to replace the pixels, and click and drag.

Here's a trick to make it easy to remove an object that comes right up to your subject—for example, a stick that comes right up to a bird's body, or another bird that's partially visible. Before you do any cloning or healing, use the Lasso tool or another selection tool to carefully outline the part of the subject that you need to protect, and then make a loose selection into the area where you'll be working, as shown in Figure 5.20. When you do your cloning and healing, Photoshop does not allow the effects to extend beyond the boundaries of the selection you just made. That way, you don't have to worry about accidentally affecting your subject.

Figure 5.20 By making a selection before you do your cloning or healing, you can protect your subject matter so you don't accidentally damage it while fixing another part of your image.

Try It! Open the image named Extra Pelicans from the accompanying CD, and remove the background pelicans while creating natural-looking water. Don't worry if it takes you more than one try. It takes many people more practice than they think it will, but once you get the hang of it, it'll be an invaluable skill to have.

Creating New Background on Empty Canvas

Sometimes your subject is too tight in the frame, whether because you framed it poorly, the subject moved, you cropped the image, or you had too long a lens for the subject. No matter what the cause, you can add canvas to remedy the situation and then clone/heal in new background.

To increase the canvas size to allow more space around your subject, choose Image > Canvas Size. (Elements users can find canvas resizing under Image > Resize >

PHOTO BY ELLEN ANON

Canvas Size.) The dialog tells you the current size of your image. In that dialog, take the following actions:

1. Check the Relative box. This tells Photoshop that the number you put in the box is the number of inches or pixels (depending on the unit you choose) to *add* to your image.

2. Fill in the desired increase in pixels or inches.

3. To specify where to add the additional canvas (top, bottom, right, or left), click in the Anchor area (shown here) to anchor the image on one or two sides. In this way, you can choose to add canvas to one, two, three, or four sides of your image, depending on where you anchor it.

4. You can also specify what color to make this new canvas:

    a. To get a jump-start on creating a new background, choose Other from the drop-down menu. This opens the Color Picker dialog.

    b. The cursor turns into an eyedropper icon; click a similar background color in the image.

    c. Click OK in the Color Picker dialog.

5. Now click OK in the Canvas Size dialog. Your newly added canvas starts out in a similar color to what will be needed.

At this point you can use the Healing Brush along with the Clone Stamp tool to create the patterns and tonalities that you would expect to see there. Don't forget to alternate between the tools as necessary. Again, you're going to have to use some artistic imagination to visualize how this additional background might have looked and then create it from pixels in other places in your image or by sampling pixels from similar images.

Note: An alternate quick way to expand your canvas is to use the Crop tool to draw around your image. Drag one or more of the side boundaries of the crop out beyond the image. Click OK, and your image will be cropped (which means expanded in this case) using the background color in your Tools panel.

Try It! Open the image named Add Canvas from the accompanying CD, and try adding canvas while making the background appear natural.

We've covered a lot of territory in this chapter, beginning with deciding on a workflow, followed by the initial steps we routinely take in optimizing our images. Each step is a building block to make your final image the best it can be. In the next chapter, we'll cover ways to improve the exposure to maximize the detail and impact of your image.

Exposure Adjustments

Nature photography—and all photography for that matter—is about light and creating a proper exposure that records that light. Once you've captured the optimal exposure, you can use Photoshop to make the most of the information you've captured. As you've already seen, we make most of our global exposure adjustments in Adobe Camera Raw (ACR). In this chapter, we'll guide you through methods to fine-tune the exposure for your images in Photoshop, many of which are quite similar to those found in ACR, and then discuss how to limit those tonal corrections to specific parts of your image.

6

Chapter Contents

Shooting for Optimal Exposure

The ability to perform exposure adjustments in imaging software leads some photographers to feel they can be a little less careful during the original capture. We strongly advise you against believing that. Creating the very best images in a digital workflow requires that you start with the very best quality. Therefore, focus on creating the best exposures in the field, and select only your very best exposures to work on in Photoshop (see Figure 6.1). By ensuring you have achieved an appropriate exposure in the original capture, you'll achieve maximum detail in the image. Your adjustments can then focus on revealing the maximum amount of detail possible and emphasizing particular areas of your image, as we'll discuss in this chapter.

Figure 6.1 Achieving optimal exposure is an important first step for any photograph. It is especially important when you need to preserve detail in shadow areas, such as in the dark areas of this scene.

As we discussed in Chapter 3, "Adobe Camera Raw," in Photoshop CS4 you can make most, if not all, your global adjustments in ACR not only for raw files, but also for JPEGs and TIFFs. However, there are times you'll choose to use the original tools within Photoshop as well. For example, you may want to tweak the settings you used for your conversion—particularly if you opted to use a converter other than ACR—or you may want to create an adjustment to apply to just one part of your image. In addition, the exposure tools in ACR and Photoshop are very similar, but sometimes they differ in significant ways that will make you favor one over the other.

When considering the best exposure, keep in mind Michael Reichmann's advice back in Chapter 1, "Thinking Digitally," to "expose to the right" in the camera.

Using CS4 Adjustment Panel

In Photoshop we make adjustments using adjustment layers rather than making the adjustments directly on the pixels themselves. This is beneficial in several ways. It allows more flexibility in the adjustments so that you can tweak them repeatedly if necessary. Additionally, it often results in a higher-quality image because the pixels themselves are not changed until the image is output. Before we talk about any of the specific adjustments—including the exposure adjustments as well as the color adjustments that we'll cover in Chapter 7—you need to understand how the Adjustments panel works.

CS4 introduced a new Adjustments panel and a Masks panel that share a panel group. You can access these directly by going to Window > Adjustments and Window > Masks. We'll talk about the Masks panel later in the chapter. If you click the Adjustment icon at the bottom of the Layers panel the way you did in earlier versions of Photoshop, the Adjustments panel will open, set to the specific adjustment you've chosen.

When you first view the Adjustments panel, it will appear as shown in Figure 6.2. Hover your cursor over the icons to see the name of each adjustment, then click on one to access that specific adjustment. Although you can choose among specific default presets, we rarely find them useful.

Figure 6.2 CS4 has a new Adjustments panel to access adjustments.

Once you open any of the adjustments, the specific dialog will be customized according to the particular adjustment, but the icons on the bottom, as shown in Figure 6.3, are common to all the adjustments. At the left of that row of icons is an arrow . Click it to return to the main adjustment panel to choose other adjustments. Next is the icon, which you can click to enlarge the dialog box or return it to standard size. The next icon toggles between making the adjustment layer affect all layers beneath it or just the layer immediately underneath it. Most of the time you'll want it to affect all the layers beneath it, but occasionally it's helpful to clip an adjustment to the layer immediately beneath it. The eye icon toggles the visibility of the adjustment layer. Toggling this icon is helpful so you can compare the image with and without the adjustment. Next is the icon that lets you preview the previous state. This is helpful when you're tweaking an adjustment and want to see whether the change you just made was helpful. Click the 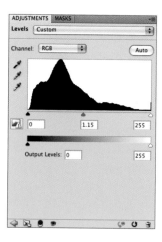 icon to reset the adjustment to its default values. Click the trashcan icon 🗑 to delete the adjustment layer entirely.

Figure 6.3 Each adjustment shares common tools along the bottom of the panel.

The amount of control that's immediately accessible from within the Adjustments and Masks panels is impressive! We'll give examples of how to use these new panels as we progress through this chapter.

Adjustment Layers

Elements users should also make their adjustments using layers rather than directly on the pixels. To access adjustment layers in Elements, click the 🖼 in the Layers palette and choose the desired adjustment. This will automatically create an adjustment layer.

Tonal Adjustments with Levels

The Levels adjustment provides good basic control over tonal adjustments for your images, with the capability to adjust contrast by independently controlling shadows and highlights within your image, as well as to adjust the overall brightness. In ACR you can make similar adjustments by setting the Exposure, Blacks, and Brightness sliders. However, there are still times you may choose to use Levels within Photoshop, particularly if you want to make changes to only one area of your image. We'll talk about making localized adjustments later in the chapter, but first we'll cover how to use Levels to make a global adjustment. We recommend using Levels to adjust contrast and brightness rather than the adjustment called "Brightness and Contrast" because the Levels adjustment offers far more accurate control of your settings. In addition, you may opt to use Curves to increase the contrast in a particular range of tonalities rather than throughout the entire tonal range. We'll talk about Curves later in this chapter.

The primary component of the Levels dialog box is a histogram display (shown earlier in Figure 6.3) that charts the distribution of tonal values within your image. Those values are represented from black at the extreme left to white at the extreme right. This gradation of tonal values appears as a gradient bar along the bottom of the histogram chart. The shape of the histogram chart tells you about the distribution of tonal values within the image. For example, histogram data that is shifted toward the left indicates that the image is generally dark. However, that doesn't necessarily tell you anything about the quality of the image; it may simply be a dark scene. Similarly, a brighter image has a histogram shifted toward the right.

The key things to watch out for on the Levels histogram are clipping and gapping. *Clipping* is an indication that information has been lost in the highlights or shadows of your image. *Gapping* is represented by gaps in the histogram and indicates tonal values that are not represented in your image.

Clipping is indicated on the histogram display by data running off the end of the chart. Clipping may be displayed in two ways. One is as a thin spike at one end of the chart. This is most commonly seen at the highlight end and is often caused by specular highlights within your image, such as reflections from water, glass, or metal. In other words, it isn't necessarily a major problem within the image because you don't expect to see detail in such highlights.

Note: As we mentioned in Chapter 1, clipping seen in a luminosity histogram always indicates that some pixels in your image are pure black or pure white, but clipping in an RGB histogram can occur when one or more channels has a value of 0 or 255. In such cases, there may or may not be black or white pixels in your image. For example, pure red would have RGB values of 255, 0, 0 and would indicate potential clipping at both ends of the histogram, even though the pixels are pure red, not black or white. The histogram in Levels shows RGB information or individual histograms for each of the channels.

The other type of clipping is more likely to represent a problem within your image, especially if it occurs in the highlights where it is usually important to retain detail. In this type of clipping, the data of the histogram gets cut off abruptly at the end of the chart (see Figure 6.4) rather than ending gracefully before the chart ends. If you think of the histogram as representing a mountain range, ideally the mountains should gradually drop down to the flatland before the chart ends. If instead the mountains end suddenly in a steep cliff, detail is lost in the area that would have gradually lowered to the base of the chart. All pixels within the "missing" tonal values have been clipped to the minimum (pure black without detail) or maximum (pure white without detail) value at that end of the histogram.

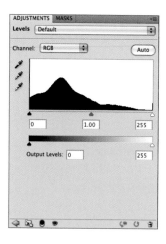

Figure 6.4 Clipping of data in your image is exhibited by a histogram chart that appears "cut off" at one end, as with the shadows here.

> **Note:** Remember, the correct shape of a histogram will vary according to the distribution of tonalities in your image. Not all subjects will have "mountains" as the correct shape of their histogram; some may have an even distribution of pixels throughout the tonal range, others may have several "mountains," and so on. Refer to Chapter 1 for more information about histograms.

Ideally, your image shouldn't exhibit any clipping when you get started with your adjustments. If it does, it is often preferable that the clipping occur in the shadows rather than in the highlights, because your eyes are usually more forgiving of lost shadow detail in a photographic image than blown highlights. However, be careful not to *produce* excessive clipping because of creating additional contrast as a result of your adjustments in Levels.

> **Note:** There are times that you may deliberately create clipping in the highlights. For example, if you are shooting a scenic and the sky is a very light and boring gray, you may choose to overexpose the scene to make it easier to replace the sky. If you do, make certain you're not also blowing out highlights in the rest of your subject matter. Additionally, if a scene is overly contrasty and you are shooting several versions of it to make an exposure latitude composite (a single image that contains data from two or more differentially exposed versions of the same scene—see Chapter 8, "Composites," for more details), some versions will have clipping in the shadows and others in the highlights.

Another potential problem to be aware of as you make adjustments is gapping in the histogram. Think of the histogram chart as a bar chart consisting of many narrow bars so that the final result typically looks like a curving data display rather than one composed of individual bars. However, when gapping occurs, you start to see the individual bars that create the data display, as shown in Figure 6.5. Gapping indicates that certain tonal values are not represented by any pixels in the image (or are represented, but only by very few pixels).

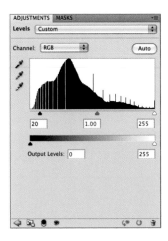

Figure 6.5 Gaps in the histogram indicate tonal values that are not represented within the image.

Gaps in the tonal values indicate that smooth and subtle transitions between tones and colors within the image may be compromised. Instead of making a gradual change from one value to another with 10 values in between, for example, the transition may be from one value to another without any transition values between them. This lack of smooth gradations is referred to as *posterization* (see Figure 6.6). This sort of flaw isn't often seen out of the camera, but rather by making strong adjustments in Photoshop, particularly in 8-bit images.

Figure 6.6 Posterization is represented by a lack of smooth gradations within an image.

Note: Gaps in the histogram rarely occur for 16-bit files because many more values are available than the 256 represented by the histogram display. Sixteen-bit files have 65,536 tonal values per color channel available, compared to 256 values per channel for an 8-bit file. As a result, 16-bit files can lose a significant number of tonal values without obvious gapping or posterization.

However, gaps in a histogram are not an absolute indication of a serious problem with your image. Minor gaps only a few pixels wide, representing just a few tonal values, aren't likely to be visible to the human eye. In fact, it isn't until the gaps become relatively extreme (at least 10 tonal values) that they are likely to be potentially visible in the final output. Although gaps certainly indicate a potential problem, they don't define image quality by themselves. If you have significant gapping in an image, use caution not to make extreme adjustments that may worsen the situation, and closely evaluate the final image at 100% magnification to ensure there isn't visible posterization.

Note: Ultimately your goal is to provide the best-looking image, not the best-looking histogram! So if a histogram exhibits gapping, consider it a caution to carefully check the appearance of your image, but don't consider gapping a problem if the image looks good.

Revealing Detail

Nature photographers are often focused on the detail within the image, so tonal adjustments often revolve around revealing and enhancing detail and texture in the photo. The Curves and Levels adjustments allows you to do exactly that by enhancing contrast and adjusting brightness to reveal the desired level of detail while maintaining an appropriate tonality within the image. The chances are you'll have made these global adjustments in ACR, but we'll describe making global Levels adjustments first and then explain how to limit them to certain parts of the image.

Let's make a Levels adjustment so you can see this in action. Begin by creating a new adjustment layer for Levels by clicking on the ⛰ icon in the Adjustments panel to access the Levels dialog. This adds a new Levels adjustment layer to the Layers panel, and the Levels dialog box appears.

Elements users should click the Create Adjustment Layer icon ◑ at the top of the Layers palette and choose Levels.

Note: We make all our adjustments as adjustment layers rather than applying them directly to the background image. This decreases the potential image degradation that occurs as changes are made to the image, as well as making it easy to modify the adjustments. To avoid any confusion when creating an adjustment, we recommend accessing the adjustment layers from the Adjustments or Layers panel rather than from the main menu.

For most adjustments with Levels, you need to adjust only three controls; you'll find all three directly below the histogram display in the Levels dialog box:

- The black-point slider (for shadows) is at the far left.
- The white-point slider (for highlights) is at the far right.
- The midtones slider is in between the two.

Together, these controls allow you to adjust the overall contrast (by shifting the black-point and white-point sliders) and brightness (with the midtones slider) of your image with excellent control.

We recommend establishing overall contrast before fine-tuning brightness. Therefore, start with the black point and white point sliders. These provide contrast adjustment by allowing you to vary the amount of adjustment being applied to the shadow and highlight areas of your image. As a result, you can, for example, sacrifice more detail in the shadows to improve overall contrast without losing significant highlight detail.

As a general rule, most nature images benefit from having the brightest pixel value set to white and the darkest pixel value set to black, to maximize contrast and tonal range within the image and to ensure that as much detail as possible is visible. In other words, after making adjustments your histogram should stretch (in most cases) nearly the full width of the chart, with few gaps in that range. Obviously there are plenty of exceptions to this, but it is a good basic rule. Because you know that the last data point at either end of the histogram chart represents the darkest and brightest pixels, you could make a basic adjustment by dragging the black-point and white-point sliders inward to the point where the data begins at each end of the histogram (see the example in Figure 6.7).

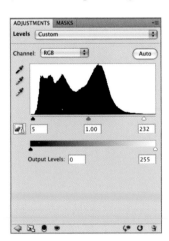

Figure 6.7 A basic start with Levels involves bringing the black-point and white-point sliders in to where the data begins on the histogram.

Of course, this is a somewhat arbitrary way to approach an image. Although it indeed produces good results for most images, it isn't an ideal solution for everyone. We recommend using clipping previews to help you set the black and white points.

The Clipping Preview

Although a basic visual evaluation of your image while making adjustments with Levels is certainly effective, it can be even more helpful to use the clipping preview display available in Levels. This display allows you to see exactly where you are losing detail within your image as you adjust the black-point and white-point sliders. As a result, you can make a much more informed decision about the settings you'd like to use for these sliders.

When you start with an image that lacks strong contrast and want to maximize the contrast without sacrificing detail in highlights or shadows, the clipping preview display allows you to see exactly where you'll begin to lose detail based on your specific adjustment of the black-point and white-point sliders.

We recommend adjusting the white point first, simply because highlight detail tends to be the more critical adjustment. To enable the clipping preview display, hold the Alt/Option key while you adjust the highlight slider/white point. Your image display initially changes to a completely (or almost completely) black display. This indicates that no pixel values (or very few) are clipped to white before you make any adjustment. As you continue to hold the Alt/Option key, slide the white-point slider to the left. You'll see more pixels showing up as you move the slider, as shown in Figure 6.8. As a general rule, we recommend adjusting the white point until pixels just start showing up in the clipping preview, and then back off just a hair. This is the point where you've maximized contrast and tonal range within the image, while sacrificing minimal highlight detail. Of course, the benefit of the clipping preview display is that you're able to make an informed decision about the amount of detail you're sacrificing to achieve the level of contrast you'd like to see and about that detail's location.

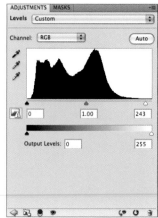

Figure 6.8 Holding the Alt/Option key gives you a clipping preview as you adjust the white-point slider in Levels, so you can see where you start losing highlight detail and in which areas of the image.

Note: The colors of the pixels that show up in the clipping preview display indicate the color channels that are losing detail within the image. The pixels won't appear as pure white or black in the image until the clipping preview shows those values. However, even if they aren't pure white or black, they are probably very close if any channels are clipping, so you can generally treat such values as though they were indeed white or black.

The process for setting the black point is nearly identical: Hold the Alt/Option key while adjusting the black-point slider, and a similar clipping preview appears, except that now it starts completely (or almost completely) white, with pixels showing up to indicate where you're losing shadow detail (see Figure 6.9). As discussed previously, we are generally willing to sacrifice more shadow detail as opposed to highlight detail to maximize contrast. The clipping preview allows you to make an informed decision about how much detail you're giving up with a particular adjustment and the location of that detail, so you can better determine the extent to which you can push the black point to produce the desired contrast level.

> **Note:** As you make changes to your image, the histogram in the Histogram panel will dynamically update to reflect those changes.

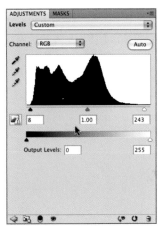

Figure 6.9 The clipping preview, while adjusting the black-point slider, shows you where you're losing shadow detail in the image.

After you've adjusted the black and white points by using the clipping preview, you're ready to adjust the midtones slider for overall brightness. Because this doesn't affect the extreme tonal values within the image, there isn't a clipping preview for the midtones slider. You need to rely on a visual evaluation of the image for this adjustment. Think of this slider as a brightness control. Moving the slider changes which pixel value within the image should be mapped to a middle-gray tonal value, but the result is a brightness shift. This adjustment doesn't have any rule of thumb you can follow in terms of positioning the slider at a particular point along the histogram chart, so you need to make a decision based on a visual review of the image.

> **Try It!** To practice utilizing the clipping preview in Levels, open the image Levels on the accompanying CD. Use the clipping preview to adjust the white-point and the black-point, and adjust the midtones slider visually.

Photography is very much a visual pursuit, so it makes sense to perform a visual review of the image and decide whether you're happy with the results of the adjustment you've made. You may want to back off the adjustments slightly in some situations to minimize the risk of introducing excessive contrast, or in other situations you may want to bring the sliders in just a bit farther to produce stronger contrast. It's up to you to determine the best adjustment for a particular image.

Note: If you're having trouble making appropriate adjustments, hold the Alt/Option key to change the Cancel button to a Reset button in any of the adjustment dialog boxes in Photoshop. If you then click the Reset button, all settings in the dialog box return to their default values.

When you've adjusted all three sliders, you've finished the basic tonal adjustment with Levels. Click OK, and the Levels dialog box closes. As with any other adjustment layer, if you change your mind about the adjustment at a later time, you can simply double-click the thumbnail icon for the Levels adjustment layer on the Layers panel, and the dialog box appears, with the sliders positioned exactly as you left them the last time you clicked OK.

Note: The Levels dialog box also includes eyedroppers that allow you to click areas of your image to automatically set the black, white, and neutral values. We'll talk more about those in Chapter 7, "Color Adjustments," when we talk about color casts.

Targeting Adjustments Using a Layer Mask

Making overall adjustments to bring out the maximum amount of detail in your images is a common goal, but one of the reasons for using the tonal adjustments within Photoshop in addition to those you already made in ACR is so that you can apply the changes to only certain areas of the image. You may want to do this to help emphasize your subject or to reveal detail in areas of your picture that have different lighting. Doing so requires the use of a layer mask to target the adjustment to a particular area of the image.

Every adjustment layer comes with a layer mask. It's the white box that appears in the adjustment layer next to the icon for the type of adjustment. The shape of the mask matches the shape of your image, as shown in Figure 6.10.

Figure 6.10 Every adjustment layer automatically comes with a layer mask.

Think of a layer mask as a visibility control for the changes you make on that layer. By default the mask is white. Wherever a layer mask is white corresponds to areas of your image where the changes made on that layer will be visible. Wherever a layer mask is black corresponds to areas of your image where the changes will not be visible. Imagine superimposing the layer mask over your image—the areas underneath white parts of the mask will show the changes you make on that layer, and the areas of the image underneath black parts of the mask will show no effects of that layer.

There are three ways ways to make parts of the layer mask black that are particularly useful for nature photographers. The first is by creating a selection before you make the adjustment layer, the second is by using the Color Range option within the Masks panel, and the third is by painting parts of the layer mask black. We'll talk about all of these approaches in more detail.

Note: A *layer mask* identifies which areas of a particular layer will be visible. In this case, we're talking about layer masks on adjustment layers, so the mask determines where the adjustment applies and where it doesn't. White on the layer mask indicates areas where the adjustment layer affects the image, and black indicates areas where it does not affect the image.

Because CS4 is nonmodal, you can work on the layer mask at any time while tweaking the adjustments. The Masks panel is the same for all adjustment layers. By default it's set to the Pixel Mask 🔲, which is what you'll want. The icon to the right 🔲 is used to select a vector mask. Since we rarely (read that as never) use a vector mask, you don't have to worry about it!

The Density slider controls the opacity of the mask. Most of the time you'll begin with 100%, but if you want to tweak the strength of the adjustment you can change this. The Feather slider enables you to soften the edges of the adjustment so that it blends more gradually into the rest of the image. However, for most of your work you'll want to use the Mask Edge option. Click it to access the Refine Edges dialog that we covered in Chapter 4, "Foundations."

If you want to invert the mask and have the adjustment affect the opposite parts of the image, click the Invert button.

Note: To use a mask on another layer, click the mask icon in the Layers panel, hold down the Alt/ Option key, and drag it to the desired layer. A dialog will appear asking whether you want to replace the existing mask. Choose Yes, and use the Invert option in the Masks panel if necessary. *All masks for all adjustment layers work this way!*

Masking a Selection

When you create a selection first and then create an adjustment layer, we refer to it as *masking a selection*. Creating an adjustment layer that is masked based on a selection is easy, especially since you've already seen some of the methods you can use to create selections in Chapter 4.

To mask an adjustment layer based on a selection, start by creating a selection that defines the subject you'd like to modify, as shown in Figure 6.11.

Photo by Ellen Anon

Figure 6.11 The first step in emphasizing a particular area of your image with a targeted tonal adjustment is to create a selection defining that area.

Then create a new adjustment layer of the desired type (in this case using Levels). Because a selection is active when the adjustment layer is created, Photoshop assumes you want to mask the adjustment layer based on the selection. Therefore, the adjustment layer applies only to the areas that were selected when you created the adjustment layer.

Notice that when the adjustment layer appears in the Layers panel, the layer mask is partially white and partially black. The white areas match the shape of the selection you originally created (see Figure 6.12). When you make adjustments to the

Levels dialog box, as in this example, the adjustment affects only the area that was selected when the adjustment layer was created.

Figure 6.12 When you create an adjustment layer with an active selection, the mask for that adjustment layer reflects the shape of the selection, so the adjustment applies only to that area of the image.

Note: On a layer mask, black blocks the layer's effect and white reveals the effect.

Using this concept, it's easy to see how you could create a selection to define the area you want to emphasize and then create a Levels adjustment (or a different type of adjustment as appropriate) to adjust that area and draw more attention to it. Remember that our eyes tend to go to areas that are brighter and more contrasty, so if you want to help make your subject stand out from the background, you could make two Levels adjustments. In the first you may adjust the background to be a little darker and less contrasty, and in the second you may adjust the subject to be a little bit brighter and perhaps more contrasty as well. (See Figure 6.13.)

Figure 6.13 By making adjustments using layer masks, you can help emphasize your subject by applying one type of adjustment to the subject and a different one to the background.

Using the Color Range Option

One of the exciting new features in CS4 is the ability to create a selection from within the Masks panel by using the Color Range option. We recommend starting to make your adjustment initially and then moving on to Color Range to define the areas you want the adjustment to affect, but you can use the options within the Masks panel at any time. Initially the adjustment is set to affect the entire image unless you began with a selection.

When you click the Color Range option, the Color Range tool appears. Use it the way we discussed in Chapter 4 to define the area you want the adjustment to affect. Think of this as an automated way of controlling where to apply the adjustment. The ability to use the Color Range tool while in the midst of making an adjustment is extremely helpful and new to CS4.

> **Note:** Sometimes it's helpful to set the Selection preview to grayscale to more easily see the selection.

Let's consider an example to see how these panels work when you're optimizing your image. Figure 6.14 shows the panels for an image where we want to lighten the subject. Rather than making a selection beforehand as you might have done in earlier versions of Photoshop, open the Adjustments panel and click on Levels. Adjust the sliders to approximately where you think you want them. Then click the Masks panel and choose Color Range. Click on the subject and use Color Range to make the best selection you can. Then use Mask Edges to tweak the edges. Now go back to the Adjustments panel and finalize the settings.

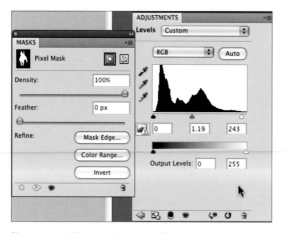

Figure 6.14 In CS4 you can have the specific adjustment dialog open while you are tweaking the mask.

Painting on a Mask

In some situations you don't want to create the adjustment layer mask based on a selection. For example, when you're going to adjust an image area that is defined by relatively nebulous edges, creating a selection to start from can be a challenge. When the edge of the area you want to adjust isn't well defined, it's often easier and more efficient to paint directly on the mask to control where the effect is visible. The concept is that you paint with white or black on the mask to control the visibility of the effects of that layer.

Almost all of us have been using a paintbrush since we were preschoolers, so creating a mask by painting is usually a very natural and intuitive approach. To use this approach, take the following steps:

1. Create an adjustment layer, in this case a Levels adjustment layer.

2. Make an adjustment so you can see an effect in the image. Concentrate on making the particular section of your image look the way you want, and don't worry that the rest of the image may be "ruined." We'll use the layer mask to restore those areas to their "before" states.

> **Note:** We recommend making an exaggerated adjustment when you're first learning to use an adjustment layer so it's easier to see exactly where in the image the adjustment layer applies.

3. To modify the mask for an adjustment layer, select the Brush tool. We usually use a soft brush (0% hardness), but in some instances you will want to use a harder brush or even a totally hard brush to make a discrete edge.

4. Press D to set the colors to their defaults of black and white, and then press X as needed to switch foreground and background colors.

5. Zoom in so you can easily see the area you want to change.

6. Place your cursor on the image, and begin painting with black as your foreground color to remove the effects of your adjustment from that area.

7. If you make a mistake, reverse your brush colors by pressing X so that white is your foreground color. Then paint over the area to correct the mistake. Layer masks are very forgiving!

To help you see exactly where you have masked the image and where the effect will appear, press the \ key. This will create a type of quick mask over your image. A transparent red layer will appear over the masked areas, as shown in Figure 6.15. As you paint with black, the red area will increase; to remove it from an area, paint with white. OK, we know it's a little confusing to paint with black and have it appear red, but remember you're not really painting on the image. You're painting on the layer mask, and the red is there as a superimposed version of the mask that's easier to see. To remove the quick mask, press the \ key again. This is one of our favorite tricks!

Figure 6.15 Pressing the backslash (\) key makes a red mask appear over the parts of your image that are masked, helping you to see whether you need to refine the mask.

Note: Another way to view the mask is to Alt/Option+ click directly on the adjustment layer mask in the Layers panel. That way, the mask appears in place of your image preview, making it easy to clean up small areas that may have been missed in painting.

One of the benefits of using layer masks is that if you decide you need to further revise the layer mask, simply click the adjustment layer to make it active and paint as needed to change the areas where the adjustment is blocked or revealed.

At times, you'll want the adjustment layer to apply to a very small area of your image, but that area won't be conducive to making a selection. In such situations, it may seem that the only solution is to paint with black throughout most of the image. An easier way is to begin with a layer mask that is already filled with black and then paint the areas where you want the effect to show with white. To do this, take these steps:

1. After creating the new adjustment layer, choose Edit > Fill from the menu.

2. Select Black from the Use drop-down list, and click OK (see Figure 6.16). This fills the layer mask with black, blocking the effect of the adjustment from the entire image.

Figure 6.16 You can use the Fill command to fill a layer mask with black and then paint with white to apply the adjustment to specific areas of the image.

3. Use the Brush tool with the foreground color set to white to paint the adjustment in the areas where you'd like it to be applied.

> **Note:** You can also use Alt+Delete/Option+Delete to fill a layer mask with the foreground color and use Ctrl+Delete/⌘+Delete to fill a layer mask with the background color.

So far you've seen how you can paint with black or white on an adjustment layer mask to target specific areas where the adjustment should be blocked or revealed. If you'd like to only partially block or reveal the effects of an adjustment layer, then the layer mask will need to be a shade of gray. The darker the gray, the more the effect will be blocked, and the lighter the gray, the more it will be revealed, as shown in Figure 6.17. Rather than using the Color Picker to select a shade of gray (because it's easy to accidentally select a non-neutral gray, which can lead to unexpected results), we recommend continuing to use the default colors of black and white but *reducing the opacity of the brush*. To reduce the opacity of the brush, use the Opacity box in the toolbar Options bar (not the Layers panel). And, as we mentioned earlier, paint with a soft-edged brush if necessary to produce a gradual transition between the areas that are and are not affected by the adjustment layer. When using a brush with lowered opacity, be careful because if you release the cursor and paint over the same spot again, you will change the gray value. At times this may be exactly what you want to happen!

> **Note:** An easy way to reduce the opacity of the brush is to press the number keys. The 1 key will yield an opacity of 10%, 2 will give 20%, and so on. Pressing 0 returns the opacity to 100%.

> **Note:** Graphics tablets such as the Wacom tablets are particularly helpful when painting on a layer mask. You can set the pen so that the pressure you use determines the opacity of the brush. That makes transitions smooth and intuitive.

Figure 6.17 You can use shades of gray on an adjustment layer mask to have the effect partially revealed within the image.

Of course, you can also combine the two approaches to creating a mask. You could start by creating a selection that defines the area you want to adjust and then paint on the layer mask to fine-tune the area you want to have affected by the adjustment. This allows you to utilize the best of both techniques to achieve the best results possible in your images.

Try It! Open the image `SelectiveLevels` on the accompanying CD, and create a rough selection of the interior of the flower using the Lasso tool. Then create a Levels adjustment, lighten the interior of the flower, and click OK. Then use the Brush tool to refine the initial selection edge, painting with white where you want the selection to apply and painting with black where you don't want it to apply. Try this exercise a second time using the new Color Range option.

Blurring the Layer Mask

If you have not used the Mask Edge option on your mask (or on the selection if you're in Elements and you began with a selection), the transition between the areas you adjusted and those you didn't will be relatively harsh, as you can see in Figure 6.18. Sometimes this works well, but other times you may want a more natural transition.

An alternative method to create a more natural transition between adjusted and nonadjusted areas is to apply a blur to the layer mask when you've finished defining its shape. By using this method, you can see the actual effect in the image rather than guessing by how many pixels you should feather a selection. Most of the time you won't need to do this, but sometimes it can improve your final results, particularly if you are planning to make a large print.

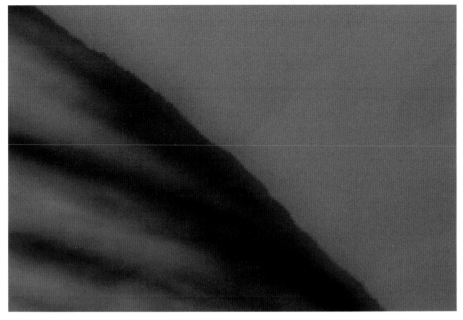

Figure 6.18 When you use a nonfeathered selection or a hard-edged brush with a layer mask, the transition between adjusted and nonadjusted areas will be relatively harsh.

Make sure the appropriate layer mask is selected first and then select Filter > Blur > Gaussian Blur from the menu to open the Gaussian Blur dialog box (shown in Figure 6.19). With the Preview check box selected, start with a value of 1 pixel, and adjust the slider up or down to achieve the desired effect in the image. You want to produce a gradual transition between the areas you're adjusting versus not adjusting (see Figure 6.20), but not soften the effect so much that the adjustment blends across too large a distance. When you've found the appropriate value, click OK to apply the blur to the mask.

Figure 6.19 Applying the Gaussian Blur filter on the mask for your adjustment layer allows you to soften the edge of the mask.

Note: We used this technique more often in earlier versions of Photoshop, before the Refine Edge options were available. However, even now, the technique can come in handy and is worth knowing.

Figure 6.20 After blurring the adjustment layer mask, the result is a more gradual transition between adjusted and nonadjusted areas of the image.

Try It! Open the image BlurMask on the accompanying CD, select the layer mask for the Levels adjustment layer, and apply a Gaussian Blur to the mask to soften the vignette effect in the image and help you gain a better understanding of the process for blurring a layer mask.

Curves

Photoshop
ONLY

The Curves adjustment in Photoshop has a reputation as being one of the most difficult controls to master. Although becoming comfortable with it can take some time and practice, it provides an incredible level of control over your images. It enables you to change the brightness values and contrast within your image by applying varying degrees of adjustments to pixels of different tonal values. Simply put, you can concentrate contrast or brightness modifications in certain tonal ranges. As with Levels, you can accomplish similar effects within ACR, but the Curves tool in Photoshop has some features that make it more convenient.

As with all controls that are available as an adjustment layer, the first step in utilizing Curves is to create a new adjustment layer from the Adjustments panel.

The key to understanding the Curves adjustment is the concept of "before" and "after" values. All adjustments in Curves are based on shifting the value of all pixels at (or near) a particular tonal value. Therefore, think in terms of brightening the midtones or darkening the highlights, for example, when working with Curves.

The Curves dialog box shows a "curve" overlaid on a grid (see Figure 6.21), all of which is superimposed over the histogram. Of course, at first the curve isn't a curve at all, but a straight line at a 45° angle. As you learn to "read" the curve, you'll see that this 45° line represents no change in the image. The gradient along the bottom of the grid represents the before tonal values, and the gradient at the left shows the after values. If you follow a vertical line up from a specific tonal value on the gradient below the grid to the point that intersects the curve line and then follow in a straight line to the left until reaching the after gradient, at this point the before and after values are exactly the same. Changing the shape of the curve alters the relationship between the before and after values, resulting in a change in the appearance in your image.

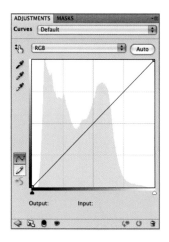

Figure 6.21 The Curves dialog box shows a "curve" that by default is actually a straight line at a 45° angle.

The grid behind the curve line is provided simply for reference, and you can set it to either a 16-square grid or a 100-square grid. In general, the 16-square grid is preferred by those working in prepress, because they tend to think about quarter tones, midtones, and three-quarter tones. However, most photographers prefer the 100-square grid, and that is the setting we recommend. To toggle between the two settings, hold the Alt/Option key, and click the cursor anywhere within the grid. Keep in mind that changing the increments has absolutely no effect on the actual adjustment being applied.

Note: The adjustments discussed in this section assume you have the gradients set with white at the top and right. If you're using them with black at the top and right, you need to reverse the direction of anchor-point movement, discussed in the "Anchor Points" section, later in this chapter.

Clipping Preview

To check for clipping, hold down the Alt/Option key while dragging the white or black points—that is, the points at either extreme of the curve. The image turns either nearly or all white, or nearly or all black. A white background is used to check for clipping in the shadows, and a black background is used to check for clipping in the highlights. Any areas where there is clipping will appear in color to indicate the particular channel that's being clipped, and if all three channels are clipped, then the area will appear black or white—whichever is the opposite of the background color. This makes it easy to see where there's any clipping and to decide whether you need to modify your adjustments to try to eliminate it. Sometimes the clipping will be in dark shadows that should be black or in specular highlights that should be pure white. At other times the clipping preview may show you that you've unintentionally lost detail in your subject.

You can use the clipping preview to accurately set the white and black points in your image. In versions of Photoshop prior to CS3, we recommended setting the white and black points in Levels because Curves didn't have a clipping preview, but this has changed. To set the white and black points in Curves, do the following:

1. Open a new Curves adjustment layer from the Adjustments panel.

2. Press and hold the Alt/Option key.

3. Click the small white triangle on the bottom right of the histogram. The image will turn black.

4. Drag the triangle to the left until colored pixels begin to appear in the preview, as shown in Figure 6.22.

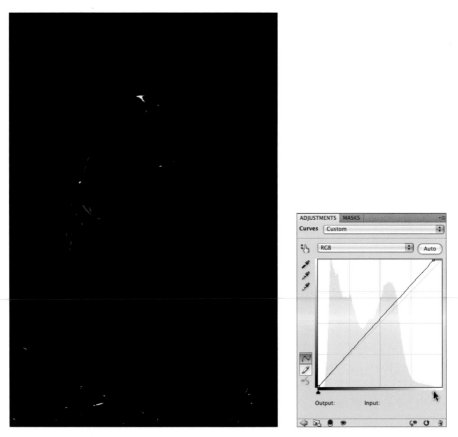

Figure 6.22 Use the clipping preview in Curves to establish the white and black points.

5. Back the slider off until there is no clipping, if possible. That sets the white point.

6. Click the small black triangle on the bottom left of the histogram, while pressing and holding the Alt/Option key. The preview turns white.

7. Drag it to the right until colored pixels appear, and then back off until there is no clipping, if possible. That sets the black point.

Dragging the triangles toward each other will increase the contrast in the image and eventually introduce clipping. For the maximum amount of contrast in your image, drag these sliders toward the center until colored pixels appear, and then back off slightly. Then, to change the overall brightness of the image or to refine the contrast within a certain range of tonalities, apply anchor points to the curve.

Anchor Points

You use anchor points for changing relationships between the before and after values in your image, which in turn creates the actual tonal adjustment. Anchor points allow you to place a handle on a particular point on the curve and adjust its position. When you do so, Photoshop automatically smoothes out the curve to connect all the anchor points, providing a seamless transition in your adjustments.

The curve always starts off with anchor points at the extreme ends. You can adjust the position of these points by setting the black-points and white-points within your image as we just described in the "Clipping Preview" section.

To see the basic functionality of anchor points, position your mouse at about the middle of the curve, and click. This places an anchor point at that position, which you can move around to change the shape of the curve, as you can see in Figure 6.23. Move the anchor point upward to lighten the image and downward to darken the image. The result is similar to adjusting the midtones slider in Levels. It differs in that the tones closest to the point you moved on the curve are altered more than tones farther away from that point. In fact, the effect tapers off toward the ends of the curve.

Of course, this hints at the incredible power of Curves. You can place up to 14 anchor points on the curve to perform adjustments on pixels at various tonal values within the image—but you'll usually need only a handful (typically one to three) to accomplish your goals with the image. By carefully positioning and adjusting these anchor points, you can exercise tremendous control over the tonal adjustments applied to the image.

CS4 makes it easier than ever to know exactly where to place anchor points. Click the targeted adjustment tool icon ![icon] in the upper-left part of the Curves dialog, place your cursor over your image in the area you'd like to lighten or darken, then click and drag up or down, and Curves will automatically add anchor points in the correct positions and adjust the curve. It just doesn't get any easier than that!

Clicking the curve to place anchor points without using the targeted adjustment tool is sort of like working blind because you don't get any feedback about which area of the image you're going to adjust. Fortunately, there is a way to make an informed decision about where to place anchor points.

PHOTO BY ELLEN ANON

Figure 6.23 To get a sense of the basic control in Curves, click at about the middle of the curve line to create an anchor point, and then drag it around to see the effect in your image.

First of all, if you point the mouse at your image and click, a small circle appears on the curve showing you where the tonal value for the pixel under the mouse falls (see Figure 6.24). If you drag the mouse around on the image, the circle bounces around as it updates its position based on the tonal value under the mouse. This display allows you to see exactly where particular areas of your image fall on the curve.

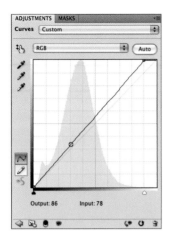

Figure 6.24 If you click your image, a small circle appears on the curve line representing where the tonal value you're pointing at with your mouse falls on the curve.

Even better, if you hold the Ctrl/⌘ key when you click the image, an anchor point is created on the curve for the tonal value of the pixel under your mouse. You can even drag around the image to review the range on the curve before releasing the mouse to place the anchor point. This allows you to place anchor points very precisely based on the area of the image you'd like to focus your adjustments on. But most of the time we've switched to using the targeted adjustment tool with Curves. By clicking the onscreen adjustment 🔲 icon and then clicking and dragging on the image preview where you'd like the image to be lighter or darker, Photoshop CS4 will automatically create and adjust anchor points for you!

> **Note:** The Curves dialog box includes eyedroppers with which you can set black, midtone, and white points in the image. We'll talk about using these in Chapter 7.

Adjusting Anchor Points

After you've created one or more anchor points, you can adjust them to change the relationship between the before and after values on the curve. You lighten or darken specific values by raising or lowering an anchor point, respectively.

You can move the anchor points by dragging them with the mouse, but you can apply a more precise adjustment by clicking an anchor point to select it and then using the arrow keys to adjust its position. You are typically thinking in terms of lightening or darkening and therefore would adjust the anchor points up or down to change the after value, but you can also move the anchor points left or right. Although doing so actually changes which before value you are adjusting, we prefer to think of this as simply fine-tuning the relationship between the before and after values by taking greater control over the specific shape of the curve.

> **Note:** At this point, you're performing only tonal adjustments with Curves. In the next chapter you'll learn how to adjust the curves for individual color channels to apply color adjustments to your images.

As you're adjusting the anchor points, you'll begin to see the relationship between the shape of the curve and the effect on the image:

- Raising or lowering the curve in a particular area affects the brightness of the pixels within the tonal range represented by that portion of the curve.

- Making a portion of the curve steeper than the original 45° line represents an increase in contrast.

- Areas that you change to be shallower than the original 45° line represent reduced contrast.

As you understand these relationships, you'll be better able to read the curve as well as apply the desired adjustments with minimal effort.

Creating the S Curve

One of the most common adjustments recommended for Curves is the S curve. This curve shape applies an increase in contrast to the midtones of your image while preserving detail in highlight and shadow areas. Because we tend to respond better to photographs with higher contrast in the midtones, you can apply this adjustment to many photographic images and have good results.

Note: Moody, foggy images do not need S curves, nor do images that are already contrasty.

To create an S curve, we recommend placing anchor points about 20% in from the black and white endpoints on the curve (see Figure 6.25). Then move the upper of these anchor points to the left and up slightly and the lower anchor point to the right and down (see Figure 6.26). You don't need to move them much to produce a nice boost of contrast in your image; often moving the anchor points by one or two clicks with the arrow keys is sufficient.

Another great feature of using Curves for such an adjustment is that you can focus your S curve on either the highlights or the shadows within your image. If you want to boost the brighter tones more than the darker ones, move the anchor point that's closer to the white endpoint farther inward than the anchor point you added near the black point.

If you're also applying more sophisticated adjustments with Curves, you may want to make one Curves adjustment layer specifically for the S curve and another for adjustments that apply to various tonal values within the image. Renaming each of these adjustment layers helps you stay organized as you move through your workflow and when you return to the image later.

Figure 6.25 To create an S curve, start by placing anchor points about 20% in from the white and black endpoints of the curve.

Figure 6.26 To complete the S curve, move the anchor points inward to achieve the desired increase in midtone contrast.

Locking Down the Curve to Limit Changes

When you move anchor points on the curve, Photoshop automatically adjusts the shape of the curve to provide a smooth transition between all anchor points. Although this is a good thing, sometimes it causes adjustments in areas where you don't want any applied. When this happens, you must prevent changes—"normalize" the shape of the curve—in the areas you don't want altered.

For example, if you're trying to focus some adjustments on the brighter areas of your image, you'll find that adjusting the anchor points causes a bend in the curve that also affects the darker areas (see Figure 6.27). To lock the curve, place a new anchor point near the existing anchor point on the side representing the tonal values to which you want to limit changes. Then place two more points on the curve close to that point. The three points together "lock" the section of the curve so that changes on one side of those three points essentially don't affect the curve on the other side (see Figure 6.28).

You can also place anchor points outside those you placed for adjustment, producing something of a barrier outside the range you're adjusting. This won't always prevent adjustments from applying to the rest of the curve, but it helps when the adjustments you're making are relatively minor.

> **Note:** If your Curves adjustment is causing undesirable color shifts in your image, change the blending mode for the Curves adjustment layer to Luminosity (using the drop-down list at the top of the Layers panel) after closing the Curves dialog box. This ensures that the Curves adjustment layer affects only tonal values, not color values, within the image.

Figure 6.27 At times you will adjust a portion of the curve that you want to affect, only to find that the entire image is being adjusted because of the shape the curve takes on.

Figure 6.28 Using an additional anchor point, you can lock down the area of the curve you don't want to have affected, bringing it back near the original starting point.

The bottom line is that you can use anchor points not just for producing desired changes within the image, but also to adjust the shape of the curve to compensate for unintended consequences of your adjustments. Think of these anchor points as handles that allow you to control the shape of the curve and use them to produce exactly the result you have in mind.

Note: The best advice we can offer for working with Curves is to use very small adjustments. It doesn't take much to cause a significant change in the image, and frustration with Curves is most often caused by adjustments that are simply too strong. Using the new targeted adjustment tool will make using Curves seem far easier and more manageable.

Curves Presets

Adobe has created a series of presets of frequently used curves that you can apply with a single click (see Figure 6.29). That way, you can quickly add a small amount of contrast or other common curves without having to re-create the curve yourself. You can also choose one of the preset curves and then modify it to suit your needs by clicking the anchor points and moving them and/or adding anchor points.

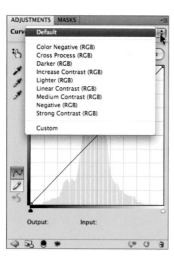

Figure 6.29 Using the new Curves presets can be a time-saver.

In addition, you can create your own presets that will appear in the drop-down menu. To create your own presets, take these steps:

1. Open an image, and create a curve. For example, perhaps you frequently add contrast just to the middle tones, and you prefer a little more contrast than what the Linear Contrast (RGB) preset applies. You could start with the preset and modify it, or you could create a completely new curve.

2. When you have the curve the way you want, click the adjustment fly-out icon and choose Save Preset.

3. In the next dialog box (Figure 6.30), give your curve a name, and make sure it's specific enough that you'll know immediately which curve is which. Leave Where set at the default folder Curves. That way, your new preset will appear in the drop-down menu.

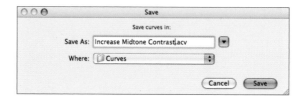

Figure 6.30 Name your curves so you can tell them apart.

4. Click Save, and your new preset appears in the Preset drop-down menu, as shown in Figure 6.31.

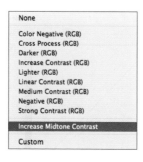

Figure 6.31 Once you create and save your custom preset, it appears in the Preset drop-down menu.

Curves

Unfortunately, Elements does not have the same advanced Curves control that Photoshop has. It does, however, provide Color Curves with easy-to-use parametric controls to adjust highlights, contrast, and more. Although Elements only provides Color Curves as a global adjustment, with a bit of trickery you can make them work like an adjustment layer.

1. Make a copy of your image layer if that's your only layer, by dragging it to the new layer icon ▓ at the top of the Layers palette. If you already have other layers, click on the top layer, hold down the Alt/Option key, and click the double-arrow icon at the top right of the Layers palette to access the fly-out menu. Choose Merge Visible and continue to hold down the Alt/Option key until a new layer appears on top of the other layers. (If only a single layer appears, you released the Alt/Option key too quickly.)

2. Select Enhance > Adjust Color > Adjust Color Curves, and a dialog window will appear as shown here.

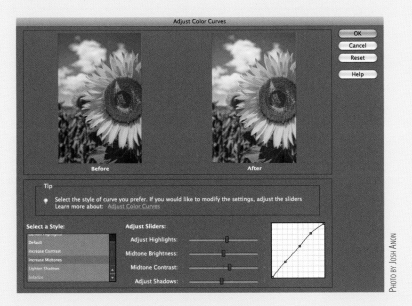

PHOTO BY JOSH ANON

3. On the left, Elements provides different preset styles. We recommend choosing Default so that there are no initial adjustments. If you're unfamiliar with curves, try selecting the different styles, and watch how both your image and the curve display on the lower right of the dialog window change.

4. Use the four Adjust Sliders to change the curve. For example, to add more midtone contrast, drag the Midtone Contrast slider to the right. Unfortunately, you can't directly manipulate the anchor points for the curve. To create an S curve, increase the Adjust Highlights slider and decrease the Adjust Shadows slider.

Tip: Elements does not provide a clipping warning for the Color Curves adjustment. However, as you change your curves, it updates your image. Arrange your windows so that the Histogram palette is visible, and use your histogram to determine if your adjustments are causing clipping.

Continues

Curves *(Continued)*

5. When you're happy with the overall adjustment, click OK.

6. To add a layer mask to this adjustment, click the Create Adjustment Layer in the Layers palette, choose Levels, and click OK without making any changes.

7. Drag the Levels Adjustment Layer from Step 6 below the layer you created in Step 1.

8. Select the topmost layer and choose Layer > Group with Previous (Ctrl+G/⌘+G).

9. Your layers setup will look similar to the following illustration. You can then paint with white or black in the Levels adjustment layer's layer mask to mask out the Color Curves adjustment.

Try It! To start getting more comfortable with Curves, open the image Curves on the accompanying CD, and make some adjustments, starting with a simple S curve adjustment and then working to fine-tune the overall tonality to your liking.

Creating a Virtual Split Neutral-Density Filter

Another tool that you can use to create an adjustment layer mask is the Gradient tool. This allows you to place a gradient on a layer mask, resulting in an adjustment that affects one side of the image completely but gradually tapers off in a given direction until it has no effect at the other side of the image. The most common example of using such a gradient is in a composition where you would otherwise shoot with a graduated split neutral-density filter, such as when you need to darken the sky without darkening the foreground of an image. But the advantage of doing it in Photoshop is that you can customize the filter to the exact size you need.

To create a virtual split neutral-density filter, follow these steps:

1. Start by creating a new adjustment layer that produces the desired effect in the area of the image to which you want it to apply. For example, you may create a Levels (or Curves) adjustment layer that darkens the sky in an image by moving the midtones slider to the right. After you've made the adjustment, click OK in the dialog box for the adjustment to apply the settings on the layer.

2. Select the Gradient tool from the Tools panel (the shortcut key is G). On the Options bar, click the drop-down list for the gradient editor, and choose the first gradient thumbnail on the list, which is the Foreground to Background gradient. Next, select the Linear option for the Gradient tool on the Options bar (shown in Figure 6.32), which is the first in the set of five buttons allowing you to choose a style for your gradient.

Figure 6.32 To use a gradient on a layer mask, select the Foreground to Background gradient with the Linear option from the Options bar.

3. Press D to set the colors to the defaults of black and white, and set white to the foreground color (pressing X to switch foreground and background colors if necessary). You're now ready to create a gradient that transitions from white to black.

4. You want to create the gradient on the layer mask for the adjustment layer you just created, so make sure that is the active layer in the Layers panel. Then click and drag the image to create a gradient: The foreground color starts where you first click, with a smooth gradation to the background color where you release the mouse, as shown in Figure 6.33. The length of the line you drag determines the distance over which the gradient transitions, and the direction determines the angle of that gradient. To lock the gradient to 45° increments, simply hold the Shift key as you drag.

Figure 6.33 Draw the gradient on the layer mask so the adjustment tapers from adjusted to nonadjusted areas.

5. In the example of darkening the sky, click the area of sky that represents the lowest area you still want the adjustment to affect completely, and drag downward to the point where you don't want any effect at all. If you're not happy with the initial gradient you created, simply click and drag again to replace the gradient with a new one. The result is an adjustment that blends smoothly, from applying completely in one area of the image to having no effect on another area (see Figure 6.34).

If your image requires an odd shape to the split neutral-density filter, you can modify the layer mask by painting on it to add or remove the effects where necessary. This can be useful when shooting in the mountains where the sky may be very light but the mountains dark, and the sky area may be V-shaped.

Figure 6.34 By applying a gradient mask to the adjustment, you're able to produce an adjustment that gradually blends, as with the sky darkened in this example.

Safe Dodge and Burn Layers

Dodging and burning are techniques borrowed from the wet darkroom, where you can use your hands or various instruments to block light from specific areas of an image. The longer the light from the enlarger strikes any given area, the darker that area will be. Blocking light to small areas during exposure is referred to as *dodging* and results in the blocked areas being lighter in a print than they otherwise would have been. *Burning* is the opposite: blocking light from *most* of the image so you can concentrate light for a portion of the exposure on one particular area, darkening that area of the print.

In Photoshop you can produce similar effects. In fact, Photoshop includes Dodge and Burn tools on the Tools panel, but we don't recommend using them because you must apply them directly to an image layer, and they don't offer the flexibility of the method we'll present here.

Setting Up

The method we recommend for dodging and burning uses one layer for dodging and another for burning, and takes advantage of layer masks and layer blending modes. Blending modes are different ways of combining layers. So far all the layers we've worked with in the examples have been in Normal mode, but Photoshop contains numerous algorithms for different ways to combine two layers. You can combine layers so that the tonal values are added together or multiplied, or the darker value used, or the lighter values, and so on. You don't have to become an expert on each of the algorithms; we'll use just two of them here: Screen and Multiply. We'll talk more about blending modes in Chapter 9, "Creative Effects."

> **Note:** We prefer this method to the older Overlay method because it's more forgiving and easier to use.

Although setting up the dodging and burning requires a lot of steps, the procedure is easy and can be automated by creating an action (see Chapter 11, "Time-Savers").

To set up layers to use for dodging and burning, do the following:

1. Create a new Levels adjustment layer, but do *not* make any changes; just click OK. This creates an adjustment layer in the Layers panel even though you aren't making any changes with it yet.

2. Double-click directly on the name of the layer (Levels1), and change it to **Dodge**.

3. In the Blending Modes drop-down menu on the Layers panel, choose Screen, as shown in Figure 6.35. The entire image will become one full stop lighter, which in most images means that it will instantly be overexposed. Don't worry—we're not going to leave it that way for long!

Figure 6.35 Take advantage of blending modes to create dodge and burn layers that can be modified easily.

4. In the menu bar, choose Edit > Fill > Use Black, and click OK. The layer mask should now be black, and your image should look the way it did before we began setting up for dodging and burning.

5. Create another Levels adjustment just as you did in Step 1, and name it **Burn**.

6. Change the blending mode of this layer to Multiply.

7. In the menu bar, choose Edit > Fill > Use Black, and click OK.

8. Select the Brush tool by selecting it on the Tools panel or by pressing B on your keyboard. Be sure to use a soft-edged brush, as shown in Figure 6.36.

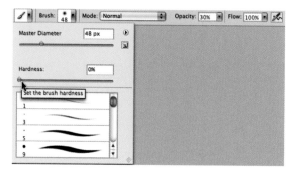

Figure 6.36 Use a soft-edged brush when dodging and burning your image with this method.

9. Set the opacity of the brush to 15%, although you may want to adjust this as you proceed since it controls the strength of the dodging and burning.

> **Note:** It's important to set the brush to the Normal blending mode in the tool Options bar, while the layer itself is set to Multiply or Screen in the Layers panel.

> **Note:** If you're using a tablet, you can also use pen pressure of the stylus to determine the Opacity setting when dodging and burning with this method.

10. Press D to set the colors on the color boxes in the Tools panel to their default values of black foreground and white background. Note that you can switch the foreground and background colors by pressing X as you're working, allowing you to easily switch between black and white.

Now you're ready to apply selective lightening and darkening to the image.

Painting with Light

With your new layers and the Brush tool properly configured, you're ready to start painting with light. Paint with white using the brush at a reduced opacity on the appropriate layer to lighten or darken your image. Although it appears that you're painting directly on your image, you're actually painting on the layer mask. Because you're painting at a reduced opacity, the result is relatively modest. If necessary, you can paint over areas multiple times to build up an effect. The best effect is usually subtle. When people look at the final image, they shouldn't get the impression that you were using dodging and burning techniques. However, when you toggle the visibility of the dodge and burn layer off and on, you'll see a difference between the images.

It's important to understand the behavior of the Brush tool when you're working at a reduced opacity for this technique. As long as you hold down the mouse button, the effect does not accumulate no matter how many times the mouse passes over a particular area. However, if you release the mouse and start painting again, the effect is uneven if you partially overlap areas you've previously painted. Therefore, it's important that you click and hold the mouse button while painting until you've covered the entire area you want to adjust. Then release the mouse and start painting again in additional areas you'd like to change.

Dodging and burning are two of our favorite techniques in Photoshop. We appreciate the capability to paint with light, bringing out details in various areas of the image or simply emphasizing particular features (see Figure 6.37).

PHOTO BY ELLEN ANON

Figure 6.37 Dodging and burning allow you to enhance detail or add drama to various areas of your image with tremendous flexibility, producing an image that has been adjusted in a subtle way but with a big difference in the final result.

Correcting Mistakes

Of course, now and then you may be less than satisfied with an adjustment you've made when using this technique. Fortunately, because you apply it using a layer mask, it's easy to fix mistakes even if it's too late to simply undo a step on the History panel.

There are two basic ways to correct your mistakes. If you were painting with white as your foreground color, make black the foreground color and set the opacity to 100%. Paint over the problematic area, and begin again.

Alternatively, if you are dissatisfied with all the dodging or burning you did, return to Edit > Fill > Use Black, and reset the layer mask to black. Then you can start over.

Try It! To practice dodging and burning, open the image DodgeBurn from the accompanying CD, and use the method presented here to add drama to the rock formation, enhancing texture and contrast.

The Shadow/Highlight Adjustment

Photoshop ONLY

The Shadow/Highlight adjustment is an excellent way to reveal subtle detail in the shadow and/or highlight areas of your images. Although you could theoretically produce similar results with sophisticated use of Curves, the Shadow/Highlight adjustment is far easier to use when you need to recover detail that has been lost in shadow or highlight areas because of excessive contrast. It's similar to the Fill Light and Recovery sliders in ACR, which we covered in Chapter 3, but it has additional controls so you can fine-tune the results.

Note: Some photographers are tempted to try to use Shadow/Highlight to fix all their exposure problems. We don't recommend that because the Shadow/Highlight adjustment works by reducing contrast. That's fine for small tonal ranges, but it's not usually a good idea to do throughout the entire image. We find it's far more effective to limit the Shadow/Highlight tool to recovering detail in the deep shadows and recovering highlights in very light areas.

Although you can't apply the Shadow/Highlight adjustment as an adjustment layer, in CS4 you can use it as a Smart Filter. As we discussed in Chapter 5, "Workflows and First Steps," a filter that's applied as a Smart Filter behaves similarly to an adjustment layer. The advantage of using it as a Smart Filter is that you can tweak the settings as needed, and you can add a layer mask to it to target the effects to certain areas of your image. For example, perhaps you have a portrait of a dark animal against a dark background. You may want to reveal details in the shadows of the animal but not in the background.

We recommend using the Shadow/Highlight adjustment early in your workflow, as the first step after you open the raw file as a Smart Object. To do so, take these steps:

1. If your background layer is not already a Smart Object, you'll need to convert it to one by choosing Filter > Convert for Smart Filters. That way, you can use Shadow/Highlight as a Smart Filter.

2.   Choose Image > Adjustments > Shadow/Highlight. Shadow/Highlight will automatically be opened as a Smart Filter, as shown in Figure 6.38.

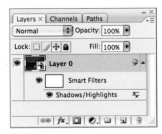

Figure 6.38 Photoshop CS4 enables you to use the Shadow/Highlight adjustment as a Smart Filter.

The default dialog box for Shadow/Highlight in Photoshop includes only the Amount sliders for Shadows and Highlights. You should never use it in this abbreviated form; instead check the option for More Options. This enlarges the dialog box to include many additional controls for fine-tuning the adjustment (see Figure 6.39) and unlocks the real power of the Shadow/Highlight tool.

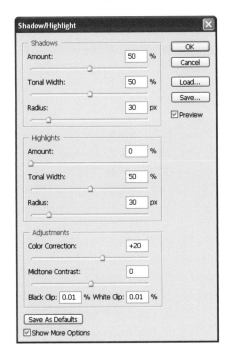

Figure 6.39 When you select the Show More Options check box, the Shadow/Highlight dialog box expands to include more controls.

The controls are divided into three sections. The Shadows and Highlights sections provide similar controls for adjusting areas of your image based on tonal value; the Adjustments section provides additional controls for improving specific aspects of the image. Using the basic Shadow/Highlight control is a simple matter of adjusting the sliders to extract the desired level of detail in the image. As you make these adjustments, use care not to overcorrect, which can create an image that is excessively flat or that has an artificial appearance.

The controls in both the Shadows and Highlights sections are the same, although they obviously target different areas of the image based on tonal value:

Amount   The Amount slider affects the strength of the adjustment you're making to the area. Think of the Amount slider for Shadows as allowing you to decide how much to lighten the darkest areas of your image. The Amount slider for Highlights provides a similar ability to darken the brightest areas. Your first reaction may be that doing so simply reduces contrast and produces a muddy image. However, keep in mind that this adjustment is designed for situations where contrast is too high or when you want to extract more detail from the darkest and brightest areas of your image. When used with modest settings, the result is an effective increase in detail without a problematic loss of contrast.

Tonal Width   To adjust the range of tonal values that will be affected by this adjustment, use the Tonal Width slider. A low value causes only a limited range of tonal values within the image to be affected, whereas a high value allows the adjustment to apply to a wider range. In other words, you expand or contract the area to be adjusted by defining a tonal range. Try to limit the tonal width to as narrow a range as possible to give you the desired results.

Radius   The Radius slider determines how far outward from pixels that fit within the defined tonal range the adjustment will spread. This provides the ability to blend the adjustment to produce a more realistic effect.

> **Note:** You'll find the best settings with experimentation. Usually you'll want the Tonal Width setting to be as limited as possible and still affect the desired tonal range. Often we find effective radius settings around the 25–40 range and again at the very high range of the scale. Don't hesitate to drag the sliders and experiment.

After you've adjusted the controls in the Shadows and Highlights sections, use the Adjustments section to fine-tune the final result. The Color Correction slider is really a saturation adjustment that affects the darkest areas of your image. This control allows you to compensate for shadow areas that often have reduced saturation compared to other areas of the image because there isn't adequate light to enhance the colors. After you've brightened up shadow areas, you'll likely want to increase the saturation slightly so those areas match the rest of the image.

Similarly, brightening shadows and darkening highlights helps extract more detail but results in an overall reduction in contrast. The Midtone Contrast slider allows you to apply some compensation by adjusting contrast for just the midtone values within the image, leaving the shadow and highlight areas you've already adjusted relatively unchanged.

The Black Clip and White Clip settings allow you to specify how much detail can be sacrificed in the image when making adjustments by using Shadow/Highlight. We recommend leaving these values to their default of 0.01% to minimize the loss of detail.

Note: Don't let the Save As Defaults button lull you into thinking you can establish one set of adjustments for Shadow/Highlight that will be appropriate for all images. Each image deserves its own custom settings.

Once you've established the optimal settings in the Shadow/Highlight dialog box, click OK to apply the adjustment to your image, as you can see in Figure 6.40.

PHOTO BY ELLEN ANON

Figure 6.40 The Shadow/Highlight adjustment allows you to extract detail in your image with relative ease.

Shadow/Highlight Adjustments

Elements' Shadows/Highlights tool has a subset of the options Photoshop CS provides, giving access to Shadows, Highlights, and Midtone Contrast. Although Elements does not provide Smart Objects, you can use the same technique explained in the "Curves" section to add a layer mask to your Shadows/Highlights adjustment.

1. Make a copy of your image layer if that's your only layer, by dragging it to the new layer icon ▨ at the top of the Layers palette. If you already have other layers, click on the top layer, hold down the Alt/Option key, and click the double-arrow icon ▶▶ at the top right of the Layers palette to access the fly-out menu. Choose Merge Visible and continue to hold down the Alt/Option key until a new layer appears on top of the other layers. (If only a single layer appears, you released the Alt/Option key too quickly.)

2. Select Enhance > Adjust Lighting > Shadows/Highlights, and a dialog window will appear.

3. Use the sliders to adjust the different parts of your image. If your image isn't changing, make sure the Preview check box is selected.

When you've finished with Shadows/Highlights, click OK and follow Steps 6–9 from the Elements "Curves" section to add a layer mask to your adjustment.

Try It! Open the image ShadowHighlight on the accompanying CD, and work with the Shadow/Highlight adjustment to extract as much detail as possible while maintaining appropriate overall contrast.

Emphasizing Your Subject

Exposure is everything in photography, and for nature photographers it can be especially critical. Being able to reveal detail hidden within your images, and to emphasize key areas of those images, can be a tremendous advantage for the final result. By practicing the adjustments covered in this chapter, you'll be able to exercise tremendous control over your images, taking them far beyond what you'd be able to achieve if you used only the camera to control your exposure.

Learn to emphasize your subject by making it subtly lighter, brighter, and/or more contrasty than the background by using layer masks. By taking advantage of the different exposure tools in conjunction with layer masks, you can tweak the tonalities in different areas of your image, creating a final print (or other output) that would have taken incredible skill and long hours in a traditional darkroom.

Color Adjustments

Color often creates strong emotional reactions, drawing you into a photo or making you pass it by. Expressive images with the most impact use color wisely to direct our attention and elicit reactions. Nature photographers have more choices to make about the colors in their images than do most photographers. Other types of photographers must maintain neutral colors, but we nature photographers are often looking for color casts, such as the warm glow of early morning light. Although we're often trying to create as natural-looking an image as possible, we also have a great deal of latitude to modify colors to make our images more expressive.

7

Chapter Contents
Recognizing Color Casts
Removing Color Casts
Adding a Color Cast
Modifying Colors to Match Nature or Add Impact
Layer Masks and Color Adjustments

Recognizing Color Casts

Sometimes, despite the fact that you may have previously adjusted the White Balance in the raw converter, you may look at your image and decide that the colors just aren't quite right. You may or may not be able to identify which color is the culprit, but you know something is off. At other times you may not even be aware there is a color cast until you do some checking. There are several ways to detect a color cast.

Using Hue/Saturation to Reveal a Color Cast

An easy way to identify a color cast is to open a temporary Hue/Saturation adjustment layer—click the Adjustments panel icon ⬛, choose Hue/Saturation ▦, and drag the Saturation slider all the way to +100. Although your picture will look weird, this will show you where there are colors that don't belong. Think for a minute about what colors you'd expect to see versus what you do see, since the colors are supersaturated. Pay attention to the hues to determine whether there are unexpected colors appearing.

> **Note:** Although it's possible to create any adjustment layer from the main menu bar—by choosing Layer > New Adjustment Layer—we recommend opening all adjustment layers from the Adjustments panel or from the ⬛ icon at the bottom of the Layers panel. (In Elements the New Adjustment Layer button is at the top of the Layers palette.) That way, you won't accidentally find yourself choosing Image > Adjustments on the main menu and working directly on your pixels.

As an example, Figure 7.1 shows a picture of a snowy egret with no obvious color cast and the same image with the Hue/Saturation slider pulled all the way to +100. Although you expect the water to turn blue or blue/cyan and the sand to turn yellowish, you do not expect the egret to be magenta. Clearly there is at least a partial magenta cast to this image.

Figure 7.1 At first glance, there is not an obvious color cast in this picture (left). Boosting the saturation to +100 reveals an unexpected magenta cast in the snowy egret (right).

Note that early-morning outdoor pictures on what will be a sunny day often have a cyan cast to them. Pictures taken in shade often have bluish casts. Magenta casts are also common, particularly with landscape pictures or images that include a partly cloudy sky.

If pulling the Hue/Saturation slider has revealed an obviously problematic color cast, it can be tempting to just go to the channel containing that color and reduce the saturation. Occasionally that approach will work, but the problem is that it reduces the saturation of that color throughout the entire image, even in areas that should be that color. There are several more useful approaches to removing the color cast that we will describe shortly.

After using the Hue/Saturation adjustment dialog box to identify a color cast, click the trash can icon to remove this layer. You need it only temporarily to give you an idea of whether you should consider doing something to remove a color cast.

Using the Info Panel to Reveal a Color Cast

When we talk about "neutral" in a digital picture, we're referring to the relationship of the red, green, and blue values for any tone, from pure white (where the RGB values are 255,255,255) to pure black (RGB values 0,0,0), as well as all tonalities of gray in between (in which the red, green, and blue values are all nearly identical). Neutral also means that pixels that should be pure red will have an RGB reading of 255,0,0; pure green will be 0,255,0; and pure blue will be 0,0,255. The farther away from these readings any pixel is that should be neutral gray or pure red, green, or blue, the more of a color cast there is. We nature photographers rarely, if ever, need to be concerned with *total* neutrality. In fact, outdoor lighting almost always imparts a color cast—sometimes warm, sometimes cool. Nonetheless, it's important to understand what neutral would be.

> **Note:** To view the Info palette in both Photoshop and Elements, choose Window > Info.

Understanding the values that neutral pixels should have enables you to check for a color cast by using the Info panel. If there are any areas of the picture that you know should be neutral (pure white, gray, or black), zoom in and place your cursor over that area. Take a look at the Info panel to see the red, green, and blue values of that point.

If the pixel is neutral, the values should be all the same (or very close). If one value is higher than the others, there will be a cast in that direction. For example, if an area that should be neutral has roughly equal blue and green values but a higher red value, the picture has a reddish cast. Conversely, if the number for one channel reads lower than the other two channels, the cast is toward the opposite color of that channel. Table 7.1 lists all the ways that one RGB channel might differ from the other two, thus creating a color cast.

Table 7.1 Identifying a Color Cast via the Info Panel

If This Value Is Off…	…This Cast Will Be Seen
Red high	Red
Red low	Cyan
Green high	Green
Green low	Magenta
Blue high	Blue
Blue low	Yellow

In Figure 7.2, a reading taken from the wing of the white pelican should be close to neutral. Instead, it shows markedly lower red values, reflecting a cyan cast throughout the image.

Figure 7.2 You know this image has a cyan color cast because the RGB values of a sample from the white wing (point #1 in the Info panel) are 139,152,150.

Note: Remembering the basic RGB colors (red, green, and blue) and their opposites (cyan, magenta, and yellow) will make your color adjustments much easier and predictable. Red and cyan are opposites, and green and magenta are opposites, as are blue and yellow. Once you appreciate this fact, you'll know to add cyan to reduce a red cast, add green to reduce a magenta cast, add blue to reduce a yellow cast, and so on.

If you have determined that there is a color cast in your image, you'll have to decide whether to eliminate it. Not all color casts are bad! Remember that part of the reason many nature photographers prefer early-morning and late-afternoon light is for the lovely warm (yellow/red) quality it imparts to their subjects as opposed to the more neutral or cooler light that may occur in the middle of the day.

Removing Color Casts

There are a number of different approaches to removing color casts, and depending upon the individual circumstances, one approach is likely to be preferable in a particular situation, whereas another approach may be more effective in another. For that reason, we'll present several ways to deal with color casts, some of which are objective and some subjective.

> **Note:** If while you are shooting you know that you will want to make sure the colors are as accurate as possible, take a shot with a gray card or other neutral gray object in the frame. That way, you can use it for the eyedropper and ensure accurate neutral color.

Subjective Methods for Removing a Color Cast

First we'll look at the subjective ways to remove a color cast from your image. Some of these approaches allow Photoshop to do most of the work for you, while others offer considerable individual control over the process and invite a great deal of personal preference.

Using the Gray Eyedropper

If there's an area that you know should be neutral—it can be any tonality from almost white to almost black and any shade of gray in between—there is a very simple way to eliminate the color cast in your picture.

1. Create a new Levels adjustment layer by clicking the Adjustments panel icon and selecting Levels.

2. Take the time to double-click the word *Levels* in the Layers panel and rename the layer; we use the name "color cast." That way, if you return to this file later, assuming you save it with your layers intact, you'll know exactly what you did in each layer.

3. Click the gray (middle) eyedropper to select it, and then click the area of your image that should be neutral. Photoshop will automatically define the point you click as "neutral" (that is, having equal red, green, and blue values) and will remap the rest of the image accordingly.

> **Try It!** Open Colorcast1 from the accompanying CD, or open an image of your own that you suspect has a color cast but includes an area you think should be neutral. First determine whether there is in fact a color cast (either use the Hue/Saturation slider method or check the Info panel). Next create a Levels adjustment layer, and click the middle eyedropper on a neutral pixel to remove the cast. Turn off the visibility of the Levels layer (by clicking the eyeball next to it in the Layers panel). Add a Curves adjustment layer, and click the same point with the Curves middle eyedropper. Then alternate viewing the Curves and Levels layers' visibility to compare the results.

You can also do the same thing using the gray (middle) eyedropper in the Curves Adjustment Layer box; the results will be just slightly different, since Levels uses a linear algorithm to do the remapping whereas Curves naturally uses a tone curve. Practically speaking, the results will be very similar in most cases. The results are also very similar to using the White Balance eyedropper in ACR.

Removing Color Casts in Elements

Elements does not have a Curves adjustment layer, and the Color Curves tool is not suitable for removing color casts. However, Elements does have a specific Remove Color Cast tool. To access it, select Enhance > Adjust Color > Remove Color Cast. Then click on part of the image that should be black, gray, or white, and Elements will remove the color cast. This is similar to choosing Levels and using the gray eyedropper.

Using a Color Balance Adjustment Layer

Photoshop ONLY

A Color Balance adjustment ⚖ may be the most generally useful approach to correcting color casts. In essence, it presents the sliders from each of the individual color channels within Levels in one interface, along with the ability to set the sliders to affect primarily the midtones, shadows, and/or highlights. As you pull the sliders, you are shifting the color values in your image toward the basic colors (red, green, and blue) or toward their opposites (cyan, magenta, and yellow), as shown in Figure 7.3.

The Tone Balance section is set by default to affect the midtones when you first open a Color Balance adjustment layer. When Midtones is checked, the changes you make on the sliders affect the majority of the pixels and tones in your image, excluding only the brightest and darkest values. Selecting the Highlights or Shadows option instead allows you to primarily adjust the most extreme tonalities in your image. You may want to adjust each of them slightly differently.

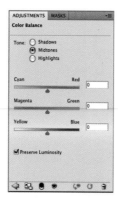

Figure 7.3 Color Balance provides an easy interface to adjust the balance within each color channel as well as to make those changes to the midtones, highlights, and/or shadows.

This can be quite useful in some situations common to nature photography. For example, if you have a white bird photographed in early-morning light on water, you may want to emphasize the warm light on the bird but not make the water appear too discolored. To do this, click Highlights and adjust the sliders to allow for more yellow and red and possibly magenta than in the midtones and shadows, where you might be attempting to limit the color cast, as shown in Figure 7.4.

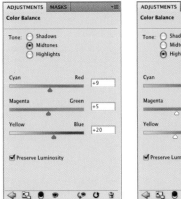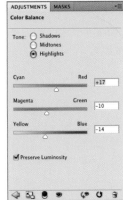

Figure 7.4 Adjusting the Color Balance sliders differently for the highlights than for the midtones enables you to leave more of a color cast on the white bird while limiting the color cast on the water.

Setting the best position for the sliders can be challenging and is a subjective, visual decision. If there is a strong color cast in your image, it's often easiest to begin by working with the corresponding slider in the midtones. For example, if your image has a strong cyan cast, start by adjusting the Cyan/Red slider for Midtones. Then, if necessary, adjust the other sliders for midtone values; after that, click Highlights and adjust, and then click Shadows to set those sliders. You may be happy with the color balance after adjusting only the midtone sliders since they affect the majority of the pixels within most pictures.

On the other hand, you may find it necessary to adjust each slider several times, and you may even discover that you can't decide which setting you like best. At that point, we offer two suggestions:

- Pull the slider that's creating a problem for you to an extreme position, and start again. You might even pull it all the way to the right, then reset it and note the setting, and then pull it all the way to the left and readjust it to where it looks best. Hopefully you'll be able to find a position that looks good to you.

- If you're still not sure, it's time to get up and walk away from your computer for a couple of minutes. When you come back, note your gut-level reaction to the picture. Are the colors good, or are they too much toward a specific color cast? Trust your immediate reaction, don't overthink it, and then make any necessary changes.

Objective Method for Removing a Color Cast

Photoshop ONLY

At times, even nature photographers want to make their images as neutral as possible, and in such cases an objective approach may be best. We've also encountered some photographers who are color-blind and who don't have the luxury of having someone close by to comment on the colors within their images. Sometimes they feel safest using an objective method to correct color casts.

To objectively remove a color cast, you use all three eyedroppers in a Levels adjustment. Initially you'll identify and set the white and black points, and then you'll have Photoshop define them as neutral.

As you already know, you can hold down the Alt/Option key while pulling the endpoint sliders within Levels to identify the lightest and darkest pixels within your image. However, you don't want to have to rely on your memories as to exactly where they're located. Instead, we'll show you how to mark them to be sure you're accurately targeting the darkest and lightest pixels within your image.

To objectively remove a color cast, follow these steps:

1. Begin by choosing the Color Sampler tool. It's located on the Tools panel with the Eyedropper tool (see Figure 7.5). Make certain to set the Sample Size option on the Options bar to 3×3 Average rather than to its default value, which is a one-point sample. The 3×3 Average option causes Photoshop to read an average of 9 pixels, which prevents you from accidentally selecting a pixel that is different from its neighboring pixels.

2. Create a Threshold adjustment layer by choosing the ▨ icon in the Adjustments Panel.

Figure 7.5 The Color Sampler tool allows you to mark particular pixels within the image (left). It's best to set the Color Sampler tool to use a 3×3 sample to avoid accidentally sampling an aberrant pixel.

3. You see a histogram with only one slider, and your image is in black and white, with no tones in between (see Figure 7.6). Move the slider all the way to the right until the image preview becomes totally black.

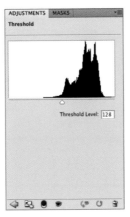

Figure 7.6 Your image will appear in black and white, with no in-between tonalities.

4. Slowly move the slider to the left, and stop when you see the first pixels begin to turn white. These are the lightest pixels in your image.

5. Zoom in by pressing Ctrl + plus to clearly identify the lightest pixels. Accuracy is vital here. Click OK.

6. Now, with the Color Sampler tool still selected, place your cursor over the lightest pixels in your image, and click. The tool leaves a small circle with the number 1 on your image. (Alternatively, you can hold down the Shift key and use the Eyedropper tool.)

7. Zoom out to see your entire image by pressing Ctrl+0/⌘+0.

8. Now move the slider all the way to the left so that the preview becomes entirely white. Gradually move it to the right, and note where the first black pixels appear. These are the darkest pixels in the image.

9. Again, zoom in as necessary to clearly see these pixels, and then click OK.

10. Place your cursor over one of the darkest pixels, and click. This time, the Color Sampler tool leaves a small circle with the number 2.

11. Zoom out again by pressing Ctrl+0/⌘+0 to see your whole image.

12. Since you no longer need the Threshold adjustment layer, click the trash can icon in the Adjustments panel to remove it. The selected pixels remain marked, and you have an objective indicator of the darkest and lightest pixels within your image, as shown in Figure 7.7.

13. Now create a Levels adjustment layer. Be sure to rename it to indicate you're using this one to remove a color cast.

PHOTO BY ELLEN ANON

Figure 7.7 The darkest pixel (bottom edge) and lightest pixel (corner of the mouth) in your image are marked with a numbered target so you can easily identify them. (Note the red circles are here for illustrative purposes only; you won't see them on your image.)

14. Next, you're going to set the values for the black and white points that you want Photoshop to use. If you have previously saved default values for black and white, you can skip this step:

   a. Double-click the black eyedropper to open the Color Picker dialog box. Type values of R = 10, G = 10, and B = 10 for the black point, and click OK. (If you have established a different set of black values for your printer, use them here.)

   b. Double-click the white eyedropper, and the Color Picker dialog box reappears. Type values of R = 244, G = 244, B = 244, as shown in Figure 7.8, for the white point, and click OK.

   c. Click OK in the main Levels dialog box. Because you've changed one or more eyedropper values, Photoshop asks whether you want to set these as your default values. Click OK.

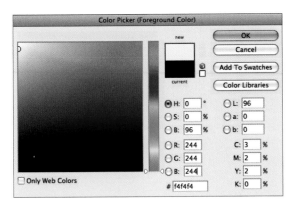

Figure 7.8 By typing values into the Color Picker, you can set the black and white values within your image and then save them as the default values for Photoshop to use in the future.

Note: Because most of our printers can't print in ways that allow us to differentiate shades of black all the way to 0,0,0 or whites all the way to 255,255,255, we have to use slightly different values. Once those are set, we can save them as default values. The actual ideal values for your printer may vary and can be determined by printing out test strips of blacks and whites at various values—(8,8,8), (12,12,12), (15,15,15), and so on—to determine where you can begin to see differences in the dark tones. You can do a similar test strip for the whites. The values suggested in Step 14 work for many people.

15. Now click the white eyedropper and then move your cursor onto your image. Carefully and accurately align the cursor with the point or the Color Sampler tool marked with the number 1. When you have precisely aligned the cursor and the sampled point, click OK. This remaps that point to an RGB value of 244,244,244, or neutral white. Verify this by looking at the Info panel, which shows you the "before" and "after" values of the targeted points.

16. Repeat the same process with the black eyedropper. In most cases, the color cast within the image is neutralized (see Figure 7.9). In some images, however, you also need to use the gray (middle) eyedropper and click somewhere in the image that should be neutral.

17. To remove the little circles with the numbers by them, reselect the Color Sampler tool and hold down the Alt/Option key. As you approach a circle, your cursor changes to a scissors. When you click, the circle is removed. Alternately, simply hide them by choosing View > Extras from the menu. This toggles the visibility of the color samples. Simply hiding them can be a time-saver if there is any possibility that you might want to modify your color-cast adjustments.

Try It! Open the image named Colorcast3 on the CD, or one of your own images, and try removing the color cast using the objective method. You can compare the results with what you obtain using your favorite subjective method.

PHOTO BY ELLEN ANON

Figure 7.9 Compare this neutral version of the heron with the original in Figure 7.7.

This approach may seem quite long, but actually it's pretty straightforward and a good way to set your black and white points as well as to remove a color cast objectively. You could also use the eyedroppers in a Curves adjustment layer to achieve similar results. You would follow the exact same procedure described in this section from within the Curves dialog box.

Objective Method for Removing a Color Cast

Elements does not allow you to mark points on an image, but there is still an objective way to neutralize a color cast.

1. Duplicate the image by right-clicking on the Background layer in the Layers palette and selecting Duplicate Layer.

2. Select Edit > Fill Layer to open the dialog box shown here:

Continues

3. Set the fill color to be 50% gray and set the blending mode to Difference. We will use this layer, which helps us identify where the gray parts of the image should be, to find a point to use with a Levels adjustment. Click OK.

4. Add a Threshold layer by clicking the Create Adjustment Layer button and selecting Threshold.

5. Drag the slider all the way to the left to make the image completely white. Gradually move it to the right until some pixels start to go black.

6. To help yourself mentally mark the point with the black pixel, select View > Grid to turn on the grid and View > Rulers to see the rulers.

7. Hide the Threshold and duplicated layers by clicking the Toggle Visibility button ⊡.

8. Select the original layer and make a new Levels adjustment layer by clicking the Create Adjustment Layer button and selecting Levels.

9. Click the gray eyedropper in the Levels dialog and click on the point you identified in Step 5. Elements will remove the color cast.

Adding a Color Cast

The reality is that nature photographers get up ridiculously early in the morning and stay out photographing until the sunset is completely over because we *like* our pictures to have the warm, special light of early and late day. We tend to prefer the color casts imparted by this light because our photos have a different feeling in them and often create more impact on the viewer than more neutral versions of the same subject. It's possible to create color casts to simulate that light using the same subjective techniques we used before to remove color casts.

For example, if you're using the middle (gray) eyedropper from within Levels or Curves and you click an area that should not be neutral, Photoshop will still be obliging and redefine the values of that point to be neutral anyway, and the rest of the image then has a color cast. This can be a good thing! You can introduce a slight warmth to your images this way by clicking a point that actually should be slightly bluish or cyanish, as shown in Figure 7.10. Conversely, you can make them appear cooler by clicking a pixel that should actually be slightly yellowish or reddish. Remember that Ctrl+Z/ ⌘+Z undoes your last step, so you can use a trial-and-error approach in finding the right spot to use. Obviously, this is a subjective way to determine the color balance within your picture that relies on Photoshop to do most of the work for you.

If you prefer to use a Color Balance adjustment layer, simply adjust the sliders to achieve the desired effect. No one but you has to know that the picture wasn't taken in the earliest morning light!

Figure 7.10 By clicking the middle eyedropper on a point that should be slightly bluish, you can impart a warmer color cast to an image.

Photoshop also offers a Photofilter adjustment . Choosing this adjustment layer allows you to select from a drop-down menu containing a variety of preset color tints, including some with familiar names like 81 or Warming Filter (see Figure 7.11). Alternatively, you can choose the specific color for the filter by selecting the Color option and clicking the color swatch. You can adjust the Density slider to control the strength of the effect. Although this is a quick and easy way to add a color cast to your image, the slight disadvantage is that it affects the entire image equally.

Figure 7.11 The Photofilter adjustment layer contains a number of familiar-sounding filters.

Modifying Colors to Match Nature or Add Impact

After you've adjusted the overall color cast of your image—whether to neutralize it or to add a color cast—you may want to work with the colors a little more to help convey the mood and impact you have in mind. Colors elicit emotional reactions from those who view your pictures. For example, pastels can be calming, while bold primary colors can be energizing, as shown in Figure 7.12. A blue cast in a snow scene can add to the sense of coldness and perhaps isolation. Warm yellow light rays drifting through trees or lighting flowers may give a sense of peacefulness and well-being or spirituality.

It's well worth the effort to spend the time to make certain the colors in your pictures elicit the reactions you have in mind. The primary tools you'll use for this are Hue/Saturation, Vibrance, and Selective Color adjustment layers.

PHOTO BY ELLEN ANON

Figure 7.12 Colors elicit emotional reactions from the viewer, so it makes sense to adjust the colors accordingly.

Adjusting Hue and Saturation

In CS4 you may opt to make most of your hue and saturation adjustments in the raw converter. However, there will still be times when you want to use the Hue/Saturation adjustment in Photoshop.

Most photographers who use Photoshop are comfortable opening the Hue/Saturation dialog box (which of course we recommend you do as an adjustment layer) and adjusting the saturation of their image. This is one of the more intuitive adjustments within Photoshop, and it can make your images come to life. However, be careful not to go to excess with saturation, not only because the colors will look fake but also because you risk losing detail as you increase the saturation. This is the result of more and more pixels being shifted toward the purest colors, resulting in a loss of detail in those areas. With most images, you'll find a modest saturation increase in the composite channel of 6 to 12 is usually effective. Of course, this varies among files from different cameras as well as individual preferences and the adjustments that you've already made in ACR.

Although you can modify the saturation of all the colors within your image by using the composite or "Master" channel (which is the default when you open the Hue/Saturation adjustment layer), one extremely useful feature is the ability to target a particular color range from the drop-down menu (see Figure 7.13). This way you can modify colors individually by selecting the desired color and changing the saturation—or hue—of a single color in your image.

CS4 has added a new, slick way to modify specific colors in your image. Click the 🖑 icon in the upper part of the Hue/Saturation dialog, and then move your cursor over your image. It will change to an eyedropper. Click on the color you want to modify and drag the slider to the right to increase the saturation and to the left to decrease it. Adding the Ctrl/⌘ key while clicking and dragging will allow you to adjust the hue rather than the saturation.

Figure 7.13 The Hue/Saturation dialog box enables you to target not only the composite channel but individual colors as well.

You can adjust several different colors using a single adjustment layer as long as the colors don't overlap. In addition you can further adjust the range of colors that are modified by using the Color Range bars, which we'll talk about in just a minute.

As with earlier versions of Photoshop and Elements, you can also target a specific range of colors to modify within the Hue/Saturation dialog. However, you can't do this from the composite channel; you have to begin within a specific color channel from the drop-down menu. Select the range of colors to modify by first clicking the eyedropper in the Hue/Saturation dialog box and then clicking the color you want to adjust.

Don't worry if you're not sure which color to choose from the drop-down menu. It doesn't matter which one you begin with, because once you click with the first eyedropper, Photoshop automatically changes to the correct color channel. You can increase the range of colors to be modified by clicking with the plus eyedropper or decrease it by clicking with the minus eyedropper.

Alternately, you can refine the range of colors to modify by adjusting the Color Range bars that appear between the two color gradients when you have specified a particular color channel (see Figure 7.14). This process is a bit more advanced than the other adjustments you've been making.

Figure 7.14 You can set the range of colors to be adjusted by moving the Color Range bars that appear between the two color gradients at the bottom of the Hue/Saturation dialog box.

To refine the range of colors to modify, follow these steps:

1. We recommend initially dragging the Saturation slider all the way to the left so that the selected range of colors is shifted to gray, as shown in Figure 7.15. This helps you to see what areas of the image you're modifying.

Figure 7.15 By moving the saturation slider to the left, the range of colors you will be modifying appears in gray on the color gradient.

2. Click the bars, and drag them to increase or decrease the targeted range of colors. This limits or expands the colors that will be affected by the adjustments you make to the sliders.

3. Click the two triangles outside the bars to define the extent of feathering of the color adjustments. These triangles control how gradual the transition is between the modified and original colors so that the adjustment is less obvious.

4. Having selected the target range of colors, move the Hue, Saturation, and Lightness sliders to achieve the desired effect.

Try It! Open the file HueSat from the accompanying CD or open one of your own images. Select a single color and then a range of colors to adjust. Try changing not only the saturation but the hue as well.

Colorizing an Image

There are times when your original image may contain very little color information and instead contain a lot of neutral values, for example this sometimes happens in pictures of fog. In such cases you may find that simply adjusting the Hue and Saturation sliders is not enough to add the color that you're after. The answer is to use the Colorize option in the Hue/Saturation dialog. Colorize changes the image into a duotone, and you use the Hue slider to select the desired color. The Saturation slider then adjusts the intensity of the color.

The Colorize option was helpful when one of our students had a lovely image of a gray covered bridge set amidst trees. He wanted to make the bridge red, but just changing the hue and saturation alone didn't work, so he used the following procedure:

1. Select the area to be colorized using any of the selection tools discussed in Chapter 4.

2. Open a Hue/Saturation adjustment layer and check the Colorize box.

3. Notice that the Hue and Saturation sliders have moved substantially. Adjust all the sliders to colorize the targeted portion of your image as desired.

Adjusting Vibrance versus Saturation

Photoshop CS4 added a new adjustment called Vibrance. To access it, click the V icon in the Adjustments panel. The Vibrance slider is similar to its counterpart in ACR and selectively increases or decreases saturation. It affects reds and yellows less than other colors and alters less-saturated colors more than strongly saturated colors. Although this was designed initially with the intent to preserve skin tones while enabling saturation of background components without using a layer mask, knowing which colors will be more or less impacted makes this a tool that can also be helpful to nature photographers. For example, in a shot of fall leaves, you can intensify the grass and sky without totally oversaturating the yellows and reds in the leaves.

The Vibrance adjustment also has a Saturation slider to enable you to adjust the overall image saturation without having to go to the Saturation adjustment.

Fine-Tuning with Selective Color

Sometimes a color may still not look right despite your best efforts at adjusting the color cast and making Hue/Saturation or Vibrance adjustments. The Selective Color adjustment ◣, accessible from the Adjustments panel in the bottom row, enables you to modify the hue of specific colors, as well as whites, neutrals, and blacks (see Figure 7.16). This tool enables far greater control over the exact hue of any specific color than is possible within Hue/Saturation, as well as the ability to adjust color casts in whites, neutrals, and blacks.

Figure 7.16 The Selective Color dialog box allows you to modify the color components of specific colors as well as the whites, midtones, and blacks within your image.

Note: Similar adjustments that can be made with Selective Color can be made in the Hue/Saturation/Luminance tab of ACR. However, ACR does not have the option to adjust the whites, neutrals, and blacks within the same dialog box.

First, select the color you want to modify by clicking the appropriate color. For example, if you've adjusted an image but the blue of the sky seems off, you can alter the shade of blue, as shown in Figure 7.17. Notice that the sliders are labeled Cyan, Magenta, Yellow, and Black this time, because Selective Color was originally designed for use with CMYK output. But it works equally well with RGB. If you increase cyan, you are decreasing red, and if you decrease cyan, then obviously red increases. Similarly, increasing or decreasing magenta alters the percentage of green used in the color, and changing the amount of yellow will alter the amount of blue. By changing the percentage of each component of a color, you have fine control over the specific hues.

So in the case of your blue sky, you might want to increase the cyan and blue components to make a better shade of sky blue (which is composed of both blue and cyan tones). If you increase the black within the Blues menu, the blue will get darker. In a sky, it's likely you'll need to work with the drop-down menus for Blue and Cyan and adjust the components within them.

Extremely precise adjustments are possible within each of the colors in the Selective Color Options dialog. Those photographers who are latent artists may particularly enjoy this ability to fine-tune colors.

Figure 7.17 Selective Color was used to improve the shade of blue in the sky by making it slightly warmer.

You will find that as you make a color more pure, there may be less need to increase overall saturation as much. This can lead to a more natural and pleasing final result in your image.

To add a little extra "pop" to your pictures, select Black as your target color, and then increase the percentage of Black by a small amount, such as 2. The actual amount varies by image. This gives many images the illusion of being slightly sharper.

You can use Selective Color to remove some stubborn color casts by choosing Neutrals in the Colors list and adjusting the sliders as needed. One of our students came to a workshop with a shot, taken under unusual lighting in a mausoleum, that had a strong cyan cast. The only method that was successful in removing the color cast was to virtually eliminate cyan from the Neutrals and Whites within Selective Color.

Layer Masks and Color Adjustments

So far we've described a variety of approaches for modifying the color within your entire image, all of which use adjustment layers and all of which adjust the color across the entire area of your photo. But there will be times when you want to target a specific part of your image to change, a part that will be determined by the subject matter rather than by a particular color range. For example, you may want to increase the saturation of your subject more than the background to help draw attention to your subject. Of course you'll use layer masks to do that. If you have any uncertainties about how to use layer masks, we urge you to take the time to refer back to the section "Targeting Adjustments with a Layer Mask" in Chapter 6. Remember that in CS4 the nonmodal adjustments make it easy to go back and forth fluidly between creating a layer mask and modifying an adjustment. Using layer masks gives you precise control over the final appearance of your images. Layer masks work the same way for all adjustments.

Using a Layer Mask for Color Adjustment

Let's apply a mask to an image of a burrowing owl with a green background. (This image is called BurrowingOwl on the accompanying CD.) To increase the saturation of the colors within the owl, but not affect the background in order to help draw attention to the bird, take these steps:

1. Create a Hue/Saturation adjustment layer by clicking the icon in the Adjustments panel.

2. Increase the saturation to make the owl look good. Ignore what's happening to the background.

3. In this case it's easier to manually paint the layer mask rather than use a selection method such as Color Range because the colors within the owl are quite similar to the background. Although we could begin with a white mask and paint out the background, it will be easier to begin with a black mask—hiding the effect of the layer—and then paint with white over the bird to reveal the effect on the bird. To quickly fill the layer mask with black, choose Edit > Fill from the menu, and choose Black for Contents.

Note: A shortcut for filling a layer mask with black is Ctrl+Backspace/⌘+Delete.

4. Now use your Brush tool to paint on your image preview using white as your foreground color. As long as your adjustment layer is still selected, you are actually painting on the layer mask and not the image itself. Paint with white over the bird to reveal the increased saturation only on the bird, as shown in Figure 7.18.

5. Next, modify the hue of the background using Selective Color. Create a new Selective Color adjustment layer (via the icon in the Layers panel), and label it **Background Hue**.

6. Modify the colors until they are pleasing, and click OK.

7. To save the time of re-creating a mask to affect only the background, click the Hue/Saturation adjustment layer to make it active.

Figure 7.18 Filling with black allows you to quickly create a black layer mask; you'll then paint with white on the mask to reveal the changes you made in that layer.

8. Hold down the Alt/Option key, click directly on the layer mask icon, and then drag it on top of the Selective Color adjustment layer. A dialog box appears asking whether you want to replace the mask. Click Yes.

9. Unfortunately, this mask is the opposite of what you need, because you want to change the background on this layer. To invert the mask, go to the Mask panel and choose Invert. The inverted mask enables you to modify the background without affecting the bird. Copying layer masks from layer to layer and inverting them as needed can be a time-saver.

> **Note:** If you've created a layer mask on one layer and want to further modify the same areas using another adjustment layer, Ctrl+click/⌘+click the layer mask icon in the first adjustment layer *before* creating the new adjustment layer. Photoshop creates an active selection based on that mask. Then when you open a new adjustment layer, the same mask appears.

> **Note:** To copy a layer mask from one layer to another, hold down the Alt/Option key, click the layer mask you want to copy, and drag it to the one you want to replace.

Using layer masks is easy and gives you incredible ability to fine-tune the color (and tonal values) within specific areas of your image. Regardless of which approach you prefer for creating your layer masks, being able to enhance parts of your image—such as the eyes of your subject—is invaluable.

Arthur Morris, a world-renowned bird photographer, offers some thoughts on how he uses QuickMasks in conjunction with Photoshop adjustments to make his bird images even more compelling. QuickMasks are another way of making a selection. Once you've created a QuickMask, any layer mask you add to an adjustment layer you create, will reflect the selection. Of course, you can continue to modify the layer mask in all the traditional ways we discussed in Chapter 6.

Digital Eye Doctor

by Arthur Morris

In *The Art of Bird Photography,* I wrote, "When viewing wildlife, or wildlife art, we tend to make immediate eye contact. Consequently, if a bird's eye is in sharp focus, it gives the photograph an impression of overall sharpness." While optimizing my images in Photoshop, I often have the chance to improve the look of a bird's eye or eyes, and I have developed a useful bag of tricks for doing just that. Doing so can add greatly to the drama and impact of an image.

For 99% of my eye repairs, I now use QuickMasks, which are simple to use and feature feathering equivalent to half the width of the brush. This results in seamless selective adjustments.

To set up for quick masking, double-click the bottom icon in the toolbar ⬚. This brings up the Quick Mask Options dialog. In the Color Indicates section, choose Selected Areas. Then change the opacity to 80% and click OK. I stick with the default bright red color, but you can change it by clicking on the red box and selecting your new color. Now you are good to go.

To toggle back and forth between RGB and QuickMask mode, press the keyboard shortcut Q.

Let's start with a simple one, darkening the pupil to increase apparent sharpness. First, make sure that you are on the Background or Smart Object layer. Then draw a small box around the eye with the Zoom tool so that the bird's eye fills a good portion of the screen. Press Q to enter QuickMask mode and then press B for the Brush tool. Check to see that the hardness is set to 0. It's best to use a brush that's not larger than half the size of the pupil. Make sure that the foreground color is set to Black by pressing D. Now click and paint the pupil with the cursor.

If you color outside the lines a bit, don't worry. Press E for the Eraser tool and erase your mistake. Press B to do more painting. Once you are happy with your paint job, press Q again to exit Quick Mask mode. Your selection will be outlined by the marching ants. Now open a Curves adjustment layer and drag the curve down a bit to darken the pupil. Do not overdo it as this will result in a black, plastic, cookie-cutter type eye. Once you go back to view the whole image, you can always reduce the effect by reducing the opacity of the Curves layer.

When you use flash to photograph birds, the pupils are often rendered quite funky. Red-eye and steel-eye (an odd-looking silvery crescent on the eye) were common when using flash with film, but with digital (which is more sensitive to flash than film), the effects are both wider ranging and even more detrimental to the image. When you examine a flashed bird's pupil (and sometimes the entire eye as well) at high magnification, unnatural highlights and lightened and artificially colored pupils are often revealed. Most folks simply ignore these problems, but the fix takes only minutes.

Prepare a QuickMask of the pupil as above, but instead of making a Curves adjustment make a Hue/Saturation adjustment. Slide the Saturation slider to the left to between −70 and −100, and then move the Lightness slider also to the left anywhere from −50 to −90. Reducing the saturation will eliminate the purples in the pupil and darkening it will make it look sharper. As earlier, be careful not to overdo it.

Though most photographers do not realize it, when we properly expose for a bird with white in its plumage, the middle tones are about a stop underexposed (and the blacks about two stops under). In addition, the eyes of many

Continues

Digital Eye Doctor *(Continued)*

birds are rather deep-set. As a result, the irises, which often range from light gray to yellow to buff, are often well underexposed. To selectively lighten the iris, prepare a QuickMask as described earlier. Then make a Curves adjustment and drag the curve up a bit to lighten the iris. Toggle the eye icon to help you evaluate the changes that you have made.

At times, a bird's eye or eyes (or more often, the bird's face or head) can use some selective sharpening even after you have darkened the pupil. Once again it is QuickMask to the rescue. Paint a QuickMask of the eye, the face, or the head as needed. Then press Ctrl+J/⌘+J to put your selection on its own layer. Then select Filter > Sharpen > Unsharp Mask and enter the following values: Amount: 15, Radius: 65, and Threshold: 0 or 1. These are the basic settings that I start with when working with a contrast mask (which increases the apparent sharpness). Depending on the image, you can try anywhere from 10 to 30 for Amount and from 30 to 130 for Radius. Again, you can see the changes that you have made by clicking the eye icon off and on. When you are happy with the degree of sharpening, click OK. When you're creating a contrast mask, the selected area is often darkened. At times this is beneficial to the image, but at times you will need to lighten the selected area. You can do this easily by making a Curve adjustment.

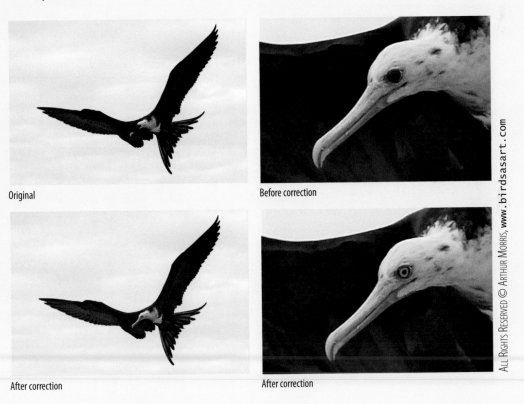

Original

Before correction

After correction

After correction

If you've followed our workflow so far, you've cropped and rotated your image if necessary, removed any dust or scratches, made any necessary exposure adjustments, and modified the colors so that your image has the desired impact. Be sure to save your image at this point with your layers intact as your master file. The following chapters provide additional ideas of ways to create and present your images.

Composites

Many nature photographers are initially loath to consider making composites, believing that this is somehow "cheating" or "dishonest." There is a clear need for photographers using Photoshop to be ethical and reveal when they have made changes to their images so that they no longer reflect the reality of what they saw and what existed. However, sometimes combining elements from several pictures can create more impact and be more representative of an experience. Ironically, compositing techniques can actually enable photographers to more accurately and realistically depict what they saw in certain circumstances, such as with a panorama, an exposure composite, or a focus composite.

Chapter Contents

Creating Panoramas

The advent of the digital darkroom freed photographers from being tied to the constraints of any one particular camera format, whether it is 35mm, medium format, or some other format. By using Photoshop or other software programs, you can stitch together a series of images to create a photograph of a particular shape that better suits the subject. An added benefit of stitching together several frames is that the larger file you create enables you to make prints that are substantially larger and more detailed than you could if you simply used a wider lens and cropped a single frame.

In-Camera Considerations

When photographing images to be combined into panoramas, following certain techniques while shooting enables you to stitch the images together with a minimum of headaches. If you choose to ignore some of the following procedures (and we admit that at times we do), you may still be able to stitch the segments together, but it's likely it will take longer and the results may not be quite what you had hoped:

- Use a tripod. We can't stress that enough!

- Not only do you need to use a tripod, but you also need to level it! If your tripod doesn't have a level built into it, place a small bubble level on a flat top surface to help get it level. This is important because you want the camera to rotate on a level axis. If you enjoy shooting panoramas, consider buying a tripod leveler such as the panning clamp with level from Really Right Stuff (www.reallyrightstuff.com).

- Level your camera as well by adding a double bubble level to the flash shoe of your camera (see Figure 8.1). Taking the time to level both the tripod and the camera means there will be a minimum of "stair-stepping" as you combine the images. Otherwise, you'll lose part of the image because you'll have to crop to get rid of the stair-stepping.

Figure 8.1 Using a bubble level on top of your camera as well as leveling your tripod will make your panoramas stitch together much more easily.

PHOTO BY ELLEN ANON

- You can shoot a panorama without a tripod, but you will lose part of the image near the top and bottom with a horizontal panorama and near the sides with a vertical panorama. When the segments are combined, you're likely to discover that you accidentally changed the relative height and angle of the camera slightly between shots. If you must shoot without a tripod, allow extra room in your framing.

- Plan your shots, allowing for an overlap of about 20–30 percent in most cases, as shown in Figure 8.2. It's helpful to identify key objects/points within each frame that you will use as anchors to help line up each segment. In the first image, this should be within the right 20–30 percent of the frame for a horizontal panorama; for a vertical panorama it would be in the bottom 20–30 percent. As you rotate the camera to take the next shot, place that same anchor point in the left (or top for a vertical panorama) 20–30 percent of the frame, and identify a new object on the right (or bottom). Repeat this process for as many frames as necessary.

PHOTO BY ELLEN ANON

Figure 8.2 Plan your shots ahead of time, allowing for an overlap of 20–30 percent between frames and an identifiable anchor point.

- Although it may seem counterintuitive, it can be quite helpful to shoot a horizontal panorama using the camera in vertical format since it reduces distortion.

- Meter the scene, and *set your exposure manually* to a compromise between the readings for the various segments. While some exposures for some of the frames that you shoot will be slightly off this way, you avoid having huge exposure variations that may result if you use one of the autoexposure techniques such as aperture priority. The autoexposure modes may set an entirely different exposure for each frame, making the final panoramic image a series of mismatched exposures. If part of your subject is white or nearly white and you need to retain the detail in that area, then use the correct exposure for that area as the manual setting for the panorama.

- If you are using a digital camera, *set your white balance manually*. Auto white balance can lead to a slightly different temperature being used in each frame.

- Avoid using a polarizer; the intensity of the polarizing effect varies as your shots vary their angle in relation to the sun, causing parts of the sky to be darker in some frames than in others.

- To minimize having to correct for distortion, use a focal length longer than approximately 35mm. However, it is now possible to use wide-angle lenses and even fish-eyes to create panoramas.

- Always start by taking the farthest left (or top) image first. This helps avoid confusion later when you combine the sections.

- When shooting a panoramic series digitally, it's beneficial to shoot a frame at the beginning and at the end of the sequence that will clue you in when you're editing that these images are part of a panoramic series. Otherwise, it's all too easy to delete images, wondering why you composed them so poorly. One trick we use is to take a shot of our hand at the beginning and end of each series.

- Compositionally, you need a logical beginning and end to the panorama, just as you would have if you were shooting a single-frame image.

Note: Photographers who shoot panoramas frequently are aware of the benefits of eliminating, as much as possible, the distortion effects of parallax. This is achieved by pivoting the lens around what is commonly termed the *nodal point*. Technically, this requires moving the camera and lens back slightly from the tripod pivoting point. Companies such as Really Right Stuff (www.reallyrightstuff.com) produce accessories, including the Omni-Pivot Package, to help with this.

Photomerge

Photomerge makes it easy to stitch even 16-bit panoramas together. Photomerge automatically arranges and blends multiple images to create a panorama with just a few instructions from you. This is a tremendous time-saver, and eliminates tediously stitching the images together manually as we did in versions of Photoshop prior to CS3. Since Photomerge can save the file in layers, we still have the option to tweak the image alignment when necessary, but Photomerge often does a surprisingly accurate job.

There are two ways to get started with Photomerge:

- The easiest way to begin is to highlight the images you wish to use in Bridge—by holding the Ctrl/⌘ key and clicking the images—and then choose Tools > Photoshop > Photomerge from Bridge's menu. If these images are raw files, Photoshop automatically converts them using whatever default you have set within Adobe Camera Raw (ACR). If you have not made any changes to the default, Photoshop uses the Auto Adjust settings.

- If you prefer, select the images to use within Photoshop by going to File > Automate > Photomerge.

  You need to set the source to use either images you have previously opened, files you specify, or a folder. Check the box to have Photomerge automatically blend the files as well as to specify the type of layout you want it to use (see Figure 8.3). Most of the time we find it helpful to use the Geometric Distortion correction option when it's available. If the images show any signs of vignetting, you'll want to check the option for Vignette Removal. Photomerge then creates a layered file containing all the images, properly placed with layer masks applied.

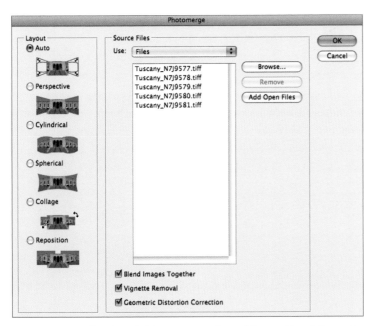

Figure 8.3 Instruct Photoshop which images to merge by specifying open files or folders, and check the Blend Images Together box, along with the Vignette Removal and Geometric Distortion corrections to have Photoshop automatically create the panorama.

You have the following Layout options:

- Use Auto to have Photomerge determine the best approach for the layout. It will read the metadata associated with the lens used and then choose which approach to use as well as apply any necessary geometric correction. Most of the time this is the choice you will use unless there is a specific reason to use one of the other options.

- Choose Perspective to have Photomerge apply corrective perspective distortion. This can be useful with some high dynamic range (HDR) alignments and other layouts with smaller angle compositions—that is, those shot with longer lenses.
- Cylindrical can be used for wide-angle compositions, including 360° compositions. Photoshop first projects the images onto a cylinder and then unwraps them.
- Spherical is also used with wide-angle compositions, particularly if the field of view is wide both horizontally and vertically. This is often the best choice (and what Auto will choose) when the images were taken with extremely wide-angle lenses, including fish-eye lenses. With fish-eyes and extreme wide-angle lenses, be sure to also select the option for geometric correction.
- Choose Reposition Only to have Photomerge create a canvas and align the images with no distortion applied.
- *Collage is similar to Reposition but enables you to uniformly scale and rotate the images while arranging them.*

In Addition to the Layout options, you can check options to Blend Images Together (which we recommend), apply Vignette Removal (only check when necessary), and Apply Geometric Distortion Correction (only check when necessary).

The panorama results will vary depending on the layout you choose, as shown in Figure 8.4. If you have Photomerge apply a distortion in the layout, the processing time increases, particularly if you're creating a panorama from numerous large 16-bit files. However, while you're waiting for your computer to generate the panorama, remind yourself it's a lot faster than doing it manually!

Reposition only

Using Auto

Figure 8.4 Using some of the layouts applies distortion, particularly at the edges of the panorama. Notice the difference between an image that was repositioned only and one where Auto was used.

Usually Photomerge does a good job, but occasionally it fails. It's a good idea to zoom in to ensure that Photomerge has done a good job of aligning each segment. If necessary, select a layer and use the Move tool to nudge a layer into place. Of course, moving one layer will make it likely that you'll need to move the other layers as well.

Note: If you are dealing with a difficult group of files to align and blend because an object, person, or animal significantly changed position between frames, it's best to open the files in Photoshop, apply a layer mask to block out the object wherever necessary, and then invoke Photomerge. Photomerge will respect the layer mask and know which frame should contain the moving thing. Otherwise, Photomerge may or may not do a good job with the alignment and blending.

Using Photomerge

To create a new panorama in Elements from Bridge, select your images just as you would in Photoshop CS4, but choose Tools > Photoshop Elements > Photomerge Panorama. If you are using Windows, select your images in the Organizer and choose File > New> Photomerge Panorama.

To select the images from within Elements, first choose File > New > Photomerge Panorama. Use the Add Open Files button to add images that are currently opened in the Project Bin to the panorama, or click Browse to browse for your images.

Within the Photomerge panel, there is no Advanced Blending option in Elements.

Advanced Image Stitching

Photoshop ONLY

In CS4 there is another way to stitch images together that can be useful with some tricky images, including HDR panoramas. To begin, in Photoshop choose File > Scripts > Load Files into Stack. A dialog box appears in which you specify which images to stack. Photoshop will create a new file containing each image as a layer. Select all the layers, and then choose Edit > Auto-Align Layers. Locking a layer 🔒 will set it as the center for any distortions. A dialog box appears in which you choose the layout; it's similar to the Photomerge dialog box discussed earlier. This places each file into the correct alignment on a correctly sized new canvas. You can apply any type of distortion or transformation necessary to each layer, as well as apply layer masks to instruct Photoshop to remove part of a layer from the final composite. The last step is to choose Edit > Auto-Blend Layers to seamlessly blend the colors and exposures. We'll discuss using the Extended Depth of Field option later in this chapter, but when creating a panorama, you would choose the Panorama option. Photoshop adds layer masks in this step that you can tweak, although the specific adjustments used in the blending are not available.

Try It! Open the Pano1a, Pano1b, and Pano1c images on the accompanying CD, and practice stitching them together. If you prefer, use a series of your own images. We recommend starting with a panorama of no more than three or four sections.

Matching the Exposures of Each Segment of the Panorama

Photoshop
ONLY

With earlier versions of Photoshop, we often had to manually create and blend our panoramas. This is rarely necessary now that the Auto-Align and Auto-Blend algorithms are so good in CS4, but it's conceivable you might shoot a series of images that Photoshop can't blend perfectly. We've seen this primarily in panoramas, including the sun at sunrise or sunset with auto white balance, as shown in Figure 8.5, or if a cloud suddenly obscured the sun in the midst of a series of manual exposures for a panorama that were calculated when the sun was shining.

Figure 8.5 Unless you manually set the white balance and exposure for your panoramas, you're likely to get some variation in colors and tonalities between the files.

If you discover that the exposures of the various segments of the panorama do not match, follow these steps:

1. Click the layer containing the second segment of the panorama to make it active.

2. Zoom in to magnify the area where the first segment and the second segment overlap and where the differences in exposure are evident.

3. Click the Channels panel.

4. Select the Red channel by clicking the word *Red*. When viewed in grayscale, the differences between the two layers are usually easy to see, as shown in Figure 8.6.

5. Choose Image > Adjustments > Levels on the menu bar. Note that this is one of the few times we'll have you working directly on the pixels. Unfortunately, when you're working within channels, you can't readily use adjustment layers.

6. Click the Midpoint slider, and drag it to match up the gray tones in layer 2 with those in layer 1. When they appear the same, as in Figure 8.7, click OK.

7. Repeat the same process for the Green and Blue channels, one at a time.

8. Repeat these steps for each frame you need to match to another until your final image matches in color and tonalities (see Figure 8.8).

Occasionally, a simple linear correction (which Levels applies) can't resolve the changes in exposure between the segments, in which case you need to use Curves rather than Levels in each channel to accurately match up the different segments. This happens more often when the quality or quantity of the lighting is changing dramatically. Follow the same procedure as described in this section, but use Curves instead of Levels.

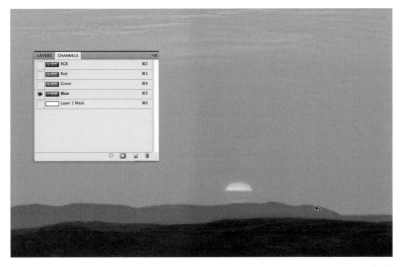

Figure 8.6 Viewing the overlapping area in each channel separately makes it much easier to see the differences.

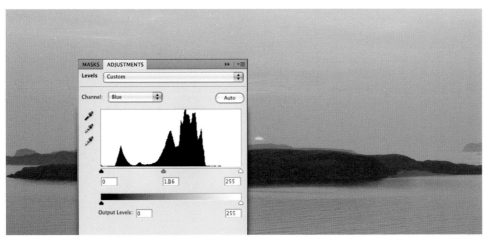

Figure 8.7 Adjusting the Midpoint slider in Levels within each channel enables you to easily match exposures.

Figure 8.8 The final image has consistent color across the various segments.

Matching Exposures

Unfortunately, Elements does not have a Channels panel and provides no easy way to see a specific color component of an image. However, thanks to the power of Undo (as well as a pencil and paper), it is possible to work around this limitation. This is recommended for advanced Elements users only.

To fix exposure mismatches in Elements panoramas, perform the following steps:

1. Follow Steps 1 and 2 from the Photoshop instructions earlier.

2. Select the first layer that is mismatched in the Layers panel and choose Enhance > Convert to Black and White.

3. In the Adjustment Intensity sliders, set the value for the channel you wish to see, such as Red, to 100, and set the other sliders to 0. Be careful with this step because the only way to see the current slider value is to hold the mouse over the slider knob and wait for the tooltip to appear; there is no way to see the value while moving the slider knob. The result will look similar to the image shown here:

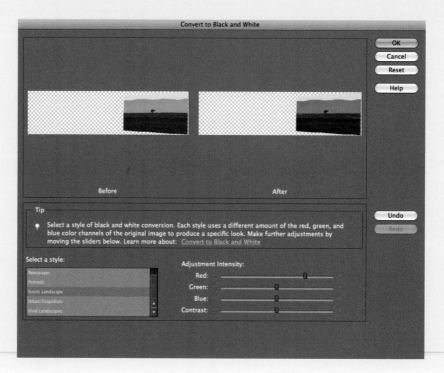

4. Repeat Step 3 for the layer you wish to match so that you are effectively looking at the Red channel in both layers.

5. Select the layer you wish to adjust, and choose Enhance > Adjust Lighting > Levels from the menu bar.

6. Change the pop-up to be the same as the channel you are working in, such as Red.

Continues

Matching Exposures *(Continued)*

7. Click the Midpoint slider, and drag it to match up the grayer tones in layer 2 with those in layer 1. When they appear the same, as you saw in Figure 8.7, write down the value you used in the Levels dialog and click Cancel.

8. In the Undo History panel, select the step immediately before Convert to Black and White to restore your image to color.

9. Repeat Steps 3 through 8 for the Blue and Green channels.

10. With the image again in color, select the layer you wish to adjust and choose Enhance > Adjust Lighting > Levels from the menu bar.

11. Set the pop-up to each individual channel and type in the values that you wrote down in Step 7. Once finished, click OK to apply the changes.

Try It! Open PanoMatch1 on the accompanying CD, and practice adjusting the exposures to get them to match. If you're looking for a challenge, open PanoMatch2, and match those exposures! (Hint: You'll need to use Curves rather than Levels to get them to match.)

Joe McDonald, one of the foremost wildlife photographers, often creates composites. He offers the following thoughts.

Composites
by Joe McDonald

Shooting digitally, my photography now has far fewer limitations. Think about it. The basic laws of optics normally restrict our vision, but for virtually my entire career I've been further limited not by what I couldn't see, but by what my camera could capture. Limitations imposed by the depth of field or the angle of view or the exposure latitude all conspired to force me to make images not as I saw them but as I knew my medium could render them. We all lived with this and probably didn't even think about it, for it was the reality of photography at the time.

Continues

Composites *(Continued)*

Digital has changed all of that for me: I now make images with the "reality" of the scene in mind. This can take any number of forms. Sometimes I simply have too much lens, but by shooting a panorama, I still get the image size and detail I wanted while encompassing more of the habitat as well. On other occasions I'll shoot focus composites, focusing on the foreground if it bears interest, and on the main subject so that the finished image lacks the unnatural dimension typical of long-lens shots. If necessary, I'll add some Gaussian blur to a background to draw more attention to the subject.

Restrictions created by a broad exposure latitude have been significantly reduced. Often I'll "shoot for the middle," knowing that I can convert a raw image twice, once biasing for the underexposure and once for the over. Usually I'll cover myself for those shots by shooting two exposures, metering for each value. That way, if the exposure latitude was indeed too broad for a single image, I'll have a good chance of recording the scene if I use two separate images.

This has simply made my photography more fun because I'm not frustrated or stymied by past limitations. I'm free to try things, probably way more than I'll ever have time to work with in the digital darkroom, but that's secondary. The fun part is the shooting, and with digital, I feel I have the potential of capturing what I truly see.

© Joe McDonald, www.hoothollow.com

Expanding Dynamic Range

Until recently, the dynamic range, or exposure latitude, that we could capture in a single image was limited by camera and film technology. Often, especially during the midday hours, there was too much contrast to be able to capture in a single shot. We had to choose to give up detail in the highlights, the shadows, or both. Photoshop enables us to combine several images of the same subject, taken using different exposures, to retain detail in the highlights and shadows while simultaneously having the midtones properly exposed. It's almost magical how we can create an image that reflects what we actually saw, no longer limited by the exposure latitude of film.

There are three techniques we'll describe to extend the exposure latitude in an image:

- Manual
- The "cookbook" approach, where Photoshop does most of the work for you
- Merge to HDR

Expanding Latitude Manually

When you encounter a situation in which there is too much contrast to capture detail in the entire scene in a single shot, take several shots at different exposure levels, and combine them using these steps:

1. Use a tripod, and take your first shot, exposing for the shadow areas. Check your in-camera histogram to ensure that the shadow areas do *not* spike against

the left side of the histogram. If they do, take another shot, adding more light to the exposure. Don't worry about the highlights in this shot.

2. Without moving the camera, take another shot, this time exposing for the highlights. This time when you check the histogram, make certain that there are no spikes against the right side of the histogram. If there are, reduce the amount of light in the exposure (see Figure 8.9). Don't worry about the shadows in this shot.

3. In some cases, you may want a third shot exposing for the midtones.

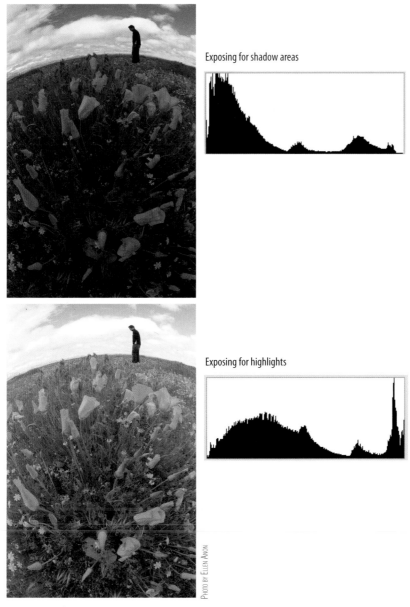

Exposing for shadow areas

Exposing for highlights

PHOTO BY ELLEN ANON

Figure 8.9 Check the histograms to make certain that the dark exposure has captured detail in the highlight areas and similarly that the light exposure has captured all the shadow detail.

4. Open each image in Photoshop.

5. Choose the Move tool, and while holding the Shift key, click one image and drag it on top of another. By holding the Shift key, they should line up in perfect registry.

6. To be certain that they are lined up perfectly, select all layers (Ctrl/⌘-click on all layers) and choose Edit > Auto-Align Layers.

7. Click the Add Layer Mask icon to create a layer mask on the top layer.

8. Choose a brush tool that is soft to medium hardness, and set the brush opacity to 100 percent initially.

9. Make sure the foreground color is set to black and the background color is set to white by hitting the D key.

10. Paint with black in the layer mask to reveal parts of the underlying image layer, leaving the well-exposed parts from each layer visible, as shown in Figure 8.10.

11. Zoom in, and work carefully.

Figure 8.10 Create a layer mask on the top layer to reveal parts of the image below that are better exposed.

12. If you make a mistake, simply switch to white (by pressing X), and paint with white in the layer mask.

13. You may want to reduce the brush opacity to partially reveal the underlying layer in areas.

14. If you have a third exposure, follow the same procedure, and add a layer mask to this layer and paint with black to reveal the underlying layers in the appropriate places.

15. You can proceed with the rest of your workflow in one of two ways:

- Flatten the image when the desired tonal range is achieved and proceed to modify it using your normal workflow as you would a single image.

- Make a Stamp Visible layer (see Figure 8.11)—a single layer containing your desired final exposure. To do this, click the top layer in the Layers panel. Then, while holding down the Alt/Option key, click the Layers panel menu at the top of the Layers panel. Continue holding the Alt/Option key, and click Merge Visible. Do not release the Alt/Option key until you see a new thumbnail icon appear in the layer you created.

Figure 8.11 A Stamp Visible layer contains all the information of the layers beneath it in a single layer that serves as the initial layer in your normal workflow.

Extending Dynamic Range Manually

To align the two layers in Elements, you will need to reduce the opacity of the top layer to 50%. If the layers are not lined up correctly, use the arrow keys on your keyboard to nudge the top layer into place. Return the opacity to 100%.

As we've mentioned previously, although Elements does not directly let you add a layer mask to a layer, we can fake it by using an adjustment layer. To do so, replace Step 7 from the Photoshop CS4 instructions as follows:

7. Select the background layer and choose Layer > New Adjustment Layer > Levels from the menu bar. Leave it blank and click OK.

Next select the top layer and choose Layer > Group with Previous from the menu bar.

Follow the rest of the steps, but before moving onto a third exposure in Step 14, select the top layer and Stamp Visible by pressing Ctrl+Alt+Shift+E / ⌘+Option+Shift+E. Your layers should look similar to the ones shown here before you move on to the next image:

The "Cookbook" Approach to Expanding Latitude

Sometimes combining two exposures is fairly straightforward, as it was in the example we used for the manual method of combining exposures. But sometimes the highlight and shadow areas are scattered throughout the image, making the manual method quite time-consuming. Fortunately, there's an easy way to have Photoshop do most of the tedious work for you in combining two images (see Figure 8.12).

Figure 8.12 You can have Photoshop use the lighter image to create a mask to use while combining two different exposures.

Take these steps to combine the two images:

1. Drag the *dark* image on top of the light image by using the Move tool while holding the Shift key. It's important that the darker image go on top.

> **Note:** For this approach to be successful, the images must align perfectly. After dragging the darker image on top of the lighter one, select both layers and choose Edit > Auto-Align Layers.

2. Add a layer mask to the dark image layer.
3. Make the background image active by clicking the background image layer, and press Ctrl+A/⌘+A to select the entire background image.

4. Press Ctrl+C/⌘+C to copy the image to the clipboard.

5. Highlight the dark image layer; hold down the Alt/Option key, and click the Layer Mask icon to make the mask appear where you usually see your image. It will be completely white at first.

6. Press Ctrl+V/⌘+V to paste the contents of the clipboard onto the white mask. Your layer mask should now appear to be a black-and-white version of the background layer, as shown in Figure 8.13.

Figure 8.13 Hold down the Alt/ Option key, click the Layer Mask icon, and then press Ctrl+V/⌘+V to make the mask appear in place of the image preview.

7. Alt/Option+click on the Layer Mask icon again to return to the normal image preview.

8. Apply a Gaussian blur (Filter > Blur > Gaussian Blur) with a radius between 0.5 and 40. *Modifying the Gaussian blur is important to make the final result appear natural.* The exact amount of blur needed can vary significantly according to the image. This is the step that people most often fail to do aggressively enough.

9. Click the image icon on the darker layer, and press Ctrl+D/⌘+D to deselect. Your image should now reflect the best of both exposures (see Figure 8.14).

10. You may want to fine-tune the tonality of the image using a Curves adjustment layer if necessary or by further modifying the layer mask.

11. Create a Stamp Visible layer, as you did in the final step of the completely manual method, and continue with the regular workflow.

Note: Open the images on the accompanying CD called CanyonDark and CanyonLight, and try combining them using the "cookbook" approach.

Figure 8.14 By using the lighter image to create a mask for the darker image, Photoshop does most of the work to create a composite using the best of both exposures.

The Elements "Cookbook" Approach to Expanding Latitude

1. Drag the *dark* image on top of the light image by using the Move tool while holding the Shift key. It's important that the darker image go on top.

2. Select the background layer and add a Levels adjustment layer by clicking the Create adjustments layer button and selecting Levels. Do not make any adjustments; simply click OK.

3. Group the top layer with the Levels adjustment layer, selecting the top layer and picking Layer > Group with Previous from the menu bar.

4. In the background layer, select the entire image by choosing Select > All Ctrl+A/⌘+A.

5. Choose Edit > Copy (Ctrl+C/⌘+C to copy that layer.

6. Alt/Option+click on the layer mask for the Levels adjustment layer to make it active. The screen will switch to the layer mask and appear white.

7. Choose Edit > Paste Ctrl+V/⌘+V to paste into the layer mask.

Continues

8. Choose Filter > Blur > Gaussian Blur and apply a very small amount (1 pixel) of Gaussian blur to the layer mask.

9. Next we will adjust the contrast of the layer mask to affect the combined images' contrast. Add a Levels adjustment to the layer mask by selecting Enhance > Adjust Lighting > Levels with the layer mask still active.

10. Drag the black and white points on the Output Levels slider until you have a moderate amount of contrast without clipping the white or black areas. The lower the contrast of this mask image, the higher the contrast of the combined image. The following image shows what the mask and Output Levels sliders might look like:

11. Perform a Stamp Visible by selecting the topmost layer and pressing Ctrl+Alt+Shift+E / ⌘+Option+Shift+E).

12. Set this layer's blending type to Overlay and adjust its opacity until you achieve the results you want. The final set of layers will look similar to those shown here:

13. Fine-tune this layer further by creating Curves or Levels adjustments.

If you have more images to blend, repeat these steps, going from the brightest image to the darkest image, until you have a final, combined image. If you used an adjustment layer in Step 13, make sure to select that adjustment layer and Stamp Visible (Ctrl+Alt+Shift+E or ⌘+Option+Shift+E) before proceeding.

Expanding Latitude via Merge to HDR

Photoshop
ONLY

Photoshop CS4 continues to improve the Merge to HDR feature. Merge to HDR is a tool to combine multiple exposures (ideally three to seven exposures of the identical subject) into one 32-bit image.

Using 32-bit enables the image to have a greatly expanded dynamic range so that the final image can contain detail in shadow areas and in highlights that normally cannot be present in a single image. In fact, 32-bit offers more latitude than what you can even see on your monitor. However, the 32-bit image can then be converted back to 16-bit or 8-bit. Merge to HDR creates an image containing the maximum amount of detail and color information possible, with very little work on your part. It ensures that the transitions among the exposures are gradual, with no harsh obvious edges. It sounds too good to be true, doesn't it?

In earlier versions, nature photographers were likely to experience several difficulties using this tool. If anything changed between exposures—a tree branch blowing slightly in the wind, a leaf, anything moving—Merge to HDR often failed to give a good final image. Similarly, if there was any camera movement, it also didn't work. In CS4 the Auto-Align algorithms have been tremendously improved. In addition, you can add a layer mask to an image to hide part of an image to help with objects that move. Although there is still no option in this version of the tool to allow you to manually align the images, it works far better than the initial version.

> **Note:** It might seem the answer would be to take a single raw file and convert it at numerous settings; however, this won't work, because the algorithms used in Merge to HDR require different *linear* data.

Situations with high contrast and static subjects are best for creating Merge to HDR composites. For example, the sun rising or setting behind a mountain offers an ideal opportunity. Normally, some of the detail in the mountain would be lost while trying to capture the colors of the sunset.

If a scene lends itself to using Merge to HDR, take the following steps in the field:

1. It's essential to use a tripod and not move your camera between exposures. Use a cable release if possible.

2. Take a series of shots, *varying the exposure by changing the shutter speed*, not the aperture (which would change the depth of field). If you use aperture priority, then you simply need to dial in different exposure compensation amounts for each shot.

3. Vary the exposures by one to two f/stops each. Don't try to bracket by small increments such as 1/3 to 1/2 stops, as you might if you were trying to capture a single well-exposed frame.

4. Check the histogram to make sure that your darkest picture includes detail in the brightest part of the image; that is, there are no spikes on the right of the histogram and no flashing highlight warnings. Similarly, check to make sure that

your lightest image (which has flashing highlights) has no spikes on the left side of the histogram. You want to make certain to capture detail in all the shadows.

5. Don't vary the lighting by using flash in one picture and not the next.

After you have downloaded your images to your computer, access Merge to HDR through Bridge directly or through Photoshop using these steps:

1. To select the files to use in Photoshop, choose File > Automate > Merge to HDR. The Merge to HDR dialog box (see Figure 8.15) appears. Click Browse to select the desired images, and then click Open, or if you have already opened the images, simply select Use Open Files.

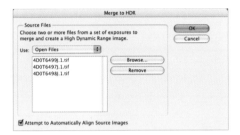

PHOTOS BY JOSH ANON

Figure 8.15 Select your desired images in the Merge to HDR dialog box.

2. Check the Attempt to Automatically Align Source Images box.

3. To select the images to use directly from Bridge, simply highlight the desired images, and choose Tools > Photoshop > Merge to HDR.

Note: Leave the "response curve" set to automatic unless you have created a custom curve for your camera. The camera response curve reflects how the camera's sensor reacts to light. The precise sensitivity of each camera's sensor differs, so ideally you need a response curve for each of your cameras if you do a lot of HDR work. There are several tutorials available on the Web to help you do this; search for *how to create a camera response curve*.

4. Click OK.

5. This leads to a Merge to HDR dialog box, shown in Figure 8.16. You can zoom in to see the results more closely, if desired, or uncheck one of the source images displayed along the left side to exclude it from being part of the final image. The image preview automatically updates to reflect this change.

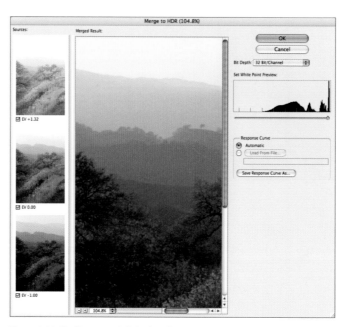

Figure 8.16 The Merge to HDR dialog box allows you to preview the results of the merge as well as specify the white point and bit depth for the composite.

6. Choose a bit depth for the merged image from the Bit Depth pull-down. To store the entire dynamic range, you must choose 32-bit.

7. Move the slider below the histogram to set the white point for previewing the merged image. In CS4 the default location is often good, but you may want to check by moving the slider to the right. This only affects the preview in a 32-bit image, since there is more information than can be displayed on a monitor (or print). You are not discarding any information yet.

8. If you choose to save the merged image as an 8- or 16-bit-per-channel file at this point, then moving this slider is applying exposure edits to your final image, and you are discarding some information. The HDR Conversion dialog box shown in Figure 8.17 will appear. There you can specify the exact conversion settings. (See Step 11 for more details on this.)

9. Click OK, and Photoshop creates the merged image.

10. Currently, there are only a few tools and adjustments that can be used with 32-bit images, but we sometimes find it helpful to use the Exposure adjustment, which was specifically designed for 32-bit images. Adjusting each of the sliders adjusts the brightness of the image slightly differently:

- The Exposure slider is calibrated in stops and increases (or decreases) brightness throughout the image, but it affects the highlights more than the shadows.

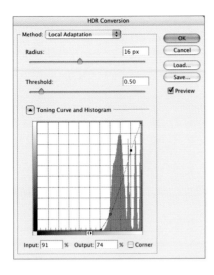

Figure 8.17 You can choose from several different approaches to convert your image back to 16-bit (or 8-bit).

- The Offset slider increases or decreases the brightness of the shadows far more than the highlights.

- The Gamma slider adjusts the brightness in a similar way to the Brightness slider in ACR. Although all tones are affected, the middle tonalities are affected the most. You may need to readjust the Offset slider as you modify the Gamma slider.

11. Although you can make a few other adjustments in 32-bit mode, including Levels, Hue/Saturation, and the Channel Mixer, you will have to convert your image back to a 16-bit-per-channel file for most adjustments and output. To do so, choose Image > Mode > 16 Bits/Channel.

12. In the HDR Conversion dialog box (shown earlier in Figure 8.17), choose from among several options in the Method drop-down list:

- Choose Exposure and Gamma to manually adjust the brightness and contrast.

- Choose Highlight Compression to compress the dynamic values in the HDR image to fall within the bounds of a 16-bit image. Photoshop automatically converts the image for you.

- Choose Equalize Histogram to compress the dynamic range of the image while trying to preserve some contrast. This is also an automatic method.

- Choose Local Adaptation (see Figure 8.18) to adjust the tonality by calculating the amount of correction necessary for specific brightness regions throughout the image. If you choose this option, you can adjust the tone curve in a manner similar to adjusting curves, as discussed in Chapter 6, "Exposure Adjustments." This is often, but not always, the most useful choice.

13. Initially your image may appear rather flat. Using adjustments such as Shadow/Highlight, Curves, and Hue/Saturation, you can increase the visible details, as well as the midtone contrast, and make the image come alive.

Figure 8.18 Using Local Adaptation and modifying the tone curve, and then making further adjustments, including Shadow/Highlight, Curves, and Hue/Saturation, allowed us to convert this HDR image to 16-bit while retaining a great deal more info in the shadows and highlights.

Try It! Open the images from the accompanying CD called HDR1, HDR2, and HDR3, and experiment with creating a 32-bit file and then converting it back to a 16-bit file.

HDR Images Using Photomatix

Most of the time we rely on the tools within Photoshop to optimize our images, and use additional software only when there is a clear benefit that justifies the expense. Photomatix software (www.hdrsoft.com) offers stand-alone programs as well as plug-in versions of their HDR program that are truly outstanding. They will work with Photoshop as well as Elements. It takes far less time to create impressive HDR images using their software. Compare the following two images; the first was created in CS4 using Merge to HDR as well as a variety of adjustments, including Curves and Hue/Saturation, and the second was created using the Tone-Map feature in Photomatix.

Extending the Depth of Field

Nature photographers sometimes encounter situations where we want to maximize our *depth of field* (the range of apparently sharp focus within an image) but we encounter technical limitations. Perhaps the range we want to be in focus is too great for the lens, or the wind is blowing, so we have to use a relatively fast shutter speed to freeze the motion. Using the faster shutter speed may mean we can't use as small an aperture as we'd like for a correct exposure without resorting to higher ISOs, which can lead to problems with noise.

Manual Method

Using a compositing technique similar to that for manually increasing the exposure latitude, you can combine two or more photographs in which you varied your focus to increase the depth of field. This can be a huge advantage at times, since you can shoot at whatever shutter speed you need to freeze the action. It can also allow you greater depth of field than would be possible in certain situations, such as macro photography.

Note: When using zoom lenses, changing the focus changes the focal length slightly, so this technique tends to work best with fixed focal length lenses.

Here are the steps you can take to extend the depth of field by combining two or more images:

1. Take two or more shots, varying the focus for each. For example, focus on the foreground in one shot and on the midground for the next shot while the camera is on a tripod, as shown in Figure 8.19.

Figure 8.19 Take two or more shots, varying the focal point.

PHOTO BY ELLEN ANON

2. Do not change the exposure; only change the focus.

3. Use your depth-of-field preview button to see what areas will be in focus and allow for overlap between the shots.

4. Open all the shots in Photoshop. If they are raw files, synchronize the settings for all the files, as discussed in Chapter 4, "Foundations."

5. Drag one image on top of another with the Move tool while holding down the Shift key to align the images in perfect registry.

6. Select all layers and choose Edit > Auto-Align Layers.

Note: Sometimes you may not be able to perfectly align the images, in which case later you'll have to zoom in and carefully create the layer mask.

7. With the top layer highlighted, click the Add a Layer Mask icon at the bottom of the Layers panel.

8. Press D to make sure the foreground and background colors are set to black and white. Press X to toggle between white and black as the foreground color.

9. Choose a medium-hard brush of the appropriate size with 100 percent opacity. You need to zoom in and work carefully, adjusting the size and hardness of your brush as necessary.

10. Paint with black on the layer mask to reveal parts of the underlying image (see Figure 8.20).

Figure 8.20 Use the layer mask to reveal the sharp areas of both images, which creates the appearance of increased depth of field.

11. Repeat this process if you have more than two shots you are combining.

12. Make a Stamp Visible layer that will be a single layer containing a flattened version of your composite image. To do this, while holding down the Alt/Option key, click the small three-line icon at the top right of the Layers panel. Continue holding the Alt/Option key, and click Merge Visible. Do not release the Alt/Option key until you see a new thumbnail icon appear in the layer you created.

13. Continue with your normal workflow.

Extending Depth of Field Manually

Elements users will again need to fake a layer mask by using an adjustment layer. To do so, replace Step 7 from the Photoshop CS4 instructions as follows:

7. Select the background layer and choose Layer > New Adjustment Layer > Levels from the menu bar. Leave it blank and click OK.

Select the top layer and choose Layer > Group with Previous from the menu bar.

Follow the rest of the steps, but before moving onto a third exposure in Step 11, select the top layer and Stamp Visible by pressing Ctrl+Alt+Shift+E / ⌘+Option+Shift+E.

Try It! Open the images called DOF1 and DOF2 on the accompanying CD, and practice combining them.

Automatic Method

Photoshop CS4 added a new feature to the Auto-Blend function called Extended Depth of Field. This uses the advanced blending algorithms to choose the sharpest areas in a series of images and composite them automatically. It's really quite impressive! To use this function, first take a series of shots with your camera on a tripod. Vary only the focus point. Begin at one extreme and slowly move the focus point back until the last area you want to be in focus is sharp. The more perfectly your images are aligned with no subject or camera movement, the better this method will work.

Photoshop ONLY

1. In Photoshop, choose File > Scripts > Load Files into Stack.

2. Select all layers and choose Edit > Auto-Align Layers > Auto.

3. Choose Edit > Auto-Blend Layers > Extended Depth of Field. Experiment with the color correction option; sometimes it helps, but it can also make it tricky to fine-tune the layer masks.

This feature can be very handy, and the more perfect the initial alignment of the images, the better the results. Ellen created the first image in Figure 8.21, which is a composite of 13 shots. By using a shallow depth of field with each shot, she was able to render the background out of focus so that it's not distracting, while obtaining significant detail in the flower. She created the second image as an example of creative use of depth of field. She combined two shots, each of which used a shallow depth of field, to capture just a single water droplet in sharp focus. The result was an image with two sharp water droplets and much of the rest of the flower out of focus. This forces the viewer to concentrate on the water droplets.

PHOTO BY ELLEN ANON

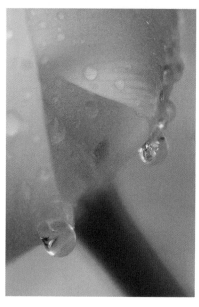

PHOTO BY ELLEN ANON

Figure 8.21 By compositing numerous shots with different focal points you can control what's in and out of focus in an image.

Using Photomerge Group Shot to Extend Depth of Field

Elements users have another option to easily combine certain types of images: Photomerge Group Shot. Group Shot was designed to help when you're taking a photo of a group, and one person has his eyes shut in one shot while another person has a weird look on her face in the next shot. Group Shot will let you load all of your shots at once, use rough lines to select areas you want, and automatically combine the images.

Nature photographers can use Group Shot to extend the depth of field in an image, whether we want to combine shots of animals or combine images with different focus points.

1. Open the images you want to combine.

2. Select them all in the Project Bin at the bottom of the screen.

3. Choose File > New > Photomerge Group Shot.

Continues

Using Photomerge Group Shot to Extend Depth of Field *(Continued)*

4. Select the image that you want to use as the base Final image. You will combine parts of other images onto this image. Drag the base image onto the right side of the screen, onto the box marked Final, as seen in the following image.

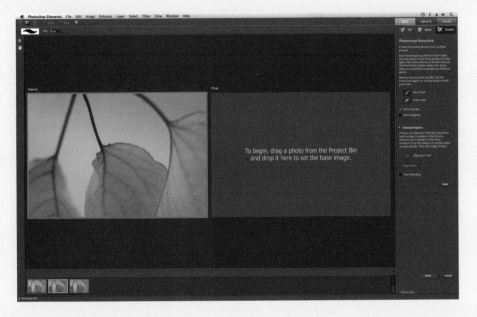

5. Select the next image from the Project Bin so that it appears on the Source box.

6. If the images are out of alignment, expand the Advanced Options area and select the Alignment Tool, as shown here. This tool will have you place three markers on matching areas of the Source and Final images to align them.

7. Click the Pencil tool to make it active, and draw on the part of the Source image that you want to merge onto the Final image. Use the Brush Size options in the upper left along with the Zoom and Hand tools to create precise strokes when needed.

8. Select the next image in the Project Bin and repeat Step 7.

Continues

Using Photomerge Group Shot to Extend Depth of Field   *(Continued)*

9. Once you have gone through all of your images, you will see results similar to those in the following image. Click the Done button. Elements will create a new file with the combined images. Especially if you are combining shots with different focus points, you might need to crop the resulting image.

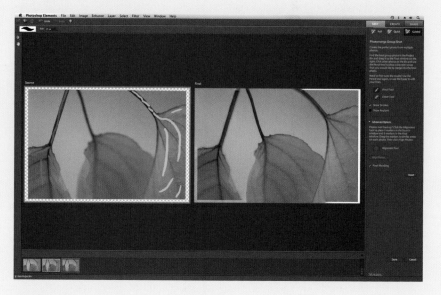

10. Proceed as normal through your workflow.

Joe McDonald, who captures extraordinary images of nature and wildlife around the world, graciously shares one of his favorite tricks for creating images with incredibly sharp detail.

Helicon Focus

by Joe McDonald

Macro, landscape, and even architectural photography can take on a whole new dimension by thinking digitally, and taking advantage of an exciting piece of software called the Helicon Focus Filter (www.heliconfocus.com.). By thinking digitally, one can envision what a final product may be, free of the constraints imposed by optics or exposure latitudes.

This can be especially productive when shooting macro subjects since depths of field are always a limitation and a dilemma, since achieving great depth often softens the overall look of an image. While it is a given that small apertures, like f22 or f32, provide great depths of field, one often does not consider the cost of using them in terms of overall sharpness. These small apertures bend and potentially distort the light, so while you may have great depth of field, the resulting image may be softer overall than it would be if shot at a wider aperture, like f11. Of course, at f11 the depth of field suffers, and you may be left with one sharp slice in an otherwise rather fuzzy image. What can one do?

Continues

Helicon Focus *(Continued)*

Enter the Helicon Focus Filter. With this piece of software one can take a series of images of a motionless subject, "rolling" the focus from near to far as you do so. The filter recognizes edge sharpness and composites an image automatically, creating a final image that is sharp from edge to edge.

The trick to using the Helicon Focus Filter is to shoot several images that cover the depth of your subject at a wide aperture that takes advantage of the maximum sharpness of your lens. Don't be stingy here—change the focus gradually so that you're certain the entire image has been covered. You may have to work relatively quickly, too, when dealing with animate subjects that might move or be blown by the wind.

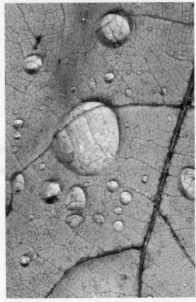

The Helicon Focus Filter isn't a plug-in, so you'll need to open the program and import the images you wish to composite. When they appear in your "Source" well, simply click on the "Run" button and let the Helicon Focus Filter take over. Within a few minutes you'll have your final result.

The Helicon Focus Filter works with raw images as well as JPGs and TIFFs, although I generally do a JPG trial first to make sure I've shot the image correctly. The Helicon Focus Filter works best with motionless subjects, so don't try shooting a field of flowers in a breeze. After you finish your composite you can open the saved file in Photoshop and continue any final fine-tuning.

Continues

Combining Elements from Multiple Pictures

When you start combining elements from various pictures, you begin to be more creative with your images. Ethically, it's important to acknowledge that what you're presenting is not a documentary photograph but rather a photo illustration or photo art. That doesn't make it inherently more or less valuable than a straight photograph—just different. Often, a photo illustration can convey the essence or spirit of a place better than a single straight photograph. But creating something that didn't exist and claiming it is not a manipulated photograph creates trouble for all photographers. The image in Figure 8.22 has impact, but it's a composite and needs to be presented as such.

PHOTO BY ELLEN ANON

Figure 8.22 Images like this can often be confused with "lucky" shots and ethically must be presented as composites.

Advanced Selection Methods

Chapter 4 covered some of the basic selection tools, but when you make composites, sometimes you need more sophisticated means of making selections. Different techniques work most effectively with different images, so it pays to understand several approaches.

If you know ahead of time that you're likely to want to use one part of a picture as a composite, it's a good idea to try to photograph it so that it contrasts as much as possible from the background. That makes it easier to select, no matter which technique you choose.

Creating a Selection from Within a Channel

This sounds a lot more difficult than it is, but don't let the sound of it intimidate you. Recall that your images have pixel information in three channels: a Red channel, a Blue channel, and a Green channel. You access these channels by clicking the Channels panel, as shown in Figure 8.23. By default, Channels shares a panel window with Layers.

Figure 8.23 To access the individual channels, click the Channels panel.

Sometimes it's easier to make a selection using one of the three color channels rather than the RGB image itself. This is the case when there is good contrast within a particular channel. For example, making a selection of a sky based on a channel is quite useful when the sky meets trees and vegetation with many fine branches.

We'll demonstrate this approach to select the sky in this poppy image:

PHOTO BY ELLEN ANON

1. Choose Channels, and then click each of the three channels, one at a time, to determine which has the best contrast in the area of interest. With the poppy picture, clearly the Blue channel offers the best contrast to separate the sky and the flower, as you can see in Figure 8.24.

Red channel

Green channel

Blue channel

Figure 8.24 Looking at the Red, Green, and Blue channels, it's clear that the Blue channel offers the most contrast between the sky and the flower.

2. Make a copy of the channel offering the most contrast—in this case, the Blue channel—by dragging that channel layer to the New Channel icon [icon] at the bottom of the Channels panel.

3. Maximize the contrast between the area you want to select and the rest of the image by choosing Image > Adjustments > Levels. This is one of the few times you make changes directly on the pixels because there is no way to create an adjustment layer for a channel. Drag in the black point and white point sliders to turn the preview nearly black and white, as illustrated in Figure 8.25. A small transition area of gray is actually beneficial.

Figure 8.25 Use the sliders in the Levels dialog box to turn this channel into black and white.

4. To fine-tune the selection, you'll most likely need to use the Brush tool and paint some areas with black and some areas with white.

5. Once you have a black-and-white preview created (which is actually a mask), click the Load Channel as Selection icon ⊙ at the bottom of the Channels panel. This creates a selection based on the mask you just created. The white areas are selected.

6. You can invert the selection (by choosing Select > Inverse on the main menu) if you find that you have selected the opposite part of the image.

7. After going through all this to make a selection, it's a good idea to save the selection by choosing Select > Save and naming it (see Figure 8.26). That way, you can refer to it in the future.

Figure 8.26 After making a time-consuming selection, it's a good idea to save the selection.

Creating a Selection Within a Channel

Although Elements does not have a Channel panel, we can fake this selection method by converting our image to black and white.

1. Duplicate the layer you wish to select in by selecting it and choosing Layer > Duplicate Layer.

2. Select Enhance > Convert to Black and White on the duplicate layer.

3. Experiment with different combinations of the Red, Green, and Blue channels (such as a value of 100 for Red and 0 for Green and Blue to let you just see the Red channel). The sidebar "For Elements Users: Matching Exposures" earlier in this chapter shows what selecting just the Red channel looks like.

4. Click OK.

5. Select Enhance > Adjust Lighting > Levels, and follow Steps 3 and 4 from the Photoshop instructions.

6. Use your favorite selection technique, such as the Magic Wand or Quick Selection tool, to select the part of the image you wish to be selected.

7. From the menu bar, choose Select > Save Selection and save this selection.

8. Delete the duplicate layer.

9. In the original layer, choose Select > Load Selection from the menu bar, and load the selection from Step 7.

10. Click on the layer mask and choose Edit > Paste from the menu bar.

Continues

Creating a Selection Within a Channel *(Continued)*

If you plan to use your selection in a layer mask, replace steps 7–9 as follows:

7. Choose Select > All from the menu bar.

8. Choose Edit > Copy.

9. Delete the duplicate layer.

Extracting an Object from Its Background

Although Photoshop CS4 does not have an Extraction filter, Elements has the Magic Extractor. To use it, follow these steps:

1. Open an image with an object you want to separate from the rest of the image.

2. Choose Image > Magic Extractor to bring up the Magic Extractor, shown here:

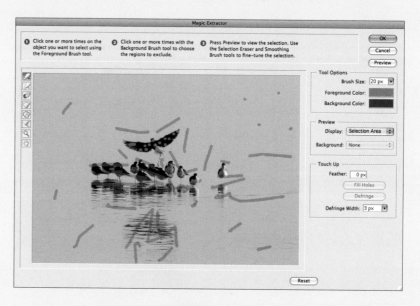

3. Using the Foreground Brush tool paint dots or lines over parts of the image you wish to extract. Zoom in and move around using the Zoom and Hand buttons, and adjust Brush Size under Tool Options to make finer selections. Use the Pointer Erase tool to remove any bad points.

4. Repeat the process with the Background Brush tool.

5. Click Preview to see the result.

6. Use the Smoothing Brush Add to Selection tool and Remove from Selection tool to adjust the edge of your selection.

7. Set the options under Touch Up, such as Feather, to do any final cleanup of your extracted object.

8. Click OK to close the Magic Extractor.

Note: For more information on making selections, see *Photoshop Masking & Compositing* by Katrin Eismann (New Riders, 2004).

Compositing the Elements

Perhaps you have several images, each containing elements that you would like to combine into a single image. Often, the relative sizes of the various elements need to be modified—you can take care of that during the process of compositing the elements. In the next example, we'll create a composite of some birds, a background, and a moon:

1. Open your destination photo (the photo that you are going to use as the main photo), set its resolution to 300 dpi (or your preferred printing resolution) by choosing Image > Image Size, and *uncheck* the Resample Image option. You don't want to interpolate the file now; just set it to the same resolution. See Figure 8.27 for our destination photo.

Figure 8.27 This is the destination photo that we'll use as the foundation for this composite.

2. Open a file containing an element you're going to use, and also set it to a resolution of 300 ppi. In our example, we'll use an image with a group of cranes flying (see Figure 8.28).

3. Use your preferred selection tool to isolate the element. In this case, it's easy to use the Color Range tool to select the cranes. Don't forget to use Refine Edges to soften the edges so that they look natural, rather than cut out and pasted.

Figure 8.28 We're going to select these flying cranes to use in the composite.

4. Choose Select > Save Selection, and type a name for the selection. This enables you to return to this selection at any time by choosing Select > Load Selection. (Note that you must save the image in order for the selection to be saved after you close the image.)

5. Use the Move tool, and drag the selection you just made to the destination image.

6. Use the Edit > Free Transform tools to size, rotate, and place these elements (see Figure 8.29). Holding down the Shift key while you grab a corner and drag it in or out will enable you to maintain the same aspect ratio and not distort the object being transformed.

Figure 8.29 Size, rotate, and place the new elements using the Free Transform tool.

7. Note that the elements you just dragged in are on their own layers. It's quite possible they may need some tonal or color adjustments to match the destination image. To make an adjustment layer that affects only a specific layer, hold down the Alt/Option key while clicking the icon to make a new adjustment layer. Check the box that says Use Previous Layer to Create Clipping Mask, as shown in Figure 8.30.

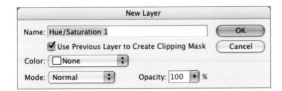

Figure 8.30 By holding down the Alt/Option key while creating a new adjustment layer, you can check the option to have only the previous layer affected by the adjustments you make.

8. Repeat this process if there are other elements from other pictures you want to include. In this case, add a moon as well (see Figure 8.31).

Figure 8.31 The final image also contains a moon that Ellen added.

9. You may want to save the composite with the layers intact as a master file so you can further modify it in the future. It's quite possible that you may want to slightly adjust the position of one of the composited items or its size.

10. Proceed with your normal workflow.

Combining Components of Various Images

In Elements, there is no option for Use Previous Layer to Create Clipping Mask (Step 7). Instead, select the Group with Previous Layer check box.

Lighting Angles Matter

It's important to pay attention to lighting angles. Many Photoshop novices create composites that would require the earth to have several suns. This detracts from the impact of the final image. Paying attention to subtle details can make the difference between an impressive image and one that evokes comments of "Oh, that was Photoshopped." Although you will be ethical and indicate when an image is a composite, you still want to elicit reactions of "Wow!"

Replacing a Sky or Other Background

Now that you've learned a variety of methods for selecting a sky, you're going to put them to use. Nature photographers often find they have a great subject with a boring sky (or other background). It's wonderful when things naturally come together and the subject, lighting, and background are all perfect. But realistically, all too often the sky or background may be great when there are no subjects, and the subjects may be great when the sky is not. Sometimes the sky is plain blue when some billowy clouds would be more interesting. This happens on African safaris, it happens while photographing birds anywhere...you name the situation, and you can bet there will be times when the sky/background just doesn't cooperate. Photoshop makes it easy to replace the dull background with one that enhances your subject matter.

To replace a sky (you can follow along using the images ReplaceSky1 and ReplaceSky2 on the accompanying CD), follow these steps:

1. Open an image that needs a new sky (your destination image), and set it to a resolution of 300 ppi.

2. Open an image of a preferred sky (or other background), and set it to a resolution of 300 ppi as well. Make sure that your new sky is at least as large as the destination image; in fact, making it slightly larger can be helpful so that you can move the new sky to position the clouds or lighting precisely where you want them. As you can see in Figure 8.32, the sky image should be a picture of just a sky and should not include other subject elements.

> **Note:** Sometimes the better sky may simply be a more dramatic cloudy sky. You don't want to combine a bright blue sky with billowy clouds and a foreground taken on a very cloudy day unless you're prepared to make some sophisticated color changes to your foreground. Paying attention to the subtleties of color will make your composites more believable.

3. Click the destination image, and make a selection of the dull sky using your preferred selection method. The Color Range tool is often the most efficient choice for selecting the sky.

4. Access the Refine Edge control by choosing Select > Refine Edge to soften and slightly expand the edges of your selection to help ensure that there are no sky pixels left.

5. Click your good sky image, and use the Move tool to drag the new sky image on top of the destination image.

6. Rename the sky image layer **New Sky**.

7. Create a layer mask on the New Sky layer by clicking the Add Layer Mask icon at the bottom of the Layers panel. Magic! Your new sky replaces the old one, since the layer mask reflects the selection you just made, as shown in Figure 8.33.

Figure 8.32 Open an image with a sky that needs to be replaced, and open an image with a better sky.

Figure 8.33 When you create a layer mask on the New Sky layer, it reflects the selection of the old sky you already made, and magically the new sky appears.

8. Sometimes you'll still need to soften the edges of the selection to make the transition to the new sky more natural. Click the layer mask to select it, and make certain the layer mask is highlighted, not the image thumbnail. Choose Filter > Blur > Gaussian Blur, and enter a value from 0.5 to 1.5 pixels. You can see the results on your image and gauge how much blur to add by what looks good. Click OK.

9. With the layer mask still active, you can further control exactly where the mask begins by choosing Image > Adjustments > Levels and moving the sliders. You are modifying the tonalities in the mask, which in turn modify the edges of each image layer. The result is that the transition edge of the new sky moves slightly so you can position it more precisely.

10. You can choose which area of the new sky (the background) you want to show by *unlinking* the layer mask on the New Sky layer. To do this, click directly on the link icon between the New Sky image thumbnail and the New Sky layer mask, as shown in Figure 8.34. Now click the image thumbnail, and choose the Move tool. You can move the new sky without affecting the mask, so you get to choose which part of the sky to show. Very cool!

Figure 8.34 By unlinking the image thumbnail and the layer mask, you can move the new sky to reveal whatever part of it best complements your picture.

Replacing a Sky

In Step 7, Elements users will again need to fake a layer mask by using an adjustment layer, as we have done in previous sections throughout this chapter.

Once you grasp the basics of compositing, you're free to create images that more accurately reflect the realities of some situations as well as images that reflect your imagination and subjective experiences. Experiment and have fun!

Creative Effects

For some nature photographers, the goal is simply to take the best shot they can to document what they see and then to optimize it in Adobe Photoshop. That's fine. Other photographers are latent artists at heart but may believe (rightly or wrongly) that they have no inherent ability to create art from a blank canvas. But given a camera as the starting point and a digital darkroom, they can make magic.

Of course, creativity is an artistic form; not every technique appeals to every photographer, and some images are more suited for one approach than another. As you read through this chapter, consider each technique as a jumping-off point for your own ideas rather than a cookbook approach to creative imagery.

Chapter Contents
Black and White
Filters
Digital Montages
Digital Multiple Exposures

Black and White

Some images lend themselves to black and white, to say nothing of the fact that right now black-and-white images are very popular. In fact, there is a timeless quality to many black-and-white prints.

Converting to Black and White

Digital cameras capture images in color, but there are a variety of ways that you can easily convert them into black and white. Although some folks may opt to simply desaturate their images by creating a Hue/Saturation adjustment layer and sliding the Saturation slider all the way to the left, or by choosing Image > Mode > Grayscale, we don't recommend those approaches because the results are often very flat and bland (see Figure 9.1). Instead, we recommend using the new Black & White adjustment layer or a Channel Mixer adjustment layer. We find that with some images we prefer the Channel Mixer and with others, the new Black & White tool.

PHOTO BY ELLEN ANON

Figure 9.1 Simply desaturating, or just changing the mode to grayscale, often converts an image to a rather bland black-and-white version.

Converting to Black and White via the Channel Mixer

Recall from Chapter 8, "Composites," that when you wanted to make a selection of part of an image, you could look at the Red, Green, and Blue channels and see what information was in each. You can use this same information to help convert to black and white. The Channel Mixer allows you to specify how much information you want each channel to contribute to the final image. It's a good idea to begin by opening the Channels panel and clicking each channel individually to see what detail is present in each (see Figure 9.2). That will give you an idea of where to begin in the Channel Mixer.

Red channel

Blue channel

Green channel

Figure 9.2 Check each channel to see what information it is contributing to the final image.

To convert an image to black and white, take the following steps:

1. Return to the Adjustments panel and choose the Channel Mixer adjustment (see Figure 9.3).

Figure 9.3 Create a Channel Mixer adjustment layer to use for converting the image to black and white.

2.   Check the Monochrome box.

3.   You can use the default settings or click in the Preset drop-down menu to try the various presets.

4.   Modify the percentages from each channel to create a more dramatic black-and-white version of your file. You can choose settings from –200% to +200% for each channel. As you adjust one, you're likely to need to tweak the other settings. Usually it's best to have the percentages from the three channels total close to 100%. Sometimes we go a little beyond 100% for a more contrasty image with a lot of punch, but you have to make sure you're not sacrificing image detail for increased contrast (see Figure 9.4). When you go above 100%, a warning triangle with an exclamation point appears by the Total percentage.

5.   Usually we leave the Constant option at its default of 0, but moving it to the left darkens the image, and moving it to the right lightens it.

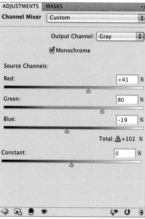

Figure 9.4 Experiment with the settings for each channel to create a black-and-white image with considerable impact.

When you first open a Channel Mixer adjustment layer and check the Monochrome box, the default values are red = 100, green = 0, and blue = 0. Although this is a good starting place for many images, most of the time you will want to further adjust the sliders. Often the Red channel provides the most contrast, but it's likely you may find some information in the Green or Blue channels that you want to emphasize; if so, you may increase those channels somewhat. When you increase one channel, you may need to decrease the other channels. You may even choose to increase one channel dramatically and then use a negative value for the other channels. Make these decisions based on your taste and the characteristics of the individual image. Often noise is more prominent in the Blue channel, so if noise is a problem in your image, you may opt to use a negative value there. There really are no typical values that apply to most images. After a little experimentation with the settings for each channel, you'll have a dramatic black-and-white image.

With the new presets that are available in Photoshop CS4, we often find it helpful to consider several versions of an image. If you're not certain that the values you have selected are the best possible combination, click the Snapshot button  in the History panel to take a snapshot of the image this way. Then reopen the Channel Mixer adjustment layer (by double-clicking its icon in the Layers panel), and try a new combination of values or one of the presets. You can repeat this process as many times as you desire. To go back to an earlier snapshot, return to the top of the History panel and click the desired snapshot, as shown in Figure 9.5. Note that snapshots disappear when you close the image.

Figure 9.5 By taking snapshots of previous combinations of settings in the Channel Mixer, you can try a variety of settings and choose which one you prefer.

Note: Because you used an adjustment layer to convert the image to black and white, as long as you save the image with the layers intact, you can go back and modify the settings.

Converting Using the Black & White Adjustment

Photoshop CS4 also has a powerful Black & White adjustment. At first glance there are a lot of sliders to adjust, but we've found that this method is both robust and easy to use. It is now our preferred method of converting to black and white.

Photoshop ONLY

We normally begin by clicking the Auto button. We can honestly say it's one of the few times we check out an "auto" anything routinely! But Adobe did a good job figuring out the Auto algorithms.

The Auto settings tend to be a little conservative for our taste, so we often proceed to tweak the sliders. At first glance, the order of the sliders may seem to be a bit random (see Figure 9.6), but if you envision a color wheel, it's easy to see that each slider represents a portion of the color wheel, and neighboring sliders are adjacent on the color wheel. When you adjust these sliders, you think in terms of the amounts of the individual colors. If you want a color to be lighter in the black-and-white image, you increase the setting for the corresponding slider, and if you want it to be darker, you decrease it. The sliders can range from –200 to +300. Using extreme settings can sometimes lead to clipping, so be sure to check the histogram.

Note: The sliders in the Black & White tool do *not* work in conjunction with their opposites, as do some types of adjustments. So to darken a blue sky, you would decrease the settings for the blue and possibly the cyan sliders, but you would not need to change the yellow or red sliders (the opposites of blue and cyan).

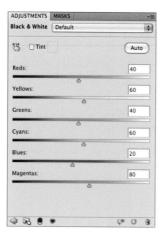

Figure 9.6 Each of the sliders works on a particular range of colors to lighten or darken the tonality of those pixels.

The Black & White adjustment also offers a choice of presets to create certain effects. You can select any of these presets and then continue to adjust the individual sliders to suit the particular image (see Figure 9.7).

Figure 9.7 We converted this image to various black-and-white renditions by beginning with several of the presets and tweaking the slider values.

PHOTO BY ELLEN ANON

In addition to controlling the tonality of each color range, the Black & White tool makes it easy to tint the image by checking the Tint option box. This automatically applies a sepia tint to the image. We often prefer to decrease the saturation of this tint slightly using the Saturation slider. If you prefer a different hue for the tint, adjust the Hue slider as desired.

Converting to Black and White

Photoshop Elements has its own Convert to Black and White tool, which works similarly to the Channel Mixer. Open it by choosing Enhance > Convert to Black and White.

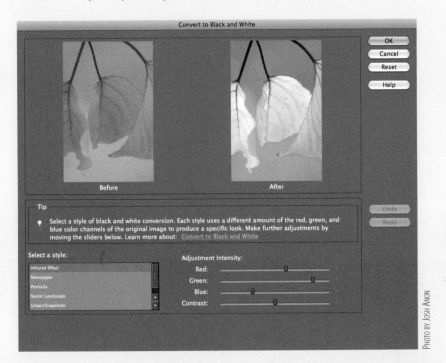

At the bottom of the dialog, you will find various presets on the left and sliders on the right to adjust the amount that each channel contributes to the image, as well as a contrast adjustment slider. Hold your mouse over a slider to access a tooltip that will indicate the percentage value for the given slider. Click OK when you are pleased with the results.

Colorizing Black-and-White Images

You may be quite content with the black-and-white rendition of your image, or you may want to experiment with adding color back into your image, depending on the effect you're after.

Photoshop ONLY

For example, you may decide that you'd like to emphasize one particular aspect of the picture by having it in the original color while the rest of the picture remains black and white. This look—popular in greeting cards—is incredibly easy. All you need to do is select the Brush tool, set it to black, make sure the Channel Mixer or Black & White adjustment layer is active (highlighted) and that the mask is selected (has a little outline around it), then paint over the areas you want to be in color (see Figure 9.8). It's that simple!

In Figure 9.8, we converted the image to a sepia tone using the Black & White adjustment tool and then applied a gradient on the layer mask to gradually transition between the original and the monotone version.

Figure 9.8 By creating a gradient on the layer mask in the Channel Mixer or Black & White adjustment layer, you can transition gradually between colorized and monochrome areas of your image.

Hopefully by now you recognize that you're using the layer mask that came with the adjustment layer to mask out the monochromatic effects. If you'd prefer the color to be more subdued, reduce the opacity of the brush by modifying the Opacity setting on the Options bar.

If you want to have a *different* color in that one area than what was originally there, create a Hue/Saturation layer on top of the Channel Mixer layer, and adjust the Hue slider (as well as the Saturation and Lightness sliders if desired) until the target item is the shade you prefer.

Some people prefer a more hand-tinted look. An easy way to create such a look is to take the following steps:

1. Create your black-and-white file using the Channel Mixer or Black & White adjustment as described in the preceding sections.

2. Reduce the opacity of the adjustment layer to achieve the desired look, using the Opacity slider in the Layers panel (see Figure 9.9). The final opacity is a matter of individual preference.

PHOTO BY ELLEN ANON

Figure 9.9 By reducing the opacity of the Channel Mixer or Black & White adjustment layer, you can create a hand-tinted look; for more impact, combine that with restoring full color to just a few areas such as the man and the window in this photo.

3. If you want to change the hue of the colors, add a Hue/Saturation adjustment layer and adjust the Hue slider to taste. The Hue/Saturation adjustment layer changes the color of the entire image, albeit with reduced saturation because of the Channel Mixer layer.

4. If you want to change the color of only part of your image and leave the remainder with the look created in Step 3, add another Hue/Saturation layer and create a layer mask so that only the areas of the mask corresponding to the areas you want to change are white and the rest of the mask is black. Adjust the Hue slider to taste.

An alternate approach to adding color to a black-and-white image is to create a Stamp Visible layer after using the Black & White adjustment layer or the Channel Mixer. Set the Brush tool to Color mode in the Options bar, and select the desired color in the Color Picker. Reduce the opacity of the brush to subdue the colors. Paint each area as appropriate.

Colorizing Black-and-White Images

As in previous chapters, we need to do some trickery to create a layer mask for our black-and-white image.

1. Before converting the image to black and white, duplicate your image layer by dragging it to the New Layer button in the Layers palette.

2. Add a Levels Adjustment Layer and leave it empty.

3. Move the Levels Adjustment Layer below the layer you created in Step 1.

4. Select the topmost layer and choose Layer > Group with Previous.

5. Select the topmost layer and convert it to black and white.

6. Select the Level Adjustment Layer's mask and paint in black to restore the color to your image.

To reduce the black-and-white conversion's opacity, select the topmost layer and change its opacity.

Creating a Sepia-Tone Effect in Elements

1. Follow Steps 1–5 under Colorizing Black-and-White Images.

2. Create a Stamp Visible layer by selecting the topmost layer and pressing Ctrl+Alt+Shift+E/ ⌘+Option+Shift+E.

3. Click the Create Adjustment Layer button and choose Photo Filter.

4. Change the filter type to Sepia and adjust the density.

5. Click OK when finished.

Another way to create a sepia-tone effect or other color effect is to create a Stamp Visible layer and then choose Enhance > Adjust Color > Color Variations. This dialog, seen in the image here, allows you to visually explore what happens as you adjust colors in the highlights, midtones, and shadows.

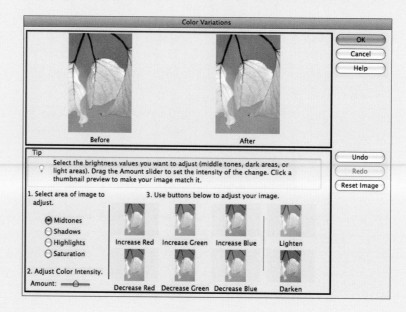

Try It! Open the image called BlackAndWhite on the accompanying CD or one of your own color images. Try converting it to black and white using the Black & White and Channel Mixer adjustment layers. Experiment with restoring color in part of it or giving it a hand-tinted or sepia look.

Filters

Photoshop includes a huge array of filters that make it easy to distort your picture in all sorts of ways. It's beyond the scope of this book to cover them all, but we'll describe a few that we find useful. However, the best way to get familiar with the filters is to open an image and begin experimenting. We'll begin by describing how to use Smart Filters and regular filters.

Note: If you opt for the "experimental" approach, it's a good idea to turn on the History Log in your General Preferences (refer to Chapter 4, "Foundations," for details) so that you can remember what you did if you stumble across something wonderful! In fact, any time you are being "creative" with your image, it's smart to turn on the History Log. You may think you'll remember exactly what you did, but if you're anything like us, at some later date you'll be frustrated because you can't recall how to replicate the effect.

Since Elements does not provide a history log, we recommend using a notepad to keep track of what you've done to your image.

Using Smart Filters on Smart Objects

CS4 has Smart Filters, meaning that filter effects can be readjusted repeatedly, even if you close and reopen the image. This is a welcome feature, very similar to the flexibility of the adjustments in adjustment layers. By using Smart Filters, you can create different combinations of filter effects that you can dynamically adjust as desired. Unfortunately, Smart Filters are available only for certain filter effects with 16-bit images but are available for all filters with 8-bit images. (For more explanation of Smart Filters and Smart Objects, refer to Chapter 5, "Workflows and First Steps.")

Photoshop ONLY

The ultimate in flexibility is to have a raw image placed as a Smart Object at the beginning of your workflow with Smart Filters applied to the raw image. Currently there are some limitations that will sometimes cause you to have to make some workflow choices. For example, a cleanup or cloning layer will not update to reflect any further changes you make to the Smart Object raw file. If you do your dust cleanup in ACR, or the cleanup layer contains only a few pixels to cover some very small dust spots and the Smart Filters you want to use are for sharpening, you'll be fine. But if you readjust the color or tonality of the raw file in any way or use a filter that causes a dramatic effect, the clone layer will be outdated and need to be redone.

We recommend that when you want to experiment with creative filter effects you create a duplicate version of your optimized image and then flatten it by choosing Layer > Flatten Image. By doing this, you can save your optimized file as a 16-bit file.

To use most of the creative filters, you'll need to convert the image to an 8-bit file by choosing Image > Mode > 8-Bit. Then choose Filter > Convert for Smart Filters. This will change the layer into a Smart Object (that will refer to the image as it was originally opened in this file, but not the original raw file), and the filters you apply will be editable.

When you want all the filter effects to apply to certain areas of the image, you can use the Smart Filter layer mask and paint the mask white or black to show or reveal the effects, just as you did with adjustment layer masks (see Figure 9.10).

Figure 9.10 Use the mask on the Smart Filter layer to control what parts of the image are affected by the Smart Filters.

If you want one filter to affect part of the image and another filter to affect a different area, it gets a little more complicated. In Figure 9.11 we added a pastel paintbrush effect to lend a painterly feel to the image. We used the layer mask to slightly subdue the effect.

1. Begin by applying the Smart Filter to the image and masking out any areas you don't want to be affected.

2. Duplicate this layer.

3. Go to Layer > Smart Object > Rasterize. This will apply the effects of the filters on the previous layer.

4. Go to Filter > Convert for Smart Filter. This will turn this layer back into a Smart Object that includes the effects of the previous layer. That way, you can apply additional filters and use the layer mask to apply the effects differently than you did in the previous layer. Use the layer mask to reveal only the portion of the image you want to be affected by this filter or to subdue the effects of the filter beyond what's available in the filter settings.

Figure 9.11 Add a layer mask to a Smart Object layer to further control the effects of the filter and where it is applied.

Using Filters Without Smart Objects

Just as with Smart Filters, since most of the creative filters work on 8-bit images only, we recommend that you duplicate your optimized master file and create a separate file to do your creative work. That way, the master file remains a 16-bit file, and the creative file is 8-bit.

If you have no use for the original file without the creative effects, you may prefer to create a Merge Visible layer at the top of the workflow by holding down the Alt/Option key and choosing Layer > Merge Visible. Be certain to continue to hold down the Alt/Option key while clicking Merge Visible. Apply the filter effects to this layer. Then you can reduce the effect later by adjusting the opacity of the layer, or you can add a layer mask to apply the filter to specific parts of the layer only.

If the filter effect you want to apply is grayed out, it means that you'll need to convert the file to 8-bit. To do so, select Image > Mode > 8-Bits/Channel.

Note: Many filters take considerable time to process. If you are going to experiment with different effects, a useful trick is to duplicate your image by choosing Image > Duplicate and significantly reduce the size of the duplicate file. Then experiment with the filters on the smaller file. When you have established a combination of filters and settings that you are satisfied with, apply the same combination to your original file.

Some filters are processed only using RAM. If a filter requires all your available RAM to process an effect, you may get an error message.

Blurs

Photoshop CS4 has an impressively long list of blurs, but we'll cover only the ones that are particularly applicable to nature photographs. We find that Gaussian blurs, and occasionally lens blurs, are the main ones we use. You may want to explore other blurs such as smart blurs, motion blurs, and zoom blurs as well.

Gaussian Blurs

Gaussian blurs produce a hazy effect and blur the image by an adjustable amount. They're quite useful when you want to blur a section of your image. However, it's important to remember that if you make a selection of the area you want to blur, a Gaussian blur considers that selection a general guideline, but not an absolute mandate, for the boundaries of the blur. This transition area between blurred and not blurred sections is more apparent the more blur you apply. At times it can create a glow around your subject, as it does in the photo in Figure 9.12.

PHOTO BY ELLEN ANON

Figure 9.12 Although the background was selected when the Gaussian blur was applied, it included some of the pink from the spoonbill, resulting in a pleasant glow around the bird.

To apply a Gaussian blur, take the following steps:

1. Make a copy of your Background layer and convert the layer for a Smart Filter by choosing Filter > Convert for Smart Filter.

2. You may choose to first select the area to apply the blur to using any of the selection tools, or you may prefer to rely completely on painting a layer mask.

3. Apply the blur to the copy layer by choosing Filter > Blur > Gaussian Blur. Using the preview as a guide, set the radius to determine how much blur you want. By using a Smart Filter, you can tweak the amount of blur at a later time if necessary.

If you have made a selection first, the mask will reflect that selection.

If you prefer to rely on a layer mask, it will be easier to begin by filling the filter mask with black by clicking on the mask and going to Edit > Fill > Use Black. Then make sure white is your foreground color in the color picker and paint the areas you want to appear as blurred. Using a reduced opacity with the brush will partially blur areas.

Lens Blur

Photoshop ONLY

The Lens Blur filter mimics the appearance of a reduced depth of field so that your subject remains in focus while the background fades away. With this filter, you specify part of the image as your subject that you want to remain in sharp focus and then set it to progressively blur other areas. You can also control the creation and appearance of specular highlights.

> **Note:** Although the Lens Blur filter can be helpful at times, it's still more efficient to use the correct aperture setting in the field.

1. Duplicate the Background layer (by dragging it to the Create A New Layer icon in the Layers panel).

The key to the Lens Blur filter is creating a *depth map*. Don't let the name intimidate you. This is where you define what parts of the image you want sharp and what parts to blur, as well as how much blur you want to add. The depth map is essentially a layer mask.

There are two ways to create a depth map; one way is to use an alpha channel, and the other is to use a selection. The easiest way, and one that works well with scenics, is to create it from an alpha channel. Figure 9.13 shows an image in which the Lens Blur filter is being used to blur the trees in the background. An alpha channel with a gradient was created to tell the filter which parts of the image to keep sharp and which parts to blur.

PHOTO BY ELLEN ANON

Figure 9.13 The Lens Blur filter was used to blur the trees in the background. The depth map was based on a gradient on an alpha channel.

2. To create a depth map based on a selection, skip to Step 3. To create a depth map using an alpha channel, follow these steps:

   a. Open the Channels panel, and create a new alpha channel by clicking the Create New Channel icon ⬚. Your preview becomes entirely black.

   b. Select the Gradient tool ⬚ from the Tools panel. The gradient is used to define a gradual transition from black to white so that the blur tapers off gradually.

   c. On the Options bar, open the Gradient picker (click the arrow next to the first field), and then click the third option in the drop-down panel (see Figure 9.14). This produces a gradient from black to white. Set the gradient type to Linear by clicking the first icon to the right of the Gradient picker in the Options bar.

Figure 9.14 Choose the black-to-white gradient to use as the basis of your depth map.

Note: You can use any style gradient that works for your particular image. For example, a radial gradient may be effective if you want to have everything blur around your subject.

d. After you apply the blur, *wherever the gradient is black, the image will be sharp; where the gradient is white, the image will be blurred.* So if you begin near the bottom of your image and drag the gradient toward the top, the blur affects the top of your image but not the bottom. Note that you can create this gradient anywhere in your image or invert it if desired. Later—in the Lens Blur Filter dialog box—you can also refine where it begins.

e. Your alpha channel is now ready, containing the gradient that determines where the blur is strongest and weakest. Click the RGB channel, and then return to the Background copy layer in the Layers panel. *Skip to Step 4.*

3. An alternate approach to creating the depth map is to create a selection first and use this selection as the basis for the depth map. This approach is frequently useful with a discrete subject such as an animal or bird that you want to separate from the background:

a. Create a selection using any of the selection methods to define the area you want to blur.

b. Save the selection by choosing Select > Save Selection. Do *not* feather the selection.

c. In the Save Selection dialog box (shown in Figure 9.15), do the following:

i. Leave the channel set to New.

ii. Enter a name that will allow you to easily recognize your selection. In this example, we used "whitepeacock."

iii. Under Operation, leave New Channel selected.

iv. Click OK.

Figure 9.15 Save your selection with an easily recognizable name as a new channel.

d. Deselect the selection by choosing Select > Deselect.

e. To feather the selection, go to the Channels panel, and click the channel you saved to make it visible. It appears as a black-and-white version of your image.

f. Choose Blur > Gaussian Blur, and using your mask as a preview, determine how soft the edge of the mask should be.

g. Click the RGB channel, and return to your Background copy. Proceed as follows.

4. Now, regardless of how you created your blur depth map, choose Filter > Blur > Lens Blur.

5. At the right of the Lens Blur dialog box, under Depth Map, set the source for the depth map to Alpha Channel 1 (shown in Figure 9.16) or to the selection, depending on which method you have followed.

Figure 9.16 Choose the alpha channel to use as the basis for your depth map (if you created a depth map using a gradient on an alpha channel) or the name of the selection (if you made a selection to serve as the basis of the map).

6. Set the preview to Faster initially to generate previews to help you select your settings. Then change it to More Accurate when you have made your final choices to preview the effect.

7. The Blur Focal Distance slider allows you to fine-tune where the blur begins. (It's similar to setting your camera at a certain focal distance.) To use it, click the part of the image you want to remain sharp. Photoshop sets the Blur Focal Distance automatically for you.

8. Drag the Radius slider to define how much blur to add, checking the preview (see Figure 9.17).

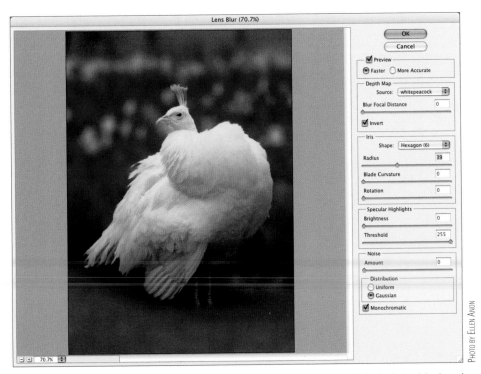

Figure 9.17 Preview the amount and placement of the blur. Note that this image uses a saved selection in the alpha channel as the basis of the depth map.

9. Once you've set your Source and Blur Focal Distance settings, adjust the other options to get the look you want, using the preview to see how the settings interact:

- The Iris settings allow you to specify the shape and size of specular highlights. Some readers will appreciate the fine control this offers, while others may prefer to use the default settings. If your image doesn't have any specular highlights, then don't worry about setting the Iris values.

- The Specular Highlights settings enable you to determine which values should be used as specular highlights. The Brightness setting allows you to specify how bright to make the specular highlights, while the Threshold setting specifies which values are to be used as specular highlights. (You can choose from 0 to 255.) True specular highlights should have a value of 255, but you may want to create specular highlights by using a slightly lower setting. Many images have no specular highlights.

  Some people choose to add some noise to simulate the appearance of film grain. If you choose to add noise, check the box to make it monochromatic. (Adding color noise will look like digital noise, which we try to eliminate!) Usually the Gaussian distribution appears more natural than uniform.

10. When you are satisfied with your settings, click OK to perform the blur.

11. If you find that you blurred areas you didn't intend to, you can modify them by adding a layer mask to your blurred image layer. Use as soft a brush as possible on the layer mask.

> **Note:** To reduce the effect of any filter immediately after applying it, choose Edit > Fade, and reduce the effect by adjusting the slider. This option exists only immediately after applying the filter.

The Liquify Filter

The Liquify filter can be a lot of fun. It's a lot like finger-painting with the pixels but with a lot more control and much cleaner hands! You can stretch, push, pull, pucker, or bloat any area to create subtle or dramatic distortions. This is one of our favorite filters to use to create artistic effects with flowers (see Figure 9.18).

Liquify can be used with 16-bit or 8-bit images, but not on a Smart Object layer. Unfortunately, it's not available as a Smart Filter. To use the Liquify filter, create a Stamp Visible layer by clicking on the top layer. Hold down the Alt/Option key and continue to hold it while choosing Layers > Merge Visible. Don't release the Alt/Option key until you see the new layer appear on top of the others. (If all the layers disappear, you released the Alt/Option key too soon!)

Be aware that unless you have a fast computer with a lot of memory, processing the Liquify effects may be slow. For that reason, you may want to convert a copy of your image to 8-bit and use the filter on that version. Once you have established effective settings for your image, you can save them and then apply them to a 16-bit version if you prefer. Don't forget to work on a copy of your Background layer or the Stamp Visible layer, both for safety and so you can apply a layer mask or reduce the opacity of the layer.

Figure 9.18 Using the Liquify filter transforms a bland picture of orchids into a striking fine-art image.

Perhaps more than any other filter in Photoshop, this is one you have to play with to use effectively. Let's look at the Liquify dialog box, which you open by choosing Filter > Liquify. A variety of tools appear in the toolbox column on the left, as shown in Figure 9.19. Some of these tools apply the distortions, while others, such as the Freeze tool, enable you to apply a quick mask to certain areas to "freeze" the effects. The Hand and Zoom tools work as usual. The primary tool we tend to use is the Warp tool, although it's worth experimenting with the others.

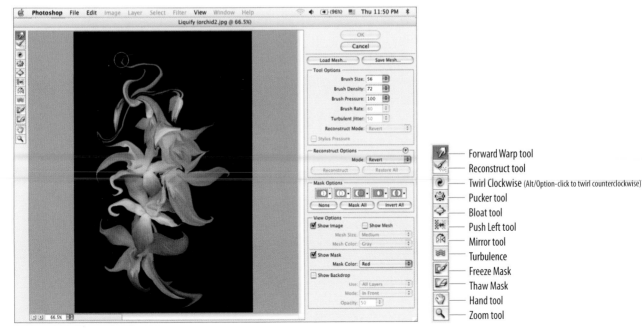

Figure 9.19 The Liquify dialog box offers several tools.

On the right side of the Liquify dialog box (shown in Figure 9.20) are options for using the tools:

Figure 9.20 On the right side of the Liquify dialog box are the controls for the various tools.

Brush Size Is as expected; it refers to the size of the brush and can be controlled by the bracket keys on your keyboard or via the setting in the dialog box.

Brush Density Controls how the brush is feathered at the edges. The effect is strongest in the center of the brush and lighter at the edges.

Brush Pressure Controls how quickly the distortions are applied when you drag a tool across your preview image. Using too large a pressure may make it difficult to stop exactly where you want.

Brush Rate Controls how quickly distortions are applied when you use a tool that can be held stationary, such as bloat or twirl.

Turbulent Jitter Sets how tightly the Turbulence tool scrambles the pixels.

Reconstruct Mode Offers additional choices for ways to reconstruct the image. Some are similar to those offered in the Reconstruction Options section, while others are in addition to those options. If you just want to return to the original state, choose Revert. The other options create further distortions.

Reconstruction Options These options allow you, with the Reconstruct tool selected, to specify a mode for the reconstruction, which can either create further distortions or revert to the original image.

When you have achieved the desired effect, if you're working on a full-resolution image, you can simply click OK to apply your work to the picture. If you are using a small-file version of your image as we suggested at the start of this section, click Save Mesh. Another dialog box appears in which you can name the effect and specify where to save it (see Figure 9.21).

Figure 9.21 After you are satisfied with the effect, save the mesh to apply to your full-sized file.

Once the mesh is saved, open your full-sized file, choose Filter > Liquify, and click Load Mesh. Choose the mesh you just saved, and click OK to perform the distortion. If you are feeling adventurous, apply a saved mesh to an unrelated image—sometimes serendipity comes into play, and you create something unexpected but wonderful!

Note: Although the Liquify tool is most commonly used to create distortions, it can also be used to correct distortions. It can even be used as a form of digital plastic surgery on photos of people. In such cases you may want to work in small increments to help avoid pixel stretching.

Liquify

The Elements Liquify filter is quite similar to the one in Photoshop. Access it from Filter > Distort > Liquify. The Elements version lacks Freeze and Thaw tools, but has specific tools for Twirl Counterclockwise and Reflection. Elements does not have options for Brush Density, Brush Rate, or Reconstruction. In addition, you cannot save the mesh to apply on other images.

Try It! Open the image called Liquify on the accompanying CD or open one of your own images, and see what you can create with it. Be sure to vary the settings and tools to get different effects.

Using the Filter Gallery

Recent versions of Photoshop (CS and newer, as well as Elements) contain a filter gallery (Filter > Filter Gallery) rather than just a simple list of individual filters. This gallery enables you to preview the effects of a variety of filters, as well as to preview the effects of combining them and reordering them. This saves a lot of time as you experiment with different effects, but unfortunately, it works only on 8-bit images. The good news is that you can use it as a regular filter or as a Smart Filter on a Smart Object layer. When it's used as a Smart Filter, you can go back and modify the filter settings, reorder, and even add and remove effects.

We often find that when using filters, one thing leads to another, and pretty soon you may have created something you love but perhaps couldn't have imagined ahead of time. The more you experiment with these filters, the more predictable they will become for you.

The Filter Gallery contains thumbnails that give you an idea of each effect. As shown in Figure 9.22, this dialog box also previews the various effects and settings on your image. You can vary the settings, combine filters, vary the order (which can substantially change their effect), and even repeat filters. The filters are applied in the order you select them, but you can drag the filter name to a different position to reorder them. To select an effect, click the corresponding thumbnail. If you want to add an additional effect, Alt/Option-click each additional filter. Clicking the eyeball icon toggles the visibility of the effect.

Figure 9.22 We used the Filter Gallery to create a painterly effect by combining the Dry Brush and Diffuse Glow filters.

Before beginning with the Filter Gallery, you should take several preparatory steps:

1. Usually when we experiment with filters, we're using files that have already been optimized. To avoid accidentally mucking up an image you've already put effort into, work on a copy of the master file by choosing Image > Duplicate.

2. Close the original file. This ensures you won't accidentally save changes to your master file, such as flattening it.

3. Flatten the image by choosing Layer > Flatten Image.

4. Choose Image > Mode > 8-Bits/Channel.

5. Duplicate the Background layer by dragging it to the Create a New Layer icon at the bottom of the Layers panel. Now you'll be adding your creative effects on a layer so that not only are you not damaging your pixels, you can also later reduce the opacity of the layer or add a layer mask to it to control where the effects are applied.

6. If you are using Photoshop CS3 or CS4, choose Filter > Convert for Smart Filters. This changes the layer into a Smart Object layer.

7. Choose Filter > Filter Gallery.

Some of the filters we frequently try are Glass (Distort grouping), Dry Brush, Poster Edges and Rough Pastels (which are in the Artistic group), and Water Paper (Sketch group). You will find your own favorites the more you experiment with the filters. However, don't forget to use the filters that are not part of the Filter Gallery as well. They are available from the Filter menu on the main menu bar.

Sometimes the distortion filters can lead to some exciting results, as shown in Figure 9.23. This poppy was distorted using polar remapping, then copied and liquified, and a bit of the original image was returned to complete the effect. Pretty wild, but that's what happens when you let your imagination go along with the filters in Photoshop!

PHOTO BY ELLEN ANON

Figure 9.23 This rather boring picture of a poppy was transformed into a fantasy image using a variety of Photoshop filters, along with a little imagination.

Additional Filter Effects

Quite a few software companies, such as Flaming Pear (www.flamingpear.com), have produced filter effect plug-ins for Photoshop. Many of these can lead to interesting effects as well. Often you can download a free sample to see whether it's something you might want to use.

Try It! Open the image called FilterGallery on the accompanying CD or open one of your own images, and experiment with a variety of filters. Try different combinations and orders of filters while varying the settings.

Digital Montages

Combining shots, or creating "slide sandwiches," has been a popular film technique for years. Traditionally, one slide had to be overexposed by about two stops and the other by a single stop to yield an acceptable exposure. At best, it's an approach that requires a lot of trial and error and bracketing.

It's not only possible to emulate these same effects in Photoshop, it's actually easier to do so! One reason is that we have the flexibility to alter exposures as needed. Another reason is that if you didn't think of using a particular image as part of a montage while you were in the field, it doesn't matter. You can make several versions of the same file in Photoshop. And in Photoshop, you can go further and combine numerous images in a variety of ways.

Before you begin to make your montages, remove any dust in your images. After all, double the dust means double the cleanup required later! Final exposure and color changes are usually best made after creating the montage.

Blending Modes

Before proceeding with ways to combine images, you need to have some understanding of blending modes.

Back in Chapter 5, you learned about layers. Recall that in many ways, pixel layers in Normal blending mode—which is what we've been using—act like prints. Whatever is on top is what you see. If you "cut a hole" in the top layer by using a layer mask to partially hide that layer, you see what's underneath. If you reduce the opacity of the top pixel layer, you see some of the top layer and some of the layer beneath it. In Normal mode, the layers blend together in an intuitive way.

However, Photoshop at its core is a series of mathematical algorithms, and there can be (and are) other instructions (algorithms) for how to blend two layers. These are called *blending modes*. Photoshop CS4 and Elements 7 have 25 blending modes. Don't panic! You don't have to memorize what each one does. Instead, you can simply scroll through the drop-down list in the Layers panel (see Figure 9.24). You'll soon realize that the most useful blending modes for photographers are Normal, Multiply, Screen, Overlay, Soft Light, Difference, and Luminosity.

Figure 9.24 Photoshop offers numerous blending modes to combine layers in different ways.

But sometimes one of the other modes will create magic for you, so don't hesitate to try them all.

Each blending mode is a different set of instructions for how to combine two layers. If you are more intuitive, don't worry about fully grasping each algorithm. Feel free to skip ahead and experiment with using the blending modes. In case you are more analytical, we're providing this explanation.

The different blending modes are grouped together in the drop-down list according to similar functions.

Figure 9.25 shows the results when a Background layer of an image is copied and flipped horizontally upon itself in six different blending modes. Note that for this image, Exclusion and Hue provided interesting results, so they were included in this illustration.

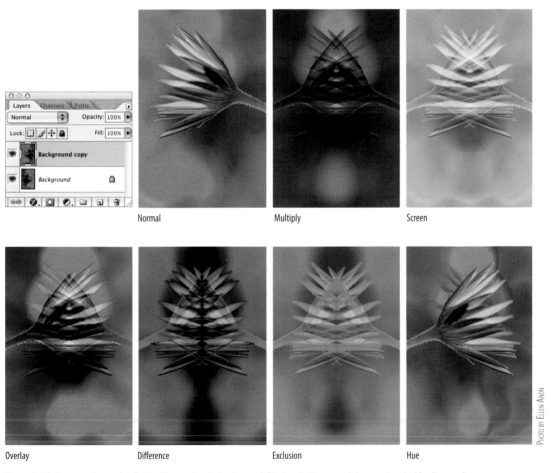

Normal   Multiply   Screen

Overlay   Difference   Exclusion   Hue

PHOTO BY ELLEN ANON

Figure 9.25 Compare the results obtained by copying the background, flipping the image, and then varying the blending mode.

Note: On a Windows system, to preview the effects of the various blending modes, scroll through them by highlighting the top pixel layer and clicking Shift++ (plus) or Shift+− (minus).

Surreal Montages

A popular effect that photographers seek is a dreamy blur. You've seen it in many artistic photos: a kind of glow or soft focus around the subject that we call a *surreal montage* (see an example in Figure 9.26). Even the most mundane subjects can become evocative when done in this way.

Figure 9.26 Surreal montages seem to have an ethereal glow around them that makes them quite evocative.

Note: The surreal montage in Figure 9.26 would not be possible using film because of the amount of white and nearly white in the image. This is a distinct advantage of digital photography.

The traditional way to capture a surreal dream montage is to take two shots with your camera on a tripod, not moving it between shots. Take one image two stops overexposed at f22 or comparable and sharply focused, and the other one stop overexposed with a wide-open aperture and blurred. Defocus in the direction that makes the blur get larger than the subject rather than smaller, because the blurred version is going to provide the glow around your subject. The first image is going to provide the detail.

With a film camera, you couldn't use a wide-angle lens because the blur would be insufficient. You were also limited to subjects that were close to middle-toned. If you wanted to do a surreal montage of a light subject, it was often impossible because you would lose all detail in the overexposed versions.

Photoshop enables you to go beyond these restrictions and create surreal montages using any lens, since you can use a Gaussian blur to blur the image as much as needed. Also, you can capture light images while retaining detail and adjust the exposure after the fact as necessary.

Note: For slightly different effects, experiment with some of the other Blur tools.

If you know you want to make a surreal montage, go ahead and capture two versions of the image as described in the preceding paragraphs. However, if it wasn't until editing your pictures that you realized an image would be great as a surreal montage, convert the same image twice, making one considerably lighter than the other. You can try plus-two and plus-one exposures in the raw converter, but we often try to avoid clipping any data, so adjust the exposures accordingly. Since some of the glow results from areas without detail, you may choose to allow some clipping. This is a matter of experimenting and seeing what effects you prefer. You can always lighten the exposure of the composite using Levels or Curves.

> **Note:** If you are using a version of Photoshop prior to CS2, you need to save and rename the first conversion before converting the image a second time.

To create the surreal montage, take the following steps:

1. Open your two images, as shown in Figure 9.27.
2. Select the Move tool ⊕, and while holding down the Shift key, drag the darker, blurred image on top of the lighter one.
3. Change the blending mode of this layer (in the Layers panel) to Multiply.
4. If the blurred layer is not as blurred as you would like, select that layer and make it a Smart Object by choosing Layer > Smart Object.
5. Choose Filter > Blur > Gaussian Blur. If you are working from an in-focus original, you may need a blur ranging from 15 to 40, depending on the amount of detail in the original image. The advantage of working this way is you can judge the necessary amount of blur in real time.
6. Adjust the overall exposure as needed with a Curves or Levels adjustment layer.

Figure 9.27 Open a light but detailed image as well as a slightly darker but blurred version of the same image.

Surreal Montages

Since Smart Filters are not available in Elements, follow the same steps as for Photoshop, but apply the Gaussian blur directly on the image layer, if needed.

You can create a similar but slightly different effect by combining two images that are underexposed by one to two stops. Instead of using the Multiply blending mode, choose Screen. Figure 9.28 shows the original image and a version created using Multiply and another by using Screen. Which approach is better will vary by image and whether the detail you want to retain is primarily in the lighter or darker tonalities.

Screen   Multiply

Figure 9.28 Creating surreal montages using the Screen or Multiply blending modes yields slightly different results. In this case, we prefer the Screen results, but in other cases Multiply will do a better job.

Note: You may want to experiment with using the Overlay or Soft Light blending modes instead of Multiply. The effect is a little different, and depending on your individual taste as well as on the particular image, you may prefer one over the other. With these blending modes you may not need the images to be quite as light as with Multiply. You'll notice an increase in contrast and saturation.

Mirror or Flip Montages

Another approach to combining images is to take the same image and combine it with a second identical shot that is rotated 90° or flipped 180°; André Gallant calls these *mirror montages*. This can yield some amazing abstract designs.

One of the keys is to experiment with the different blending modes. Often, Multiply, Overlay, Difference, Exclusion, Luminosity, or Color yields some interesting results. Usually you begin with well-exposed images and lighten the montage as needed after you combine the layers. Depending on the choice of blending mode, you may or may not need to adjust the exposure.

To create mirror or flip montages, take these steps:

1. Open an image, and duplicate the Background layer by dragging it to the Create a New Layer icon.

2. Ctrl+click/⌘+-click the icon for the Background copy layer to select it.

3. Choose Edit > Transform > Rotate, and select 90° in either direction or flip horizontal or vertical. The choice depends on the particular image and what you think might look good.

4. Scroll through the different blending modes to see what looks good. Sometimes nothing works, and sometimes you hit a winner, as you can see in Figure 9.29.

5. If you have elected to rotate your image 90°, chances are you will want to crop and use the center square formed by the overlap of the two images.

6. Sometimes you can repeat the process and copy the montage, rotate, or flip it and blend it to create a virtual kaleidoscope.

Figure 9.29 Flipping this image horizontally and selecting the Difference blending mode resulted in a dramatic abstract design.

Try It! Open the image called Flip on the accompanying CD, or open one of your own. Duplicate it, and then rotate or flip it to create various effects. Be sure to scroll through the blending modes to see how they affect the montage.

Mirror Images

Mirror images are very similar to flip montages, except that the two images are side by side rather than on top of each other. This creates an obvious dramatic symmetry that can be quite compelling. Natural phenomena that have strong design components, such as sand dunes, rock formations, waves, and even trees, lend themselves to this approach. Remember that the center of your image is formed by what is on the edges of your file, so your subject may need to be placed toward the edges of the original rather than your typical composition.

To create a mirror montage, take the following steps:

1. Open your file (see Figure 9.30), and duplicate it by choosing Image > Duplicate. This is easier for this technique than simply copying the Background layer, as you did earlier.

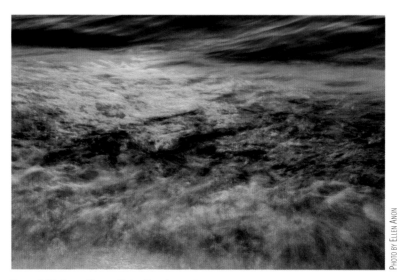

Figure 9.30 Open a file you think will work as a mirror.

2. Select your original file, and choose Image > Canvas Size to determine the size of your image.

3. If you are going to create a horizontal montage, double the width of the canvas, but leave the height alone (see Figure 9.31). Anchor the original to the right or left as desired by clicking the anchor arrow ⬚. (If you are creating a vertical montage, then double the height and leave the width alone. Anchor the image at the top or bottom as desired.) Click OK.

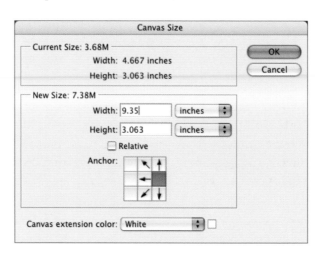

Figure 9.31 Double the canvas size in width if you are creating a horizontal mirror, or double it in height if you are creating a vertical mirror.

4. Select the copy of the image, and drag it onto the original using the Move tool.

5. Select the Background copy layer, and choose Edit > Transform > Flip Horizontal (or Vertical).

6. Use the Move tool to align the flipped layer next to the original.

7. When you get close, it's easier to use the arrow keys on your keyboard to nudge the layer into place.

Using this technique creates symmetry that sometimes creates what appears to be odd creatures or faces (see Figure 9.32). These often add to the intrigue of images created this way.

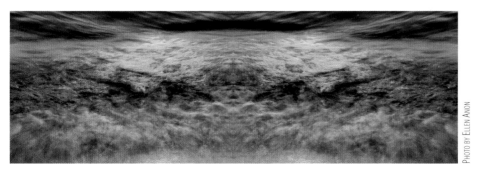

PHOTO BY ELLEN ANON

Figure 9.32 The symmetry of mirror montages often creates what appear to be creatures in unexpected places.

Multiple-Subject Montages

So far, we've been describing a variety of ways to combine two versions of the same image, but it's also possible to combine two different images. One approach to combining two different images is to have one image provide the texture and have the other provide the subject matter. You can stack one on top of the other, rotate, or flip one as desired. And of course, the effect is going to vary dramatically depending on the way you combine the two images. You could simply reduce the opacity of the top image and leave it in Normal blending mode, or you could choose any of the other blending modes.

> **Note:** Shots of wood, tree bark, textured glass, frost, rocks, snow, rain, and lots more can be used as texture.

Figure 9.33 shows a flower image and a shot of the rain on the greenhouse wall. The greenhouse-wall file was dragged on top of the flower using the Move tool. Scrolling through the blending modes, the image jumped to life in the Difference mode. However, the flower was a little too unrecognizable, so we added a layer mask to the second layer and used it to reveal the center of the original flower in the layer below.

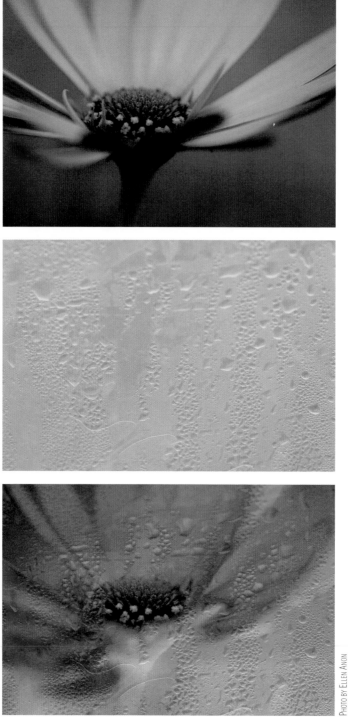

PHOTO BY ELLEN ANON

Figure 9.33 Combining two very different shots in the Difference mode led to this striking image.

There are no simple rules or absolutes to follow when creating montages. You are the artist, and you have to decide what works and what doesn't. It's your chance to apply all the knowledge you've gained in the previous chapters!

For example, you could add texture to a surreal montage created from the steps in an earlier section:

1. Open two versions of an image that you want to use to create a surreal montage, and follow the steps described earlier. We'll use the surreal montage shown in Figure 9.34.

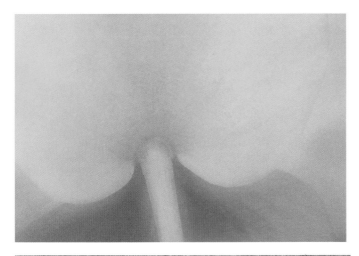

Figure 9.34 We'll combine this surreal montage with a texture shot of wood siding.

2. Open a shot that you want to use as texture.

3. Drag the texture shot on top of the other layers by using the Move tool.

4. Reduce the opacity of this layer in the Layers panel so that it provides a subtle, but not overpowering, texture. Often you may be in the range of 10% to 20% opacity, but of course, this varies depending on the particular images you're using.

Note: Beyond relying on reducing the opacity, experiment with changing the blending mode of the texture layer as well.

The final result (see Figure 9.35) should be subtly different than a straight shot, and it is this unexpected texture that captures your viewer's attention.

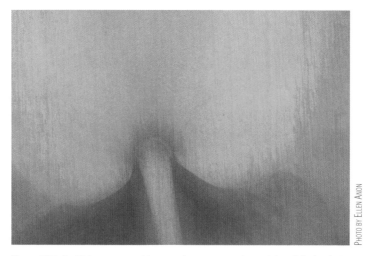

Figure 9.35 Combining a texture with a surreal montage can give a subtle, soft feel to the image.

On occasion, we have combined all of the techniques discussed so far into one image. Figure 9.36 is the result of two totally different images of sand dunes montaged together and then mirrored horizontally. Note that unlike in the previous examples, two different images were combined equally as the foundation for the montage. That entire montage was then duplicated and mirrored vertically, and the image was cropped.

Note: Montages can also consist of two totally different images combined using blending modes or opacity.

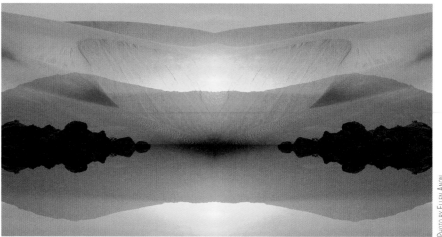

Figure 9.36 Almost all the techniques described so far in this section were combined to create this dramatic image.

The ways to combine images in Photoshop is infinite. The only limit is your imagination!

Digital Multiple Exposures

Ever since Ellen was exposed to some of Freeman Patterson's in-camera film-based creative multiple exposures, she decided there *had* to be a way to create the same effect digitally. Although some methods were available on the Internet, none worked reliably and well. It took some time and experimentation, but at last she figured out how to create multiple exposures of as many images as desired in Photoshop. Since then Nikon has offered the ability to create multiple exposures in some of its cameras, but most other camera manufacturers have yet to follow suit.

For those not familiar with Freeman's techniques, he uses film and takes multiple images (9, 16, or 25), moving his camera slightly between shots. Sometimes he moves the camera in a vertical or horizontal direction, depending on what would be a natural movement for the subject. Sometimes he zooms the camera between shots, and at other times he combines zooming the camera with rotating it slightly between shots. The results are artistic, soft-abstract renditions of familiar subjects (see Figure 9.37).

PHOTO BY ELLEN ANON

Figure 9.37 Multiple exposures can render familiar subjects in pleasing, artistic, abstract ways.

To use a digital camera to create multiple exposures, you can still shoot the original files in RAW. Then batch-process the images in ACR so that all are adjusted the same way (as described in Chapter 3). Be sure to remove dust when possible. Although normally you could go ahead and open the files, there is a potential problem; the issue is memory. For example, with a 1DsMKII camera, each 16-bit converted file is roughly 95MB. If you have 9 or 10 images to combine, your multiple-exposure file is going to be close to 1GB in size before you do anything else to it. You're going to need a lot of RAM and hard drive space to deal with files that large. If you don't have enough memory, you can convert the raw files to JPEGs first by choosing Save in the raw converter. Create the composite using the JPEGs and then save the composite as a TIFF. That way, you'll maintain image quality and maximize the use of your computer's resources.

The steps to combining multiple images within Photoshop are as follows:

1. Choose File > Scripts > Load Files into Stack.
2. Choose Files, or choose Folder if all the images are in their own folder.
3. Click Browse, navigate to the desired images, and select them.
4. Do *not* check the option Attempt to Automatically Align Source Images (see Figure 9.38)—that will defeat the purpose!
5. Click OK.

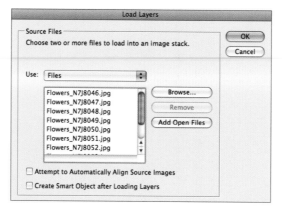

Figure 9.38 Using a script to layer all the images is far more efficient than doing it manually.

6. Reduce the opacity of the second image to 50% in the Layers panel.

7. If you have a third image to add, drag it on top of the others, but reduce its opacity to 34%.

8. For a fourth layer, reduce the opacity to 25%; a fifth layer is 20%; a sixth layer is 17%; a seventh layer is 15%; an eighth layer is 13%; and a ninth or tenth layer is 10% (see Figure 9.39).

> **Note:** The trick is to set the opacity for each layer according to the number of images you are using. If you are using two images, the first is 100% and the second is 50%—that is, 100 divided by 2. The third layer's opacity is 100 divided by 3, the fourth is 100 divided by 4, and so on.

9. Leave the blending mode for these layers set to Normal except for the final layer, which you may want to set at Overlay or Soft Light to add a little punch to the image.

10. You can adjust the exposure using a Levels or Curves adjustment layer, and you can adjust the color using any of the color adjustment layers.

Figure 9.39 Reduce the opacity of each layer according to how many layers you are combining to create abstract expressive images.

Simulating Multiple Exposures

It is possible to create digital multiple exposure images in Elements, but because the Load Files into Stack command is not available, it takes a bit of extra work. Replace Step 1 from the preceding process as follows:

1. Open the bottommost image.

2. Open the second image.

3. Select the Move tool, and while holding the Shift key, drag image 2 onto image 1. You must hold the shift key for proper image alignment.

4. Close image 2 and repeat Step 3 with the remaining images.

The ability to create digital multiple exposures opens up entire worlds of creativity. The only downside is the need for a lot of memory, both compact flash card space as well as computer memory. Often it's a good idea when shooting a multiple exposure to do it more than once; subtle differences in the amount you moved the camera can make a huge difference in the success of the image.

When shooting multiple exposures, be sure to shoot a blank shot between groupings so that you'll know where each series begins and ends.

The number of ways to modify an image to creatively express your vision is limited only by your imagination and time. The more familiar you become with the basic and more advanced adjustments, filters, and blending modes in Photoshop, the more freedom and ability you'll have to express what you feel in addition to what you saw. To give you another example of a creative expression of an image, we asked Nikon Legend Behind the Lens Tony Sweet to share the behind-the-scenes of one of his images.

Creative Vision and Extreme Color

by Tony Sweet

Being a big fan of "extreme color," I'm always on the lookout for various ways to intensify color in image situations. This scene was shot in the fall in New Hampshire. There was a small patch of birch trees, orange fall color, and a surprising foreground patch of purple flowers. This is a tremendous scene for color interpretation.

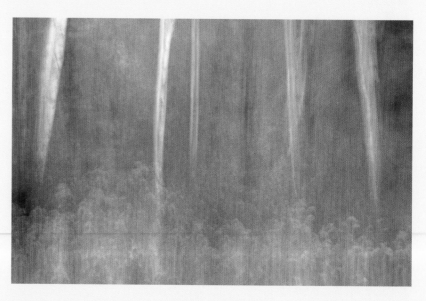

A straight shot of the image was OK but didn't render the color I was seeing in my imagination. Smoothly panning this scene for one second was an excellent way to fill the frame with color more than a straight shot. I was able to "paint" over the picture space by panning the camera in an up-and-down fashion, keeping in line with the birch trees as much as possible, creating a colorful abstract of line and color.

Continues

Creative Vision and Extreme Color *(Continued)*

Postprocessing in Photoshop, I used three adjustment layers:

Curves adjustment layer #1: I placed the point in the middle of the graph and used the arrow key to slightly move the point downward to darken the image a little.

Curves adjustment layer #2: I created and saved a small S curve to slightly increase contrast and loaded the curve for this adjustment layer.

Hue/Saturation layer: Because this is an abstract image, I felt free to boost saturation to achieve the image I see in my imagination. Here, I increased the saturation in the master window to 25.

© Tony Sweet, www.tonysweet.com

Note: The key to any creative endeavor is to wonder "what if . . ." and then find out.

This chapter has only touched the tip of the iceberg in terms of what you can do with your images. We hope you'll use these ideas as a starting point to create imaginative versions of some of your own photographs.

Output

*Spending time outdoors in nature capturing
beautiful images is often inspirational,
and it's a driving force for many of us, but
creating lasting output to share with others
and to view time and time again is also
special. In earlier chapters we focused on
optimizing the images, and in this chapter
we'll take a look at how to produce the
best output. We'll talk about printing your
images, creating slide shows, and creating
a web gallery to share your images with an
even broader audience.*

Chapter Contents
Output Workflow
Printing Your Images
Creating Busines Cards
Using Adobe Output Module

Output Workflow

The output workflow actually starts very early in the process of optimizing your photographic images in Photoshop. Of course, we could go so far as to say that every optimization step is part of the output workflow, since you're generally trying to make the image look its best in order to produce the best output. However, what we're referring to here is saving the image. Although we tend to talk about saving the image near the end of the workflow, in reality you should be saving from early in the workflow. As a general rule, every time you perform any significant optimization step on your image, you should resave so you won't lose any changes should something go wrong.

The idea is to save a master image (in addition to archiving your original capture) that contains all of the image and adjustment layers in a single file, which becomes your master image, to be used as the basis for all future output (see Figure 10.1). After you've saved the final result safely, you're ready to move on to preparing that image for output.

Note: Save your master file as either a TIFF or PSD file. Both formats support layers.

Figure 10.1 Your master image file should contain all of the image and adjustment layers used to create the optimal output.

Duplicating the Image

By this time, you can well imagine how important your master image is. As you'll see in the next few sections, the process of preparing your image for output can result in changes to the number of pixels in your image as well as to the actual color and tonal values for the image. Therefore, if you are using our *traditional workflow*, we recommend using a working copy of your image while preparing it for output. This ensures that the original master image remains safely saved without risking a permanent loss of pixels.

Note: Although technically using our traditional workflow you could use your master image to prepare for output and then do a Save As, it's risky because it's far too easy to accidentally do a Save on the image and override your master file. That's why in our standard workflow we recommend getting in the habit of working on a duplicate copy.

As a result, the first step in the *traditional output workflow* is to create a duplicate copy of the image by choosing Image > Duplicate (File > Duplicate in Elements). The Duplicate Image dialog box (shown in Figure 10.2) appears, allowing you to enter a name for the new image document. The name in the text box is simply the name of the document you are duplicating with the word *copy* appended to it. You can enter a different name if you want, which becomes the filename if you save this duplicate image later.

Figure 10.2 The Duplicate Image dialog box allows you to specify a name for the image, as well as to specify whether you want to flatten the image by enabling the Duplicate Merged Layers Only check box.

The Duplicate Image dialog box also contains a check box labeled Duplicate Merged Layers Only. This check box is enabled only if the image you're duplicating contains multiple layers. If you check it, the duplicate image is a flattened version of the original image. We recommend checking this box for two main reasons. First, it flattens the image into a single layer, thus reducing the amount of memory required by the image. (Remember, the master image with all layers intact has already been saved, and you're working on a duplicate copy.) This can speed up the process of preparing the image for output and sending the data to the printer. Second, sharpening can be applied only to a single layer, so if you have multiple image layers in the image, this streamlines the sharpening process.

When you have established the desired settings, click OK to create the working copy of your image file, and then close the original master image.

If you are using our *flexible workflow* and you don't have a separate Clone/Healing brush layer with significant changes, you don't need to duplicate your master file. You can apply sharpening and other output adjustments as Smart Filters directly on the background Smart Object layer. Since the Smart Object layer references the original file, you won't lose quality as you repeatedly resize the image for each different type of output (see Chapter 4, "Foundations"). However, you will still need to adjust the sharpening settings each time you resize the image, because the amount of sharpening necessary will vary according to the file size, resolution, and amount of detail. The advantages to applying the sharpening as a Smart Filter are that you will have one master file with all the layers and adjustments, including the sharpening, and that you can readjust the amount of sharpening at any time. However, if you do have a clone layer where you've done more than just dust cleanup, you will need to duplicate the master file and follow the steps for the standard output workflow.

Note: If you are using our *traditional workflow*, we also recommend applying sharpening and noise reduction as Smart Filters so that you can adjust the settings as necessary. Sometimes after you see the final output, you'll realize your settings need tweaking. By using Smart Filters, that's easy to do.

Resizing

Chances are the native size of your image doesn't match the final output size you're targeting, so you need to resize it. This involves setting both the resolution and the actual output size. To change the size of the image, choose Image > Image Size, which opens the Image Size dialog box shown in Figure 10.3. (In Elements, choose Image > Resize > Image Size.)

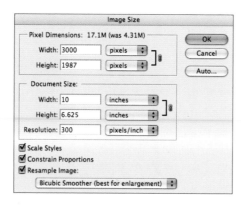

Figure 10.3 The Image Size dialog box allows you to resize your image for the final output.

Although you would normally start at the top of a dialog box and work your way down, in the case of the Image Size dialog box, it makes more sense to start at the bottom and work your way up. At the bottom, be sure the Resample Image check box is checked, which enables Photoshop to resize the image using interpolation, changing the number of pixels within the image. The drop-down list to the right of the Resample Image check box provides options for the algorithm to use for interpolating the data in your image, as shown in Figure 10.4.

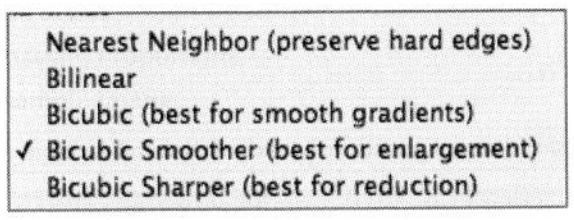

```
Nearest Neighbor (preserve hard edges)
Bilinear
Bicubic (best for smooth gradients)
✓ Bicubic Smoother (best for enlargement)
Bicubic Sharper (best for reduction)
```

Figure 10.4 You can choose from five options for the interpolation algorithm in the Image Size dialog box, but you generally use only Bicubic or Bicubic Smoother.

Bicubic is an all-purpose option. If you're creating a particularly large enlargement from your original, the Bicubic Smoother option is a better choice, and you can use it any time you're enlarging. Bicubic Sharper is designed to maintain sharpness when reducing the size of an image, but we prefer to control the sharpening ourselves and therefore don't usually use this option, although some people use it to save time when preparing images for display on the Web. The other two options—Nearest Neighbor and Bilinear—are not appropriate for producing high-quality photographic output and should not be used.

The Constrain Proportions check box ensures that you maintain the aspect ratio for the image. If you clear this check box, it's possible to stretch the image in one direction or the other. Although this might not be a problem when done to a very small degree, it can produce a distorted result if taken too far, and we recommend eliminating the possibility altogether by keeping this check box selected.

The Scale Styles check box determines whether layer styles are scaled when you resize the image or whether they are kept at their same size. This isn't an issue at this point since you have already flattened the image. However, you generally want to scale any layer styles, so if you are resizing an unflattened image, keep this check box selected.

The Resolution box in the Document Size section of the Image Size dialog box determines how the pixels are distributed when the image is output, and it plays a role in determining how many pixels are required in the final image. For digital display (monitors and digital projectors, for example), this number is irrelevant. However, because some software applications where you may import your images do indeed look at this number, we recommend setting it to about 96 pixels per inch (ppi) for those situations. For printing, the best resolution depends on the output method being used, but 300 ppi is a good standard value.

Note: If you're working with film scans, it's particularly important to keep an eye on the Resolution setting. If you've scanned at 4000 dpi, you don't want to resize to a 20˝×30˝ print without changing the resolution to a more appropriate value, or you'll produce an absolutely huge file that takes forever to resize and likely crashes your computer.

The next step is to set the output size. For images that will be printed, this should be done in the Document Size section, setting either the Width or the Height. You can change the unit of measure with the drop-down list to the right, and if you have the Constrain Proportions check box selected (as we recommend), setting the Width or the Height causes the other to be adjusted automatically.

> **Note:** When you make adjustments that affect the actual pixel dimensions of the image in the Image Size dialog box, the current size is displayed after the Pixel Dimensions label, with the starting size shown in parentheses.

For images that will be displayed digitally on a monitor or digital projector, the size should be adjusted using the Width or Height text boxes in the Pixel Dimensions section. This allows you to set the specific pixel sizing for your intended purpose. For a digital slide show, for example, you might set these dimensions to fit within the resolution of your digital projector. For a website, you might set them to a standard output size you deem appropriate for your specific site design.

> **Note:** Check the resolution of your projector, and use those values to set the height or width to resize images that you'll use in a slide show. Many projectors have a native resolution of 1024×768, while others may be 1400×1050, and so on. Your images must fit within those specifications.

Once you've established the sizing parameters in the Image Size dialog box, click OK, and Photoshop resizes the image accordingly.

> **Note:** Some people are tempted to wait and resize in the Print dialog box. We don't recommend that because for best results you need to sharpen your image based on its final size. If you wait to resize in the Print dialog box, you have to do the sharpening before resizing. You'd be surprised how different the results can be.

Reducing Noise

Although you could insert steps to reduce noise earlier in your workflow, noise often becomes more apparent as you are preparing your image for output. We recommend applying any noise reduction before sharpening to make sure the process of sharpening won't exaggerate the noise, so this is a good time to apply such a correction, if you haven't done so already.

Photoshop has a noise-reduction filter called Reduce Noise (found under the Filter > Noise submenu). If noise exists in your image, it's most likely found in the dark shadow areas, although sometimes it can also be found in the midtones or even the lighter tones. To check for noise zoom in on the dark shadow areas and look for pixels with random colors that don't match their surroundings, as shown in Figure 10.5. If you find noise that is problematic in the image, try using Reduce Noise to minimize it.

PHOTO BY ELLEN ANON

Figure 10.5 Noise is most often found in the dark shadow areas of an image when high ISO settings or long exposures are used with a digital camera.

If you have opted to use our *flexible workflow* beginning with a raw file placed as a Smart Object, you can click the Smart Object layer and use the Reduce Noise filter as a Smart Filter directly on that layer. However, if you have used other Smart Filters in conjunction with a layer mask, you will need to duplicate the background Smart Object layer by dragging it to the New Layer button at the bottom of the Layers panel. This will create a new Smart Object layer. If you have a separate Clone/Healing brush layer in your workflow with significant changes, you will need to follow our traditional workflow.

If you are using our *traditional workflow*, you'll also need to create a new separate layer for this correction. Begin by creating a copy of your background image layer by dragging it to the New Layer button at the bottom of the Layers panel. This ensures that you are preserving the original image data, as well as gaining the opportunity to mask out any areas of this layer if the noise reduction isn't needed or introduces color problems.

To use the Reduce Noise filter, choose Filter > Convert for Smart Filters, and then choose Filter > Noise > Reduce Noise from the menu. This first changes the layer into a Smart Object so that you can apply the noise reduction as a Smart Filter. The Reduce Noise dialog box opens, which includes a number of parameters that allow you to adjust its behavior.

Make sure to zoom in on the preview image in the Reduce Noise dialog box so you can see detail in the image clearly. We often zoom in to 200% or even 300% magnification. You can adjust the zoom percentage for the preview using the plus and minus buttons below the preview image. You can click the preview image to see the "before" version without the effect of the Reduce Noise filter, releasing the mouse to see the "after" version again.

Note: It's a good idea to set all of the settings in Reduce Noise to 0 before starting so you'll be able to see the effect of each individually as you work to find the best settings.

The most important setting in the Reduce Noise dialog box is the Reduce Color Noise slider. This setting determines how aggressively color noise, exhibited by random color variations (as opposed to luminance noise exhibited by tonal variations) should be reduced in the image. The potential risk is that you'll reduce the overall color in the image by using a setting that is too high, because it causes an averaging of pixel values within the image. To help ensure you're getting the best results with a minimum of unintended effects, we recommend starting with a very low setting and then gradually increasing the value until you have effectively minimized the noise.

The Strength setting controls the amount of noise reduction you'd like to have applied to luminosity noise in the image—that is, noise exhibited by tonal rather than color variations. This is noise that is exhibited by tonal variations at the pixel level; generally, this isn't a significant issue in digital images, and increasing the Strength setting too much effectively blurs the detail out of your image. However, we still recommend adjusting this setting for images that have significant noise to see whether it provides a benefit.

The Preserve Details slider controls the amount of edge detail you want to maintain. Adjusting this too high reduces the effect of luminosity noise reduction controlled by the Strength setting (and in fact, this setting is available only if the Strength is set higher than 0). However, generally you want to use a relatively high setting here, such as 50% to 60%, to ensure you are maximizing the amount of detail in the image (see Figure 10.6).

After you've reduced the noise in your image, you may want to enhance detail slightly to compensate for the slight loss caused by the noise-reduction process. The Sharpen Details setting allows you to enhance edges within the image. We recommend starting with a low setting and gradually increasing the value until you have achieved the desired level of edge enhancement, without creating any quality problems within the image.

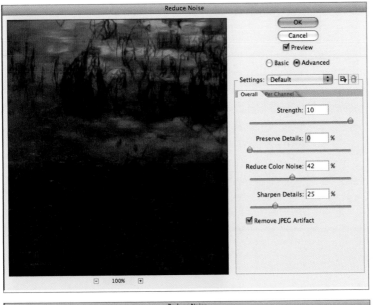

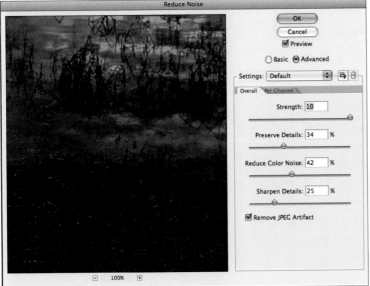

Figure 10.6 You can use the Preserve Details slider to ensure that maximum detail is maintained in the image despite the changes being applied by Reduce Noise.

Reducing Noise

The Reduce Noise filter is available in Elements in a more basic form. It includes just the controls from the Basic tab excluding the Sharpen Details slider. Elements users should follow the basic workflow to apply this filter.

Noise Reduction Advanced Settings

If you discover that you have significant luminosity noise in an image, we recommend returning the Strength setting to 0 and selecting the Advanced option. Additional per-channel settings become available that enable you to adjust the noise reduction individually for each color channel in your image. When you select one of the color channels from the drop-down list below the smaller preview on the Per Channel tab, that preview is updated to reflect that channel, and you can adjust the Strength and Preserve Details settings individually for the channel, as shown in Figure 10.7.

 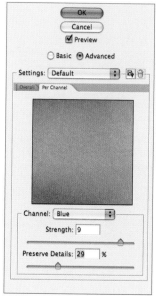

Figure 10.7 The Per Channel tab allows you to adjust the Strength and Preserve Details adjustments individually for each channel in your image.

The greatest benefit of these advanced settings is the ability to target additional noise reduction to a single channel, such as the Blue channel, which is often where the most noise exists within digital images. If you have an image with strong noise, it's helpful to examine each of the channels and set individual settings for each to minimize the amount of noise each channel contributes to the overall image, while simultaneously minimizing the amount of noise reduction that's applied to each channel. You can use much higher settings in one particular channel and lower settings in the other channels. This will help preserve details while at the same time reducing the luminosity noise. Then when you have selected the best settings for each channel, return to the initial part of the dialog box and set any additional overall luminosity noise reduction that's needed.

Once you have applied appropriate noise reduction to your image (if necessary), click OK in the Reduce Noise dialog box to apply the settings to your image.

When you're applying any noise reduction to an image, no matter how carefully you do it, there is a risk of some loss of image detail. One way to limit the amount of detail lost is to restrict the application of the filter to just those areas of the image where noise is an issue. For example, you may not notice the noise in detailed parts of your image, but many nature images have large out-of-focus backgrounds where noise may be more obvious. To apply noise reduction selectively, add a layer mask to the Noise Reduction filter layer by clicking the Add Layer mask button at the bottom of the Layers panel. If you're using a Smart Filter, use the smart filter mask. Then paint with black to remove the noise reduction from areas. Or, as you learned in earlier chapters, you can begin by filling the layer mask with black (Edit > Fill > Use: Black), and then paint with white to selectively apply the noise reduction to parts of the image. Of course, you can reduce the opacity of the brush to partially reveal the noise reduction in other areas of the picture.

Note: As with most tasks in Photoshop, there are other ways to go about noise reduction. Some people find it helpful to duplicate the image layer, blur it, and then reduce the opacity of the layer to taste. This option may work well with a particularly high-noise image, but you'll also need to add a layer mask to remove the blurred effect from your subject. Another good way of reducing bothersome noise is to duplicate the background layer, blur it, and change the blending mode to Color.

Removing Noise Using a Mask

To apply noise reduction with a layer mask in Elements, you will need to use the same technique we've used in previous chapters to create a layer mask. Follow these steps:

1. Duplicate your image layer by dragging its row in the Layers palette to the New Layer button.

2. Add a Levels adjustment layer and leave it empty.

3. Move the Levels adjustment layer below the layer you created in Step 1.

4. Select the topmost layer and choose Layer > Group with Previous.

5. Select the topmost layer and apply noise reduction.

6. Select the Levels adjustment layer's mask and paint in black to remove the noise-reduction filter.

Note: A number of third-party noise-reduction plug-ins are available that can help with unusually severe noise problems. One that we have had particularly good results with is Noiseware Pro, available at http://www.ellenanon.com/Ellen_Anon/Products.html. In fact this is our preferred way of reducing noise. The controls are easy and intuitive, and the software does an excellent job with noise removal. You do have to be vigilant with any noise-reduction software to avoid being overly aggressive in removing noise and accidentally creating a watercolor effect.

Try It! Practice removing noise from your photos by opening the image Noise.tif on the accompanying CD and applying the Reduce Noise filter to it.

Sharpening

Sharpening is an important aspect of preparing your image for output and is of particular importance for nature photographers who are often concerned with maintaining maximum detail in their images. It's not a way to make up for poor in-camera techniques, and you can't make a blurry picture tack sharp. However, you can compensate for the small amount of softening that occurs in the digital process by applying a sharpening filter. The sharpening filters enhance edge contrast, which helps improve the overall perceived detail in your images. In other words, they create an illusion of increased sharpness.

Although it's important to evaluate the effect of your sharpening settings based on a view of the actual pixels in your image, we don't work with the image set to 100% scale while applying sharpening. Doing so allows you to view only a portion of your image (in most cases). Instead, we prefer to set the image to fit the screen (View > Fit on Screen) and use the 100% preview in the dialog box for the sharpening filter being used to make judgments about the settings. This allows you to then click any area of your image to set the preview to show that area.

Note: Although most images benefit from sharpening, it's important to keep in mind that images without significant detail—such as a photo of the sky at sunset with no foreground detail—may not need to be sharpened.

At this point in the *traditional output workflow*, we're working on a flattened version of our master image file that may or may not contain a noise-reduction layer. The initial flattening of the original image is important so we can apply sharpening—which affects only one layer at a time—to the entire image in the event that we have additional pixel layers for tasks such as image cleanup or object removal. When preparing nature images for print, particularly for large prints, we recommend creating a copy of the background layer for the sharpening. That way, you can add a layer mask and apply the sharpening just to the subject and not to the background. Many nature images have out-of-focus backgrounds that should be blurry. Furthermore, by sharpening the subject and not the background, you can help the subject to stand out from the background.

If you've created a noise-reduction layer, duplicate that layer rather than the background layer. If you used a layer mask on the noise-reduction layer, click the layer mask on the new layer, and drag it to the trash can. In the event you opt to use a layer mask on your sharpening layer, you'll need a different mask than the one you used for the noise reduction. We'll talk more about targeted sharpening later in this chapter.

If you are using the *flexible workflow* and have done all or most of your cleanup in the raw converter and do not have a clone layer with significant changes, you can apply your sharpening as a Smart Filter to the background layer. If you have used other Smart Filters on the background layer using a mask, duplicate the background layer for the sharpening. Rasterize that layer by choosing Layer > Rasterize Smart Object. That will apply the filters you originally applied. Then choose Filter > Convert for Smart Filter to prepare that layer to be sharpened using a Smart Filter for flexibility. That way, you can add a mask to apply sharpening to selected areas only.

Since sharpening is so important to the final appearance of your image, you may wonder why it comes so late in the process. One reason is that the sharpening settings you use vary based on the output size and should be optimized for the output size and printing process you're using. Another is that sharpening, while beneficial to the image, is a destructive process in the standard workflow in that it alters pixel values, so we want to apply it as part of our output workflow rather than to the master image.

The Unsharp Mask Filter

It used to be that the most common tool for sharpening images was the Unsharp Mask filter. Since the introduction of Smart Sharpen it has become the sharpening tool of choice for some nature photographers. Nonetheless, we begin by talking about Unsharp Mask, because understanding how it works will help you use the Smart Sharpen filter.

The Unsharp Mask filter provides excellent control over the sharpening process, enabling you to improve the overall appearance of the image without introducing quality problems in the process. To use Unsharp Mask, first choose Filter > Convert for Smart Filters to change the layer into a Smart Object, and then choose Filter > Sharpen > Unsharp Mask from the menu. The Unsharp Mask dialog box appears (see Figure 10.8), which contains three settings you can adjust to modify the sharpening effect: Amount, Radius, and Threshold. Because you're using it as a Smart Filter, you can readjust the settings at any time.

Unsharp Mask operates by enhancing contrast along the edges of objects within your image. In other words, it's enhancing contrast where contrast already exists. Adjusting the controls in the Unsharp Mask dialog box allows you to change how this contrast enhancement is applied.

The Amount setting determines how much the contrast is enhanced along edges. Think of this as an intensity control. The higher the setting, the more intense the edge contrast is in your image.

The Radius setting allows you to determine the size of the area to be affected by the boost in contrast along the edges. For images with high detail, you generally want to have the impact affect only a small area for each edge.

The Threshold setting determines how much difference must exist between two pixels for the sharpening to be applied. With a minimum Threshold setting of 0, virtually all pixels are affected by sharpening. As you increase the value, fewer areas are sharpened because they must exhibit a certain amount of contrast before they're considered to be an edge. This helps you maintain smooth textures in areas of the image where that is important.

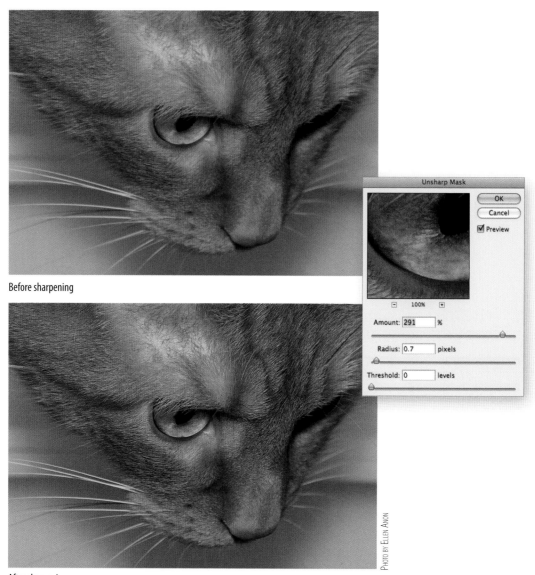

Before sharpening

After sharpening

PHOTO BY ELLEN ANON

Figure 10.8 The Unsharp Mask dialog box allows you to control the sharpening effect on your image with three individual sliders called Amount, Radius, and Threshold.

The most common question photographers ask is what settings they should use. And the response is generally different no matter who they ask! In fact, you can choose among a variety of ways to get good results from the sharpen filters, so we feel that rather than give you a priori values to use, it's better if you develop an understanding of how the different settings work. That way, you can choose what works best for your image. Ellen, along with Rick Holt, has developed a demo, which we show you in Figure 10.9, that is useful for understanding the different settings.

Figure 10.9 demonstrates how the sharpening works. Contrast is added to every edge. If a pixel is white, then the contrast is black; if it's black, the additional contrast is white; if it's yellow, the contrast is blue; if it's red, the contrast is cyan; and so on.

The contrast is the opposite of the pixel. You control the intensity of the contrast with the Amount slider, how far out the contrast extends with the Radius slider, and whether the contrast is applied by the Threshold slider.

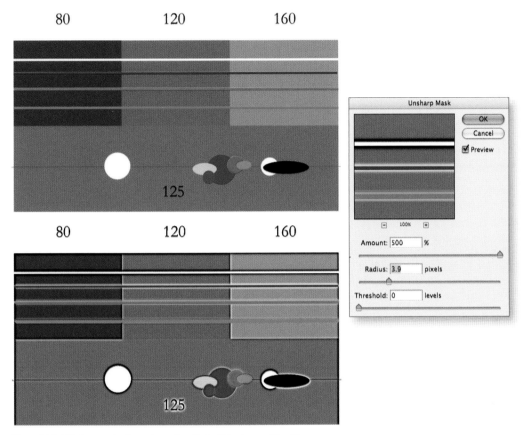

Figure 10.9 This demo makes it easy to see the effects of the sharpen filter sliders.

Try It! Download the file named SharpenDemo, and experiment with a variety of different settings. Adjust the sliders to extremes to see the effects.

Having said that, we will offer the following as some guidelines. Generally, you can combine a very low (0.2–0.2.0, depending on file size and detail) Radius with a very high Amount (200–500) and get good results. That is often Ellen's pre-ferred method when using Unsharp Mask (see Table 10.1). Alternatively, you can use a smaller Amount (70–50) and a larger Radius (0.8–2.25) and also achieve very good results. A third approach is to use a very low Amount (15–40) with very high Radius settings (usually double the amount). This will increase the contrast within the image and sometimes avoid artifacts. For high-detail images, such as most nature images, you should use a Threshold setting of 0. That way you can enhance small differences so that details like feathers appear more distinct. Conversely, if you're sharpening a portrait of your significant other, a Threshold setting of 8–12 is probably appropriate.

(You won't win points from anyone if you sharpen every wrinkle and imperfection in their face!)

Table 10.1 Typical Unsharp Mask Settings for High-Detail Nature Images

	Amount	Radius	Threshold
Low-res image	200% to 500%	0.2 to 0.8	0
High-res image	200% to 500%	0.8 to 2.0	0

Note: As digital cameras continue the megapixel race, newer cameras may appear with even higher resolutions that can use higher Unsharp Mask settings.

It's important that you evaluate the effect of Unsharp Mask on a 100% preview of your image. When your image is set to Fit on Screen, it's often at an odd magnification that causes temporary artifacts to appear on the monitor. These artifacts make it difficult to judge the sharpening amounts. When you change the magnification to 100%, those artifacts disappear. You can change the zoom percentage for the image to 100% by choosing View > Actual Pixels from the menu. This enables you to evaluate the sharpening effect looking at the actual effect in the image on which you're working. If you prefer to see the entire image while you're working so you can choose which areas you want to evaluate for the best sharpening effect, set the zoom to fit the image on screen by choosing View > Fit on Screen from the menu. Then click anywhere in your image to set that as the preview area in the Unsharp Mask dialog box. It's important to realize, however, that when you work this way, you must use the preview within Unsharp Mask (not the actual image) to evaluate the results.

Once you've established your settings for Unsharp Mask, click OK to apply the effect.

Unsharp Mask

In Elements, you'll find Unsharp Mask under Enhance > Unsharp Mask instead of the Filter menu. Since Elements lacks Smart Filters, you'll need to duplicate your Master file (File > Duplicate) and choose to flatten the layers in the new image. Resize the new file, and then sharpen it.

The Smart Sharpen Filter

As we mentioned earlier, Smart Sharpen is the sharpen tool of choice for some nature photographers. The Smart Sharpen filter includes the ability to mitigate the sharpening in highlights and shadows in your images individually, which can be very helpful—especially when you have artifacts or noise in shadow areas of the image. That way you can decrease the sharpening applied to the noisier parts of the image. In addition, it provides a much larger preview window for viewing the effects at 100%, and it offers the ability to change the type of blur algorithms it uses to create the sharpening. Although it lacks a specific Threshold control to maintain smooth textures throughout the image, Ellen has found that it does a good job with most of her nature images. To use Smart Sharpen, create duplicate layers as necessary as described at the beginning of the "Sharpening" section, and choose Filter > Sharpen > Smart Sharpen from the menu. The Smart Sharpen dialog box (shown in Figure 10.10) appears, with the large preview area set to the default of 100%.

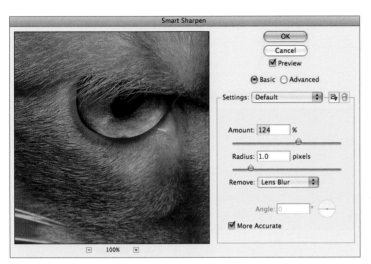

Figure 10.10 The Smart Sharpen dialog box includes a large preview and settings to help you control how sharpening is applied to your images.

Note: The key setting in the Smart Sharpen dialog box is the Remove drop-down list, where you choose a blur type. Choose Lens blur.

As with the Unsharp Mask filter, you can click and hold on the preview image to see what the image looks like without sharpening applied, and you can release to see it with the effect. You can also drag within this preview area to change your view to a different area of the image. Clicking the actual image centers the preview on that position, similar to what you're able to do with Unsharp Mask. The Preview check box controls whether the effect is visible in the actual image, as opposed to being visible only in the preview area within the Smart Sharpen dialog box.

Below the Preview check box are options for Basic and Advanced. With Basic selected (which is the default), only the Sharpen settings are available. When you select Advanced, tabs appear for Shadow and Highlight, as you can see in Figure 10.11. Although these settings are worth considering, in many nature photographs it's often more important to distinguish between applying the sharpening to the subject or the background rather than the highlights or shadows. Nonetheless, the Advanced settings enable you to apply sharpening to most of your subject while reducing how much is applied to any shadow or highlight areas.

Figure 10.11 When you select the Advanced option in Smart Sharpen, tabs are added that enable you to reduce the sharpening in the shadows and/or highlights.

The Basic settings in Smart Sharpen include the Amount and Radius settings you're familiar with from Unsharp Mask, as described in "The Unsharp Mask Filter" section earlier. The settings function in the same way, with Amount controlling the intensity of the halos created along edges in your image and Radius controlling the size of those halos. As a general starting point, the default values of 100% for Amount and 1.0 for Radius are good. Refer to the settings recommended in the previous section for more details on how you might adjust these basic controls.

At the bottom of the Basic sharpening section is a More Accurate check box. This is in effect the Threshold command. More Accurate results in selecting more "edges," while leaving the box unchecked results in fewer areas being categorized as edges. Although this option requires additional processing time, it also produces better results for most nature images and enables you to use lower Amount and Radius settings. We recommend keeping this check box selected for most images you are sharpening with Smart Sharpen.

The blur-removal settings are the key controls in the basic settings for Smart Sharpen and in fact are what differentiates this section the most from the features available in Unsharp Mask. Instead of applying simple edge contrast with a fixed approach (with the specific application varying based on settings used) as with Unsharp Mask, the Smart Sharpen filter takes an intelligent approach based on the settings you establish. The primary control here is the Remove drop-down list, which controls the algorithm used to process the image when it comes to reducing the appearance of specific types of blur in the image (see Figure 10.12). We'll describe these options in more detail in a moment, but the point is that instead of just applying added contrast to the image as Unsharp Mask does, Smart Sharpen can counter specific causes of blur in your images to help you produce the best results possible. We recommend leaving this option at Lens Blur for most images.

The default setting of Gaussian Blur causes the Smart Sharpen filter to process the image with the same algorithm used by Unsharp Mask. With this setting selected, the results achieved with Smart Sharpen are very similar to the results achieved with Unsharp Mask with the same settings.

Figure 10.12 The Remove drop-down list provides various options for reducing the effect of blur in your image to improve the perceived sharpness.

The next option for blur removal is Lens Blur. This option adds another element to the "smart" aspect of the Smart Sharpen filter. It causes the filter to detect edges and texture detail within the image. The sharpening effect is adjusted in those areas to maintain fine detail and reduce the size of halos. This is the setting we recommend using for most images because it does the most to achieve the typical goals of the photographer applying a sharpening effect to an image.

The final option for blur removal is Motion Blur. This option is designed to compensate for blur caused by motion of either the camera or the subject during the capture. Unfortunately we have found this tool to be only minimally helpful—it sounds good theoretically, but practically speaking it's very difficult to effectively remove motion blur, especially motion blur reflecting camera movement, because the movement may not be limited to a single direction.

When you select the Advanced option in the Smart Sharpen dialog box, two additional tabs appear: Shadow and Highlight. These tabs contain additional settings that allow you to reduce the sharpening effect in these particular areas (see Figure 10.13).

Figure 10.13 Among the Advanced options are settings that allow you to control the mitigation of sharpening in the shadow and highlight areas of your images.

Although there are separate tabs for limiting sharpening for both shadow and highlight areas within the image, the controls and behavior of each are identical. Both tabs allow you to adjust how much you want to reduce the sharpening effect in each area, as well as contain controls for determining how broad a range of shadow and highlight values should be affected. We discuss the controls here collectively. You simply need to apply the settings as needed on the Shadow or Highlight tab (or both of them) to apply the desired adjustment in the particular tonal areas of the image where you need it.

When adjusting the settings on the Shadow tab, we recommend zooming in to the darkest areas of the image and, for the Highlight tab, zooming in on the brightest areas. This allows you to better evaluate the settings as you adjust them on each of the tabs.

Here are the settings available on the Shadow and Highlight tabs:

Fade Amount   The Fade Amount setting controls how much the sharpening effect should be reduced within the shadow or highlight areas of the image. A value of 0% means the sharpening effect is not reduced at all, and the maximum value of 100% means the sharpening effect should be completely removed from the affected area of the image. Start with a value of 0%, and gradually increase the value until the sharpening effect is reduced in the target areas to the extent desired.

Tonal Width   The Tonal Width setting allows you to specify how broad a range of tonal values should be affected by the reduction in sharpening effect. Very low values mean sharpening is removed only from the very dark pixels in shadow areas, and a high value causes the effect to be removed from a broader range of tonal values, extending into the midtone values. We usually use a value in a range from about 10 to 50 so the reduction in sharpening affects only the true shadow areas of the image, but evaluate all shadow areas to determine the best value for your particular image. Since noise is often worse in shadow areas, you may want to focus your attention there.

Radius   The Radius setting provides control over how far out from each pixel Photoshop should look when deciding whether a particular pixel is contained within a shadow area. Frankly, even large adjustments of this control have a minimal effect on the final results achieved, so we recommend just leaving it at the default value of 1 pixel.

Keep in mind that the settings you establish on the Shadow and Highlight tabs are "sticky," which means that whatever settings you use for one image will remain selected the next time you use Smart Sharpen. So if you use the Advanced features at times, it's a good idea to get in the habit of checking and returning the Fade Amount settings to zero while setting the rest of your sharpening. Otherwise, you may be reducing the amount of sharpening in the highlights or shadows without realizing it.

Smart Sharpen

Smart Sharpen is available in Elements under the Enhance > Adjust Sharpness command, but there are no Advanced options. In addition, "More Accurate" is called "More Refined" in Elements.

Targeted Sharpening

Although at times it can be useful and efficient to sharpen the whole image at once, in many nature images it's advantageous to sharpen only portions of your image. Localized sharpening is particularly helpful when there is a specific subject against an out-of-focus background, such as often occurs with bird or flower photography. In such situations, it can be nearly impossible to find a Threshold setting in the Unsharp Mask filter that adequately sharpens the subject and does not affect the background. The Smart Sharpen filter using the Lens Blur setting often does a good enough job, particularly with small images, that you may not feel the need to block the sharpening from background areas. However, when you are creating a large print, you will still want to control which areas are sharpened.

The best method in such cases is to use a layer mask or filter mask (with a Smart Filter) to precisely control which areas are affected. The mask allows for various gradations of the sharpening within the image as well as eliminates the sharpening effects from areas, such as sky or water, that sometimes show increased noise when sharpened.

This approach is extremely precise, quick, and easy. If you are using the *traditional output workflow*, you must do the sharpening on a copy of the background layer, on the duplicate image. If you are using the *flexible workflow*, you may be on the background layer if there are no other Smart Filters being used or on a copy of the background layer if there are. Then, to selectively apply the sharpening, take the following steps:

1. Choose Filter > Sharpen > Smart Sharpen, setting the values as described earlier in this chapter.

2. While holding the Alt/Option key, click the Create Layer Mask icon to add a black layer mask to the sharpening layer. This temporarily hides the effect of the sharpening from the entire image.

3. Select the Brush tool by pressing the B key, and select the default colors of black and white by pressing the D key. Make certain that white is the foreground color, pressing X to swap foreground and background colors if necessary. Use a soft-edged brush at 100% opacity to reveal the sharpening in your primary subject. If there are areas that need some sharpening but not full sharpening, paint those areas with a reduced opacity. By using a soft-edged brush, you don't have to worry about precisely following the edges of your subject. This should be a quick mask to create, not a painstaking one.

Note: You can also use this layered method with the Unsharp Mask filter in place of the Smart Sharpen filter. In addition, you can use layer masks with Smart Filters.

Targeted Sharpening

To sharpen just a portion of your image, follow these steps:

1. Duplicate your image layer by dragging its row in the Layers palette to the New Layer button.

2. Create an adjustment layer with no changes and click OK.

3. Move the Levels adjustment layer below the layer you created in Step 1.

Continues

> **Targeted Sharpening** *(Continued)*
>
> **4.** Select the topmost layer and choose Layer > Group with Previous.
>
> **5.** Select the topmost layer and apply noise reduction.
>
> **6.** Select the Levels adjustment layer's mask and paint in black to remove the noise reduction filter.

Printing Your Images

Once you've prepared the image through the output workflow, you're ready to produce a print, which is typically the ultimate goal for nature photographers. When sending the image to the printer, it's important that you use the appropriate settings to ensure accurate color and optimal quality.

> **Note:** Remember that getting an accurate print depends on a calibrated monitor display. If your monitor isn't calibrated, you can't trust the colors displayed to be accurate, and therefore you can't be assured of a matching print.

Soft Proofing

Photoshop ONLY

An optional additional step that can be helpful before actually sending your image to the printer is *soft-proofing*, which enables an on-screen preview of what the print will look like. A printed image often looks slightly different from what you see on the monitor, even when using the correct printer/paper profiles in a color-managed work-flow, because of the particular qualities of the paper and ink. There may be some loss of contrast, brightness, and/or color saturation. Soft-proofing offers you a chance to preview those differences and make some adjustments so that the print looks the way you expect.

To soft-proof an image, first create a duplicate copy of the image by choosing Image > Duplicate. That way, you can compare the file the way you've been viewing it to the way it will appear when printed. You can configure and enable a soft-proofing display by choosing View > Proof Setup > Custom from the menu and configuring your output print settings. When you click OK, the image simulates the final printed output, and you can tweak the soft-proof by making a few small adjustments to make it more similar to the original. You then make the print from the soft-proof version.

Although the print dialog now contains soft-proofing options, taking the time to soft-proof this way enables you to see the soft-proofed version in more detail so you can make more accurate compensatory adjustments.

Configuring the Print Settings

To get started, choose File > Print. The Print dialog box shown in Figure 10.14 appears.

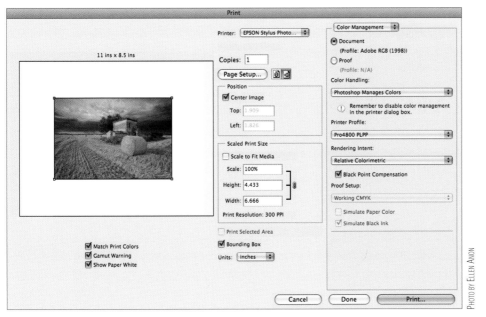

Figure 10.14 The Print dialog box, accessed by choosing the Print option from the File menu, allows you to control the basic color-management settings for output.

If you are using a Mac, you must begin by clicking the Page Setup button. As shown in Figure 10.15, this elicits an additional dialog box where you choose your printer, paper size, and format. Windows users access similar options later in the Printer Properties dialog box.

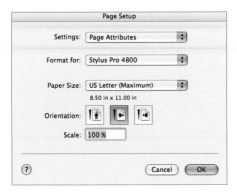

Figure 10.15 On a Mac you must use the Page Setup dialog box to specify your printer, paper size, and orientation.

We recommend checking the three boxes under the image preview. (These are available only within Photoshop.) Match Print Colors modifies the image preview to simulate the way the printed colors will appear. The Gamut Warning will highlight any colors that are out of gamut so you can decide which rendering intent to use (more about that shortly.) The Show Paper White option simulates the shade of white of the paper. Together these options help you make last-minute decisions about the color and contrast in your image. Although the preview is small, it's a quick way of previewing how the print will look before you actually use the paper and ink. You can always opt to go back and do a full soft-proofing, as we mentioned earlier in the chapter.

Make sure the Color Management option is selected from the drop-down list at the top right of the dialog box. Set the option to Document, not Proof, so the working space or embedded profile is used to determine the color values from your image being sent to the printer.

Beneath that are the key settings related to color management. From the Color Handling drop-down list, select Photoshop Manages Colors. The Printer Profile drop-down list is where you need to specify the profile appropriate for the printer, ink, and paper you're using to produce the print. Many printers now include "canned" custom profiles, which are designed for the printer, ink, and paper combination their name implies, but were not created specifically for the printer sitting on your desk.

Note: Using the Photoshop Manages Colors option assumes you are using a specific profile for your printer, ink, and paper combination. If you aren't (which we don't recommend), you need to use the Printer Manages Color option instead.

Rendering Intent deals with how colors that your printer can't produce (out-of-gamut colors) are changed to colors it is able to print. We recommend that for most images you select Relative Colorimetric, which ensures that colors your printer can produce are rendered accurately, while any color it can't produce is shifted to the closest in-gamut color. However, some images, often those with very saturated reds, may look better if you use the Perceptual rendering intent. Perceptual compresses the entire color gamut of your image into the printer's gamut, rather than adjusting only the colors that are actually out of gamut, but in some cases this can result in a more natural-looking result. You can experiment with the various rendering intents from the drop-down list and see the differences to your output in the preview.

Beneath the Rendering Intent drop-down list, select the Black Point Compensation check box so that black in your image is mapped to black in the output.

When you have set the appropriate settings in the Print dialog box, click the Print button to bring up another Print dialog box (shown in Figure 10.16). The dialog boxes differ between the Mac and Windows platforms. In Windows, select the printer you're sending the image to in this dialog box, and then click Properties. The Properties dialog box for the particular printer you are using appears (see the example in Figure 10.17). The settings you use in the printer Properties dialog box depend on your particular printer model, but in general, you need to set the appropriate paper type and size, quality settings, and color-management settings. Find the least invasive color-management choice—such as a "no color adjustment" or similar option—to ensure that the printer doesn't try to alter the color values in the printing process. As unintuitive as this may be, it enables Photoshop to handle the color management for the print, which is what you want. Otherwise, your print will have some unusual colors and tonalities.

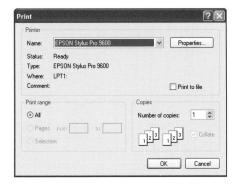

Figure 10.16 The Print dialog box allows you to select the specific printer you want to use for printed output.

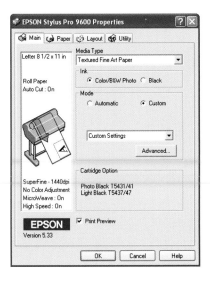

Figure 10.17 On Windows, clicking the Properties button in the Print dialog box opens the Properties dialog box for the printer you selected.

On a Mac you will need to specify your printer in the next Print dialog box (see Figure 10.18) and then select Print Settings from the Copies & Pages drop-down menu. You will need to reselect your printer and specify your media type. We recommend you choose Advanced Settings under Mode and select SuperFine—1440dpi for Print Quality. The precise options that are available vary by printer and paper type. We recommend choosing Finest Detail when possible.

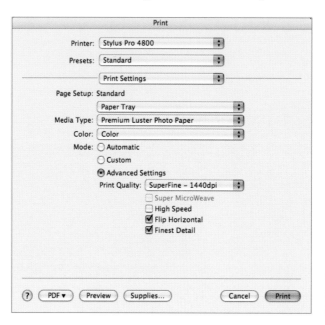

Figure 10.18 Although the specific settings may vary by printer and paper, set the media type and quality settings in the Print Settings dialog box.

Next, select Printer Color Management from the drop-down menu, and choose Off (No Color Adjustment) (see Figure 10.19). As mentioned earlier, for Windows you must choose No Color Management in order to have Photoshop manage your colors so that your output appears as you expect it to appear. Otherwise, you will get unpredictable results and waste time, paper, and ink…to say nothing of feeling very frustrated!

With all settings established for the print, click OK in the printer Properties dialog box, and then click OK in the Print dialog box to send the job to the printer.

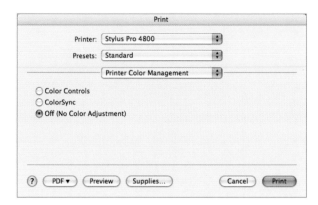

Figure 10.19 Choosing No Color Management is essential for having your print match your monitor.

Printing

Elements' Print panel (as shown here) is similar to the one in CS4. Unfortunately, there are no soft-proof preview options.

Peter K. Burian is a stock photographer, the author of *Mastering Digital Photography and Imaging* (Sybex, 2004), and the coauthor (with Tim Grey) of *Photoshop Elements 5 Workflow* (Sybex, 2006). As a regular contributor to several photo magazines, including *Shutterbug*, *Here's How*, *Photo Life*, and *Australian Photography*, he frequently tests digital cameras, lenses, scanners, and printers.We asked him to give us his picks for black-and-white printers.

Ideal Printers for Black-and-White Outputs

by Peter K. Burian

Photographers who love black-and-white prints are often disappointed with their ink-jet outputs. Although it should be possible to make a truly neutral monochrome print with color inks, few machines are designed to do a competent job without a frustrating process that involves constant fine-tuning in the printer driver and making test prints until one is very close to neutral.

At one time, there was another issue, especially with printers using pigmented inks, such as the now-discontinued Epson Stylus Photo 2200. This problem was *metamerism*: the tendency for inks to change color under different types of illumination. A print may look quite different under incandescent light, fluorescent light, and sunlight, for example.

Epson, Canon, and Hewlett-Packard have solved the technical problems, and all three now market certain ink-jet printers (using pigment inks) that are optimized for making monochrome outputs. As a bonus, all those machines also accept fine-art media, including thick papers such as "canvas." The most popular of these can make prints as large as 13×19 inches on sheet paper. Epson's new Stylus Pro R2880 (which replaced the R2400) is the latest model in this category; as a bonus, this machine also accepts roll paper (unlike its direct competitors from HP and Canon) for making panoramic prints as large as 13×44 inches. The R2880 employs the eight-color UltraChrome K3 pigmented inkset, including Photo Black or Matte Black plus two gray inks. (The K3 pigments are also used in the current wide-format Epson models, including the Stylus Pro 3800, 4880, 7880, and 9880.)

PHOTO BY PETER BURIAN

My tests of the R2880 confirmed significantly reduced metamerism and also a very even gloss effect over the entire print area. The color outputs show a very wide range of color and great vibrancy. This Epson machine also features a remarkably versatile driver option—Advanced Black & White printing mode. When selected, only one gray and two black inks are used for making prints without any apparent color cast. The driver provides many of the features that previously

Continues

required the purchase of a separate raster image processor (RIP), an advanced printer driver that provides maximum control over the entire printing process. With simple adjustments, you can create neutral, warm, cool, or sepia-toned prints and fine-tune the settings as desired; this feature expands the range of options available to the monochrome fine-art print maker.

The black-and-white prints—on paper as thick as 1.3mm—are completely neutral and, to my eye, perfect in every respect. They match the best silver halide prints that I had seen in the past thanks to a remarkably high maximum density and ultrawide tonal range. The Display Permanence Rating provided by Wilhelm Imaging Research (WIR) ranges from 83 years to 118 years, depending on the Epson media used, and even longer when the prints are displayed under glass with a UV filter.

HP was the first of the companies to employ a pigmented inkset that virtually eliminated metamerism and also satisfied dedicated black-and-white print makers. Its 13"×19"-format machines, the Photosmart Pro B9180 and the newer B8850 (similar but without an Ethernet port), employ seven colors of Vivera pigments, including a light gray plus photo black or matte black. Both accept paper as thick as 1.5mm and the prints are instantly dry, waterproof, and extremely resistant to fading. (HP's current large-format DesignJet series also employs Vivera inks and includes a built-in spectrophotometer for creating custom color profiles for virtually any media.) Although designed to make vividly saturated color outputs, the Photosmart Pro machines are highly suitable for monochrome printing. The WIR Display Permanence Rating is impressive, too: 250 years when using certain premium-grade HP or Hahnemühle papers.

The HP printers provide advanced color-management options, including a Black & White Printing mode that's optimized for making prints without a color cast. However, black-and-white toning options are not available. For truly neutral monochrome prints, use the Gray Inks option for printing with black and gray ink only. In my view, the Pro B9180 or B8850 is a fine choice for monochrome printing because it produces very good results with pure whites, excellent shadow detail, and a pleasing tonal gradation; for a snappier effect, it's worth boosting contrast in the driver software.

Canon's 13"×19"-format PIXMA Pro9500 employs 10 Lucia pigments, including two blacks (Photo or Matte) as well as a gray ink for enhanced black-and-white outputs. It accepts moderately thick papers, with a weight up to 200gsm (grams per square meter); heavier 350gsm paper can be used but not for borderless printing. The Pro9500 is bundled with both Canon's Easy-PhotoPrint software and Easy-PhotoPrint Pro, a versatile Photoshop plug-in, the ideal feature for serious printmaking. For the best results in monochrome printing, use the black and gray inks only. According to WIR, the estimated Display Permanence Rating is 104 years for Semi Gloss or 95 years for Fine Art Photo Rag paper, and nearly twice as long when UV filtered glass is used. Black-and-white prints made in Grayscale mode are very good, with particularly rich, dark blacks; snappy contrast; smooth tonal gradation; and a very slight warm cast.

Several wider-format Canon models are also available, employing a full 12 Lucia pigments, including two gray and two black, for making even better monochrome prints. The imagePROGRAF iPF5000, the 17"-format desktop model, includes a versatile driver with

Continues

Choosing the Best Paper

The choice of paper when producing a print is a very subjective decision. When we're asked by nature photographers what paper should be used, our typical response is that you really need to try various papers for yourself to find what you like best. However, as subjective as this decision is, here are some general guidelines to help you decide.

A big part of the decision has to do with the type of effect you want to produce in the print. The first consideration is the surface type. For images where you want to have maximum detail, contrast, and vibrancy of colors, a semi-gloss paper is a popular choice. For example, a crisp high-detail image of highly saturated flowers or a strong landscape image with a silhouetted foreground subject generally works well on a semi-gloss paper such as Epson's Premium Luster and similar papers from other manufacturers. Full-gloss papers are less popular because they tend to produce strong reflections, so it's difficult to see all the detail in the image.

Many professional nature photographers use matte papers for their prints. Velvet papers, available from a variety of companies, often provide a rich look to the prints, with full detail readily visible. However, if you're accustomed to the type of prints you get from a photo lab, it may take you a while to adjust to the look and feel of a print on matte paper.

For images that are more artsy, such as delicate flowers with subtle colors or a photo captured under diffuse lighting on an overcast day, or abstracts, you may want to maintain the subtle mood by choosing an art-style paper such as a watercolor paper. These are usually matte papers formulated for ink-jet printers with various textures. Art papers often tone down the colors, contrast, and details in your image to produce a print that looks more like a painting.

Decisions about what texture paper to use depend on personal style and on the content in the image. When in doubt, most people opt for a smooth paper surface. However, many other textures are available that add to the aesthetics of an image. Images with deep, rich colors, such as the greens of a rain forest, can produce beautiful results with a canvas surface that lends a painterly look to the image. Images that have smooth or subtle textures can be enhanced by a textured paper that adds a certain random aspect to the surface.

We strongly recommend that you test a wide variety of papers to find the ones you feel work best for your images. Many third-party paper manufacturers offer "sampler" packs that provide an economical way for you to test many papers as you discover your new favorites. Above all, experiment with many different papers so that you can find options that enhance the qualities of your images and that help define an individual style for you.

> **Note:** The website www.Inkjetart.com/samples.html offers a variety of inexpensive sampler packs so you can experiment to see which papers you prefer. The site www.redriverpaper.com/samples/index.htm also offers sample packs, including greeting card kits.

Adding Borders

Although your images are no doubt beautiful all by themselves, as you gain more knowledge of optimizing those images with Photoshop, you may want to find ways to add expressive touches to your images. One way to add a creative effect without altering the basic content of the image is to add an artistic border around your image.

You can choose among a variety of methods to add such a border to your image. One of these is a plug-in, called PhotoFrame, from OnOneSoftware (www.ononesoftware.com). This software includes thousands of photo edges you can apply to your images, making the process very easy.

However, you can produce similar effects in Photoshop with no special software. Rather than removing pixels from your image to create the edge effect, we recommend adding a new layer above the image layer to serve as the artistic border around the image. So, start by creating a new layer above your image layer by clicking the New Layer button at the bottom of the Layers panel. Then select Edit > Fill from the menu, choose white from the Use drop-down list, and click OK to fill this layer with white (see Figure 10.20). Of course, you don't really want to cover up the entire image with white, but this provides the foundation for this technique.

Figure 10.20 The first step in creating an artistic border around the edge of your image is to create a new pixel layer and fill it with white.

To help you better identify the area you want to apply the border effect to, turn off the visibility of the new layer you filled with white by clicking the eye icon to the left of its thumbnail on the Layers panel. Next, choose the Rectangular Marquee selection tool, and drag from *near* the top-left corner of the image to *near* the bottom-right corner (as shown in Figure 10.21). This becomes the area along which the edge effect is added, with anything outside the selection hidden and anything inside the selection retained, so be sure to position this selection accordingly. When you've finished, turn the visibility of the white layer you created back on by clicking in the box where the eye icon was.

Figure 10.21 Create a selection with the Rectangular Marquee tool to define the area where the border will be created.

The next step is to switch into Quick Mask mode, which allows you to modify the selection with a bit more flexibility. To switch to Quick Mask mode, press Q on your keyboard, or click the button on the right side directly below the Color Picker on the Tools panel. The selection is now displayed using a mask display, with a color (red by default) showing the area that was not selected and no color (which therefore allows the white layer to appear) in the selected area (see Figure 10.22).

Figure 10.22 Switching to Quick Mask mode causes the selection to be displayed as a color overlay, with the overlay representing areas of the image that are not selected.

To apply a creative shape to this edge, apply a filter to the Quick Mask display. Choose Filter > Filter Gallery from the menu (see Figure 10.23). Start by selecting an initial filter to work with from the sections in the center of the dialog box. We prefer the filters in the Brush Strokes and Distort sections for this purpose, but anything is fair game if you like the final result. Ellen's favorite is Spatter, which is in Brush Strokes. As you're adjusting the settings for this filter along the right side, keep in mind when you're looking at the preview that white areas are where the image will be visible and black areas are where the image will be blocked in the final result.

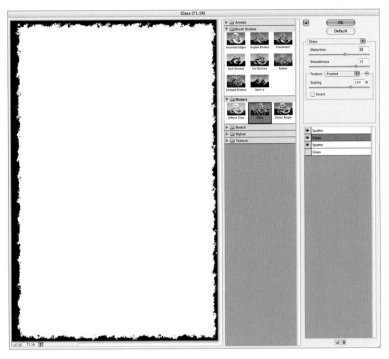

Figure 10.23 Use the Filter Gallery to apply filters that distort the edge of the selection on your image.

After you've established settings for the filter you've selected, you can actually add other filters to create a more complex pattern. To do so, click the New Effect Layer button at the bottom right of the dialog box. This initially duplicates the first filter you added, but you can then select a different filter to change it, adjusting the settings as desired.

Once you have a basic shape for the border you want to apply to your image, click OK in the Filter Gallery dialog box. The shape of the Quick Mask display is altered based on your filter selections. Switch back to normal mode for the selection by again pressing Q or by clicking the button on the left below the Color Picker on the Tools panel. The selection reflects the edge shape you created by applying filters in Quick Mask mode.

> **Note:** The selection shape may not perfectly reflect the result of filtering in Quick Mask, because the "marching ants" border of the selection follows the line along the division only between pixels that are at least 50% selected and those that are less than 50% selected.

Because you want to retain only the outer portion of the white layer that was added to this document, the selection needs to be inverted to include only the outer border area. Choose Select > Inverse from the menu to invert the selection. You can then use this selection as the basis of a layer mask to block out the white layer where it isn't selected. To do so, simply click the Add Layer Mask button at the bottom of the Layers panel. The result is a white border around your image that blocks the outer edge, but with an artistic shape to that edge that can help enhance the textures and mood of the image (see Figure 10.24).

Figure 10.24 When you add a layer mask with an active selection you have modified with the application of one or more filters, the image is masked based on that selection to hide areas outside the selection, resulting in an artistic edge effect.

Adding Borders or Frames

Elements provides more direct ways to add photo frames, but doesn't support the technique we describe for adding frames in Photoshop. To apply a frame in Elements, take the following steps:

1. Select Window > Effects.
2. Click the Photo Effects button ▢.
3. Select Frame from the drop-down menu.
4. Select the type of frame you wish to add (a drop-shadow frame is shown here) and click Apply.

Continues

Adding Borders or Frames *(Continued)*

Elements offers another method of adding a huge variety of frames. To begin, click the Create button. From the first drop-down menu in the Content panel choose By Type, and in the next drop-down menu choose Frames. Some of the options are pretty outlandish, but there are also some more conservative options. After applying the frame, it may mask out part of your image. If that happens, click the handles on the marching ants box and drag them out to the ends of your image. Be warned that Elements will not let you continue to edit your image after you apply a frame this way.

Try It! To practice the methods described in this section for applying a border to your image, open the image Border on the accompanying CD, and apply this method to the image. Save the result for the next section.

John Shaw is one of the foremost nature photographers. He has graciously agreed to share his technique for creating a presentation frame with our readers.

Making a Presentation Frame

by John Shaw

Here's an easy method to make a presentation frame to set off your favorite image. I'll use a photo of a winter oak with some small bamboo at its base. I shot the photo in Hokkaido, in the north of Japan.

Open a master image in Photoshop, a picture that you have already tweaked to a finished state. If you have any layers showing on the Layers panel, duplicate the image and flatten it. Size the image as you desire, and sharpen as you would normally. You want a totally finished, ready-to-go image.

The first step is to add a hairline around the image, and then some canvas space. I'm going to use black/white as my foreground/background colors in Photoshop. These are the default colors, and just to confirm they are present I press the D key on my keyboard. Of course I could use other colors, but I'll stay with these for now.

I select the entire image by choosing Select > Select All or using Ctrl+A/⌘+A. Next I choose Edit > Stroke.

I set Width to 3 pixels, and check the Inside Location button. Right now there is nothing "outside" of my image, so "inside" is the only possible location. Yes, I'm going to cover up a minute portion of my photo, but I think this amount can be spared. I make sure the Color setting is black, and hit OK. After the Stroke is finished, I deselect by pressing Ctrl+D/⌘+D.

Next, I'll add just a bit of canvas space. I use Image > Canvas Size and make sure the Relative box is checked. I'll add 0.2 of an inch of white space (the default background color) all the way around the image. Depending on the size of your image, you might have to adjust this number.

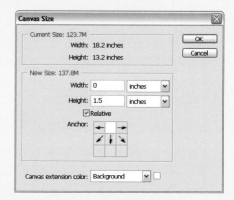

Now I do a Select > All and Edit > Stroke once again to add another stroke around the extended canvas.

Next I extend the canvas again by choosing Image > Canvas Size.

This time I'll add 3" of white canvas all around. But now I want to weigh the bottom space to make it the largest area, so once again I choose Image > Canvas Size and add 1.5" to the bottom area. Note that I selected the center-top square as my anchor position.

And now I have the presentation image ready for type.

Continues

Making a Presentation Frame *(Continued)*

I select an appropriate type face and size. I'll use AvanteGarde Bk for my name, in a 30-point size, and set the letter spacing to 250% in the type options.

Since the type is on its own layer, I can use the Move tool to position it where I want, in this case centered below the photo.

Now I'll add a decorative line. I open the rulers by choosing View > Rulers and drag out vertical guides to either side of the image. Then I make a new layer topmost in the Layers panel.

I select the Brush tool with a 5-pixel hard edge; then, while holding down the Shift key, I draw from one guide to the other just above my name. Holding down the Shift key keeps this line perfectly horizontal.

I want to remove the center portion of this line, where my name will be positioned. I select the Rectangular Marquee tool, set zero feathering to get a hard edge, and draw a box around my name and over the line. What I've done is select the portion of the line I want to eliminate. I hit the Delete key on my keyboard, and that section is gone. Then I use the Move tool to reposition what's left of the line.

I'll add the name of the image on the left using a different type face; here I used Technical at 18 points.

You can make all sorts of variations on this theme by changing colors, canvas sizes, and how much type you add. Play around to discover what you like.

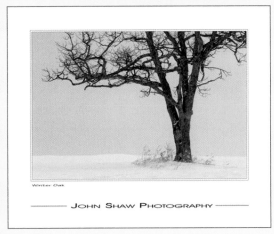

Creating Business and Greeting Cards

A great way to share your work with others is to create cards that feature your favorite images. You can create business cards to hand out or greeting cards for personal use or to sell. We've placed instructions for creating a greeting card on the accompanying CD

Creating a business card is in many ways similar to creating a greeting card. In some ways, it's easier since you don't have the issue of folding the final print and the related layout issues to contend with. First we'll describe how to create a business card and then we'll cover how to create the print layout.

Creating a Business Card

To create the card layout, start by making a new document for this purpose. Select File > New from the menu, and create a document that is 3.5" wide and 2" tall (the standard dimensions for business cards) at 300 dpi (see Figure 10.25). Be sure the Color Mode is set to RGB, and leave the bit depth at 8-bit. Use White for Background Contents. Click OK to create your new document.

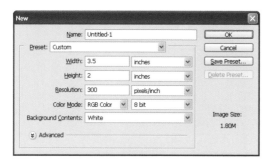

Figure 10.25 Create a new document with the dimensions of your individual business card to get started.

Note: If you prefer to make a vertical business card, simply switch the Width and Height settings when creating your new document for the business card layout.

The next step is to add an image to the layout. To do this, follow these steps:

1. Open the image you want to include, and create a duplicate copy, flattening it in the process.

2. Resize it to fit the dimensions of your business card.

3. Use the Move tool to drag the image into the business card layout, as shown in Figure 10.26.

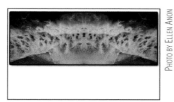

Figure 10.26 Use the Move tool to bring your image into the business card layout.

You have these options:

- If you want to rotate the image, select Edit > Transform > Rotate from the menu, move the mouse outside the bounding box, and drag to rotate. When you're happy with the rotation, press Enter/Return, or double-click inside the bounding box.

- You can also resize the image by selecting Edit > Transform > Scale, holding the Shift key as you drag a corner to resize, and pressing Enter/Return or double-clicking inside the bounding box to apply. Use the Move tool to fine-tune the position of the image as needed.

- To include multiple images, simply repeat the process, making sure the correct image layer is selected in the Layers panel when you rotate, resize, or move the image.

Adding Text

Of course, although it may be tempting to consider the photograph the key component of the perfect business card, you'll need text for it to actually serve the intended purpose! Creating text layers in Photoshop is quite easy, and you can exercise tremendous flexibility in the appearance of the text. To add a text layer, select the Text tool from the Tools panel, and click the image close to where you want the text to appear. You can reposition the text later, so don't worry if it's not in the precise position you want. A flashing cursor appears, allowing you to start typing immediately. Make sure the text is set to an appropriate size before you start typing so you'll be able to see and manage the text. On the Options bar (shown in Figure 10.27), there is a drop-down list for text size with two Ts of different sizes to the left of it. We recommend starting with a point size of 12 initially.

Figure 10.27 The Options bar for the Text tool contains a number of settings related to the overall appearance of your text.

As you type your initial text, don't worry about the font attributes, because you'll change those in a moment. Just type the text you want to appear. When you've finished, *don't* press Enter/Return as you may be inclined to do if you want to create multiple lines of text. In terms of adjusting the final layout of your text, it's much easier if each text element, or line of text, is created as a separate text layer. When you've finished typing that block of text, simply switch to the Move tool, and get yourself ready to fine-tune the position of the text.

> **Note:** When you create a text layer, the name of the layer automatically changes whenever you change the text itself, with the name reflecting that text.

With the Move tool active, drag the text to the desired position, using the arrow keys on your keyboard to get the text into the perfect position. You're then ready to adjust the attributes of the text. To do so, double-click the thumbnail icon for the text layer on the Layers panel. This selects the text associated with that layer so that any changes you make to the attributes affect all of the text.

On the Options bar, the first setting to consider is the font type. The Font drop-down list provides a WYSIWYG (What-You-See-Is-What-You-Get) sample preview, showing you what the font actually looks like to the right of the font name. To the right of the Font drop-down list is another drop-down list that allows you to select the style for the text. Your options are Regular, Italic, Bold, or Bold Italic. Keep in mind that some fonts do not support all of these style options directly.

You specify the font size to the right of the font and font style drop-down lists. You'll use the same point-size system you may be familiar with from using word processing software, with 12 points the standard for most documents, but 10 or even 8 points often necessary for the reduced real estate of a business card.

To the right of the font size drop-down list is the anti-aliasing drop-down list. This controls how the lines within the text are refined to avoid a stair-step pattern along curved lines. Choose among the various settings to get a preview of the effect, but we generally find that the Sharp option provides excellent results.

The next set of buttons allows you to control the text alignment, with the standard choices of left, center, and right represented by icons on the buttons. Since you're not going to be creating paragraphs of text, the default setting of left alignment is probably adequate, but at times you may find it helpful to use a different option to help you align text properly.

The colored box to the right of the text alignment buttons defines the color of the text. It reflects the current color of the active text layer; click this colored box to open the Color Picker and select a new color. Note that the selected text appears inverted, so you don't see the final result until you apply the change to your text (for example, by selecting the Move tool as discussed earlier).

The Warp Text button brings up the Warp Text dialog box (shown in Figure 10.28), where you can adjust the shape of the path upon which the text is written. Normally, the text simply flows across a straight line. However, you can have it move across a curved line or have the text itself warped into a particular shape. The Warp Text dialog box includes a Style drop-down list, where you can specify the particular shape you'd like to use, along with settings to adjust the particular style you've chosen.

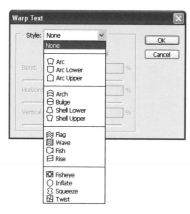

Figure 10.28 The Warp Text dialog box allows you to distort the text so it flows along a path that isn't straight.

Note: For advanced users, the last button on the Options bar for the Text tool opens the Character panel, which provides more options for fine-tuning the text appearance.

Applying Layer Styles

Once you've created the basic layout for your card, experiment with adding some layer styles to your text or image layers. These allow you to add dimension to the elements that compose your business card design. To add a layer style, first select the desired layer on the Layers panel. Then click the Layer Style button *fx.* at the bottom of the Layers panel. A list of available layer styles pops up (see Figure 10.29). Let's start with a simple drop shadow to add some depth to the current layer. When you select an option from the list, the Layer Style dialog box (shown in Figure 10.30) appears. Along the left side are the available styles, and in the center are the options for the currently selected style. You can add more than one style to the current layer by selecting it from the left. Be sure to click the text rather than the check box so the option is activated and the options for that style are shown at the same time.

Figure 10.29 When you click the Layer Style button, a pop-up list provides the available options for the effects you can apply to elements within your text or image layers.

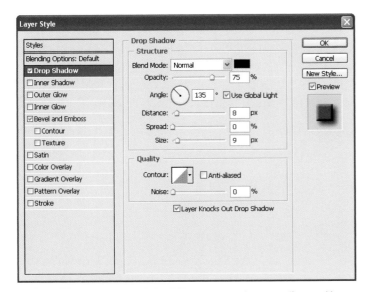

Figure 10.30 The Layer Style dialog box allows you to select the various effects to add to the current layer and adjust the settings for those effects.

Adjust the settings in the center section of the dialog box as desired. Remember that a subtle effect is generally best because it provides the impression of depth without overwhelming the viewer. The best settings are usually those you feel are a little too subtle. To get you started, add a Drop Shadow layer style and a Bevel and Emboss layer style to your text layers. When you've added the desired settings, click OK to apply them to the current layer.

Chances are you want to apply a consistent style to all the text elements in your business card layout. When you add a layer style to a layer, an icon that matches the button you clicked initially at the bottom of the Layers panel is added on the right side of that layer in the Layers panel. To copy the layer styles to other layers, hold down the Alt/Option key, and click and drag the Layer Style icon to the desired layers. You can copy the layer styles to as many layers as you need.

To adjust the Layer Style settings later, simply double-click the icon on the right side of the layer on the Layers panel. The Layer Style dialog box appears, where you can select the style on the left and adjust the settings in the center. Click OK when you've finished making adjustments. You will have to drag the updated layer style icon to other layers using the same styles—they won't automatically update otherwise.

Note: If you create a combination of layer style settings that you particularly like, you can save them so you can easily use them on other projects. For example, you might create a combination of styles that you like for your business cards. To save them, click New Style while in the Layer Style dialog box. A new dialog will appear in which you can name the style and specify whether to include the Layer Effects and/or Blending Options. You could call it **Business Card Styles**. Then this new style will appear as the last icon in the Layer Style panel. When you want to create a new business card, click Styles, at the top left of the Layer Style dialog and choose the Business Card style icon. That style will immediately be applied to the text. You can create customized styles for nearly any purpose. To remove a layer style, drag it to the trash can, or Alt/Option-click it, and use the little scissors that appear to click and remove the style.

Layer Styles

In Elements layer styles are effects and not layers that can be modified later. To apply a layer style, select Window > Effects, click the Layer Styles button , select the style you want, and click Apply.

Saving the Layout

Once you've added image and text layers to the layout, fine-tuned their settings and positions, and applied layer styles as desired, you should have a business card that you're proud to distribute. Be sure to save this document as a TIFF or PSD file with all layers intact so you can make revisions as desired at a later date. This master file will be the basis of the print layout we'll create in the next section.

Try It! Open the image BizCard on the accompanying CD, and create a business card layout.

Creating the Print Layout

With the business card layout created, the next step is to create a print layout that includes multiple business cards so you can print sheets of them at a time. Although prescored business card papers are available, most of them that we've seen don't provide a material that is adequate for photo-quality printing. In addition, when you separate them along the scored edges, the result does not look very professional. Therefore, we recommend using a paper designed specifically for producing photo-quality output on your photo ink-jet printer for this purpose. In general, you'll get the best results from coated matte papers.

For this example, we'll assume you're printing to an 8.5"×11" sheet of paper that produces good results on your photo ink-jet printer, but you could certainly use a larger paper size if you prefer. The first step is to create a new document with the dimensions of the paper. Select File > New from the menu, and in the New dialog box, enter dimensions of **8.5"** for Width, **11"** for Height, and **300 dpi** for Resolution, and make sure the document is set to RGB with a bit depth of 8-bit. Click OK to create the new document.

Add new vertical guides at 0.5" and 4.5" to mark the left edge of each business card by selecting View > New Guide from the menu (shown in Figure 10.31). Guides are nonprinting lines that you can place at any horizontal or vertical position within a document to provide layout guidance. Then add new horizontal guides at 0.5", 3", 5.5", and 8", marking the top of each business card (see Figure 10.32). This provides a framework for you to place each business card into this document.

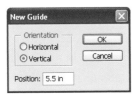

Figure 10.31 The New Guide dialog box allows you to place a guide at a specific position within your page layout document.

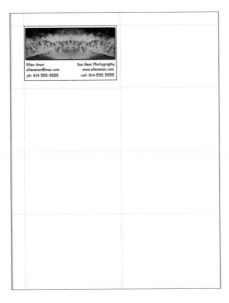

Figure 10.32 Add guides to the page layout for your business cards to provide a reference for where each individual card should be placed. Then move the first business card into the print layout in the first position at the top left of the document.

If you don't still have the business card layout document open, open it now. Then create a working copy by selecting Image > Duplicate from the menu. Select the Duplicate Merged Layers Only check box to flatten the image in the process, and click OK. Then use the Move tool to drag this flattened duplicate into the new document you created for your print layout.

Drag this business card layer to the top-left position defined by the guides you added to the document. By default, the layer snaps into the corner identified by the guides you added as you get close; if it doesn't, choose View > Snap to turn on this feature.

At this point, it's a good idea to add a Stroke layer style to this image layer, which makes it easier to cut out the individual business cards after printing. To do so, click the Add Layer Style button at the bottom of the Layers panel, and select Stroke from the pop-up menu. Set the size to about 2 pixels, with Position set to Outside (see Figure 10.33). Click the Color box to bring up the Color Picker and set a color for this stroke. (We recommend using black and cutting this area out of the final business cards, but you could also set a color you like and keep it as a frame for the cards.)

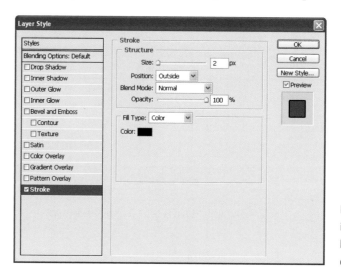

Figure 10.33 Add a stroke to the individual business card layer so you have a reference for cutting each card out later.

Once you have positioned the first business card layer, select the Move tool, then hold down the Alt/Option key and drag a copy of your card to the next position on the page. Repeat this process to place a business card layer at every position you defined with the guides you added to the document. You can opt to use several versions of your card on one large sheet, as shown in Figure 10.34.

When you have finished creating a complete page layout, save it as a TIFF or PSD file so you can always refine the layout later if desired. You're then ready to print this document as you would any other and then cut out the individual business cards.

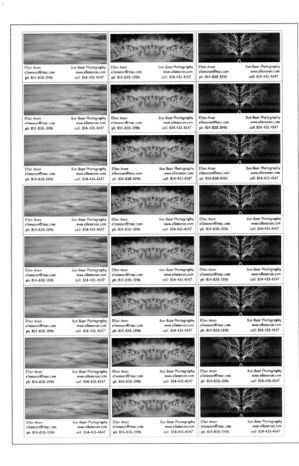

Figure 10.34 When you have placed a business card at each position within your page layout, save the file and use it as the source for printing your cards.

Creating a Page of Business Cards

Creating a page of business cards is slightly harder in Elements, because Elements doesn't have guides. Here are the steps we recommend:

1. Create a new, blank 8.5×11 document at 300dpi with a white background.

2. Flatten your business card document and, using the Move tool, drag it onto the blank document.

3. Drag the layer Elements created in Step 2 onto the Create New Layer button to duplicate it, and repeat until you have five layers worth of business card images.

4. Select one layer and move it to where you want the top card to be (both on the top and left).

5. Select another layer and move it to where you want the bottom of the bottom card to be.

6. In the Layers palette, select all of the layers you created in Steps 2 and 3.

7. From the workspace buttons area, click Distribute > Vertical Centers. Elements will spread the layers out vertically.

Continues

Creating a Page of Business Cards *(Continued)*

8. In the workspace buttons area, click Align > Left Edges. Elements will align the left edge of the layers, as shown in the following graphic.

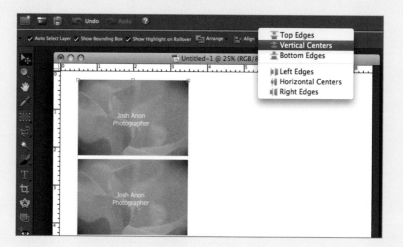

9. With all of the layers still selected, choose Layer > Duplicate Layer and just click OK in the dialog window that appears with duplicate options.

10. Select the Move tool, and use the right arrow key on your keyboard to nudge these layers to the right to form the right column (use Shift+Right Arrow to nudge the layers faster).

By using the Distribute and Align commands, Elements will spread your images out over the page, aligned nicely so that you can make a straight cut against each edge. By using the keyboard in Step 10 rather than the mouse to create the second column of images, you ensure that the top and bottom of the second column stay aligned with the first column, thus making it easier to cut out your business cards.

Using Adobe Output Module

Adobe Output Module was added to Bridge CS4 to create PDF and Web output. You choose the PDF option to create various types of PDFs, including contact sheets as well as slide shows, and the Web Gallery button to create output for the Web, including galleries, slide shows, and journals. The interface takes a little getting used to, but it's pretty intuitive once you get accustomed to using it.

To begin, click the 🔳 icon near the top left of the Bridge interface or go to Window > Workspace > Output. The interface changes to appear as shown in Figure 10.35.

Figure 10.35 Choosing the Adobe Output Module accesses the Output panel, which contains options for PDF and Web output.

Contact Sheets

Creating contact sheets is useful when you want to create output with multiple images on a page, such as a CD cover. The Adobe Output Module contains a series of options, as shown in Figure 10.36, that make this easy. To create a contact sheet, follow these steps:

1. Begin by selecting the images you want to use in the Content panel.

2. In the Document section, specify the document size. For example, if you're making a CD cover you might use 4.25" by 4.25". The page preset will change to Custom automatically unless you are using a standard preset.

3. Click the ▣ or ▣ icon to specify a horizontal or vertical layout.

4. Normally we choose High Quality—this uses a dpi of 300, whereas Low Quality uses 150.

5. Since we typically do not need to add passwords for contact sheets, leave the Open Password and Permission Password options unchecked.

6. In the Layout panel, specify the number of rows and columns to use.

7. Check the option to use Auto Spacing. Normally we leave the other two check boxes unchecked.

8. If you want to have text appear with the filenames, complete the Overlay panel options.

9. If you want a watermark to appear over your images, complete the options in the Watermark panel. We suggest using an opacity of about 20%.

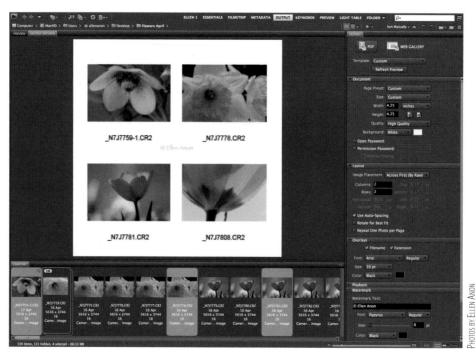

Figure 10.36 The Adobe Output Module offers many options for creating contact sheets.

Note: In order to see a preview of the changes you make in the various panels in the Output panel, you need to click the Refresh Preview button near the top.

The Output Module can only create contact sheets that are PDFs, not JPEGs. Nonetheless, you can print from a PDF.

To create any other type of PDF output of your images, you will follow similar steps, beginning with choosing the template. One of the less well-known types of PDFs is a slide show PDF. This is just a basic slide show of images with transitions but no music or other special effects.

Many programs are available for creating intricate digital slide shows, and we recommend you take advantage of them when doing a formal presentation. But if you want to generate a slide show that someone might view on their computer, you can use a PDF slide show.

Note: As we discussed in Chapter 2, "Bridge," you can quickly create a slide show in Bridge (by selecting images and choosing View > Slideshow) and even rate or delete images while viewing the slide show. Some photographers find that quite helpful while editing. However, you can't save that type of slide show and show it again later or on another computer. Instead, you can create a PDF slide show.

The PDF Presentation dialog, shown in Figure 10.37, allows you to establish the settings for a basic slide show that can be played using the Adobe Reader software used to read PDF documents. Here's how to create a slide show in Photoshop as a PDF document:

1. Choose the Output workspace and click PDF.

2. Select the images you want to use—for best results, presize your images to the size you want to use in the slide show. You can use the Image Processor for this (see Chapter 11, "Time-Savers").

3. In the Document panel, specify the width and height. We recommend black for the background color.

4. If you want to require a password to view the slide show, check the options and specify the password in the Document panel.

5. In the Layout panel, specify 0 for Top, Bottom, Left, and Right.

6. Choose Repeat One Photo per Page (unless you want to view multiple photos at a time) in the Layout panel.

7. In the Playback panel, check the option to open in Fullscreen mode, then specify how quickly to advance to the next page (slide) and whether to loop after the last page. Choose a transition—we prefer Fade—and the speed of the transition. Some of the effects are relatively amateur in appearance and can be distracting, so be careful.

Figure 10.37 The Adobe Output Module contains options for creating basic slide shows that can be saved as PDF documents.

8. Specify whether to include filenames and extensions along with the images in the Overlay panel.

9. As with a contact sheet, you can watermark the images if you choose. When you're done, click Save. Photoshop will generate a PDF that will play as a slide show. You can then open that PDF file with Adobe Reader (in most cases, you can simply double-click the file to do so), and the slide show starts automatically. To return to a normal screen, use the Esc key.

Note: It's a good idea to create copies of your master images to use for this purpose, resizing them down to about the display resolution you intend to use for the slide show. Otherwise, the PDF file used for the final presentation can become very large. It's also a good idea to convert the images to the sRGB color space (Edit > Convert to Profile) to ensure the best color possible for monitor or projector display.

Creating a Web Gallery

Prints aren't the only form of output nature photographers want to produce. Displaying images on the Web is becoming more popular, providing a great way to share your images with a large audience easily and affordably. Although building a professional-quality website can require either many hours of learning and designing or a considerable budget, Photoshop makes it easy to create a basic gallery of your images to display on screen through the Output Module.

To get started, choose Bridge > Output and click Web Gallery. Choose a template from the template drop-down menu, as shown in Figure 10.38.

Figure 10.38 Bridge provides a variety of templates for your web page, including web journal or gallery style pages with slide shows.

Complete the Site Info panel with the information you want to appear on the page, as shown in Figure 10.39. In the E-mail Address box, enter your email address if you'd like it to be displayed in the contact information on the gallery you're creating. This provides a simple link for people to use if they want to contact you with questions about your images or (better yet) how to purchase an image.

The Color Palette contains options for the appearance of items. To change any of the colors, click on the color swatch. A color picker will appear. Choose the color you prefer and click OK. The color swatch will update to reflect your choice.

The Appearance panel has controls for the web page slide show. Again, we prefer the Fade transition and urge caution when choosing some of the other effects as they can be distracting.

Figure 10.39 The Web Gallery dialog box allows you to establish settings that enable Photoshop to create all the files necessary for a basic gallery for your images on the Web.

In the Create Gallery panel, name your gallery—presumably with the same name you used in the Site Info panel. Choose whether to save the web page to disk or upload it to your server.

If you're reviewing your images in the Bridge application, select the images you want to include in a web gallery, and then choose Tools > Photoshop > Web Photo Gallery from the Bridge menu to open the Web Photo Gallery dialog box with the selected images automatically set as the source for the gallery.

PDF Contact Sheets, Slide Shows, and Web Photo Galleries

Elements does not have a specific Output Module, but nonetheless it's possible to create contact sheets, PDF slide shows, and web galleries.

Contact Sheets

To create a contact sheet in Elements, choose File > Contact Sheet II. A dialog appears, as shown here, in which you navigate to the files or folder to use. In the Document section, specify the output size for the contact sheet. Within the thumbnail section, specify the number of rows and columns. There's also an option to choose font style and size if you want the filenames included.

Continues

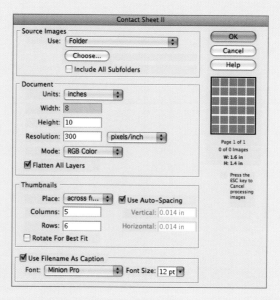

CHAPTER 10: OUTPUT ■

Note that you can use premade templates for CDs or DVDs from Create > Projects > More Options. Using the Contact Sheet II method will give you more control over the output.

PDF Slide Shows

Create a PDF Presentation in Elements by clicking the Create button at the top right of the screen, and under Projects, choose PDF Slide Shows. In the dialog that appears you can opt to use files that are open (but already saved) or browse to the images you want to use. Select Presentation and the background color. (We use black.) Check any file information you want to appear. Then specify the Presentation Options, including how fast to advance, whether to loop the show (have it run continuously), and which transition to use. When you click Save, another dialog appears in which you name the PDF and specify where to store it.

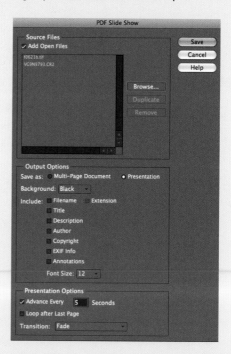

Web Galleries

To create a Web Gallery in Elements, click the Create button at the top right of the screen, and under Projects, click the Web Photo Gallery button. A dialog appears in which you choose how you want the gallery to appear and what images to use.

Continues

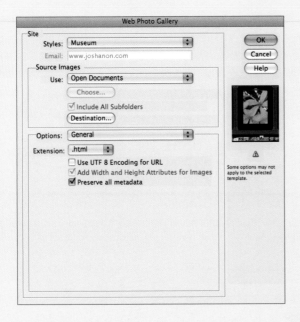

At the top of the dialog box is a Styles drop-down list where you can choose the overall appearance of the website. Because the names don't provide a completely clear indication of what the site layout will look like, we recommend that you select the first option from the drop-down list and then use the up and down arrow keys to cycle through the various options. A thumbnail display on the right side of the dialog box gives you an indication (though very small) of how the layout will look.

In the E-mail box, enter your email address if you'd like it to be displayed in the contact information on the gallery you're creating. This provides a simple link for people to use if they want to contact you with questions about your images or (better yet) how to purchase an image.

In the Source Images section, specify both the source of images and the destination for the files to be created as part of your gallery. From the Use drop-down list, select Folder if you want to specify a particular folder containing image files you want to use in your gallery. If you have selected images in Bridge that you want to include in the gallery, choose the Selected Images from Bridge option.

If you have set the source to Folder, click the Browse button to open a separate dialog box, where you can identify the folder where the images to be included in the gallery are stored. If there are additional folders within the source folder with images you want to include in the gallery, select the Include All Subfolders check box.

If you're going to be using a folder as the source of images, you may want to copy those images into a new folder so you can more easily manage the collection of images to be included in the gallery.

Continues

To select the folder where you want all of the files for your gallery to be saved, click the Destination button. As with the Browse button for setting the source, this opens a dialog box where you can specify a folder or create a new folder.

The Options section of the Web Photo Gallery dialog box contains a large number of settings, broken down into various sections that are accessed by choosing a category from the drop-down list at the top of this section.

George Lepp, one of the Canon Explorers of Light and Print Masters, has always been at the forefront of the digital evolution. He has been experimenting with a new way to present digital images—High Definition Time Lapse photography. He graciously shares his techniques in the following sidebar, and a sample of a movie he created is included on the CD that comes with this book.

High-Definition Time Lapse with DSLR Cameras

by George Lepp

You've seen the time-lapse imagery on the evening news where the clouds go screaming by, and the wonderful video on the Nature Channel where a day passes before your eyes in mere seconds. Well, you can create the same kind of movies in high definition with your digital SLR (DSLR) camera.

You'll need a couple of pieces of equipment and some software, but after that it's all about being creative. The first tool you'll need is a good tripod. The camera needs to be immobilized during the filming sequence. In order to fire the camera at a specific timed interval, you need an intervalometer. This accessory is a timer that is either already in your camera or can be connected through your electronic cable release input. Some of the cameras that have built-in intervalometers are from Nikon—the D200, D300, D2X, and D3. For those cameras from Nikon that don't have this feature, Nikon offers the MC-36 Multi-Function Remote Cord, which plugs into the camera. Canon does not have any built-in intervalometers, so for these DSLRs you will need the TC-80N3 Timer Remote Controller.

The third item you will need is software to assemble the time-lapse movie from your images. One that I've used extensively is Apple's QuickTime Pro. Regular QuickTime is free from the Apple website, but you need to go one step further and purchase QuickTime Pro for $29.95. The advanced program has the needed assembly feature. In the Pro version, click File > Open Image Sequence and then click on the first image in a folder that holds just the series of images you want to make into a time-lapse movie. A simple video program like Adobe Premiere Elements will also assemble a series of stills into a movie.

Start your project by choosing a subject, and determine the optimum firing rate for the camera, depending on the result you want to achieve. It can be an image every hour or even one a second. I often use one frame every 5 seconds for a smooth yet time-lapse look. Set the camera

Continues

High-Definition Time Lapse with DSLR Cameras *(Continued)*

exposure to Aperture Priority and choose an f/stop that can be maintained if the time lapse goes into a low-light situation, as when you shoot throughout the day from sunrise to sunset, or in overcast. You can obtain interesting results by using slow shutter speeds throughout the sequence, a choice made possible by neutral density filters. Set the resolution of your DSLR to its smallest JPEG. This resolution will be better than HD TV and will take up only the smallest space on your recording media. I've taken a full day's images (4,000) on a 4GB CompactFlash card.

Your next problem will be power. If you're going to shoot for hours, you will run out of power from your camera battery. The answer is auxiliary power, from an additional battery system, a household AC supply, or a plug-in or power inverter from a vehicle. Now capture your series of images.

Place all your JPEGs from the series in one separate folder, and then compile your movie. The program will ask you what frame rate you will want to play the series at; the normal video rate is 29.97 frames per second. You can choose a slower rate if you want to slow things down, but it may be jerky. When you play the rendered movie back on Apple QuickTime, be sure to check Play All Frames under the View menu to get the proper effect.

I've had great fun with time-lapse movies of such subjects as a balloon festival, traffic patterns, water filling and emptying a bay, and a few hours in the life of an elephant seal colony. With these tools and basic software, you'll be ready for any great subject that comes your way.

© George Lepp

In this chapter we've explained methods for sharing your images after they have been optimized. This is only a starting point for producing great output, and we encourage you to be creative in how you prepare your images for display. In the next chapter, we'll demonstrate some additional time-saving techniques for optimizing your workflow.

Time-Savers

Throughout this book, we've provided you with the best techniques for inputting, optimizing, and outputting your images at every stage of the digital workflow. In this last chapter, we'll present some ways to help you save time and improve your efficiency. Adobe Photoshop has a variety of ways for you to automate many of the tasks that you perform repeatedly. That way, you can spend less time optimizing images and more time being creative either in the field with your camera or in Photoshop!

11

Chapter Contents
Actions and Batch Processing
Using the Image Processor
Creating a Copyright Brush
Individualizing Keyboard Shortcuts

Actions and Batch Processing

Time is in short supply for most of us. And if we're offered a way to get a job done with equal quality but in far less time, most of us would eagerly choose the more efficient method...if for no other reason than ultimately it means we'll have more time to get back to the things we love, such as taking more photos!

When it comes to becoming efficient with repetitive tasks in Photoshop, one of the keys is creating actions and applying those actions to a group of images in batch. Actions allow you to automate just about any series of steps you can perform in Photoshop. You can record a series of steps and then have those steps applied to additional images in exactly the same way. Batch processing allows you to apply the action to a group of images at once. The result can be a significant boost to your productivity.

Let's look at an example where we'll create an action to add the Safe Dodge and Burn layers that we covered in Chapter 6, "Exposure Adjustments."

Creating an Action

Photoshop ONLY

The Actions panel is "Command Central" for creating and managing your actions. So, start by selecting the Actions panel (shown in Figure 11.1). If it isn't visible, choose Window > Actions from the menu or use the keyboard shortcut Alt+F9/Option+F9.

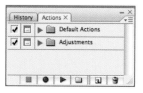

Figure 11.1 The Actions panel is "Command Central" for creating and managing your actions.

In this panel, actions are organized into folders called *sets*. Photoshop includes a Default Actions set with a variety of included actions, but you should divide your actions into sets that define logical groups. For instance, in this example you may create a new set called Adjustments to contain the various actions you may utilize when optimizing images. You may create other sets for actions you use for creative effects or for output—such as setting up the template for a business or greeting card, as we discussed in Chapter 10, "Output." The important thing is to create sets that are logical to your particular workflow and that will enable you to quickly locate an action.

> **Note:** Click the fly-out menu on the top right of the Actions panel to access some additional action sets that Adobe includes. Some of these may save you the time of creating an action yourself, and/or you may discover a fun effect to add to an image. However, often it's best to create your own actions to meet your specific needs.

To create a new set, click the Create New Set button ▭ at the bottom of the Actions panel. In the New Set dialog box (shown in Figure 11.2), enter a name and click OK.

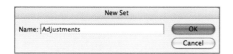

Figure 11.2 The New Set dialog box allows you to create a new set that helps you manage the various categories of actions you're creating.

Note: When creating an action, it's a good idea to work with a copy of one of your images. Duplicate your file before you start creating the action, and use that as the file you adjust in the process of recording the action.

With this set active, the next step is to start recording your new action. Click the Create New Action button ◼ at the bottom of the Actions panel. In the New Action dialog box (Figure 11.3), enter a descriptive name for this action. For this example, let's use **Dodge and Burn Layers**. The Set option defaults to the one that was selected when you created the new action, but you can choose a different set from the drop-down list if desired. The Function Key option allows you to set a shortcut key for the new action you're creating, which can be convenient if you're applying this action individually to single images. Finally, the Color setting determines what color the action displays in if you use Button mode for the Actions panel; this allows you to color-code the individual actions. Although some people find this useful for categorizing certain types of actions, we prefer using the default system of grouping actions into sets, so we leave the Color setting at None.

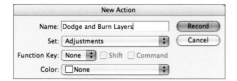

Figure 11.3 In the New Action dialog box, specify a name for the new action, the folder you want it stored in, and a function key to use as a shortcut key to run the action.

Once you've established the panel characteristics for the new action, click Record to start actively recording the action. Don't worry, though—time isn't an issue. Photoshop doesn't record the time you take between your steps but instead records the final result of each step you perform so those steps can be repeated as quickly as possible when you apply the action to an image. You can perform any adjustment or command on an image as part of an action. However, keep in mind that any step that depends on specific positioning within the image can be problematic because image dimensions vary from one photo to the next. In those instances, you may have to include a Stop or Modal control in the action. We'll cover how to do that later in this chapter.

Note: When recording an action, be sure to perform the steps in the order you want them repeated when you run the action. Sometimes it's helpful to write down the steps ahead of time. But you can revise the settings as often as you need to while recording the action; Photoshop will use only the final result of each step. Note that it will record errors and corrections of steps so that, for example, if a selection is made and then Deselect is used, both commands will be in the action. The steps in the action can be edited, reordered, turned off, duplicated, or deleted later.

We'll record an action to create Safe Dodge and Burn layers as an example. This is a good one for you to try as well.

1. Open the image being used as the example for the action.

2. Select the Actions panel.

   a. (This step is optional.) Create a new set; we created one called Adjustments.

   b. Click the new action icon, and name the action. We called ours Dodge and Burn Layers.

   c. Click the Record button.

3. Open a Curves adjustment layer using the icon for the Adjustment panel at the bottom of the Layers panel, but make no adjustments to the curve.

4. In the Layers panel, change the blending mode for the layer to Multiply. Initially the entire image will appear too dark.

5. Double-click directly on the word *Curves*, and type **Burn**.

6. Make certain the layer mask is selected by clicking it, and then choose Edit > Fill > Black. This step fills the layer mask with black to completely hide the darkening effect we introduced in Step 3.

7. Open a second Curves adjustment layer, by clicking the left facing arrow at the bottom of the Adjustment panel and then clicking the Curves icon again. Again make no adjustments to the curve.

8. Change the blending mode for the layer to Screen. Initially the entire image will appear too light.

9. Double-click directly on the word *Curves*, and type **Dodge**.

10. Choose Edit > Fill > Black.

11. Click the Brush tool to select it.

12. Change the opacity of the brush in the toolbar to about 15%. Including Steps 11 and 12 in the action will mean that you're ready to start the actual dodging and burning on the image after you run the action.

13. Click the Stop button to stop recording.

Note: Although selecting any brush-based tool is recordable, actually using the brush to perform any brush strokes is not recordable. So if you try to paint in the layer mask, that will not be recorded.

You've now created an action, which you can now apply to an individual image or to many images at once by using batch processing. Each step in the action can be viewed within the Actions panel, as shown in Figure 11.4. Anytime you want to run the action, have the image open, open the Actions panel, select the action, and click the Play icon. If you created a keyboard shortcut for the action, just press the shortcut key to run the action on an open image.

Figure 11.4 The Actions panel will show each of the steps in the action.

When you create an action that you're likely to use on a batch of images, we recommend saving the image and closing the file as the last steps in the action. Obviously this isn't practical in an action such as the one we just created—but that's an action geared primarily toward use on one image at a time. By saving and closing the file within the action, you help ensure that each processed image is saved and closed correctly.

Always save your action set after recording a new action. A system crash or improper shutdown will wipe out any new actions. To prevent accidentally losing the action, you must save the action set by using the panel menu in the Actions panel, shown in Figure 11.5, and choosing Save Actions.

Figure 11.5 Saving your action set is essential so you don't accidentally lose your actions.

Advanced Controls in Actions

Creating a basic action is pretty simple and straightforward, but at times you may need to do something a little fancier. For example, perhaps you want to be able to change the values used in some of the dialog boxes in the action. In that case, you need a modal control. A *modal control* pauses the action at the point where you need to fill in the appropriate settings. You can also use a modal control to enable you to use any of the tools, such as Crop or Transform, that require you to press Enter/Return to apply them. When the action comes to that step, it pauses and cues you to perform the necessary task. When you're done, you click OK in the dialog box or press Enter/Return, and the action resumes playing. Essentially, the modal control simply turns on any dialog box associated with the step.

To create a modal control for a specific step of an action, click the empty box to the left of that step (see Figure 11.6). Clicking the icon toggles it on and off. If you toggle the modal control off, the action will use the settings you used while recording the action. An action that contains modal controls will have a red modal icon by its name.

Figure 11.6 New modal controls enable you to change settings in dialog boxes while running an action.

Note: Sometimes you'll encounter a problem with an action if the image you're applying it to has a different size or orientation from the one on which you recorded. Changing the Ruler to Percent while recording sometimes corrects such problems.

Although many tasks can be automated using actions, any task that requires something to be done at a specific position in the image may present a problem with images of different sizes, resolutions, or orientations. For example, creating a single action to apply a copyright to the lower-right corner of an image is more challenging than it would seem because of different image sizes and resolutions. Most tools can be recorded, but some—such as the painting tools—cannot.

One thing that can help is to insert a Stop into the action. A Stop lets you perform a task that cannot be recorded—such as creating a selection. To include a Stop in an action, click the command just prior to where you want the Stop to occur. Click the Actions panel drop-down menu (Figure 11.7) and choose Insert Stop. This will cause a message box to appear in which you type instructions to yourself so you remember what you need to do. When you're done, click the Play button to continue the action. You can insert the Stop while recording the action or after you're done.

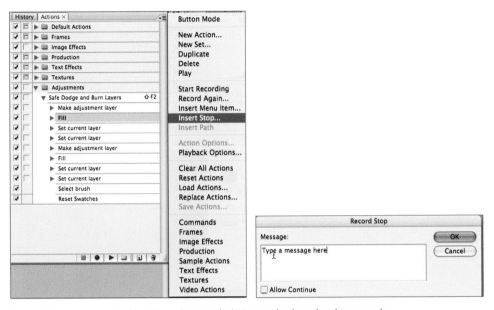

Figure 11.7 Choose Insert Stop from the panel menu in the Actions panel and complete the message box.

Another use of Stops is to record a reminder or message as to what should be done at a particular step. To do this, you follow the same steps as we just described, but you must check the option Allow Continue. When the message box appears during the action, the user can read the message and then click Continue rather than stopping the action.

Inevitably there will be times you'll record an action with steps you no longer want included, or you'll realize that you left something out. Although you could start over and record a new action, sometimes it's easier to revise the existing action.

Removing a step from an action is easy. Choose the action in the Actions panel, and reveal the steps by clicking the expansion arrow. Choose the step you want to remove, and either drag it to the trash can icon or click the trash can icon.

To add one or more steps to the action, choose the action and use the expansion arrow to reveal the steps. Choose the step just prior to where you want to begin the additional steps. Click the Record button and record the missing steps. When you're done recording the additional steps, click the Stop button.

Custom Actions

Unfortunately, it is not possible to record actions directly in Elements, but Photo Effects are in essence prerecorded actions. With a bit of hacking, it is possible to load certain other pre-recorded actions from CS4 into Elements as additional Photo Effects. However, because this is not a supported workflow and is sometimes unreliable, we will not cover it here. There are third-party tools (such as Add-O-Matic available at http://www.graficalicus.com) that automate the hackery and make it easy to load CS4 actions into Elements. Just keep in mind that the actions aren't guaranteed to function properly. Also, feel free to see if your favorite set of third-party actions has installation instructions for Elements.

Batch Processing

Photoshop ONLY

As you can see, recording an action is relatively straightforward. Just start recording, perform the steps you want included in the action, and then stop recording. Where many photographers run into trouble is in attempting to apply the action in a batch to a series of images, which is, ironically, where you achieve the real benefit of actions. The problem is with the confusing choices that are offered to you in the Batch dialog box.

To get started, select the action you want to apply to a group of images from the Actions panel. Then choose File > Automate > Batch from the menu, which brings up the Batch dialog box (shown in Figure 11.8). Because you selected an action first, the Set and Action drop-down lists default to the one you want to apply to your images.

Note: When you're applying an action to a group of images in batch, we recommend copying the image files to a separate folder to protect the originals.

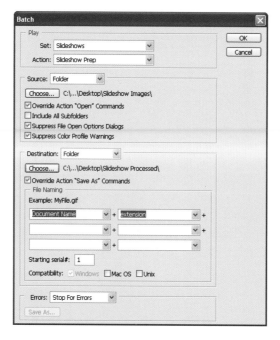

Figure 11.8 The Batch dialog box allows you to specify the action you want to run on a group of images, as well as other settings that determine which images should be processed and how they should be handled.

The Source section provides a number of options related to the images you'll be processing with the action. The Source drop-down list allows you to specify where the source images are located:

- The Folder option lets you specify a location where you've copied the images to be processed. This is the option we use most often.

- The Import option applies to images being imported from a particular source at the time the action is run.

- The Opened Files option applies to all images currently open in Photoshop.

- The Bridge option applies the action to all images currently selected in Adobe's Bridge.

If you have included an Open step in your action, select the Override Action "Open" Commands check box so the action actually opens and processes the files you specified in the source folder, rather than having the same image you used to create the action opened repeatedly. If your action does not contain an Open command, then you must not check this box; otherwise, the Batch command won't open the files you've selected for batch processing. In other words, don't check this option if the action was recorded to work on an image that's already open or if the action contains Open commands for specific files that are used as part of the action.

If you have used the Folder option in the Source section and there are more images in subfolders below your selected folder, select the Include All Folders check box so those images are also processed.

The Suppress File Open Options Dialogs option causes all images to be opened with default values without bringing up any Options dialog boxes that may be associated with the particular open operation. The most common situation where this would be an issue is for raw files—normally the ACR dialog box is displayed when a raw file is opened. By checking this option in the Batch dialog box, the default or previously specified settings are used instead of opening the ACR box. As a general rule, keep this check box selected, since the point of using batch processing is to allow a group of images to be processed without any user intervention required.

Similarly, select the Suppress Color Profile Warnings check box so the action won't pause for missing profiles or profile mismatches in any of the images you are processing. With this option selected, the default action specified in the Color Settings dialog box is performed when either of these situations occurs.

The next section of the Batch dialog box is Destination, which allows you to specify parameters for the output that is generated by the batch process. From the drop-down list, select the Folder option so that the processed images are saved into a specific folder and don't overwrite the original files. The other options are None (which leaves the file open unless the action recorded a Save command) and Save and Close (which causes each image to be saved as it is processed, replacing the existing files). If you use the Folder option, click the Choose button to bring up the Browse for Folder dialog box, where you can specify which folder you'd like to save the processed images in (you can choose to create a completely new folder for this purpose instead).

One of the biggest points of confusion for photographers using the Batch dialog box relates to the Override Action "Save As" Commands check box. You use this option so you can specify a Save As command in the action and then have the new files saved to whatever folder you specify in the Batch command, rather than the one you used when you created the action. It causes Photoshop to ignore the specific filename and folder you used when creating the action. If you don't use this option and you specify a filename in the Save As dialog box when you record in the action, then when you run the action, the new file will be renamed to the same name you used when creating the action.

If you want to save the processed images using their original filenames but in a different folder than you specify in the Batch command, you must save your image when recording the action. Then in the Batch processing dialog box, check Override Action "Save As" Commands and specify the destination folder. If you don't check this option, then Photoshop will save the images in two places: the folder that you specify as the destination, and the folder you used while creating the action. Note that the action must contain a Save As command to use this option. If you try to use it with an action that doesn't contain a Save As command, the batch processing won't save the processed files.

In the File Naming section, you have considerable flexibility in naming the files that are created. You can type specific text into the option boxes or select a variable from the drop-down list. For example, if you want to save the images with a filename in the structure `Slideshow_0001.jpg`, enter **Slideshow_** in the first box, select 4 Digit Serial Number from the drop-down list in the second box, and then select the Extension option from the third drop-down list. The default values of Document Name and Extension cause the original filenames to be retained. If you're using a serial number option, specify the starting value in the Starting Serial # box, which defaults to 1.

In the Errors section, choose either Stop for Errors or Log Errors to a File. The latter option has Photoshop log errors without interrupting the batch processing. We prefer to use the Stop for Errors option so we know right away if there is a problem we need to correct.

When you've set all the settings you want to use for the action you are applying to a group of images, click OK, and Photoshop processes all of the images specified in the Source section with the action specified in the Play section, saving the resulting output based on the settings in the Destination section. This processing is done automatically at top speed, making the process very efficient.

Whenever you find yourself performing the same task on a group of images, such as applying a watermark, consider making an action to automate that process. The small amount of time spent creating the action pays significant dividends when you apply that action in batch to a large group of images.

Al Ward, in addition to being the technical editor for this book, is the brain behind ActionFx.com, a website dedicated to Photoshop presets (actions, shapes, brushes, layer styles, and so on), and has nearly 110,000 presets available for download at the time of this writing. In the accompanying sidebar, he provides tips for creating watermarks.

Creating Watermark Actions

by Al Ward

The ability of actions to record nearly every process in Photoshop sounds great, but few users actually wrap their minds around these incredible handy tools and utilize them in their work. Not so many years ago there simply wasn't much documentation on actions, and a natural assumption was that they required some degree of programming skill. This could not be further from the truth. If you can navigate a Photoshop panel and have had experience with a tape recorder, VCR, DVD-R, or other media-capturing device, then you already have the concept behind actions mastered; you just don't realize it yet. This chapter gives you an excellent start on working with actions, and I encourage you to go through the information carefully.

With that said, you may still be wondering what actions can do for you as a photographer. The answer is plenty, whether you're interested in photo correction, photo manipulation, simple productivity, or even web design and funky special effects.

One repetitive function an action can perform with ease over and over again so you don't have to is the creation and placement of a watermark. Photographers who display their work online and don't want to suffer the thieves of this world running off with their livelihood can quickly set up an action that will place a watermark on a single image or on an entire folder of images when using the action with the Batch command.

Note that these types of actions are often dependent on an image's resolution and size. I recommend creating actions of this nature for specific image orientations and resolutions. For instance, the action outlined here works well on a portrait photo, 8×11, at 300 ppi. Although the action will work regardless of the image size and resolution, the text may spill off the edges on an image with a different resolution. Build an entire toolkit of watermark actions using variable image sizes in a single action set, and name each action in the set based on the photo orientation and resolution it is designed for. An example may be `WM_Portrait_8x11_300ppi`, placed in a set of actions called My Watermarks.

Here's the process to create such an action:

1. Open the Actions panel. Create a new action set, and call it Watermarks.

2. Open an image. Create a new action in the set, and give it a name; something like Watermark-001 will do for this trial run. (It can be renamed as you see fit later.) Click Record.

3. Anything you do in Photoshop is now recording. First ensure the rulers are displayed (View > Rulers). Then right-click the ruler bar on the top or side, and select Percent. This will ensure the watermark appears with the same positioning no matter the size of the image, the resolution, or the orientation (landscape or portrait).

4. Select the Type tool. Change the foreground color to whatever color you would like your watermark to be, and then select the font and font size you want to use. For instance, a light gray/white foreground color and a semi-bold font set to 14–20 pixels works well for most of my photos. Also, for watermarks I place in the middle of images, I set the justification to Center.

Continues

438

Creating Watermark Actions *(Continued)*

5. Move the mouse to the spot where you want to start typing. If you would like the water-
    mark to be placed directly in the center of each photo, watch the top and side rulers as you
    move the mouse, and click when both the side and top ruler markers are at 50%. Type your
    watermark information (such as **Copyright 2008, mygenericwebsite.com**). Once it's
    typed, you may edit the text as needed (Transform > Rotate, Transform > Scale, and so on).

6. To make the text appear embossed rather than have a simple color fill, open the layer
    styles for the text layer, and apply a simple bevel. Accept the style by clicking OK, and then
    reduce the fill opacity for the layer to 0, or a slightly higher percentage if you want some
    color to remain yet still be transparent. You may also opt to add a drop shadow, outer
    glow, or other text-enhancing setting with your style.

7. When you are happy with the new watermark, stop recording and *save the action set* to a
    folder on your hard drive where you can easily find it later.

8. Open another image, preferably with a different orientation, and rerun the action. If you
    followed the directions in this sidebar, you'll see the watermark in the same position on
    the new image, despite orientation or resolution.

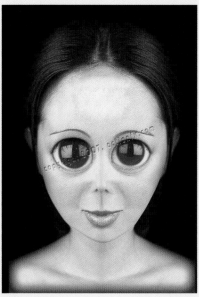

© Al Ward, ActionFx.com

Now you are set to add a watermark to all your photos. Use the information in this chapter to set
up a batch process using this action, and ensure the batch saves copies of the images and does
not save over the originals. Again, the authors describe this process, so please take care in reading and practicing on "throwaway" files until you are sure you have it mastered.

On a parting note, you may want to create watermark actions using varied fonts, colors, and
watermark positions. Save them to the same action set, and create an entire toolbox of Watermark actions. Trust me; your life will be a lot easier if you incorporate actions into your Photoshop mind-set. Enjoy!

Batch Processing

The Elements version of the Batch Processing tool is designed to let you apply certain pre-defined actions, rather than custom actions, to multiple files. To pull up the dialog box seen here, select File > Process Multiple Files.

Similar to the CS4 Batch tool, the Elements Process Multiple Files tool gives you a variety of choices for file sources (e.g., Folder or Bridge), you can set a specific destination, and there is a convenient way to rename multiple files. In addition, Process Multiple Files provides a quick interface for resizing, converting file type, watermarking, and auto-correcting.

Resizing a Group of Images

When you have a group of images that need to be resized, gather the horizontals together in one batch and the verticals in another, then follow these steps:

1. Select File > Process Multiple Files.

2. Follow the instructions for Photoshop CS4's Batch tool to select source and destination locations.

3. Check the Resize Images check box under the Image Size box.

4. Type in the desired destination size. By leaving Constrain Proportions checked, you need to type in only a width or height, and Elements will figure out the other dimension for you.

5. Pick a resolution.

6. Click OK.

Continues

Batch Processing *(Continued)*

We would not recommend using the Quick Fix tools, as you will usually want more manual control over your adjustments than those tools allow. In addition, Process Multiple Files doesn't let you set any options for these adjustments. While it's tempting to run Resize Images and Sharpen at the same time, we recommend against it because you don't want to accidentally oversharpen your images.

Setting a Watermark

Elements users are fortunate in that the Process Multiple Files tool provides an easy way to add copyright text to multiple images. To do so, follow these steps:

1. Select File > Process Multiple Files.

2. Follow the instructions for Photoshop CS4's Batch tool to select source and destination locations.

3. In the Labels section of the dialog box, choose Watermark from the pop-up menu.

4. Type in the copyright text.

5. Select a position, font type and size, and color and opacity.

6. Click OK.

Creating a Droplet

Photoshop ONLY

A droplet provides a way to run an action on a single image, a group of images, or a folder of images, directly from your desktop (or elsewhere). You create a droplet icon for the action and then drag the images (or folder) onto it to run the action. Using a droplet can save you time since you don't have to bother with the Batch dialog box in order to run the action.

You must create the action first. Then, follow these steps to create a droplet:

1. Choose File > Automate > Create Droplet. This launches a dialog box similar to the Batch dialog box except that it begins with a Save Droplet In drop-down menu (Figure 11.9).

2. Specify where to save the droplet. Usually if you want the convenience of a droplet, you'll want it to be on your desktop, but you could create a special folder just for droplets or you could choose to store them elsewhere, such as in Documents. You'll also need to name the droplet. We recommend using a name that readily identifies what the action does.

3. Choose the set and the action.

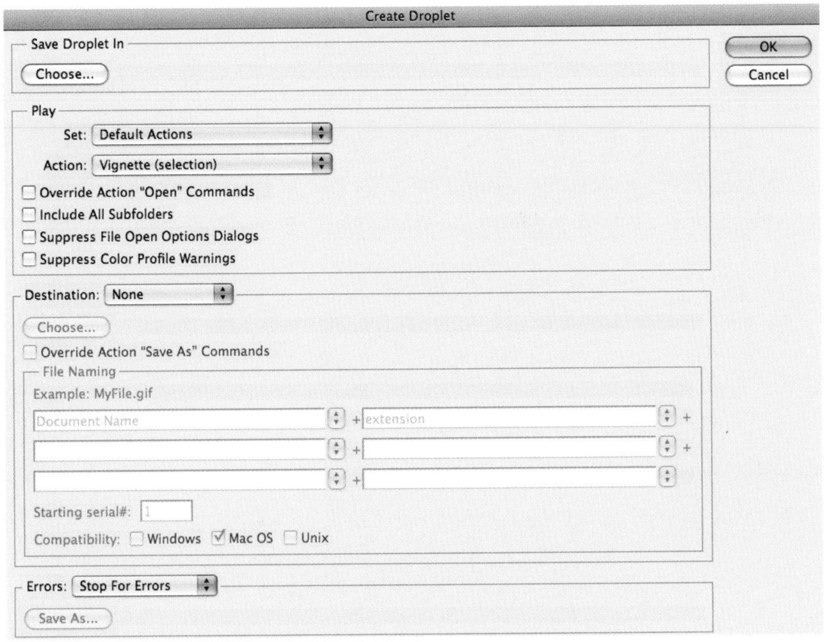

Figure 11.9 The Create Droplet dialog box is quite similar to the Batch dialog box.

4. Complete the rest of the options, which are identical to those we described in detail in the section on batch processing.

5. Click OK, and the droplet will be saved wherever you specified.

To use the droplet, drag any image or folder containing images onto it. Photoshop will automatically launch if it's not already running, and you can be off taking more photos!

Using the Image Processor

The Image Processor was introduced in Photoshop in CS2 and is a major time-saver. It allows you to convert images into different sizes and formats that you specify and it stores them wherever you choose. That's a huge time-saver as you prepare images for the Web, emails, a slide show, and so on. It's similar to a batch command except that you don't have to create an action to make it work. In addition, it takes advantage of a Fit Within command so you don't have to separate your horizontal and vertical images.

The Image Processor can convert files to JPEG, TIFF, or PSD formats, or to two or more different formats simultaneously (see Figure 11.10). In addition, it can resize images to fit within specific dimensions for each format. It can also embed a color profile or convert the JPEGs to sRGB, run an action, and/or include copyright metadata in the converted images. That's a lot of convenience in one dialog box!

Photoshop ONLY

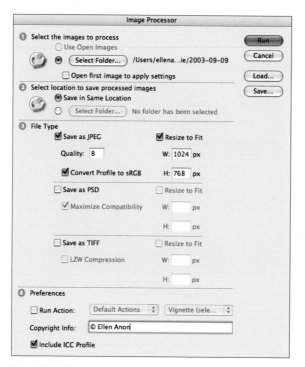

Figure 11.10 The Image Processor makes it easy to resize images for different outputs.

To use the Image Processor, follow these steps:

1. To access the Image Processor from Bridge, choose Tools > Photoshop > Image Processor. To access it from within Photoshop, choose File > Scripts > Image Processor.

2. Specify the images you want to process. You can use open files or select a folder of images.

3. If you are using raw files, you may want to check the option to Select Open First Image to Apply Settings. That way, you can customize the raw settings to apply to the first image, and the Image Processor will apply those same settings to the remaining raw files. That can be very helpful if the images were shot under similar lighting conditions. If you don't check this option, the Image Processor will use the existing settings for each image. If you have customized the settings for each image in ACR, you should not check this option.

4. Select a location to store the processed images. If you choose Save in Same Location, the Image Processor will automatically create a separate folder within that folder for the processed images. Each file format will have its own folder.

5. Select the file types and options. The Resize to Fit option is particularly convenient. You can specify the maximum height and width in pixels for the image. The Image Processor will retain the aspect ratio of the original file but resize the image to fit within the dimensions you specify. For example, if you are processing images to use in a slide show and your projector has a resolution of 1024×768, you would set those dimensions.

6. Select an action to run if you choose. Some people create a sharpening action for their web-sized or slide show images and have the Image Processor run it.

7. Fill in the copyright information, but remember that this is metadata. It will not appear as a copyright symbol and text on the image itself. (To do that, you can use the copyright brush that we'll cover next in this chapter or use a watermark action as Al Ward described in the sidebar "Creating Watermark Actions.")

8. Keep the Include ICC Profile option checked.

9. Click Run. If the settings you have established are ones that you will use frequently, you can opt to save them for even more time efficiency. That way, when you open the Image Processor you'll just need to click Load, select the settings, and select the Source folder.

Creating a Copyright Brush

One of the tasks that most nature photographers wish they could automate is adding a copyright to an image. Al Ward showed you in an earlier sidebar how to create an embossed watermark. However, some people are more comfortable using a copyright brush. The effect is just slightly different. To create a customized brush that contains your copyright, follow these steps:

1. Choose File > New File, and create a new document. The exact size is not important, but it is helpful to make it with a transparent background, as shown in Figure 11.11. Set the resolution to 96 since the main use for the copyright is likely to be for email and web images.

2. Select the Text tool and the font you want to use. Ellen uses Snell Roundhand, Crisp, or Papyrus, but any font you like will work. We use an 18-point font size.

3. Select the color for the text in the Text tool Options bar at the top of the monitor (see Figure 11.12). This will become the default color for the brush. We suggest using either white or black. You'll adjust the opacity of the brush when you use it, so don't worry about it being too obvious and distracting.

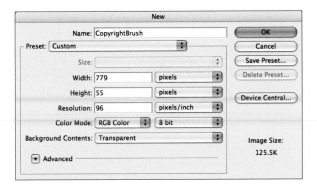

Figure 11.11 Be certain to set the background to Transparent when creating the new file to use for the copyright brush.

Figure 11.12 Select the font, size, and color for your copyright brush in the Text tool Options bar.

4. Click on the image and type © and your name. Include the year if you choose. To access the © symbol on a Mac, type Option+G. In Windows, it's a little more difficult; hold the Alt key while pressing 0169 on the number pad. You must use the number pad, not the numbers immediately above the keyboard. On a laptop you may have to use the function key as well to access the number-pad numbers.

5. Ctrl+click/⌘+click the text layer icon in the Layers panel to select the text (see Figure 11.13).

Figure 11.13 You must turn the text into a selection before converting it into a brush.

6. Select the Brush tool. Make sure that Hardness is set to 100%.

7. Choose Edit > Define > Brush Preset. Name the brush **Copyright** and include the name of the font (see Figure 11.14). (In Elements, this menu command is Edit > Define Brush from Selection. If you are using white as your brush color and receive a message that says "Could not complete the Define Brush from Selection command because no pixels are selected," change your text color to something other than white and try again.)

Figure 11.14 Be sure to name your copyright brush in a way that makes it easy to find.

8. Click OK.

9. You don't need to save the document; you can simply close it. You now have a brush that is your copyright.

To use your copyright brush on an image, follow these steps:

1. Select the Brush tool, and then go to the Brush presets in the tool Options bar (see Figure 11.15). Choose the copyright tool you just made.

Figure 11.15 Choose your copyright brush from the Brush presets.

2. Create a new layer on your document (optional). By placing the copyright on a new layer, you can adjust the opacity of the copyright symbol after you make it by adjusting the opacity of the layer in the Layers panel. Alternatively, you can set the opacity of the brush to 60%, although at times you may want it more or less opaque.

3. To change the color of the text, click the foreground Color Picker, and select the desired color.

4. To change the size of the copyright, use the bracket keys just as you do with any other brush tool.

5. Position the cursor, and with a single click, apply the copyright!

> **Note:** Placing a copyright on an image gives some protection against illegal use of the image, although for full protection you must register your images with the U.S. Copyright Office. For more information about how to register your images, see Carolyn Wright's excellent website and free blog, www.PhotoAttorney.com.

Individualizing Keyboard Shortcuts

As you've noticed, there are a lot of shortcuts in Photoshop. Some of them become second nature to almost everyone who uses Photoshop regularly and are major time-savers, while others are quite esoteric. People vary greatly in their feelings about using shortcuts. We find that they are often useful to help us work more efficiently, and throughout the book we recommend our favorites to you.

Photoshop ONLY

Amazingly, even with the abundance of shortcuts in Photoshop, there isn't a shortcut for everything! You may decide that there's a step you perform repeatedly that you'd like to create a shortcut for. For example, there is no longer a shortcut to the Annotation tool. If you frequently make notes about images, you might want to create your own shortcut.

1. In the menu, choose Edit > Keyboard Shortcuts. This will bring up the dialog box shown in Figure 11.16.

2. Within the Application menus, scroll down until you see Annotations. Click on it.

3. If a shortcut already exists for the command, it will appear in the white box. Since creating an Annotation doesn't have a default shortcut, the box is blank initially. In the box, type the shortcut you want to use. In this case, we used Ctrl+R/⌘+R.

4. Click OK. If the shortcut is already in use, a warning dialog will appear. If you click OK, the shortcut will be reassigned to your new command.

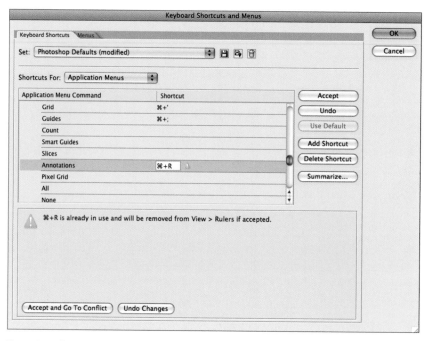

Figure 11.16 You can create your own customized shortcuts for most steps that you perform regularly.

You'll find that most shortcuts are already taken, so you may have to reassign one that you don't tend to use. Of course, this means you'll get accustomed to using certain shortcuts on your home machine that won't work on other machines.

In this chapter we've presented some methods for you to improve the efficiency of your workflow and share your images in a variety of ways. As with all the chapters in this book, the underlying theme has been producing the very best results possible with your images and then sharing those images. Now that you have learned many techniques to help you achieve these goals, we hope you'll find an increased passion for your photography, a growing desire to share your images with the world, and a heightened level of skill in achieving exactly the results you envision for your photographs!

About the Companion CD

What You'll Find on the CD

The following sections are arranged by category and provide a summary of the items you'll find on the CD.

Chapter Files

You will find sample images for you to use to practice the techniques in the book. They are arranged by chapter. Use them to follow along with the instructions and to try each new technique as it is presented. Taking the time to use these images will reinforce what you're reading. In addition, the Chapter 10 folder contains the Time-Lapse movie that accompanies George Lepp's sidebar.

Photoshop Videos and Elements Videos

You will find a series of training videos to augment the materials in the book. Topics for Photoshop are:

- Adobe Camera Raw Part One
- Adobe Camera Raw Part Two
- Bridge Part One
- Bridge Part Two
- New Views in Photoshop
- Using the Adjustment Panel
- Using the Masks Panel
- Spring Loaded Tools

Addition information includes:

- Instructions for creating greeting cards for Photoshop and Elements users
- Creating a web page for Elements users

Topics for Photoshop Elements videos are:

- Developing a Workflow
- Applying Curves
- Creating Layer Masks
- Processing Multiple Files

For updates to any of the CD material, go to www.sybex.com/go/nature.

System Requirements

The techniques in the book and the video tutorials on the CD are geared primarily for users of Adobe Photoshop CS4 and Photoshop Elements 6 for Macintosh or Windows. Some of the techniques shown are applicable to previous versions of the software. Go to www.adobe.com for further information on system requirements for Photoshop and Photoshop Elements. There is no software available on this CD.

Using the CD

To copy the items from the CD to your hard drive, follow these steps.

1. Insert the CD into your computer's CD-ROM drive. The license agreement will appear.

> **Note:** Windows users: The interface won't launch if you have autorun disabled. In that case, click Start > Run (for Windows Vista, Start > All Programs > Accessories > Run). In the dialog box that appears, type **D:\Start.exe**. (Replace *D* with the proper letter if your CD drive uses a different letter. If you don't know the letter, see how your CD drive is listed under My Computer.) Click OK.

> **Note:** Mac users: The CD icon will appear on your desktop; double-click the icon to open the CD and double-click the Start icon.

2. Read through the license agreement, and then click the Accept button if you want to use the CD.

   The CD interface appears. The interface allows you to access the content with just one or two clicks.

Troubleshooting

Wiley has attempted to provide programs that work on most computers with the minimum system requirements. Alas, your computer may differ, and some programs may not work properly for some reason.

The two likeliest problems are that you don't have enough memory (RAM) for the programs you want to use, or you have other programs running that are affecting the installation or the running of a program. If you get an error message such as "Not enough memory" or "Setup cannot continue," try one or more of the following suggestions and then try using the software again:

- **Turn off any antivirus software running on your computer.** Installation programs sometimes mimic virus activity and may make your computer incorrectly believe that it's being infected by a virus.

- **Close all running programs.** The more programs you have running, the less memory is available to other programs. Installation programs typically update files and programs, so if you keep other programs running, installation may not work properly.

- **Have your local computer store add more RAM to your computer.** This is, admittedly, a drastic and somewhat expensive step. However, adding more memory can really help the speed of your computer and allow more programs to run at the same time.

Customer Care

If you have trouble with the book's companion CD-ROM, please call the Wiley Product Technical Support phone number at (800) 762-2974. Outside the United States, call +1(317) 572-3994. You can also contact Wiley Product Technical Support at http://sybex.custhelp.com. John Wiley & Sons will provide technical support only for installation and other general quality control items. For technical support on the applications themselves, consult the program's vendor or author.

To place additional orders or to request information about other Wiley products, please call (877) 762-2974.

Index

Note to the Reader: Throughout this index boldfaced page numbers indicate primary discussions of a topic. Italicized page numbers indicate illustrations.

459

■ INDEX